ALLENDE'S CHILE
and the Inter-American Cold War

The New Cold War History   Odd Arne Westad, editor

Tanya Harmer

ALLENDE'S CHILE
and the Inter-American Cold War

The University of North Carolina Press
CHAPEL HILL

© 2011 The University
of North Carolina Press
All rights reserved

Set in Arnhem & Franklin Gothic

Manufactured in the United
States of America

The paper in this book meets the
guidelines for permanence and
durability of the Committee on
Production Guidelines for Book
Longevity of the Council on
Library Resources.

The University of North Carolina
Press has been a member of the
Green Press Initiative
since 2003.

15 14 13 12 11   5 4 3 2 1

Library of Congress
Cataloging-in-Publication Data

Harmer, Tanya.
    Allende's Chile and the Inter American
      Cold War / Tanya Harmer.
    p. cm.—(The new Cold War history)
    Includes bibliographical references and index.
    ISBN 978-0-8078-3495-4 (hardback)
    1. Latin America—Politics and government—
1948–1980. 2. United States—Foreign relations—
Latin America. 3. Latin America—Foreign relations—
United States. 4. United States—Foreign relations—
1945–1989. 5. Chile—Foreign relations—1970–1973. 6.
Cuba—Foreign relations—1959–1990. 7. Brazil—
Foreign relations—1964–1985. I. Title.
    F1414.2.H317 2011
    980.03—dc22   2011011686

To my parents, Anita and Jeremy

Contents

Maps and Illustrations

Acknowledgments

I am indebted to many people for their support and guidance during the many years that I have been researching and writing this book. First, I owe an enormous debt to Arne Westad—my graduate teacher, doctoral supervisor, mentor, and friend. His inspiration, warm encouragement, energy, and enthusiasm for history and learning have been invaluable to me. As a student and now a lecturer at the London School of Economics (LSE), I have also been incredibly fortunate to benefit from the exciting intellectual, research, and teaching environment of the International History Department, the LSE's Centre for Diplomacy and Strategy, LSE IDEAS, Arne Westad's Wednesday afternoon Cold War Research Seminar, and the LSE's Latin America Research Seminar. Within this context, my particular thanks go to Nigel Ashton, Antony Best, Jeff Byrne, Steve Casey, Vesselin Dimitrov, Arne Hofmann, Artemy Kalinovsky, Ed Packard, George Philip, Kristina Spohr-Readman, Thomas Field, Victor Figueroa Clark, and Erica Wald, all of whom at one point or another read earlier portions of the book and offered helpful comments. I am also enormously grateful to Anita Prazmowska for helping me locate Polish documents that are referred to in this book while on sabbatical and then for spending hours translating them for me over coffee and baklava. The same goes for my former graduate student at the LSE, Laura Wiesen, who translated East German materials for me with great enthusiasm and professionalism. Without a doubt, the contents of this book are far richer as a result of the support and inspiration that the LSE has provided me with since I first arrived there as a rather nervous graduate student in 2001.

Beyond the LSE, I am profoundly grateful to Piero Gleijeses and to Jim Hershberg, who took the time to read the manuscript version of the book. Not only did they express interest and faith in the project, but they also offered detailed comments and insightful suggestions, which I have done my best to incorporate into the final version. Alfredo Riquelme, Joaquín Fermandois, and Fernando Purcell at the Pontificia Universidad Católica

(PUC) in Chile have also been incredibly supportive. For their advice and interest in my research, their collaboration in the LSE IDEAS Latin America International Affairs Programme, and their invitation to Chile during the spring of 2010, my thanks. Over the course of my research trips to Chile, I have also been warmly welcomed at Chile's Foreign Ministry Archives and assisted by its staff. My thanks therefore go to those who helped make my visits there so fruitful, and particularly to the archive's director, Carmen Gloria Duhart. In Cuba, the process of research is as complicated as it is exciting, and it would have been far more daunting without the support and guidance of Antoni Kapcia, Hal Klepak, and members of the Cuba Research Forum based at the University of Nottingham and the University of Havana. For their help in obtaining the right visa, introducing me to the right people, and providing a welcoming environment to discuss research in Cuba, I am greatly indebted. In Havana, my thanks go to Jorge Hernández and Luis René Fernández at the Centro de Estudios Sobre los Estados Unidos at the University of Havana, the staff at Casa Memorial Salvador Allende, and Carlos Alzugaray at the Instituto Superior de Relaciones Internacionales. I am also grateful to others working on Latin American and U.S. history with whom I have enjoyed stimulating conversations and from whom I have received invaluable feedback and support, not least Andrew Preston, Jim Siekmeier, Vanni Pettina, Andy Kirkendall, Alessandro Santoni, Olga Ulianova, Eugenia Palieraki, Matias Spektor, Hal Brands, Andy Scott, and Kristian Gustafson. Over the years, I have also been pushed forward by the many insightful comments and questions about my research at various conferences and seminars in the United Kingdom, Chile, Italy, France, and the United States. To those who were there and whom I have not mentioned in person, thank you. For their help in the final stages of the writing process, I am also enormously grateful to Charles Grench, Beth Lassiter, Brian MacDonald, and Ron Maner at the University of North Carolina Press, and to Michael Taber, who took the time to help me improve the manuscript. Needless to say, any errors or mistakes that follow are entirely my own.

The research and years I have dedicated to this project would simply not have been possible without the generous financial assistance I received as a doctoral student from the Arts and Humanities Research Council (AHRC), the International History Department at the LSE, and the University of London's Central Research Fund. In particular, the AHRC's doctoral scholarship and Study Abroad Grant allowed me to kick-start the project by funding extended research trips to Washington, Santiago, Brasilia, and

Havana in 2004. The University of London's Central Research Fund and the International History department's travel bursaries and staff research fund then provided me with funds to return to Washington, Cuba, and Chile over the course of the next six years to conduct further archival research and interviews. I am also grateful to the Institute of History at the PUC in Chile for having paid for my travel to and living expenses in Santiago over the course of my stay there as a visiting professor in 2010.

Last but by no means least, I would like to say a special thanks to my friends outside of the world of academia and to members of my family, who either read bits of the book, gave me their heartfelt support over the years, or both. Words are not enough to express the gratitude I feel toward them, and I would certainly not be where I am now without them. I would especially like to thank my sister Jessy, Mark and Claire Plumb, Katie Plumb and Ian Jasper, Lindsay Evans, Kate Annand, Erin O'Connor, Javier Urrutia Denicola, Frederico Matos, the girls from 45 Ash Grove, and Tom Newman. Most of all, however, I would like to thank my parents, Anita and Jeremy, who not only endured the worst of a lengthy writing process with me but also made the best of it possible by opening my eyes to the world, encouraging me to discover it, and offering me love and support along the way.

Abbreviations

AID	Agency for International Development, Department of State, United States
ARA	Bureau of Inter-American Affairs, Department of State, United States (The abbreviation is based on the bureau's earlier name, Office of American Republic Affairs.)
CIA	Central Intelligence Agency, United States
CODE	Confederación Democrática (Democratic Confederation), Chile
COMECON	Council for Mutual Economic Assistance
DGLN	Departamento General de Liberación Nacional (General National Liberation Department), Ministry of the Interior, Cuba
DIA	Defense Intelligence Agency, United States
ELN	Ejército de Liberación Nacional (National Liberation Army), Bolivia, Chile
ENU	Escuela Nacional Unificada (Unified National School System), Chile
ERP	Ejército Revolucionario del Pueblo (Revolutionary Army of the People), Argentina
Eximbank	Export-Import Bank, United States
G77	Group of 77
GAP	Grupo de Amigos Personales (Group of Personal Friends)
GOC	Government of Chile
IBRD	International Bank of Reconstruction and Development
IDB	Inter-American Development Bank
INR	Bureau of Intelligence and Research, Department of State, United States
IPC	International Petroleum Company
ITT	International Telephone and Telegraph Corporation

JCR	Junta Coordinadora Revolucionaria (Revolutionary Coordinating Junta)
MAPU	Movimiento de Acción Popular Unitario (Movement of Popular Unitary Action), Chile
MINREX	Ministerio de Relaciones Exteriores (Foreign Ministry), Cuba
MIR	Movimiento de Izquierda Revolucionaria (Movement of the Revolutionary Left), Chile
NSC	National Security Council, United States
NSDM	National Security Decision Memorandum
NSSM	National Security Study Memorandum
OAS	Organization of American States
OLAS	Organización Latinoamericana de Solidaridad (Organization of Latin American Solidarity)
PCCh	Partido Comunista de Chile (Chilean Communist Party)
PDC	Partido Demócrata Cristiano (Christian Democrat Party), Chile
PN	Partido Nacional (National Party), Chile
PS	Partido Socialista (Socialist Party), Chile
SRG	Senior Review Group, National Security Council, United States
UNCTAD	United Nations Conference on Trade and Development
UP	Unidad Popular (Popular Unity), Chile
USG	United States Government

ALLENDE'S CHILE
and the Inter-American Cold War

Chile

INTRODUCTION

On 5 November 1970, thousands of people crammed into Chile's national stadium to mark the beginning of Salvador Allende's presidency and what was being heralded as the birth of a new revolutionary road to socialism. For some, Allende's inauguration two days earlier had been a cause for mass celebration. Along the length of Santiago's principal avenue, musicians, poets, dancers, and actors had performed on twelve open-air stages specially erected for the occasion, and crowds had partied into the evening. Now, on a sunny spring afternoon, along with foreign journalists and invited dignitaries from around the world, they flocked to hear the president's first major speech. As Allende rose to the podium to deliver a message of national emancipation and rebirth, he looked out on a sea of flags in optimistic anticipation of what was to come. He then proclaimed that Chile was ready to shape its own destiny.[1]

The way foreigners in the audience interpreted his speech depended largely on where they came from and what they believed in. Delegates from Havana, Brasilia, and Washington respectively watched in jubilation, horror, and disdain—uncertain what the future held but conscious that Allende's inauguration had significantly changed the way it would unfold. Indeed, right there, the seeds of what would develop into a new phase of a multisided inter-American Cold War battle were already firmly in place. And although the roots of this struggle lay in previous decades, its outcome would now be decided in a bitter contest over the course of the next three years.

What follows is the story of those years, the people who lived through them, and the international environment they encountered. On one level, this is a history of Chilean foreign relations during the country's short-lived revolutionary process that ended with a brutal right-wing military coup d'état and Allende's death on 11 September 1973. Yet, it is also an examination of Chile's place within what I call the inter-American Cold War. Rather than a bipolar superpower struggle projected onto a Latin

American theater from outside, this inter-American Cold War was a unique and multisided contest between regional proponents of communism and capitalism, albeit in various forms. With the Soviet Union reluctant to get more involved, it was primarily people across the Americas that fought it and, although global developments often interacted with regional concerns and vice versa, its causes were also predominantly inter-American. However, much remains to be understood about it, especially in the period after the Cuban revolution triumphed in 1959. From this year forward, the Cold War in the Americas changed, being definitively shaped thereafter by the clash between Havana and Washington as the polar opposites of revolution and reaction on the continent. An array of other Latin Americans were also involved, some of whom shared Washington's or Havana's views and were inspired by them, others who surpassed even their ardent zeal for combating each other, and far too many others who were caught up in the middle. In the early 1970s, for example, Brasilia's role as a staunch anticommunist actor in the inter-American system was a particularly decisive dimension to this conflict, as were the tens of thousands who lost their lives in the dirty wars that engulfed the Southern Cone toward the end of that decade. But until now the story of how all these different groups interacted with each other has not been fully told.

Although it is beyond the scope of this book to examine the inter-American Cold War in its entirety, what follows is one vital chapter of it: the Chilean chapter in the early 1970s. Sandwiched between the better-known histories of Ernesto "Che" Guevara's death in Bolivia and Cuba's intervention in Angola, or between the Alliance for Progress and Operation Condor, the Allende years certainly deserve more attention as a moment of profound transition in inter-American affairs. For one, Allende's decision to shatter the Organization of American States' isolation of Cuba by reestablishing diplomatic relations with the island in November 1970, together with the Cubans' own shifting approach to regional affairs in the early 1970s, makes this an interesting episode in the history of Cuba's relationship with the Americas—and, by extension, an important period for those of us trying to incorporate Havana's side of the story into an international history of inter-American affairs. As it turned out, this period was the beginning of Cuba's formal reintegration into the inter-American system after collective OAS sanctions had been imposed on the island in 1964. Moreover, if Allende's election was the most important revolutionary triumph in Latin America since the Cuban revolution in 1959, his overthrow three years later was the most important victory for counterrevolutionary forces in the region since the right-wing Brazilian coup of 1964. On a broader scale, the rise and fall of Allende's Chile was also tangled up in several momentous global narratives including the burgeoning North-South debate on modernization and development, Cuba's intervention in Africa, and the rising importance of human rights in international affairs.

Intriguingly, all these upheavals occurred during a period of purported détente in international affairs. From today's vantage point, détente's characteristic trademarks—triangular diplomacy, Ostpolitik, the Strategic Arms Limitation Talks, and the Helsinki Accords—seem starkly removed from Cold War battles being played out simultaneously in Latin America and the wider Third World. Yet this was not necessarily understood by those in the Americas, Africa, or Asia when the process of détente began. To the contrary, for many in the global South, détente initially at least appeared to offer breathing space in which to advance toward modernization and development without the risk of incurring U.S. and/or Soviet intervention. And, to begin with, Allende's peaceful democratic election in September 1970 seemed emblematic of a more mature, tranquil mood in international politics that offered hope of a peaceful alternative to violent revolution and reaction. Together with the heterogeneous left-wing coalition he represented, Unidad Popular (Popular Unity, or UP), Allende not only challenged the rules of socialist revolution but also attempted to redefine Chile's place in the world on the basis of "ideological pluralism" in international affairs. But in doing so at the same time as striving to help reshape the world's economic and political system in line with the global South's needs, he and his government put the concept of détente— or at least the idea that détente might benefit and incorporate the global South—to the test.

On the surface, Allende's chances of succeeding appeared promising— East-West tensions were diminishing when he assumed power, the world's postwar economic system was showing signs of collapse, radical transformation in Latin America looked imminent, and the Third World was increasingly demanding a more equitable share of the globe's wealth and power. To many, restrictive Cold War ideological divides also seemed to be a thing of the past, especially when Nixon traveled to Beijing and Moscow in 1972. However, by the time he did, it was already clear to the Chileans that the game of détente was both temporary and conditional on where countries were located in the world. While statesmen in the global North pretended to ignore ideological disagreements with each other, the Cold War continued in the South, and as it did, the struggle between different modes of social, political, and economic development often grew fiercer, more radical, and more violent. And alongside the wars that raged in southern Africa and Southeast Asia in the 1970s, there was no meaningful inter-American détente. Despite brief moments of attempted rapprochement between Washington and Havana in 1974–75, and at the tail end of détente in the late 1970s, relations between the United States and Cuba remained deeply antagonistic while the U.S. economic blockade of Cuba continued. For their part, Soviet leaders do not appear to have pushed for a U.S.-Cuban détente. Cuba rarely came up in U.S.-Soviet negotiations between 1969 and 1972, and when, on one occasion in early 1972, Kissinger briefly raised the hypothetical possibility of an improvement in U.S.-Cuban relations in one of his back-channel talks with the USSR's ambassador in Washington, Anatoly Dobrynin, the latter was unimpressed. As the ambassador noted in his journal after talking to Kissinger and consulting with Latin American foreign ministers attending an OAS summit in Washington, there were actually "no changes in U.S. policy towards Cuba."[2]

Détente was also not the opportunity for Allende that his government ardently hoped it would be. Not only did it fail to prevent U.S. intervention in Chile, but it also diminished the Soviet Union's already slim ability and desire to assist the UP at a time when it faced decisive opposition. Moreover, at the height of détente in the mid-1970s, right-wing military dictators either held on to power or seized control and engaged in brutal wars against "communism" in the majority of states in South America. As one senior U.S. official argued in 1970, Latin America was a "key area" in "a mortal struggle to determine the shape of the future of the world."[3]

Within this inter-American context, Chile's revolutionary process—the so-called Chilean Road to Socialism or La Vía Chilena—determined how this "mortal struggle" evolved. Immediately after Allende's election, Fidel Castro committed Cuba to protecting the new president's life and supporting his revolutionary goals, while Richard Nixon issued instructions to ensure they failed. Having initially regarded Latin American affairs as a low foreign policy priority, Nixon now also told his National Security Council that, although Chile, like Cuba, had been "lost," Latin America had not, and he wanted Washington do everything possible to "keep it."[4] The United States then employed various tactics throughout the continent to do just that, ranging from newly focused containment of Chilean and Cuban influence to "rolling back" left-wing advances, often with Brasilia's help and encouragement. Primarily, U.S. officials concentrated on the Southern Cone, where they assisted local right-wing dictators and enabled counterrevolutionary military elites to take power in the few countries where they were not already in control. Henceforth, rather than merely a geographical collection of states at the southern end of Latin America, the Southern Cone became a historically significant grouping as a result of what happened in the 1970s. Defined here in its broadest sense to incorporate Brazil and Bolivia as well as Chile, Argentina, Paraguay, and Uruguay, this was later to be the home of "Operation Condor," the now-infamous state-sponsored anticommunist network that unleashed repression and terror throughout the Americas and Europe from the mid-1970s until the 1980s.

Of course, knowing what came after Allende's presidency makes it very difficult not to regard his efforts to usher in a peaceful road to socialism and a new international order as idealistic and naive. Yes, the Chileans who entered government in November 1970 understood that Allende's revolutionary agenda would face major obstacles at home and abroad when it came to pursuing a revolutionary agenda, but they did not fully anticipate or understand the vehemence of their enemies' hostility toward them. On the one hand, they mistakenly believed economic factors were at the heart of such hostility and, on the other hand, they were very much caught up in the possibility that the United States' influence in Latin America was in trouble, that its difficulties in Vietnam limited its foreign policy agenda at home and abroad, that U.S. officials' reassurances were genuine, and that their own apparently persuasive reasoning would allow them to neutralize the threats La Vía Chilena faced. Ultimately, as a committed socialist, Allende also firmly believed that Chileans, Latin Americans, and the world beyond would eventually—even after his own death, if need be— be persuaded of the merits of his ideological cause and march hand in hand toward a historically determined future. And he was not alone in this regard. As the former *Washington Post* journalist John Dinges has argued, all those who study Latin America during this period need to appreciate "one improbable fact"—that "radical social revolution was a real possibility for millions of people, coloring everyday life with hope or dread depending on the circumstances and political views of each individual."[5]

With this "improbable fact" in mind, this book deals with the impact external actors had on Chilean domestic politics; how Chile affected regional developments; and, beyond this, the degree to which inter-American affairs and global trends such as the growing North-South divide in global politics and superpower détente interacted with each other. Because of their centrality to the events that unfolded, I have focused first and foremost on Chilean, Cuban, and U.S. perspectives when addressing these questions. Among these three, the Chileans were the key determiners of their country's foreign relations and its future rather than being passive bystanders viewing—and being affected by—the actions of outsiders. Beyond them, Cuba and the United States were the external powers that had the greatest impact on Chilean affairs, and the relationships that Santiago's new leader had with Havana and Washington would be his most decisive. As indicated already, others also stood alongside them, not least the Southern Cone's revolutionary movements, who sought refuge in Chile during the Allende years, and Brazil's military regime, whose regional role is examined in detail for the first time in this book. Indeed, as the United States' representative at Allende's inauguration, Assistant Secretary of State for Latin American Affairs Charles Meyer privately told Chile's new president the day after his inauguration, bilateral relationships were "not only played in a direct and immediate way but also in multilateral arenas."[6] And these intersections—between the domestic and the international, the bilateral and the multilateral—are the main themes of the story that follows.

BEFORE EMBARKING on an examination of the evolution of the Chilean chapter of the inter-American Cold War, it is perhaps worth pausing to explain why an alternative perspective on Allende's presidency and the Cold War is necessary. First and foremost, the issue is one of "decentering" the story and viewing it from different perspectives and then weaving these together in one integrated narrative. As Hal Brands has argued, what he sees as "Latin America's Cold War" consisted of "a series of overlapping conflicts" that "drew together local, regional, and global conflicts."[7] Moreover, as Leslie Bethell and Ian Roxborough have urged, rather than "forcing the rich diversity of Latin American politics into a Cold War template," we need to "use that diversity to provide a framework helpful in understanding the indigenous origins of the Latin American Cold War."[8] While I would argue that the United States' place within this diverse tapestry in the Americas has to be included on account of its highly consequential relationship with the region, this is an important observation. In the past, formulaic research centering on U.S. interventions in various Latin American countries has not only tended to retrospectively give the United States the power to dominate Latin America's history but has also resulted in a rather sporadic crisis-driven narrative of inter-American affairs.[9] Or as one historian recently noted, for far too long a Latin American event seemed to count among Cold War scholars only when "high-level American government policymakers participated in its planning and execution."[10]

The attention that the rise and fall of La Vía Chilena has received is no exception. As far as there is an existing *international* history of Allende's presidency, it has been taken over by a crowded field of studies that began appearing in the 1970s regarding Nixon and Kissinger's intervention in Chile first to prevent Allende's inauguration and then to bring down his government—what has become a cliché of U.S. interventionism during the Cold War. While there is now a broad consensus that the United States cannot be held exclusively responsible for Allende's failings and subsequent overthrow (or death), the extensive declassification of U.S. documents from the late 1990s onward led historians to eagerly reexamine the details of Washington's covert operations in Chile in the hope of finding evidence either to support or to reject this conclusion.[11] Overall, however, a narrow historiography of blame for Allende's downfall has shaped discussion with particular emphasis on (re)exposing Henry Kissinger's individual role and his desire to subvert democracy.[12] Two of the most recent works in this regard are Jonathan Haslam's *The Nixon Administration and the Death of Allende's Chile: A Case of Assisted Suicide* (2005) and Kristian Gustafson's *Hostile Intent: U.S. Covert Operations in Chile, 1964–1974* (2007). Reflecting the longevity of a polarized debate, they actually reach different conclusions about U.S. responsibility for the Chilean coup, with the former arguing Nixon and Kissinger were individually responsible for masterminding it (albeit within a conducive atmosphere created by Allende's "suicidal" economic and political policies) and the latter exaggerating the extent to which they were not. Haslam's suggestion that in mid-1973 Nixon and Kissinger sidestepped the CIA and used the Pentagon's contacts with the Chilean military to embark on an ultrasecret operation to kill off Allende's ailing government is perhaps the most original new contribution to the "who did it?" debate.[13] Nevertheless, the details of his argument—drawn from anonymous interviews—are questionable and unpersuasive. For example, Haslam suggests that Nixon's confidant, the U.S. defense attaché in Paris and soon to be deputy director of the CIA, General Vernon Walters, was in Chile on the day of the coup, personally helping the Chilean armed forces to mount it from his hotel room in Santiago. Yet Walters's personal diaries show that he was not in Santiago at the time.[14]

More important, it seems to me that focusing on Nixon and Kissinger's skullduggery or CIA machinations in Chile tells us only one part of one side of a far more interesting and complex story. Decentering even the United States' side of the story alone reveals much more, particularly when it comes to explaining motivations for U.S. policy, the process by which it occurred, and its consequences. As the historian Jussi Hanhimäki has asserted, the key is to draw on the growing wealth of declassified documentary material to place Kissinger's role, in particular, in context. He thus argues that "the important story" is "why certain policy options prevailed over others, how the implementation of policy functioned, and why it produced positive or negative (long- and short-term) results."[15]

In this respect, a couple of things stand out immediately. First, consensus turns out to have been more frequent in the Nixon administration when it came to Chile and Latin America than has previously been acknowledged. Although they disagreed on priorities and tactics at various points between 1970 and 1973, the president, Kissinger, Secretary of State William Rogers, the U.S. State Department's Bureau of Inter-American Affairs, the Defense Department, and the Treasury Department *all* opposed Allende and wanted him removed from office. In an attempt to find Kissinger guilty, Nixon's role as the principal guiding force behind the United States' renewed Cold War Latin American policies in late 1970 has also been underplayed. Meanwhile, the State Department's contribution to the formulation and execution of policy has been misrepresented as the moderate and moral wing of U.S. foreign policy making. As the declassified record demonstrates, Secretary Rogers showed no sympathy or tolerance for Allende or La Vía Chilena. And as chapter 7 details, interagency contingency planning for a successor regime over a month before the Chilean coup took place reveals much about who led policy as well as what lay at the heart of the protagonists' "hostile intent." Rather than merely opposing Allende by 1973, the Nixon administration as a whole—State Department officials, CIA operatives, Kissinger and Nixon included—had developed a clear idea of what it wanted to happen in Chile: it *wanted* authoritarian rule patterned on Brazil's dictatorship and a war against the "Left" as the only remedy to reverse the damage done by Allende's presidency. Even more striking are decision makers' fears that Chilean military leaders were not Brazilian enough, either in terms of their readiness for repressing the Left or in their ideological sense of a mission. Not only does this demonstrate with clarity exactly what they wanted to achieve, but it also shows how ignorant they were of those whom they were pinning their hopes on—who turned out to be far more ideological and violent than they could have dreamed of. Partly as a result of these misguided notions, there was also broad agreement in Washington about the need to encourage Chilean military leaders who eventually toppled Allende's government to seek help from other regional dictatorships and to cooperate with them to impose a new counterrevolutionary order in the Southern Cone.

This broader regional dimension was the second factor to leap off the page when I began my research into the U.S. side of Chile's international relations during the Allende years. To date, the story of U.S. intervention against Allende has been treated as *the* case study of the Nixon administration's Latin American policy. In fact, it is generally agreed that Nixon and Kissinger were "indifferent" to the region and that they did not regard it as "important" beyond their general preference for military leaders and disdain for expropriation.[16] Yet a mountain of newly available documentation shows that this was simply not the case. True, Washington officials' animosity toward Allende was based on general calculations about the impact he could have on the global balance of power, but Allende was more than an isolated threat in a geostrategic superpower contest.[17] He was viewed in a regional context to such an extent that after September 1970 Chile directly shaped a new phase of the United States' Cold War agenda in Latin America. At one point, Kissinger's chief aide on Latin American affairs even went so far as to warn that the region was a potentially greater test of the Nixon administration's foreign policy than Southeast Asia.[18]

Latin America's location was the key to this concern. After all, this was the United States' backyard and an area that was commonly perceived as underpinning its superpower status. It was also an area where Washington's prestige and political influence were particularly weak in 1970. And it was precisely because Chile had magnified the United States' deteriorating regional position that Allende's election was treated with such alarm. Protecting corporate economic interests was not the main issue at stake here—the Nixon administration did not even properly address this problem vis-à-vis Allende's election until early 1971. The Soviet Union was also not believed to be on the verge of imminently taking over the United States' sphere of influence. Instead, it was internal developments within Latin America and Chile's importance for them that were considered ominous. Allende's election starkly showed that those within the United States' traditional sphere of influence were rejecting Washington's prescriptions of economic and political development and opting for socialism, albeit "irresponsibly," as Kissinger put it.[19] More important, considering the climate of upheaval in the inter-American system, their actions and anti-imperialist agenda threatened to be particularly catching. U.S. policies therefore focused on stemming the tide and on winning back political influence throughout the hemisphere. To argue that the Nixon administration subsequently developed a sophisticated or comprehensive strategy toward Latin America would be an exaggeration. But not to examine U.S. policy toward Chile in the context of its reenergized approach to regional affairs after Allende's election is to fail to get to the core of its intervention in Chile.

Latin American sources also now show that the United States did not act alone but worked with regional actors and was sometimes dragged into further involvement in inter-American affairs by them. Brazil's military regime was the United States' most obvious ally in this respect and was often far more concerned, zealous, and impatient about combating Castro and Allende than the Americans. Working alongside right-wing leaders in Chile, Uruguay, Bolivia, Paraguay, and Argentina, the Brazilians were key players in the increasingly "Latin Americanized" counterrevolutionary crusade that came to dominate the Cold War in the Southern Cone by the mid-1970s. Far from being pawns of the United States, these right-wing leaders that had once relied on U.S. funding and support to reach their objectives would increasingly take ownership of the Cold War in the era of realpolitik and détente, overtaking the United States' own anticommunist mission and standing as powerful alternatives to Cuba's revolutionary example.

So what of the other side of the story—the side that Washington so vehemently opposed, namely Castro's Cuba and Allende's Chile? In contrast to the detailed account provided in Piero Gleijeses's groundbreaking history of U.S. and Cuban "conflicting missions" in Africa, the story of the intense competition between these two countries closer to home has not been adequately told.[20] Although far more is known about bilateral U.S.-Cuban relations, we are "desperately lacking a study of Cuba's role in Latin America," as the Mexican-based historian Daniela Spenser recently lamented. This is partly due to the lack of archival sources in Havana, but oral history can help considerably to begin righting this situation. Fortunately, the Cubans who participated in Latin American events during these years were keen to step forward and tell their stories to me, conscious that because of their silence their roles were being distorted or ignored.[21]

Havana's involvement in Chile during the Allende years clearly needs clarification. On one hand, the Cubans have been depicted as subverting

Chilean democracy and establishing a sinister base in Chile for supporting regional insurgency, a view that was propagated by Nixon, Kissinger, and the military junta that seized power on 11 September 1973.[22] On the other hand, some left-wing Chileans have argued that the Cubans not only failed to offer enough arms to defend the revolution but also "abandoned" Allende to his fate.[23] The best study of Cuba's influence in Chile is Haslam's *Assisted Suicide,* in which the author agrees with the former of these two interpretations. Examining Havana's growing influence in Chile from the 1960s onward and its impact on the polarization of Chilean society as a reflection of global Cold War developments, Haslam draws on U.S. and East German intelligence sources to argue that Castro's relationship with Allende was disrespectful, subversive, and tense. The Cubans in Chile, in Haslam's words, were "ominously and somewhat impatiently in the wings, the perennial ghost at the feast."[24]

I argue that the relationship was actually far more respectful and that the Cubans should not be regarded as having either "abandoned" Allende or "subverted" his presidency (the potency of the "subversion" idea clearly lies in Washington's calculated efforts to "play up" Cuba's role at the time of Allende's presidency as a means of discrediting him).[25] There *were* intense disagreements about revolutionary tactics between Allende and Castro, some of which are revealed for the first time in this book. However, the Cubans ultimately accepted that Allende was in charge. Chilean-Cuban ties were based on a close personal friendship between Castro and Allende forged over a decade before 1970 as well as the intimate relationships that the Cubans who were stationed in Chile during the Allende years had with their Chilean counterparts. Havana's preparations to resist a coup, which its leaders increasingly believed was only a matter of time, also show that Cubans stationed in Santiago were ready to fight and die alongside Allende and Chilean left-wing forces in a prolonged struggle to defend the country's revolutionary process. That they did not end up doing so was, in part, because Allende urged them not to on the basis that he did not want a battle between Chile's armed forces and the Cubans on Chilean soil. The Chilean president was therefore far more in control of Cuba's involvement in his country than previously thought.[26] And, as it turned out, Allende's unrelenting commitment to nonviolent revolution in Chile meant that he committed suicide in the wake of military intervention rather than retreating to the outskirts of Santiago to consolidate his forces and lead a future resistance struggle as the Cubans wanted him to do.

Alongside Castro's respect for Allende's final say in what happened in his country, the Cubans faced other decisive obstacles when it came to supporting and safeguarding the Chilean Road to Socialism. One was the sheer difficulty of defending Chile's revolutionary process in the U.S. sphere of influence and against the numerical power and strength of the combined branches of Chile's armed forces that struck, especially as the Cubans had not suspected that Pinochet would join in a coup. With neither Allende's permission to build up a substantial number of armaments and trained military cadres in Chile nor any apparent support from the Soviet bloc to do this on a scale that would have begun to redress the huge imbalance of forces, they faced a formidable task. And on top of this, they had to deal with the division within Chile's left-wing forces. Ultimately, the Cubans believed that Allende was the only leader who could unite such disparate forces, but they were increasingly frustrated because he not only was unable to do so but also refused to lead the Left in a direction more akin to Cuba's revolutionary experiences. Altogether, the advice that the Cubans gave to Chile's left-wing parties—to unite and to coordinate preparations to resist a military confrontation—was only as good as the influence they had on the Chileans they worked with. Last but by no means least, because the Cubans had to protect both Allende's legitimacy and their own country's reputation within Latin America, they were circumscribed by effective propaganda campaigns launched by the CIA and the Chilean Right accusing the Cubans (both falsely and justifiably) of interfering in Chile's internal affairs, trying to provoke armed conflict, and delivering arms to the Left.

On the Chilean side of our story, these allegations obviously shaped perceptions of Allende. Not only did the questions of who he was and what he stood for spark endless debate at the time, but they have also done so ever since. Mainly, this is because Allende was a highly contradictory figure. His friend, the Chilean writer and diplomat Gonzalo Rojas Pizarro, probably described him best when he depicted him as simultaneously having had the body and mind of a democratic statesman and the heart of a revolutionary.[27] For Allende, the two were not mutually exclusive and were able to coexist as a result of his faith in Chilean exceptionality— the belief that Chile's circumstances and commitment to constitutional democracy made it different from other countries in Latin America, where armed struggle was the only route to true independence and socialist revolution. Even so, this apparent contradiction has led to multiple portraits of Allende, which depict him as being everything from a saintly martyr to a villain and a misguided democrat hopelessly intoxicated—or in some cases "bewitched"—by Fidel Castro. And in what is the most comprehensive study of twentieth-century Chilean foreign policy to date, the Chilean scholar Joaquín Fermandois argues that Cuba's revolution was a "concrete model" or "paradigmatic horizon" for the UP government.[28]

Although this is an exaggerated snapshot of Allende's admiration for Castro's revolution, it does underline a central trend: the effort to understand exactly who Allende was by examining his international friends.[29] And yet, because Allende simultaneously embraced ties with Cuba and sought amicable relations with the United States, proclaimed nonalignment but journeyed to the Kremlin in search of aid, and gave sanctuary to Latin American revolutionaries while promising not to export revolution, tying Allende and the heterogeneous coalition he led to neat categorizations has proved impossible. To some, his policies were ad hoc, even "schizophrenic," whereas to others he was a passive instrument of the KGB, and to others still he was a "principled pragmatist."[30] So which of these labels is most accurate?

Like other accounts of Allende's presidency, this book argues that he acted to avoid isolation and manage conflict without sacrificing the ideals he fought for. However, I think it would be a mistake to view Chilean foreign policy as a cohesive strategy of "principled pragmatism," as others have.[31] For one, Allende led a broad left-wing coalition of parties that spanned the Chilean Left's various Marxist and non-Marxist tendencies and proved hard to unite when it came to putting policy into practice. Broadly speaking, from left to right, the coalition included Allende's own heterogeneous party, the Socialist Party (PS); the Movement of Popular Unitary Action (Movimiento de Acción Popular Unitario, or MAPU), the country's principal left-wing party; the pro-Soviet Communist Party (PCCh); the Radical Party (PR); and two smaller parties. Furthermore, the PS increasingly stood to the left of Allende and the other members of the coalition to such an extent that Allende ultimately ended up siding against his own party with the more moderate PCCh. As a result of these differences within the UP government and between arguing foreign policy advisers—a problem that basically paralyzed Chile's U.S. policy from mid-1972 onward—Allende pursued an international strategy toward the United States that was more often hesitant, imprecise, and reactive than purposefully pragmatic.

To be sure, Chile's impressive outreach to Latin America and the Third

World during this period was prescient. It is also an interesting picture of how the global South interacted with world politics in the early 1970s. Not only did Santiago host the third United Nations Conference on Trade and Development in 1972, for example, but Santiago's foreign minister was a pivotal figure in attendance at the G77's meeting in Lima in October 1971 and the Non-Aligned Movement's Summit in September 1973. In the early 1970s, Chile also significantly contributed to the radicalization of the global South's agenda as it prepared what would be the groundwork to fight for a New International Economic Order in 1974. Indeed, Allende defined Chile's foreign policy as a "reasoned rebellion" in an age of decolonization and Third World emancipation. And asserting his country's independence, he demanded that he and other Third World nations be allowed to dissent from U.S. prescriptions on economic and political relations.

However, Allende obviously overestimated the power of Chile's ability to resist U.S. intervention and the extent to which Chile could rely on Third World or Latin American unity for concrete assistance, not least because of his government's hopeful reading of détente. Unable to solve his main dilemma of how to lessen Chilean economic dependency on the United States without losing U.S. financial credits, trade, and economic aid, Allende was also increasingly stuck between his goal of independence and Chile's greater dependency on foreign powers.

It must be noted that he had no easy alternatives. Both an outright confrontation and capitulation to the United States on key issues that offered Washington public reasons to oppose him—namely, his relations with Cuba and the UP's nationalization program—had their drawbacks. The former risked repeating Cuba's experience, something the Chileans were very consciously keen to avoid. And the latter entailed Allende giving up lifelong political aims and alienating members of the UP. Yet access to the declassified record demonstrates that the Chileans had more room for maneuver early on than they realized. True, U.S. sources show conclusively that the Nixon administration's destabilization measures in Chile had begun *before* Allende even came to power and enacted his program. But it is now clear that U.S. policy makers privately felt far more vulnerable and threatened by Chile's example than they let on. They were especially eager to do what they could to avoid an open confrontation or exposure of wrongdoing at a time of growing domestic and international criticism of U.S. foreign policy in the context of the Vietnam War. In fact, Washington was so concerned with Chile's potential to become another Third World

"David" pitted against "Goliath" that U.S. diplomats expended considerable time reassuring the Chileans that the Nixon administration meant no wrong and opting for tactical shifts at key moments to lessen the appearance of hostility, and thus to limit Allende's chances of rallying support on an anti-American platform. It is just possible, then, that the Nixon administration might have been backed into an uncomfortable corner and been forced to tactically retreat and modify either its covert operations in Chile or efforts to restrict credits to the country (or both) had Allende opted for a harder, more openly vociferous line when he was strongest, in the first six months of his presidency.

Certainly, when he embarked on a more active campaign to publicize U.S. hostility to his government, Washington felt intimidated enough to step away from more overt opposition to his presidency. But by then it was largely too late, not least because Allende's "excess profits" ruling—by which profits reaped by private U.S. copper companies in Chile since the 1950s would be deducted from compensation owed to expropriated firms—provided a handy pretext that the United States was able to retrospectively apply when justifying their refusal to grant credits to him. When Allende opted to accept protracted negotiations as opposed to outright opposition with the United States at the end of 1972, the United States gained even more of the initiative when it came to U.S.-Chilean relations. By this stage, Washington needed the negotiations far less than the Chilean government, which was internally divided, battling growing opposition at home and a mounting economic crisis. And while Chile just managed to cover its financial deficit by September 1973 as a result of juggling assistance from socialist countries, Western Europe, and Latin America, this was far from sustainable. The more obvious the difficulties of this juggling act became, the more confident the United States was that Allende would ultimately fail. Indeed, Washington officials were thus prepared—and happy—to stage-manage lengthy, but cyclical, bilateral negotiations with the Chileans that promised little and avoided any resolution of core ideological or political differences, safe in the knowledge that Allende's government was running out of time.

All of which leads me to one final point with regard to how we study the history of inter-American affairs (and international history more generally). U.S.-Chilean relations and the ties between Cuba and Chile were changing, dynamic, and interactive processes rather than static and inevitably determined structures. On the one hand, Latin American actors had considerable agency when it came to the decisions they took and the way that the relationship between the United States and Latin America unfolded. On the other hand, what follows offers key insights into the rather haphazard way in which policy makers often navigated their way through different options, alliances, and policy choices. True, the balance of economic and military power between different actors in the story that follows circumscribed the paths they followed. But as Forrest Colburn has written with regard to Third World revolutionary processes, "A revolution is an explosive interaction between ideas and reality, between intention and circumstance, between political activity and social context."[32] The same can also be said of counterrevolutionary responses to the prospect of radical transformation. All sides had strategic objectives and interests, but rather than following predetermined paths and being constrained by inanimate social forces, each of them responded tactically to domestic, regional, and international developments they encountered in a far more fluid dynamic process than is sometimes accepted. As we shall see, who held the initiative against whom and for what purpose also changed repeatedly over the course of only three years as policy makers argued between themselves within government and states maneuvered around each other to shape the future. But if chance, coincidence, and personality mattered when it came to the decisions that were ultimately taken, the question here is *how* leaders chose which path to follow, how effective those choices were vis-à-vis their opponents, and what consequences these had for Chile and the inter-American Cold War.

Only by weaving various perspectives together in a multidimensional narrative is it possible to see the shifting patterns of the past. In doing so, we appreciate Castro's involvement in Chile as being the result of Allende's invitation and his previous ties with the Cubans in the 1960s as well as the effect that Cuba's experience in Chile had on Havana's already shifting regional policies. On the other side, we can also see how effectively the Nixon administration deceived the Chileans about its real intentions, the extent to which Chile's international campaign to publicize its cause temporarily offset the United States' economic and strategic advantage against Chile, the serious disagreements between policy makers in the United States about how to respond, and the fact that, in the end, it was only because certain U.S. policy makers arguing for tactical retreat won out over their hard-line colleagues that the United States was able to avoid what many within the Nixon administration feared might end up being a detrimental full-scale confrontation with Santiago. As a direct result, we also see how Chilean opportunities for making the best of a clash with Goliath dissipated. In addition, a multidimensional narrative shows that a new counterrevolutionary offensive in the Southern Cone had taken its toll on the prospects for progressive change in the region by the end of 1972, leading many of the region's revolutionary movements to seek refuge in Chile, which in turn boosted targeted attacks on the UP for letting "foreign extremists" flood the country. Well before September 1973, in fact, the Nixon administration found itself less concerned about "losing" Latin America than it had been and, hence, less desperate with regard to when and how Allende would be overthrown. Finally, an international history of the rise and fall of La Vía Chilena demonstrates that, while U.S. policy makers hesitated and waited in the wings for events to take their course, it was Chilean military leaders who launched the coup with the help of sympathetic Brazilian friends, not the United States. And our effort to understand why they did inevitably leads us back to the Cuban involvement in Chile and Latin America.

Incorporating Cuban, Chilean, and U.S. perspectives in a woven narrative, this book is divided into seven chronological chapters. Chapter 1 examines the inter-American system prior to Chile's presidential election, focusing on changing Cuban strategies for supporting revolution in Latin America, the origins of Allende's relationship with Castro, and the Nixon administration's initial approach to inter-American affairs in the period before September 1970. Chapter 2 examines how Cuba and the United States reacted to Allende's election, arguing that their subsequent aims and approach toward Chile were determined by their conceptualization of regional affairs. Chapter 3 then turns to the view from inside Chile, focusing on Santiago's international relations during Allende's first nine months in power and the beginning of a new phase of the inter-American Cold War. Chapter 4 subsequently charts the beginning of Allende's declining fortunes and the shifting balance of power in the Southern Cone. During the latter half of 1971 Allende nationalized Chile's copper industry, Fidel Castro paid a long visit to Chile (in the process becoming convinced that Allende would one day have to face a military confrontation), there was a coup in Bolivia, Uruguayan elections resulted in a decisive left-wing defeat, Brazil's president was welcomed with open arms in Washington, and Chile built up considerable sympathy and support through an ambitious international campaign.

As chapter 5 then shows, Allende's growing domestic and international battles in the first ten months of 1972 began to take their toll, particularly as many occasioned serious disagreement between Chile's left-wing leaders. As Santiago's policy makers gradually began realizing that the era of peaceful coexistence did not offer Allende the space to implement his peaceful road to socialism, or the opportunities for the global South to assert itself on the international stage, the United States began implementing new more flexible, and relaxed, tactics for winning back influence in Latin America. In chapter 6, we see that, although Allende faced growing difficulties abroad in late 1972 and early 1973, the UP's parties did surprisingly well in Chile's congressional elections in March 1973 precisely at the moment that his allies abroad began dissecting the reasons for his likely defeat. Finally, chapter 7 examines the cataclysmic end to La Vía Chilena. By detailing the interaction between international actors and Chilean politics in the months immediately before and after Allende's overthrow, it demonstrates the final impact that the inter-American Cold War had on Chile and vice versa. On the one hand, details of the Cubans' experience during the coup and the coup leaders' ferocity against Havana's embassy in Santiago on the day of the coup underscore the military's concerns about that country's role in the country. On the other hand, when the Cubans fled Chile, Washington sprang into action to help Chile's new military regime and encouraged it to coordinate with others in South America to battle against the Left in all its various guises.

As it turned out, the United States did not have to do much coordinating. Three years after Allende's inauguration celebrations, Chile's national stadium once again became a focal point of Chilean politics. This time, however, it was a detention and torture center for seven thousand prisoners rounded up by a military junta that seized power on 11 September 1973. Within its walls, Brazilian intelligence officials were to be found, assisting the representatives of Chile's new military dictatorship in their repression of the Left while rooting out Brazilian exiles who had previously found sanctuary in the country. Allende was dead, and within three months another twelve hundred were murdered by the military junta's new regime.[33] Back in Havana, Cuban leaders also concluded that the prospects of revolution in South America were minimal, leading them to focus on nonideological diplomatic and economic ties in the region while simultaneously shifting their revolutionary hopes to Africa. Indeed, rather than having been the harbinger of a red tide, Chile's "road to socialism" had actually been a moment of profound transition in the other direction, spanning a period of decisive defeat for left-wing forces in South America.

Of course, for those that had gathered to hear Allende speak at the national stadium back on a warm spring day in November 1970, what lay ahead was still unimaginable. And difficult as it may be, we must cast our minds back to that moment of uncertainty when hope and dread shaped the way in which peoples and leaders throughout the Americas conceptualized the prospect of revolutionary change. This is, after all, the only way to understand why and how history unraveled the way it did. It is also where an international history of Allende's Chile and the inter-American Cold War in the early 1970s must begin.

1 IDEALS
Castro, Allende, Nixon, and the Inter-American Cold War

"It is hard to imagine," a Chilean Socialist Party militant mused as he looked back on the late 1960s more than forty years later. Back then, when you walked into any bookshop, there were lots of Marxist publications, and news of Latin American guerrilla struggles reached Chile all the time. Especially toward the end of the decade, Che Guevara's ideas and Régis Debray's books were also endlessly discussed within Chile's different left-wing parties, and everyone was engaged in what seemed like a permanent ideological debate.[1]

This ideological fervor in Chile resulted as much from internal as from external factors. International developments had profoundly influenced Chilean politics throughout the first half of the twentieth century despite it being the country furthest away from both superpowers, nestled between the Andes and the Pacific at the southernmost tip of the Americas. Whether affected by the result of the Great Depression of the 1930s or the Korean and Vietnam wars, Chile's export-orientated economy fluctuated with global copper markets, the Santiago-based United Nations Economic Commission for Latin America expounded theories of dependency that were taken up by many others in the Third World, and new ideas from abroad fertilized those already present and growing within Chilean society. On the Left, divisions within the international communist movement over Stalin's leadership or the Soviet invasions of Hungary and Czechoslovakia, for example, had had a profound impact on the character of and relations between Chile's left-wing parties. And the United States–led "Alliance for Progress" had invigorated the country's centrist Christian Democrat government in the mid-1960s, encouraging—and funding—President Eduardo Frei Montalva's reformist program to bring about a "Revolution in Liberty."

However, it was the Cuban revolution that had had the most pivotal external impact on Chilean political debates in the 1960s. For the Socialist Party, in particular, Cuba's revolutionary example had a special resonance. As the Chilean scholar, diplomat, and politician Heraldo Muñoz explained, "the Cuban Revolution symbolized and synthesized the essential tenets of [Socialist] party thought on international affairs. In short, Cuba constituted a nationalist, anti-imperialist, popular, anticapitalist, and Latin-Americanist experience . . . with which Chile and Chilean Socialists could identify fully—that is, politically, culturally, geographically, historically, and economically; unlike the various nationalist-populist experiments in Latin America, Cuba was to build socialism from below and not as the imposition of foreign troops, within the Western hemisphere and merely ninety miles away from the United States."[2]

Beyond Chile, the Cuban revolution had also fundamentally changed the narrative of inter-American affairs and politics. Before Fidel Castro entered Havana in January 1959, efforts to bring about revolutionary change in Latin America had suffered decisive setbacks, most notably in Guatemala, where the nationalist leader, Jacobo Arbenz, had been overthrown as a result of a CIA-backed invasion in 1954. After the Cuban revolution, however, the situation was reversed and everything seemed possible: left-wing parties in Latin America not only had evidence that revolution could *succeed* but also proof it could even do so in the United States' immediate backyard. True, Fidel Castro's strategy for gaining power may have been more violent than the one advocated by long-established communist parties throughout the region. But it also undoubtedly energized those who believed that socialism was the answer to Latin America.

As a Chilean Socialist Party senator, Salvador Allende was one of many left-wing politicians in Latin America who flocked to Havana after 1959 to see what the revolution was like and who left Cuba impressed. In the era of Che Guevara's internationalist missions to Africa and Bolivia during the mid-1960s, the island then became home to an impatient younger generation of radicalized Latin American volunteers who aspired to follow in Guevara's footsteps. One such Chilean later described how he went to Cuba looking for his own Sierra Maestra. "The only thing that tormented me was a sense of urgency," he recalled, "if I did not hurry up, this world was not going to wait for me to change and perhaps I would not have time to get to my mountain."[3]

Of course, the task of bringing about socialist revolution throughout Latin America was far more complex than a question of enthusiastic young revolutionaries heading off into the mountains. By the end of the 1960s, even Havana's leaders had begun to acknowledge this and, as a result, were already reviewing their earlier insistence that armed struggle and the guerrilla *foco* was *the* road to revolution. Their examination of the alternatives available for bringing about progressive, if not yet socialist, change responded to the scars of the new intensified inter-American Cold War that had emerged after 1959. Cuban support for armed revolution in Colombia, Argentina, Peru, Venezuela, Guatemala, and Bolivia had failed.[4] The reformist government of João Goulart had also been toppled and replaced by a military dictatorship in Brazil in 1964; U.S. forces had invaded the Dominican Republic in 1965; a highly politicized military elite had emerged in the region that believed it had a role to play in the region's future; and, devastatingly, Che Guevara had been killed trying to spark a revolution in Bolivia in late 1967. At the same time, the continent's left-wing movement—the heterogeneous Chilean Left included—had become deeply divided over Castro's call to arms. As some went in search of their own Sierra Maestras, others berated the idea of the guerrilla foco and continued to advocate forging broad alliances as a means of gaining political power.

Meanwhile, many on the right and center of Latin American politics shared left-wing frustrations about the region's lack of economic progress during the United Nations' "development decade" of the 1960s. Not only did it seem that Latin America had failed to keep up with a rapidly changing world, but President John F. Kennedy's $20 billion Alliance for Progress had failed to "immunize" the hemisphere from revolutionary currents and had clearly fallen far short of its illustrious goals. Even President Frei in Chile suggested that the alliance had "lost its way" and demanded new answers to Latin America's underdevelopment.[5] After all, the region continued to face challenges of inequality, political instability, exploding population growth, economic dependency, and military interventions. Toward the end of the 1960s, it was also characterized by a surge of radical nationalism and growing resentment toward a world economic system that seemed destined to ignore its needs, so much so that many predicted that revolution (of one form or another) was "inevitable."[6]

The incoming Nixon administration in Washington was not oblivious to this. As one internal U.S. study warned at the end of 1969, "rapidly intensifying change" was sweeping through Latin America.[7] Nasser-style nationalist revolutionary military leaders had seized power in Peru, Panama, and Bolivia, adding a new dimension to inter-American relations that challenged U.S. influence in the hemisphere.[8] And in Chile, one of Latin America's few long-standing democratic countries, politics seemed to be moving left. Moreover, as Allende would later say, what happened in Chile was not "isolated or unique."[9] Years later, a senior member of Cuba's Communist Party echoed this verdict, arguing that to understand Allende's election and his presidency, one needed to understand what the Americas and the world looked like in the late 1960s and early 1970s.[10]

Castro's Cold War

Combining ideas of social justice that had come to prominence during Cuba's nineteenth-century struggle for independence with Marxism and anger at U.S. interventionism, Havana's revolutionary leaders extolled defiant, radical nationalism and an internationalist commitment to accelerate Latin America's "second independence." As Castro proclaimed in his "Second Declaration of Havana" (1962), it was "the duty of every revolutionary to make revolution" and "not for revolutionaries to sit in the doorways of their houses waiting for the corpse of imperialism to pass by."[11] This notion of revolutionary internationalism did not come from nowhere in 1959. Before this, Fidel Castro had not only called for Cuba to become the "bulwark of liberty" in the Americas but had also acknowledged that his "destiny" would be to wage a "much wider and bigger war" against the United States.[12]

Revolutionary Cuba's foreign minister echoed this sentiment more than a decade later when he explained to Havana's socialist bloc allies what the Cubans' approach to Latin America was. In his words, they were "fighting for the freedom of Latin American nations" in an "emancipatory and revolutionary battle" reminiscent of "the Latin American people's fight for liberation from Spanish colonial oppression in the first half of the nineteenth century" led by Simón Bolívar and José de San Martín.[13] As Piero Gleijeses has written, "history, geography, culture, and language made Latin America the Cubans' natural habitat, the place closest to Castro's and his followers' hearts."[14] And Manuel Piñeiro, who headed Cuba's Latin America policy for three decades after the revolution, quite simply explained that the Cubans saw their country as an "inseparable part of Latin America." "Our revolution is a part of the Latin American revolution," he argued. "Each of our triumphs makes the fraternal countries stronger. Every Latin American victory strengthens our revolution. Our battle won't have ended until all of the peoples of Our America have freed themselves of the neocolonial yoke."[15]

With these ideas in mind, Havana offered the most radical and consistent challenge to the United States' influence in Latin America during the 1960s. While the Cubans sustained their regional battle against what they considered to be U.S. imperialism, the USSR tended to accept the region as Washington's sphere of influence. Particularly after the Cuban Missile Crisis, this meant trying not to provoke the United States' hostility by prioritizing nonideological economic ties over riskier support for socialist revolution. It also meant reasserting Moscow's long-held view that Latin America was a place where revolution would progress gradually, through class alliances and constitutional means and in two stages (national bourgeois and then socialist). Indeed, in the postwar era as a whole, Moscow's policies toward the region had mostly been reactive and focused on saving revolutionary processes rather than igniting them. When Nikita Khrushchev stressed the need for peaceful coexistence in the mid-1960s, this in turn led to a fierce rejection of what the Soviets—and Soviet-affiliated communist parties in Latin America—regarded as "adventurist" Cuban efforts to spark revolution through armed insurgency.[16] The pro-Soviet Venezuelan Communist Party also denounced Fidel's "role of judge over revolutionary activities in Latin America, the role of the super-revolutionary" and "his claim to be the only one who decides what is and is not revolutionary in Latin America."[17]

Havana was meanwhile unrepentant about its radical brand of revolutionary activism. In March 1967 Castro publicly attacked Venezuelan Communists along with "shilly-shalliers and pseudo-revolutionaries" on account of their objection to guerrilla insurgency.[18] And a month later, the Cubans published Che Guevara's infamous call to fight decisive cumulative wars against the United States ("two, three, many Vietnams").[19] According to U.S. intelligence sources, the Cubans had already trained fifteen hundred to two thousand Latin Americans in guerrilla warfare between 1961 and 1964, a number that undoubtedly rose during the latter half of the decade.[20] One of those who underwent such training later remembered Cuba as a "fascinating . . . link between revolutionaries from diverse countries," the place to meet "proven combatants," left-wing intellectuals, and guerrilla leaders. In secret training camps in Cuba, Uruguayans, Venezuelans, Colombians, Peruvians, Argentines, Bolivians, Brazilians, and Chileans could be found within groups of about thirty to forty receiving classes on firearms, explosives, artillery, mines, urban struggle, and topography. The cost and commitment that the Cubans expended on such training was immense; on one training exercise, for example, participants were expected to fire two hundred bullets a day over the course of several weeks. However, as a graduate of the training camps remembered, this was "not the place to make friends" because everyone hid their real names and remained reluctant to share revealing information with each other. More ominously for the prospects of a continental-wide Latin American revolution, not all nationalities got on.[21]

Overall, however, Cuba's offensive against U.S. influence in Latin America in the 1960s was far more restrained than was its offensive in Africa, a factor that Gleijeses ascribes to the perceived risks involved and problems of promoting insurgency as opposed to working with sovereign leaders.[22] More important, Havana's Latin American policies were also less successful. Guevara's Bolivian adventure, which was Cuba's biggest Latin American foreign policy venture before its involvement in Chile, had been quite literally the least-worst option for trying to spark a revolutionary insurgency in Latin America.[23] After his failed mission to the Congo, Che Guevara had been impatient to embark on another revolutionary campaign, preferably in Argentina but otherwise on its border. With limited prospects for starting a successful foco elsewhere, and Castro desperate to stop Che Guevara from going to Argentina, which was considered acutely dangerous, Bolivia had therefore been an unsatisfactory compromise. Even those closest to Che and the preparations for creating a foco in Bolivia later recalled that the Argentine was searching around for just about any location to create a "mother column" to power a continental revolution.[24]

As the historians James G. Blight and Philip Brenner have argued, Fidel Castro then decided to "wait and hope for good news from Bolivia, even though the outlook was bleak. . . . If Che pulled off a miracle in Bolivia, many things might be possible."[25] Although Guevara had regarded Bolivia as a suitable base for pursuing guerrilla operations in Argentina and Peru since 1963, there were multiple reasons why fermenting a Bolivian revolution—or a continental war from Bolivia as a result of internationalizing the foco—was impracticable. As Régis Debray later explained, a tree bearing revolutionary fruits needed a seed with roots, and the attempt to start a guerrilla struggle in Bolivia "had nothing in common with the horticulture." Among other things, it had been hastily organized, undermined as a result of divisions between Che Guevara and the Bolivian Communist Party led by Mario Monje, and strangled by the lack of concrete support it received from Bolivia's rural peasant population.[26]

The "trauma" of Che's death forced a drastic reevaluation of Cuba's Latin American policies, which coincided with rising ferment and nationalist upheaval throughout the continent. "New dynamics," as Cubans termed the rise of revolutionary nationalism, appeared to indicate that a new—albeit significantly different—phase of revolution was on the horizon. Like leading U.S. officials who had formulated policy toward Latin America in the early 1960s, the Cubans grew particularly interested in nationalist military elites after witnessing the growing roles they assumed in Peru, Panama, and Bolivia from 1968 onward.[27] Cuba was especially enthusiastic about Lima's new military government, which expropriated the U.S.-based International Petroleum Company with great fanfare and made immediate efforts to build ties with it.[28] In fact, Fidel Castro would personally tell one Chilean diplomat he was "very especially interested" in its leader, Juan Velasco Alvarado, whom he considered to be a man of the Left. To be sure, the new military leaders in Peru after 1968 were not Marxists. But Havana regarded their nationalization projects and social reform programs as a progressive step in the right direction—away from U.S. influence and toward some sort of economic and social justice.[29]

Although the Cubans acknowledged this type of revolutionary development would be slow, they also observed that Velasco Alvarado, together with Panama's Omar Torrijos (1968–81) and the two presidents that ruled Bolivia in quick succession at the end of the decade, Alfredo Ovando (1969–70) and Juan José Torres (1970–71), were promoting independence from the United States. And, crucially for an island suffering the results of economic sanctions, they also seemed to be reconsidering Cuba's isolation.[30] In this context—and with Che's death as a painful indication of the obstacles facing guerrilla struggles in Latin America—Havana began embracing a variety of non-Marxist nationalists and reformists after a decade of denouncing them as reactionaries. As a key protagonist of Cuba's policy toward Latin America later put it, Cuba did not unilaterally change its policies but instead responded to regional transformations.[31]

Yet, by adapting to local conditions and working with a broad assortment of regional actors, Havana *did* change its approach to Latin America. As Cubans examined the continent's shifting dynamics, Castro began to talk about many roads to revolution and adopt a more careful policy. On the one hand, he recognized that the United States' growing intervention in Latin America to prevent "another Cuba" had hampered Havana's regional approach and made it increasingly dangerous. Not only had the United States played a pivotal role in funding and training local armed forces in Latin America throughout the 1960s, but Johnson's invasion of the Dominican Republic had also raised loud alarm bells regarding the

United States' willingness to use gunboat diplomacy again to achieve its aims. Finally, Richard Nixon's election in 1968 deeply worried the Cuban leadership that worse was still to come. On the other hand, Cuba began to question the capabilities and prospects of its various different allies in Latin America. Having once been relatively unquestioning about the revolutionary movements and groups that it supported, its leadership now began to be more selective. Crucially, for example, at the end of 1968 Havana withdrew the Cubans who had been training to take part in a second major effort to ignite a guerrilla insurgency in Bolivia led by one of the survivors of Che's column, Inti Peredo. Although those involved in the guerrilla effort never knew exactly why the Cubans had been recalled at the last minute, it appears that Castro had decided he wanted to see a guerrilla movement develop and flourish on its own before he committed more of his own people to Bolivia.[32]

CIA analysts observing Cuba's approach to Latin American affairs in years to come would notice this new caution. As one of their reports later acknowledged, Havana had "sharply reduced its aid to guerrilla-orientated revolutionary movements in Latin America" after Che Guevara's death and had embarked on what seemed to be "a more realistic approach to international relations . . . a less violent approach that is more likely to diminish Cuba's isolation than continuation of support to guerrilla groups." According to this analysis, "Training in guerrilla warfare and other paramilitary subjects" was henceforth "given only to small, select groups. Logistical support still continues to some rebel groups but it is restricted to very small amounts of arms, ammunition, and communications equipment. . . . Subversive groups in Nicaragua, Colombia, and Venezuela are considered too disorganized, undisciplined, and untrustworthy to merit more than token Cuban support."[33] Although Cuba continued its long-standing support for Uruguay's urban guerrillas, the Tupamaros, Cuba's foreign minister, Raúl Roa, also privately explained to Cuba's socialist allies that the guerrilla group could not be considered Marxist and was very unlikely to ever gain power, even if it provided a useful check on Uruguayan security services.[34]

Overall, Luis Fernández Oña, a Cuban intelligence officer who would serve in Chile during Allende's presidency, described Cuba's representatives abroad in the early 1970s as "more conscientious," no longer revolutionaries "of impulse" but rather "revolutionaries of the heart *and* thought," schooled in revolutionary theory.[35] What he did not say, of course, was that they were also schooled in the implications of failure. At the very least,

Cuba remained diplomatically and economically isolated in the Western Hemisphere. And this fact, together with the changing nature of Latin American politics, called for a shift in tactics. As Jorge I. Domínguez, the author of a seminal study on Cuban foreign policy, argued, Havana's leaders "are neither dogmatic nor stupid: they have learned from past mistakes."[36]

Castro's growing flexibility regarding the ultimate character and pace of Latin America's revolution was also a consequence of Cuba's domestic situation. By the late 1960s, it became clear that earlier hopes of skipping stages of socialist revolution had been idealistic. Facing Cuba's failure to achieve a sugar harvest of 10 million tons, Castro publicly admitted responsibility in July 1970 for having been misguided. "We leaders of the Revolution have exacted too high a price [in] doing our apprenticeship," he acknowledged. "More often than not we made the mistake of minimizing difficulties, and complexity of problems. . . . The going will be hard—harder than it seemed at first . . . building socialism is difficult . . . learning to build the economy is much more difficult for revolutionaries than we imagined."[37] Later that year, Castro was then openly and uncharacteristically acknowledging the need to "proceed slowly so as to reach our destination soon, slowly so as to reach our destination well . . . slowly so as to reach our destination safely."[38]

During this period, Cuba also realigned itself toward the Soviet bloc and began looking in earnest at what Moscow's development model could offer the island. After Soviet-Cuban relations had reached an unprecedented low in 1967–68 as a result of Cuba's radical approach to Latin America, disagreements over the best path to development, and Cuban disdain for what it saw as Moscow's halfhearted support for Third World allies, various factors had persuaded Castro to seek a rapprochement with Moscow. In the context of Cuba's perpetual—and justifiable—fear of U.S. intervention, these included both Moscow's warning that the Soviets would not intervene militarily to protect Cuba if Castro provoked the United States in Latin America and the USSR's curtailment of oil shipments to the island in late 1967.[39] But it was also influenced by Castro's new approach to the task of building socialism after the failure to advance rapidly in the 1960s. As a high-level Polish Communist Party delegation would report after visiting Havana in 1971, the Cubans were embarking on "significant" changes to overcome earlier mistakes that had been founded on an "unrealistic approach to social and economic development." Now, Havana's leadership had returned to the practice of offering material—as opposed to moral—

incentives to the country's workers, stressed the importance of Soviet help to the Cuban revolution, and recognized the *"need to benefit from the experience of other countries."*[40]

The extent to which Castro's rapprochement with the USSR from 1968 onward transformed Cuba's regional policy is nevertheless unclear and debatable. Cubans maintain that Moscow never had any decisive role in directing Havana's relations with Latin America, and to a large degree this is borne out by what we now know about the Soviet-Cuban relationship vis-à-vis Africa.[41] It also appears that the Cubans' review of their Latin American policies began before this and that, if anything, this reappraisal may have pushed Castro back to the Soviet Union rather than the other way round. Certainly, members of the Soviet bloc continued to report on Fidel Castro's position on Latin America as something somewhat alien to them—a particularly Cuban cause and principled obsession.[42] Furthermore, even after Soviet-Cuban relations began to improve toward the end of 1968, Castro did not feel secure enough to abandon his efforts to make Latin America—and the world—safe for the survival of his revolution. "Will the Warsaw Pact divisions be sent to Cuba if the Yankee imperialists attack our country?" Castro asked, as he simultaneously endorsed the invasion of Czechoslovakia.[43] To make Cuba safer, and the hemisphere less threatening, the Cubans therefore continued to pursue their own, independent efforts to end their isolation and secure their revolution's future in Latin America.

The Soviet Union was nevertheless pleased with Castro's new flexibility toward the region. In early 1970, Moscow's diplomats announced to U.S. State Department officials and Latin American ambassadors in Washington the arrival of a "new Castro" who had "matured," was "willing to live in peace and harmony with his neighbors," and was "prepared for a more responsible role in international affairs."[44] Two years later, an internal Polish Foreign Ministry memorandum would then detail what Soviet bloc analysts regarded as having been "the Cuban leadership's realistic revision and review of the situation in Latin America." After a period of "adventurism"—when the Cubans had made theoretical and practical "mistakes" (e.g., by succumbing to "a false assessment of the revolutionary situation in Latin America" or supporting "pseudo-revolutionary groups")—Warsaw recorded that important changes had taken place: Havana had broken off ties to "extremist and demagogic groups" in the region, there had been an adjustment in the Cuban cadres who dealt with Latin America (the Poles were actually wrong about the extent to which this had taken place), and

Havana had responded well to the emergence of progressive governments in the region.[45]

As Havana's subsequent policy in Latin America clearly moved more in line with the Soviet Union's, this opened up possibilities of cooperation, perhaps most extensively in Peru.[46] Yet, where Chile was concerned, there are no indications to suggest that the Cubans coordinated their efforts with the Soviets or that they were acting on the Soviets' behalf. Havana's leadership had maintained close relations with Chile's various left-wing parties throughout the 1960s despite—or, in some cases, precisely because of—its divergent position toward Moscow. To be sure, relations between Cuba and the pro-Soviet Chilean Communists had deteriorated in the mid-1960s, but as Castro's strategy toward Latin America changed at the end of the decade, and as Cuban-Soviet relations improved, this tension diminished with what appears to have been a nudge from Moscow to its loyal allies, the Chilean Communists. When the PCCh leader, Volodia Teitelboim, arrived in Cuba for a visit in June 1970, the Chilean Communist Party reported to East Germany that this was "an initiative pushed by Moscow in order to improve relations between brother parties."[47] Be that as it may, this made it far easier for Cuba to support the Unidad Popular coalition as it began campaigning on behalf of its presidential candidate, Salvador Allende.

Cuba, Chile, and Salvador Allende

Allende had been the key to Havana's ties with Chile since 1959. As Fidel Castro recalled in 2008, over the course of more than a decade he had had "the honor of having fought next to [Allende] against imperialism . . . from the time of the triumph of the Cuban revolution."[48] Of course, the Chilean leader had been an advocate of socialist revolution and a determined challenger of U.S. imperialism before Castro had even reached adolescence. Their experiences and methods were also poles apart. However, both shared a common set of values and a world outlook that brought them together at a critical moment in Latin American history. As a Chilean senator throughout the 1960s, Allende had denounced Washington's aggression against Cuba, vociferously supported Castro's revolution, and shown sympathy toward the Castroite far Left in Chile (to which his nephew Andrés Pascal and his daughter Beatriz belonged). Indeed, Allende's political standing and his loyalty to the Cuban cause meant that Havana's leaders regarded him as a highly significant ally.

By 1970 Cuban revolutionaries could also look back on more than a decade of friendships with Chilean left-wing leaders and at least some internationalist collaboration with them in Latin American revolutionary struggles. Certainly, before Chile severed diplomatic relations with Cuba in 1964 along with other OAS members—and with more difficulty after—Cuban intelligence officials passed through Chile to coordinate Havana's support for revolution elsewhere in Latin America.[49] Many Chileans also spontaneously volunteered to go to Cuba to offer their assistance to the revolution at the start of the decade, among them the future manager of Chile's Central Bank during the UP years, Jaime Barrios. As a Cuban intelligence officer who worked in Chile in the early 1960s recalled, this early support for the revolution was "powerful."[50]

Meanwhile, many of the young Cubans who arrived in Chile during this period (among them Cuban intelligence officials) were often rather frustrated and culturally bemused by Chilean "formality" and the "strictness" of legalistic strategies for revolution.[51] And Havana's leaders were also deeply skeptical of the concept of a peaceful democratic road to revolution. Yet in many respects they had always regarded Chile as a unique case in Latin America, lacking the prerequisites for armed insurgency. Two-thirds of Chile's population lived in towns and cities, it was one of the most industrialized countries in Latin America, and its established left-wing parties participated in a stable constitutional democracy. When Che Guevara had pored over maps of the region to decide where he could locate a guerrilla motor to power a continental revolution, he likewise had not seen Chile as a viable location. With its arid desert in the north and Patagonia in the south, its climate extremes and its isolated position between Argentina's armed forces over the Andes and the Pacific on the other side, it was never regarded as being a good base for a guerrilla movement.[52] As such, Cuba's deputy prime minister, Carlos Rafael Rodríguez, later noted that Chile had always been "one of the few exceptions" where peaceful revolution could possibly succeed.[53]

Even so, some Chileans were eager to persuade the Cubans that their country was ripe for armed insurgency in the 1960s and were frustrated by the Cubans' "respect" for the traditional Chilean Left's emphasis on non-violence.[54] In 1965 a group of young educated students in the southern city of Concepción established the Movimiento de Izquierda Revolucionaria (Revolutionary Left Movement, or MIR), an unmistakably Cuban-inspired party. This was initially a small group, comprising only three hundred members, and even U.S. intelligence analysts believed the MIR's strength to be "far more miniscule" than the three thousand members press arti-cles suggested it had in 1970.[55] Moreover, the MIR's initial attempt to cre-ate a guerrilla base camp in the cordillera of the Andes on the border of Argentina was a complete disaster.[56] The MIR's relationship with Cuba also complicated Havana's relationship with Chile's other left-wing par-ties, especially when the group launched urban guerrilla insurgency cam-paigns in the late 1960s. Its violence and mobilization efforts certainly tarnished the Left's constitutional reputation in Chile and undermined the PCCh's and PS's efforts to gain power peacefully. And in this context, Cuba's association with the MIR became a core issue dominating Chilean intra-Left struggles.

However, when Havana reduced its emphasis on armed struggle and moved closer to Moscow at the end of the 1960s, it had distanced itself from the MIR's actions. As Chile's future chargé d'affaires in Havana remem-bered, members of the MIR—or Miristas as they were known—enchanted the Cuban leadership, reminding it of its own youthful revolutionary fervor.[57] But, increasingly, Cuba limited its support to funding the MIR's newspaper, *Punto Final*, and instructed Miristas that they would have to finance their own insurgent activities (which they did through bank raids they euphemistically called "expropriations").[58] Did the Cubans also force the MIR to support Allende's campaign in 1970, as some have argued? The answer is complicated. In the run-up to the elections, the MIR suspended its urban guerrilla actions not because the Cubans instructed it to so much as because of Allende's direct request that it do so and the MIR's own con-fidence that when Allende lost—as it believed he surely would—its com-mitment to armed action would gain credibility.[59] More important, it now appears that Allende personally offered to pay the MIR to stop its violent actions in Chile. In a meeting with the group's leadership during his presi-dential campaign, he listened sympathetically to the MIR's argument that it would not be able to survive without funds generated from its expropria-tions, and he therefore offered to help the group economically. As one of those who was present at the meeting later remembered, he offered the MIR $80,000—"a lot of money in those days!"[60] In February 1970, when the MIR announced its "critical support" for the UP, the Cubans were never-theless pleased that it was getting behind Salvador Allende's election cam-paign.[61] After all, it was the presidential candidate and *not* the MIR that was, had been, and would be Havana's main ally in Chile.

As noted, the relationship between Castro and Allende rested first and foremost on a similar view of Latin America's predicament. Both leaders shared a belief that they faced similar challenges of dependency and underdevelopment in an unequal capitalist world and that they were circumscribed in their efforts to redress this system by the overbearing power of the United States in Latin America. As Allende told the crowds that gathered to celebrate his inauguration as president, Chile's backwardness was the result of a "dependent capitalist system which counterposes the rich minority to the needy majority internally and the powerful nations to the poor nations externally."[62] And as far as the Socialist Party was concerned, "worldwide exploitation involved not only social classes but also nation-states."[63] Allende—a lifelong Socialist himself—saw Chile as just one front line in a wider battle between the world's poorest peoples and its richest nations in which he and Castro were fighting on the same side.

Like many others in the global South, including Castro, Allende also adopted Marxism—and Marxist-inspired theories of dependency—as a means of understanding his country's backwardness and of solving it.[64] Two decades before becoming president, he had argued that human destiny was "marked out by the road of socialism . . . not just because it represents technological and economic progress but also because of its different concept of communal life, because it puts the common heritage at the service of all."[65] This did not entail an automatic allegiance to the Soviet Union. To the contrary, the Socialist Party's very identity was based on its opposition to the PCCh's pro-Soviet stance, and, as a founding member in the early 1930s, Allende argued the need to find Chilean—as opposed to Soviet—solutions to his country's problems. During his presidential campaign in 1964, when faced with what Chileans at the time referred to as a "terror campaign" that linked his candidacy with the prospect of Soviet tanks rolling into Santiago, he had also clearly stated that reduced dependency on the United States need not mean new subservience to the USSR. Chile would be no one's partner in the Cold War struggle, he insisted.[66]

Indeed, rather than a strict division of the world between East and West, it was the split between the global North and South that conditioned Allende's worldview. In prescribing socialism as a route to economic development, equality, and emancipation for the Third World, Allende subscribed to what Forrest Colburn has termed the "vogue of revolution in poor countries."[67] The new Chilean government shared a view of historical inevitability that drew on Marxist notions of progress, what another scholar, Robert Malley, describes as "a well-defined, if misinterpreted, progression of events from the fall of the colonial order to independence and to the victory of 'revolutionary' Third World movements."[68] Certainly,

Allende would refer to his own victory as "a monument to those who fell" in Chile's "social struggle, who sprinkled with their blood the fertile seed of the Chilean revolution" and made it possible.[69] And looking toward the dawn of a new world, Chile's foreign minister during the Allende years, the Socialist Clodomiro Almeyda Medina, later argued that "the current of history" tended "to strengthen the efforts of developing countries" and aid their efforts to close "the gap . . . that irrationally separates the developed capitalist world from the peoples of Asia, Africa, and Latin America."[70] As some of the young Chileans that would work closely with President Allende recounted, the war in Vietnam, student protests in Paris in 1968, and the rise of Third Worldism also imbued them with enthusiasm and a sense that their country's political developments were part of a major shift in global politics.[71] As one such Chilean recalled, by the late 1960s, they believed that world revolution was imminent and that it would be determined in the global South.[72]

Back in 1959, Castro's revolution had reinforced Allende's beliefs and inspired him. In March of that year he had arrived in Cuba to see for himself what it and its leaders were like, whereupon Carlos Rafael Rodríguez, who had spent some time in Chile during the 1950s, introduced him to the country's new leaders. When Allende met Fidel Castro and Che Guevara, he had been immediately impressed. As if to prove his allegiance to the ideals Havana's leaders espoused, but to distinguish himself from their methods, he often exhibited Che Guevara's dedication to him that read: "To Salvador, who by other means is trying to obtain the same." Allende later also explained to Régis Debray that in Cuba and Vietnam, which he visited in 1969, he had found inspiration in "a united people, a people with political conscience, a people whose leaders have moral strength."[73] And in a speech he had given while visiting Havana in 1962, he also proclaimed that the enemy of the Chilean people was the same enemy Cuba faced. "Cuba is not alone," he pledged. "Cuba has the solidarity of all the oppressed peoples of the world! We are with you because your revolution which is Cuban and national is not only your revolution but the revolution of all oppressed peoples . . . as a people you have opened, in words and in action, a great road of liberation in Latin America."[74]

This message of liberation was central to Allende's objectives. For Chile, which had after all gained its political independence in the early nineteenth century, the issue of "liberation" centered on the quest for "second independence" through the eradication of U.S. economic penetration of the country. But instead of sugar, as in Cuba's case, it was copper that dominated Chilean trade with the United States. Copper, "the salary of Chile," as Allende termed it, accounted for 80 percent of Chile's foreign exchange earnings.[75] From the 1920s until the late 1960s, four U.S. companies had also dominated 80–90 percent of Chile's large-scale mining. After a period of intense foreign investment in Chile during the 1950s, President Frei had then begun the process of nationalization by buying out 51 percent of the country's Gran Mineria.[76] But by 1970, foreign investors still controlled a quarter of Chilean industry.[77] Meanwhile, Chile had rising unemployment, inequality, and poverty. Explaining why a country rich in copper and mineral resources had "failed" to solve the "grave crisis" facing Chilean society, Allende, and the Unidad Popular coalition he represented in the election of 1970, pointed to Chile's economically dependent status and charged "imperialist exploitation" of Chile's riches. "By nationalizing copper, we shall cease to be poor," a Communist Party slogan promised.[78]

Allende's commitment to nationalizing Chile's raw materials and reducing U.S. economic and political dominance in Latin America was long-standing. As a junior minister in Pedro Aguirre Cerda's Popular Front government in the late 1930s, he had regarded himself as participating in a struggle to secure Chile's economic independence.[79] In the 1940s, he had condemned Washington's tolerance and support for dictators in the region.[80] In the 1950s, he was also one of the Chilean "Friends of Guatemala" who had denounced the United States' intervention against President Jacobo Arbenz in Guatemala.[81] In Allende's words, Arbenz had shown other nations in the Americas the way toward "progress and liberty." When U.S. secretary of state John Foster Dulles called an emergency meeting of the OAS to address Arbenz's supposed threat, Allende then described the meeting as "an instrument of the Cold War" and took off on a six-month tour of the Soviet Union, the People's Republic of China, and Europe. In an article published in *Pravda* while he was in Moscow, he subsequently underlined his preoccupation with the struggle for independence: Chileans, he wrote, "want peace and do not want war; we want respect of our sovereignty, not forced dependence; we want social justice, not exploitation."[82] Later, throughout the 1960s, Allende was a vehement critic of the Alliance for Progress, on the grounds that it did not solve Latin America's "basic problem": its dependency.[83]

In this context, Castro's struggle against the United States had radicalized Allende's approach to inter-American affairs, for, as he later told Debray, Cuba's experience had "indisputably" shown the lengths imperialism would use to defend its interests.[84] In the early 1960s, he had therefore recommended that Castro's Second Declaration of Havana be the region's "Magna Carta"; he had broken off his friendship with the Venezuelan leader Rómulo Betancourt because of differences regarding Cuba; and although he believed Chile's particular circumstances made it unsuitable for armed struggle, he had established close ties with revolutionary movements throughout the hemisphere and financially and logistically aided those who adopted violent means of bringing about revolution in Latin America.[85] Publicly, at least, he was not shy to proclaim that "militant[s] of the Latin American revolution" had "a legitimate duty and honor to lend . . . solidarity—human and ideological—to militant *compañeros* of the same revolution."[86]

Allende's personal relationship with Fidel Castro was cemented through his numerous visits to Cuba during the 1960s. In 1966 he participated in the Tricontinental Conference of African, Asian, and Latin American revolutionary and national liberation movements in Havana. Subsequently, he was one of those who proposed the formation of the Organization of Latin American Solidarity (OLAS), which came into being the following year. As it turned out, OLAS was largely ineffective as a functioning collective organization. But it was also highly symbolic and feared by an increasingly ideological anticommunist elite in Latin America, which regarded it as being far more powerful than it actually was. To this elite, OLAS embodied dangerous currents in continental affairs and, in the words of one right-wing Brazilian newspaper, was "responsible for all acts of terrorism" in Latin America.[87] Highly exaggerated as these allegations against OLAS were, Allende received extensive criticism for his association with the organization back in Chile. According to those who attacked him, he was antipatriotic and had sold out to Fidel. Or as Allende wrote at the time, he felt as if he had been subjected to his "own Vietnam and personal Bay of Pigs" as a result.[88]

The most important meeting between Allende and Castro occurred during one weekend in late October 1967 at a rural farmhouse in Manzanillo at the foothills of the Sierra Maestra. Luis Fernández Oña, who had been assigned to Chilean affairs since 1964 and who went by the name of "Demid" at the time, accompanied his boss, Manuel Piñeiro, and Fidel at this meeting, where he would also first get to know his future wife, Allende's daughter, Beatriz. As Oña recalled more than thirty years later, it was on this occasion that Allende and Castro's friendship grew, as they played ping-pong and talked about ideology and the future long into the night.[89]

Salvador Allende (wearing hat) in Cuba, 1969. Luis Fernández Oña is at the far left.
Courtesy of Luis Fernández Oña private collection.

Shortly after this, a small group of Chilean Socialist Party militants had also become involved in Cuba's internationalist mission in Bolivia. As noted already, following Che Guevara's death at the end of 1967, the Ejército de Liberación Nacional (National Liberation Army, or ELN) had begun exploring the prospects of a second guerrilla operation in Bolivia. And directly as a result of her trip to Cuba in 1967, Beatriz had become one of the leaders of a Chilean branch of the ELN working toward this end with the tacit support of her father.[90] Then, in February 1968, Allende inspired Havana's unswerving gratitude when he accompanied the three Cuban survivors of Che's guerrilla column in Bolivia out of Chile to safety after their escape into that country. By coincidence, Oña had been in Santiago clandestinely when the survivors escaped to Chile and recalled that Allende, as president of the Chilean Senate, immediately ensured the survivors were treated correctly and freed from police custody. Allende then focused on how the survivors would leave Chile. The Cubans had a small plane, a pilot, and a tank of fuel but not enough to go far. Moreover, Allende agreed with Oña that if they flew out of Chile, the Cubans would be vulnerable and could easily be shot down, perhaps by the CIA. As a result,

Oña later remembered studying maps with Allende to discuss the best possible route the survivors could take before finally reaching the decision to have Allende publicly accompany the survivors on a flight to Tahiti, where the Cuban ambassador to Paris collected them.[91]

In contrast to this obvious—and politically risky—display of support for Cuba's revolutionary mission in Latin America, Castro's ability to support Allende's presidential campaigns was oblique. Because Allende refused to countenance the prospect of violence as a means of furthering revolution in Chile, it was somewhat difficult for a generation of Cuban leaders trained in guerrilla insurgency to support him. During Chile's 1964 and 1970 presidential elections, the CIA had also launched propaganda equating an Allende victory with a Castroite dictatorship as part of a broader "terror campaign" against him. Despite this scaremongering, Allende's enemies actually had little evidence of Cuban involvement in the country. (It was only after Allende's election that the CIA estimated Cuba had given $350,000 to Allende's 1970 campaign, a figure that has been widely circulated as fact ever since but never corroborated.)[92] Although there is much that is still unclear about Castro's support for Allende during the election, Cuba's Chilean operations had also clearly become increasingly difficult after 1964. With no diplomatic relationship with Chile and therefore no continuous presence on the ground, the Cubans had had to rely on separate clandestine missions, covert radio signaling, and information from Chileans who visited Havana in circuitous journeys via Prague or Paris.[93] This situation improved slightly in February 1970, when Frei reopened commercial relations with Havana in a move to placate the Chilean Left (the agreement was worth $11 million for that year alone). But Castro appears to have refused to accept Santiago's overtures later that year to reestablish diplomatic relations on the grounds that this would give the Christian Democrats a useful issue with which to attract left-wing support in Chile's forthcoming election.[94] Beyond denying the PDC's candidate, Radomiro Tomic, campaigning material, the Cubans generally feared that they could do more damage than good by intervening on Allende's behalf, and, at least during the months leading up to the election, it therefore seems that the senior Cuban intelligence officers who would play the largest role in Allende's Chile stayed away. As Oña later recalled, the Cubans "played so that Allende would win." And in 1970, playing to win meant keeping a low profile.[95]

Certainly, the possibility that the United States could exploit Allende's relationship with the Cubans to undermine his election campaign was considered a very real one in Havana and Santiago. Yet, to some extent, both Castro and Allende drew strength from growing anti-Americanism in the hemisphere and the international challenges that the new Nixon administration faced, both in Southeast Asia and in Latin America. As Allende told a Canadian reporter on the day of his election, the United States had to "understand" that Latin Americans could not live indefinitely in "misery and poverty" while financing the "richest and most powerful country in the world."[96] More than two years later, he would still be insistent on this point, informing U.S. secretary of state William Rogers that "something must have happened for this welling up of feeling to have come about in Latin America"; there was "a definite, palpable feeling running in Latin America . . . that there must be change."[97] But of course the big question ahead was whether the new Nixon administration was predisposed to respond to such an appeal for understanding and how it would react to the prospect of an Allende presidency.

The Nixon Administration and Latin America

Richard Nixon was no stranger to Latin America when he assumed the U.S. presidency in January 1969, but, at least initially, he did not regard the region as a U.S. foreign policy priority. As Viron Peter ("Pete") Vaky, Kissinger's first assistant for Latin American affairs, recalled, the president's "heart and soul" were far more focused on Vietnam, détente, and the opening to China.[98] As such, Nixon stalled when it came to addressing Latin American concerns, and U.S. policy toward the region was somewhat adrift until late 1970. This also had something to do with Henry Kissinger's views on the region. In contrast to Nixon's previous engagement with Latin America, the new president's national security adviser was neither particularly well informed about nor interested in inter-American affairs.[99] In 1969, Kissinger even went so far as to tell Chile's foreign minister, Gabriel Valdés, that what happened in the "South" was unimportant. "History has never been produced in the south," he told the Chilean diplomat; "the axis of history starts in Moscow goes to Berlin, crosses over to Washington and then goes to Tokyo."[100] Meanwhile, those in Washington who did believe that the United States' relations with Latin America were worth focusing on generally agreed that U.S. influence and prestige in the region were in serious decline. While policy suggestions varied, the general—if unenthusiastic—consensus among these officials was that a more wary, careful, "low profile" approach was called for as a means of rescuing Washington's standing in the Americas. And yet this tricky and untested concept clashed with certain prevailing attitudes within Washington regarding "irresponsible" "Latins" who were not equipped with the "maturity" to resist communist influences on their own.

Nixon's own views on Latin America had primarily been shaped by his visits to the region and by his period in government as President Dwight Eisenhower's vice president. In 1955 he had traveled to the Caribbean, where he embraced the Cuban dictator, Fulgencio Batista, and the Dominican Republic's Rafael Trujillo. Then, in 1958, he had personally come face-to-face with widespread anti-American protests when he visited Uruguay, Peru, and Venezuela. Those who had gone out onto the streets to protest his presence—or, as in Caracas, to throw rocks at him—had been demonstrating for a variety of reasons, among them U.S. intervention against Arbenz, Washington's support for dictatorships, its imposition of tariff barriers against Latin American goods, and a general lack of enthusiasm within the United States for addressing Latin American development needs.[101] Yet Nixon shared the views of many others in Washington who immediately blamed an international communist conspiracy, dismissing demonstrators in Caracas publicly as a "mob" of tobacco chewing, spitting, irrational, and "bloodthirsty" youths manipulated and controlled by global communism.[102]

The trip had subsequently provoked a sudden new U.S. interest in Latin American affairs as a result of this perceived communist threat. When Nixon had listened to Latin American leaders repeatedly asking for more economic assistance during his tour, he had told them that the answer to prosperity lay in private investment rather than commodity agreements. However, in answer to the Brazilian and Colombian presidents' appeal for a Marshall Plan for Latin America to the tune of $40 billion—"Operation Pan America" as Brazil's President Juscelino Kubitschek called it—the administration had begun moving gradually toward a broader consideration of economic assistance, which foreshadowed the Alliance for Progress and included the creation of the Inter-American Development Bank worth $1 billion (of which the United States supplied 45 percent) and a $160 million military aid program. This new approach was nevertheless limited. Indeed, after a brief moment of soul-searching after Caracas, the Eisenhower administration essentially maintained the line that Nixon had personally delivered to Latin American leaders regarding the importance of private enterprise as a means of achieving accelerated development.[103]

By the end of the 1960s, Nixon viewed the prospect of upheaval and revolution with even more concern than he had done a decade earlier but still resisted the idea that U.S. development or aid programs could solve the problem. The handwritten notes he made during a private trip to Peru, Chile, Argentina, and Mexico in 1967 are revealing in this respect. As far as he was concerned, the "battle of ideas" in Latin America had yet to be decided, whereas in Asia it had essentially been "won." There, he noted, Japan, South Korea, Taiwan, Malaysia, the Philippines, and Thailand were showing the path to developmental progress while China, North Vietnam, North Korea, Indonesia, and Burma were proving "what did not work." Unless Latin America wanted to "fall hopelessly behind" and become a "permanent depressed area," Nixon wrote to himself, it needed "a new Revolution . . . Not of Arms but attitude." Unlike the Japanese, he observed that the Latin Americans had not learned how to "copy" or "improve" on what the West had to offer. And, as yet, South America's younger generation was seeking a "religion—a cause." According to him, its nationalist reformist leaders, in Chile, for example, had no right-wing support and were not "exciting enough" to attract left-wing followers, while the New Left was "dissatisfied with [the] slow rate of progress" but had "no plan (Castro doesn't work; Communists too conservative)." In obvious contrast to Allende's and Castro's prescriptions, Nixon's answer to these challenges was not state-led redistribution and nationalization but rather private foreign investment, albeit in a way that did not "subsidize & perpetuate unsound institutions." As he saw it, the Alliance for Progress had thrown good money away while the battle of ideas continued unabated; complaining about the Latin Americans he spoke to, he noted that "they *want* even *more*—[yet] are *less satisfied!*"[104]

During this 1967 trip, Nixon was also able to get a direct glimpse of domestic Chilean politics and made some telling observations along the way. Looking forward to the country's presidential elections in 1970 and reflecting on the left wing's appeal throughout the country, he concluded that Chilean politics were on a "razor's edge . . . could go either way." If Allende ran again and won, he mused that the United States might "have to let them [the Chileans] go through the wringer—stop aid." When Frei warned him personally that, on the contrary, the country might turn to the "military right" if the center failed, Nixon privately noted that this seemed like a "Good prophecy."[105] Nixon had long since believed that the military was a "great stabilizing force" in South America, of "outstanding quality." And while he had advocated preferential American support for democratic leaders in Latin America after his disastrous South American trip in 1958—

"a formal handshake for dictators; an *embraso* [*sic*] for leaders of freedom," as he put it—he ultimately believed Latin Americans were "frighteningly" naive about international communism and in need of strong military leaders under U.S. influence.[106]

In fact, a prevailing, condescending view in the United States was that North Americans not only were wiser and more capable of governance but had a duty to save reckless, vulnerable Latin Americans. In 1950, Louis Halle, a State Department official writing under the pseudonym "Y," had published an article in *Foreign Affairs* that laid out these views explicitly. Democratic rule, this article argued, was "not an absolute condition to be assumed by a people as one puts on an overcoat."[107] The State Department's George Kennan had also drawn scathing conclusions after a trip to Latin America earlier that year. Where "concepts and traditions of popular government are too weak to absorb successfully the intensity of a communist attack," he advised Secretary of State Dean Acheson, "we must concede that harsh governmental measures of repression may be the only answer; that these measures may have to proceed from regimes whose origins and methods would not stand the test of American concepts of democratic procedure." In Kennan's view, it was "unlikely that there could be any other region of the earth in which nature and human behavior could have combined to produce a more unhappy and hopeless background for the conduct of human life"; he saw the region as an unfortunate blend of Indian civilization, Spanish conquerors, and "Negro slave elements," all of which proved to be "handicaps to human progress" and contributed to "exaggerated self centeredness and egotism—in a pathetic urge to create the illusion of desperate courage, supreme cleverness, and a limitless virility where the more constructive virtues are so conspicuously lacking."[108] These types of views were by no means new or fleeting. More than a century before, Thomas Jefferson had lamented that independent South American nations were not ready for "free government." "Their people are immersed in the darkest ignorance and brutalized by bigotry & superstition," he wrote.[109] And nearly two hundred years later, Nixon and many of his closest advisers still maintained that democracy was simply "a very subtle and difficult problem" for "Latins" as a whole, be they South American, French, or Italian.[110] As Nixon—hardly the pillar of open democratic governance himself—privately remarked, they "governed in a miserable way" and had to be saved from themselves.[111]

These views were neither aberrations within Washington's policy-making establishment nor the preserve of Nixon's Republican Party. As a telephone call between Henry Kissinger and his predecessor as secretary of state during the Kennedy and Johnson eras shows, U.S. policy makers were generally rather arrogant and dismissive when it came to what was necessary to sustain a positive U.S.–Latin American relationship:

[Dean] R[usk]: . . . We should do something about the feeling of neglect they [Latin American countries] seem to have fallen into. I think you ought to get Latin American Ambassadors and Ambassadors from the OAS to take them on a boat ride, give them some drinks and just make them feel . . .

K[issinger]: Well, I am giving a lunch on Friday in New York for Latin American representatives at the UN. I know that's not exactly it, what you are suggesting, but . . .

R: That's right, that kind of courtesy, flattery if you like. It is greatlsy [sic] appreciated by the Latinos, who respond to that sort of thing more so than people from other parts of the world. . . . On the second day of President Johnson's administration he called in all the Latin American Ambassadors to the White House as one of the first acts of the administration. They were so flattered that it was one of the first things he did and it made a big difference for quite a while.

K: Excellent idea.

R: It doesn't have to be aimed at a particular subject, or anything. It is just one of those cour[t]esies they will appreciate.

K: I think you're right.

R: Just give them a chance, its [sic] important to these Ambassadors, to send a telegram back hom[e] saying I was on the river with the Secretary of State, and I said to him and so forth, sort of build themselves up back home, you see.

K: I may do it next week.

R: Before the weather closes in . . . [112]

Despite suggesting such superficial remedies for the underlying causes of Latin Americans' "feeling of neglect," Rusk nevertheless highlighted a real problem for the United States: the regional sense of disenchantment with U.S. policies. Moreover, compared to Castro, who was eagerly embracing such disenchantment at the end of the 1960s, the Nixon administration seemed to be moving lethargically to address the situation when it assumed power in 1969.

Partly as a means of introducing a new type of U.S. policy toward the region, Latin American foreign ministers attended a conference in Viña del Mar, Chile, in May 1969 to establish a common position vis-à-vis the new Nixon administration. The conference called for decisive change in U.S.–Latin American relations and the inter-American system. It also formalized Latin American frustrations with progress toward previous development goals and disdain for inequality in the Western Hemisphere that conference delegates saw as being largely the United States' responsibility. Subscribing to popular notions of Dependency Theory and led by Chile's foreign minister, Gabriel Valdés, participants posited that Latin America was underdeveloped precisely because it was financing U.S. economic growth. They also reemphasized the principle of nonintervention as a guiding principle for inter-American relations and argued U.S. aid should no longer be tied to purchasing U.S. goods or issued on the grounds that the recipient adopted "one determined political, social and economic model."[113] It was the struggle against economic dependency and underdevelopment—as opposed to interstate conflict—that had become central to questions of national security for many of those present at Viña, delegates argued.[114] In sum, although Latin Americans may have been asking for help from Washington—thereby demonstrating their ongoing dependency on the United States—they were also trying to fundamentally remold the way they received it.

Unsurprisingly, Nixon was unsympathetic and affronted when Valdés delivered the "Consensus of Viña del Mar" to him in person in June 1969.[115] But there was a sense within Washington that something—as yet undefined—had to be done to improve U.S.–Latin American relations. In July, an interagency study concluded that Washington had to try to reinvigorate a "Special Relationship" with the region.[116] As policy analysts noted, nationalism posed "a significant threat to U.S. interests, particularly when taken in conjunction with a Soviet presence and a Soviet willingness— partial or hypothetical—to offer itself as an alternative to Latin dependence on the U.S." They also underscored that the United States could benefit from pursuing "enlightened self-interest and humanitarian concern for economic and social development."[117]

Around this time, Nixon also received a rather more alarmist report on regional affairs from his special envoy to the region, Governor Nelson Rockefeller. Pointing to the deteriorating state of U.S.–Latin American relations, Rockefeller warned that "the moral and spiritual strength of the United States in the world, the political credibility of our leadership, the security of our nation, the future of our social and economic lives" were at stake in Latin America. If the "anti-U.S. trend" continued in the region, he underlined, the United States would be "politically and morally isolated from part or much of the Western Hemisphere." And because the United States' relationship with Latin America had a vital "political and psychological value" beyond traditional strategic interests, "failure to maintain that special relationship would imply a failure of [the United States'] capacity and responsibility as a great power."[118]

Kissinger would have surely agreed with his former boss's conclusions had he taken more time to concentrate on Latin American affairs. As he had noted in 1968, the "deepest problems of equilibrium [were] not physical but psychological or moral. The shape of the future will depend ultimately on convictions which far transcend the physical balance of power."[119] Yet, for now, he and the president pushed Rockefeller's alarmist conclusions to one side. And with little serious input or interest in Latin American affairs from the White House, the State Department's Bureau of Inter-American Affairs (ARA) was therefore free to draft a new public policy toward the region, which was finally unveiled by Nixon at a meeting of the Inter-American Press Association on 31 October 1969. As one of those who helped put together the president's speech for this occasion argued, the Rockefeller Report exaggerated the threat of growing communist subversion in Latin America and lapsed into a paternalistic tone that Latin Americans would find difficult to swallow.[120] By contrast, the ARA's policy was a clear recognition of the United States' difficult predicament in Latin America and an apparent promise to intervene less and listen more. In a clear swipe at Kennedy's Alliance for Progress, it also heralded the beginning of inter-American "Action for Progress" and a "mature partnership" with the region. "If our partnership is to thrive, or even to survive," Nixon promised when he announced the policy, "we must recognize that the nations of Latin America must go forward in their own way, under their own leadership."[121]

The way in which this approach would work in practice was nevertheless unclear. On the one hand, the ARA's director, Assistant Secretary of State for Latin American Affairs Charles Meyer, declared before a U.S. congressional committee, "Dissent among friends is not a disaster, and tolerance of differences is no tragedy."[122] After a National Security Council meeting in mid-October, the president also agreed to untie aid to countries in the region from previous conditions. On the other hand, Nixon held firm to his belief that private enterprise and foreign investment were the answer to development, launched limited economic sanctions against Bolivia and Peru when they nationalized U.S. companies, and insisted that Washington should continue assisting Latin American military leaders (albeit more discreetly).[123] Many were therefore unconvinced by the suggestion either that the "mature partnership" signaled anything new or that the Nixon administration had devised an adequate response to nationalist trends in South America. While Latin Americans (including Allende himself) decried evidence of U.S. intervention in Peru, private businesses in the United States complained about what they perceived to be an excessively soft, "apologetic" approach to a region where U.S. investments totaled $12 billion.[124] Yet, for now, Nixon and Kissinger were not sufficiently concerned or interested to do anything about any of this.

In fact, far from a coherent recipe for "action" or "progress," the Nixon administration's initial attempt to deal with "rapidly intensifying change in the Americas" was a rather halfhearted acknowledgment of reality rather than any substantial redefinition of U.S. policy. Not only were Latin American affairs not at the top of the White House's priority list, but the concept of a "mature partnership"—laudable as it sounded—was too ad hoc, too ill-defined, and too ephemeral to significantly reshape policy toward Latin America. In prescribing that U.S. policy makers deal with regional developments on a case-by-case basis, "Action for Progress" was also by nature a reactive policy. But just how the Nixon administration would react to future challenges in the hemisphere was not clearly thought through. In the period before late 1970, Rockefeller's analysis was left hanging in the air, even if Nixon, for one, was predisposed to fearing the worst. As he had concluded back in 1967, the "battle of ideas" was still waiting to be won in Latin America and the region's leaders were not yet mature enough to win it. Beyond the president, Kissinger was also likely to react to challenges in the hemisphere in the context of his general perception that the power of the United States was in dangerous decline. As he had written in 1968, "The essence of revolution is that it appears to contemporaries as a series of more or less unrelated upheavals. The temptation is great to treat each issue as an immediate isolated problem which once surmounted will permit the fundamental stability of the international order to reassert itself. But the crises . . . are symptoms of deep-seated structural problems . . . the age of the superpowers is nearing its end. The current international environment is in turmoil because its essential elements are in flux simultaneously."[125]

Conclusion

Having neither decisively won nor lost the battle to influence inter-American affairs during the 1960s, both the United States and Cuba were surveying their past struggles against each other at the end of the decade to determine how best to turn new hemispheric dynamics to their advantage. This was by no means a straightforward process. For the Cubans, it meant completely reappraising the tactical cornerstones of their previous efforts to support revolutionary change in Latin America through armed struggle. And for the incoming Nixon administration, it involved a coordinated and concentrated effort to deal with the many challenges the United States faced, which had simply not materialized yet. At their core, U.S. and Cuban reappraisals—as evolutionary as they might have been at this stage—were nevertheless still essentially based on the same values and strategic aims that had guided their policies throughout the 1960s.

Allende, too, remained true to the ideals that had driven him into politics. To a large extent, Cuba's revolutionary example, the inter-American Cold War struggle it had fought with the United States in the 1960s, and his previous presidential campaigns had radicalized him. Yet he also remained wedded to the prospect of peaceful democratic change within Chile and to his ambition to reach the country's presidential palace, La Moneda. Remarkably, Allende also believed that because of his democratic methods for achieving power, he would be able to reason with the United States on an equal footing—something that it is very clear Nixon and his advisers were never predisposed to allow, given their attitudes toward Latin America and Washington's previous Cold War policies in the Americas.

Meanwhile, within Chile, Allende's three unsuccessful presidential campaigns meant that there were many who believed Allende would neither be selected as a candidate again nor be able to win power. Allende himself often joked that his gravestone would read: "Here lies Allende, future president of Chile." And in the months before his nomination, he had had to expend considerable efforts to convince those within his own party—and particularly those on the left wing of the PS such as Carlos Altamirano—that he was the person best placed to stand for president and usher forth a revolutionary process in Chile.[126] Finally, with the announcement that the UP coalition had chosen him as its presidential candidate, he had another shot at realizing that dream.

However, as presidential campaigns in Chile got under way at the beginning of 1970, a lack of White House attention and the State Department's new "low profile" approach to the hemisphere resulted in anti-Allende operations that were far less extensive than those employed by the CIA in 1964. As a later postmortem of U.S. policy toward Chile during the election concluded, "there was no systematic analysis or consideration at the policy-making level on questions of how great a threat an Allende Government would be to U.S. interests"; "attention paid to the Chilean election at the policy-making level was infrequent and late"; "an Allende victory was not considered probable"; "there were philosophical reservations [within the United States] about intervention in a democratic country"; and "there was concern about the risks of exposure if we provided substantial support."[127] In 1970 CIA officials did advise the U.S. multinational company International Telephone and Telegraph Corporation on the best means to channel $350,000 to the right-wing candidate, Jorge Alessandri (another group of U.S. businesses matched that amount). However, fearing that "any significant sum arriving from the U.S. would be as discreet as a moon launch," as the U.S. ambassador in Santiago put it, the CIA itself channeled only $1 million—a third of what it had provided six years earlier—toward "spoiling" propaganda that aimed to discredit Allende by linking him to images of murderous Soviets and Cuban firing squads.[128] In 1970 this propaganda was considered something of a joke by many Chileans, who saw it as too obvious, too alarmist, and too obviously linked to the CIA. True, the substance of the "new Castro" was still unclear and untested. But the idea of direct Cuban intervention or Soviet armies marching into Chile appeared somewhat ludicrous to even the staunchest Chilean anticommunists. Perhaps more important than this, both U.S. and Cuban analysts joined the majority of commentators in Chile and Latin America in predicting that Allende would probably lose the election. And, as such, no one thought too seriously about what would happen if he won.

2 UPHEAVAL
An Election in Chile, September–November 1970

Fidel Castro was in the offices of Cuba's official newspaper, *Granma*, when he heard that Salvador Allende had narrowly won Chile's presidential election late at night on 4 September 1970. "The miracle has happened!" he exclaimed, when Luis Fernández Oña walked through the door. Oña then joined Fidel, Manuel Piñeiro, and others as they debated the election's significance for Chile, for Latin America, for the cause of socialism worldwide, and for Cuba. Castro also instructed the next day's edition of *Granma* to categorically proclaim the "Defeat of Imperialism in Chile." Later, he signed a copy for Allende and, having been up most of the night, he called Santiago at dawn to congratulate his friend on what he considered to be the most important revolutionary triumph in Latin America since his own victory a decade before.[1]

Conversely, in Washington, President Nixon and Henry Kissinger were furious. Kissinger, who had dismissed the South as being "unimportant" only a year before, now went so far as to argue that Chilean events had a bearing not only on United States–Latin American relations but also on the developing world, on Western Europe, on the United States' "own conception" of its world role, and on U.S.-Soviet relations.[2] As Kissinger recalled years later, his reaction was one of "stunned surprise."[3] The South, it seemed, had suddenly become *very* important.

These reactions were as automatic and immediate as they were diametrically opposed. Primarily, Havana and Washington were motivated by their assessments of the impact that Allende's election would have on the inter-American balance of power. As such, Chile became inextricably linked to their broader desire to win support and influence throughout Latin America. Havana therefore celebrated Allende's election as the most potent example of a new regional revolutionary wave destined to undermine U.S. influence. And Washington viewed it as an instant "loss" in what it suddenly considered to be a significant area of a global zero-sum game against communism. Indeed, the "rapidly intensifying change" in Latin America that Nixon's National Security Council had discussed a year before now came into acute focus.[4] Moreover, although it was not immediately clear how leaders across the Americas would respond to Chile's news, Allende's victory immediately epitomized the possibility of radical transformation. In view of these regional and global concerns, economic considerations were of secondary importance. Nixon, after all, believed that he was fighting "a mortal struggle to determine the shape of the future of the world" in which more than financial gain was at stake.[5]

Automatic as these responses may have been, the contours of the policies Havana and Washington would adopt were complicated by the anomalous nature of Allende's victory and his so-called Chilean Road to Socialism. For the Cubans, who were used to assisting rural guerrilla insurgents, the question was how to boost a constitutional democrat's chances without undermining his democratic credentials. And for policy makers in the United States, the challenge was to stop a democratically elected president from being inaugurated without too obviously forsaking the democratic ideals they purported to stand for. As Secretary of State William Rogers recognized, "After all we've said about elections, if the first time a Communist [sic] wins the U.S. tries to prevent the constitutional process from coming into play we will look very bad."[6]

Indeed, as both Cuban and U.S. decision makers tried to define appropriate strategies to match these challenges, they were conscious that the "wrong" policy could have disastrous consequences for the new, more mature profiles they had been trying to promote within the inter-American system. In view of potential domestic and international criticism that interference in Chilean internal politics was likely to cause, they were thus both concerned that others (and each other) would perceive their policies as being "correct." In the short term, this ironically led them to fall back on covertly pursuing not-so-correct policies as they developed longer-term public and private postures toward Allende's Chile. As Kissinger would argue to Nixon, the way policies were "packaged" was important.[7]

Notwithstanding these concerns, the period between September and November 1970 was a time of rapid—if not always effective—reaction to fast-moving Chilean domestic developments in Havana and Washington. Because Allende had received only 36.4 percent in a three-way presidential race, he had to wait for a congressional vote on 24 October to confirm (or deny) his victory. In the intervening weeks, Havana agreed to protect the new president's life, albeit cautiously, while the Nixon administration simultaneously launched a series of covert operations against him later known as Track I. Mistrusting—and blaming—Washington's bureaucracy for having allowed Allende to win in the first place, the president also instigated a second track that risked greater exposure of U.S. operations in Chile but that was to be carried out without the knowledge of the State Department and the U.S. Ambassador in Santiago. "Track II," as it became known, had a more explicit and tightly focused remit than Track I, namely to provoke a coup that would bring a decisive halt to Chile's constitutional process and at some unspecified date allow military leaders to call a new election in which Allende would somehow be prevented from standing or winning. However, Tracks I and II ultimately had the same aim: to stop Allende from assuming the presidency. While the former focused on working with—and manipulating—the outgoing Chilean president, Eduardo Frei Montalva, Chilean congressional leaders, senior military figures, and media outlets, the latter concentrated on fueling a violent putschist plot against Chile's constitutionally minded commander in chief of the army, General René Schneider, to clear the way for a more interventionist role on the part of the country's armed forces. Indeed, the story of Schneider's subsequent murder and details of Tracks I and II are well known, thanks to the U.S. Senate's Select Committee investigations in 1975.[8]

Rather than retracing this well-researched story, what follows contextualizes immediate reactions to Allende's election within the broader dynamics of the inter-American Cold War. It thus looks at not only why Castro and the Nixon administration intervened in Chilean domestic politics in the way they did but also how this affected their broader approaches to Latin America. In doing so, it argues that when the Cubans and the Americans formulated their policies toward Chile, they were both responding to shifting hemispheric trends, lessons they had drawn from the 1960s, and their concerns about provoking regional hostility by intervening too obviously in Chilean affairs.

Cuban Celebrations

Castro would later tell Chilean crowds that Allende's victory had demonstrated the power of Cuban ideals.[9] Indeed, to Havana's leaders, La Vía Chilena was instantly considered as a leap in the direction of socialism and Latin American emancipation. Despite Allende being one of revolutionary Cuba's most loyal and intimate comrades, the Cubans nevertheless adjusted reactively to events as they unfolded rather than acting in line with a fixed contingency plan or preset goals. In the first instance, Allende's personal request for security assistance began a new phase of Cuban involvement in Chile. And although Castro responded favorably to this request, both the Cubans and the Chileans feared that exposed involvement would provoke Allende's enemies, which in turn constrained Havana's room to maneuver. Castro certainly did not want to endanger either his own revolution by undermining Havana's new "maturity" in the hemisphere or Chile's nascent revolutionary process through an association with its newly democratically elected president that was too close or visible.

As mentioned already, Allende's victory sparked intense debate in Havana. A month before Chileans had gone to the polls, Castro had finally acknowledged that the ballot box could lead to socialism.[10] But there were still serious doubts within the Cuban leadership. Now that "the miracle" had taken place, various questions were still on the horizon: Would the Chilean congress confirm Allende's victory, and would he be allowed to assume office? Would the UP be able to consolidate the "illusory power" of government if the real reins of power were still in the hands of the oligarchy, the bourgeoisie, and the military? How would the president-elect protect himself against counterrevolutionary forces and their international backers?[11]

While this debate ensued in the fortnight after Chile's election, Allende's daughter and his private secretary arrived in Havana. Beatriz Allende (or Tati) and Miria Contreras Bell (or La Paya), with whom Allende was romantically involved, were Allende's most intimate confidants and, in the case of Beatriz, his most direct channel to the Cubans. Beatriz had spent considerable time in Cuba since her second visit to the island with her father in 1967 and had subsequently become romantically involved with the Cuban intelligence official Luis Fernández Oña, whom she married during her stay in September 1970. Moreover, she had become deeply attached to the Cuban revolution, to its emphasis on armed insurgency, and to the prospect of following Che Guevara's footsteps. Despite her repeated requests, the Cubans had nevertheless refused her the intensive military training that she wanted because of who her father was. However, during her stays in Cuba between 1967 and 1970, she *had* learned to shoot and, more important, she had been given radio communications training. Not only was she able to assist in transmissions between Cuba and the Chilean branch of the ELN, but she also controlled the secret codes for transmitting radio signals between Santiago and Havana before full diplomatic relations were established in November 1970.[12]

With these intimate ties already established, Beatriz and La Paya arrived in Cuba on 14 September 1970 to ask for assistance in guaranteeing Allende's safety. Beatriz had little faith that the Chilean Right, together with the United States, would allow her father to assume the presidency, let alone lead a revolution by peaceful and democratic means, and on the night he had been named a presidential candidate, she had left him a note expressing her skepticism of his chances.[13] Then, when Allende won, she and La Paya were among a group of close advisers who strongly believed he could be assassinated. Consequently, they wanted to provide the president-elect with a well-trained, armed personal escort.[14]

During his presidential campaign, Allende had relied on a small ad hoc group to protect him, which included young Socialist Party militants, members of the Chilean branch of the ELN, and close personal friends.[15] But in a country of 10 million people, this was a relatively insignificant and ineffective escort, with just eight pistols, no means of transport, and only four safe houses. Because of these weaknesses, Allende is said to have had to rely on military contacts and information supplied by UP parties and the MIR for news on potential plots against him.[16] Although Allende later told Régis Debray that there had been two attempts on his life, no concrete incidents appear to have sparked the fear that he was in danger. Instead, there was a general feeling that his security needed to be improved, given doubts about the loyalties of Chile's armed police force, the Carabineros; fears about CIA plots; and rumors that the armed forces might launch a coup.[17]

In this context, Castro was willing to help. In the eleven years since coming to power, his security apparatus had grown to counter the persistent threat of assassination or attack by Cuban exiles and the CIA. The nature of Cuba's policy toward Latin America in the 1960s also meant that those at the head of policy formulation toward the region were militarily trained, skilled in the art of covert operations, and experienced in practicing revolutionary internationalism.[18] Indeed, after 1964, when all Latin American countries except Mexico had severed relations with the island, Cuba's Foreign Ministry had closed its Latin American department, and Cuba's Ministry of the Interior had taken full control of policy toward the region.[19]

Even so, when it came to responding to the Chileans, Castro insisted on doing so carefully. He therefore sent only three Cubans to Santiago in the first instance to assess exactly how the Cubans could help.[20] The three Cubans represented three different branches of Cuba's intelligence and security apparatus, namely the Tropas Especiales, the Ministry of the Interior, and the Departamento General de Liberación Nacional (General National Liberation Department, or DGLN), also at Havana's Ministry of the Interior. Led by Manuel Piñeiro and later to become the Department of the Americas, the DGLN's mission differed from the broad intelligence work done by the Ministry of the Interior in that, instead of being involved only in information gathering and espionage destined to support Cuba, it was proactively concerned with supporting revolutionary movements and parties abroad. In the context of a more general review of Cuban foreign policy at the end of the 1960s, it had been established just before Allende's election, replacing the Interior Department's "Technical Vice Ministry," which had previously been in charge of supporting revolutionary and anti-imperialist struggles in Latin America and the Third World.[21] More important, it was the DGLN that ultimately coordinated Cuba's policy toward Chile during Allende's presidency. Below Fidel Castro, Manuel Piñeiro was personally in control of the DGLN, and beneath him was Ulises Estrada, a senior intelligence officer who was now put in charge of the DGLN's new Chile desk.[22]

Of the three Cubans who were sent to Chile in September 1970, the most important was Beatriz's new husband, Luis Fernández Oña, a member of the DGLN and long since involved in coordinating Cuba's relations with Chile. Having departed almost immediately after Beatriz and La Paya left Cuba and taken a long circuitous route to Chile, he and his two companions arrived in Santiago clandestinely as part of a delegation to a Pan-American congress of veterinary scientists.[23] Once in Chile, however, his parameters for action were minuscule. Although Oña had instructions to talk to Allende directly, finding time and a safe place to do so was difficult. For more than a month, the Cubans were frustratingly confined to a safe house in Santiago, venturing out only occasionally (mostly at night) and trying not to speak lest they revealed their Cuban accents. When Oña finally journeyed to meet Allende in a mutual friend's home in late October, he escaped identification by armed policemen only because they failed to ask for his papers when they stopped the car he was traveling in.[24] Then, after he had conducted a taped interview with Allende, it took weeks for the recording to reach Castro and Piñeiro, as it was considered safe to be delivered only by hand.[25]

The three Cubans' capacity to bolster Allende's defensive bodyguard was therefore initially limited, despite the Cubans believing that the group—soon to be known publicly as the GAP, after the president described it as a Grupo de Amigos Personales (Group of Personal Friends)—urgently needed help. More than three decades later, Oña recalled that, when he arrived, the bodyguard "knew nothing" and had far fewer weapons than right-wing paramilitary groups. It was for this reason that he had brought ten new pistols for the GAP with him from Cuba. (They were smuggled through Chilean customs in a suitcase by a female veterinary delegate who feigned an injured leg and sat on it as it was wheeled through airport security.)[26]

Meanwhile, the GAP was also reinforced with new members. In the hope of benefiting from the MIR's preparations for armed struggle and integrating it into Chile's constitutional road to socialism, Allende had asked its leaders to join the GAP.[27] As one former Mirista, Max Marambio, recalled, the MIR did not consider protecting a president who represented bourgeois Chilean institutionalism to be particularly "honorable." Nevertheless, he was one of three members of the MIR who accepted Allende's request. In fact, Marambio was appointed the GAP's first leader on account of his previous military training in Cuba and, by his own recollection, his very good relationship with the Cuban leadership.[28] Later, after November 1970, Cuba began supplying the GAP with more arms, while other members of Cuba's Tropas Especiales—including members of Castro's own bodyguard—began arriving in Chile to offer logistical training.[29]

For now, though, Havana's involvement in Chile was circumscribed. Although the Cubans were able to deliver a suitcase of weapons and the promise of more meaningful assistance in the future, Castro was effectively restrained by sensitivity to "intervention" in Chilean affairs. He also wanted more information about Allende's future plans and strategies for consolidating his revolutionary road to socialism before acting. In this initial and hastily organized phase of Cuban support, communication was also problematic and the three intelligence officials sent to Chile had inadequate cover stories to justify their prolonged presence in Santiago.

While the parameters of Cuba's collaboration with Allende were being worked out, the fundamental principle governing Chilean-Cuban relations over the next three years was nevertheless established. As the democratically elected leader of Chile and a longtime Cuban ally, Allende would be in charge, and Cuba would respect his sovereign authority.[30] Aside from this central relationship, Havana would also maintain separate relations with Chile's left-wing parties: the Communist Party, the Socialist Party, the

MIR, and MAPU. Of course, historical ties and shared views meant that relations with the PS and the MIR were closer than those sustained with others (the PCCh had far closer relations with communist parties in the East, primarily in the Soviet Union and East Germany). The decision to simultaneously maintain good relationships with these different parties would also become complicated if their revolutionary paths diverged.

For the time being, the Cubans were both hopeful and uncertain about the UP's chances. Although Havana judged Allende to be supported by the majority of Chile's armed forces, the Cubans feared that he faced potential danger from right-wing paramilitaries and/or the CIA.[31] While the Cubans suspected that the United States was already involved in undermining Allende's victory, and although rumors of a possible coup to stop Allende hung loud and heavy over Chilean politics, Havana also lacked definitive intelligence on CIA activities, let alone an ability to counteract them. Certainly, Oña recalls that no one contemplated a scenario in which the Right—aided or not by the United States—would kill the commander in chief of Chile's army in a botched attempt to provoke a coup.[32]

Panic in Washington

Although Nixon's foreign policy team was notoriously divided, all U.S. officials had instantly agreed Allende's victory was "bad news."[33] What they differed on was *how* bad it was and what to do about it. Policy makers quickly also found themselves torn between their instinctual desires to intervene and fears that, by doing so, U.S. prestige in Latin America and beyond could be damaged. Indeed, State Department officials voiced concerns that misguided intervention could be worse than doing nothing. The president and his national security adviser vehemently disagreed. In an essay on foreign policy formulation in 1969, Kissinger had already advocated acting first and thinking later when faced with crises in a revolutionary period.[34] Moreover, he had *already* rejected a modus vivendi with Allende back in August. In his view, the idea that Allende might want accommodation—something that was never studied in great detail—was "so doubtful" it was "meaningless."[35] Nixon, too, believed he had to act quickly. As he later recalled, he perceived Allende's victory as a test of U.S. power comparable to the Cuban Missile Crisis, the Vietnam War, and tensions in the Middle East, albeit a more subtle one.[36]

It was this subtlety that made efforts to overturn Allende's election so difficult. Persuading international and domestic audiences that a small, far away, democratic Chile threatened U.S. national security would obviously be challenging. What is more, it was particularly awkward for the world's self-proclaimed champion of democracy to challenge a democratically elected president, especially at a time when the Nixon administration was trying to extricate itself from Vietnam "with honor" and prove its commitment to replacing an era of Cold War confrontations with negotiation and dialogue. Nixon certainly did not want "a big story leaking out that we are trying to overthrow the Govt." Yet, in his own words, he believed that he had to take risks to stop Chile "going to hell so fast."[37] He thus approved a variety of haphazard, desperate—and ultimately disastrous—covert efforts to stop Allende's inauguration. As it turned out, however, the Chileans the United States relied on could not be secretly bought, cajoled, or effectively controlled. And it was only when this became obvious, and covert operations were failing, that the administration finally began articulating the precise threat that Allende posed and how to systematically counteract it in the long term.

Although the White House retrospectively believed an Allende victory could have been avoided, it had paid little attention to Chile's elections before it was too late. True, the U.S. ambassador in Santiago had been warning that an Allende victory "would mean the emergence of a Castro-type government in Chile" for over six months before Chileans went to the polls. In addition Kissinger had ordered an interagency study on the ramifications of an Allende victory (National Security Study Memorandum 97, or NSSM 97), but less than a month before the election those who compiled it had concluded that "no vital interests were at stake" in Chile. While it did acknowledge the "considerable political and psychological costs" that would follow an Allende victory together with the "definite psychological advance for the Marxist idea" that it would bring, reports from Santiago predicted Allende would lose. Consequently, policy makers postponed discussion of what they would do if he won, and Kissinger decided to sit back and wait.[38]

When Allende won, inertia then turned to panic and recrimination. Kissinger ordered a major postmortem of U.S. policy toward the election, and Robert Hurwitch, a member of the Inter-American Bureau at the State Department (ARA), was called before the president's Foreign Intelligence Advisory Board shortly afterward to explain what had gone wrong. As John Crimmins, deputy assistant secretary for Latin American affairs, recalled years later, Hurwitch "was really shaken up" by the violent reaction he received; the board—and particularly Nelson Rockefeller—apparently could not understand why the ARA had failed to "arrange the election."[39] While an internal investigation into why the United States had not done more to stop Allende being elected would find the policy-making level of government guilty of neglecting the issue, Kissinger shirked responsibility by characterizing the election result as a "sad record for the ARA" and the fault of "wishy-washy" bureaucrats.[40] Indeed, he generally had little respect for those who ran the ARA and would often rant about their failings. In his words, Assistant Secretary of State Charles Meyer was a "weakling" and the others were hopelessly misguided "Alliance for Progress men."[41] Fearing that the ARA did not now want to do anything to overturn Allende's election, in private Kissinger personally vowed not to let Chile "go down the drain."[42]

To ensure it did not, Kissinger first convened the 40 Committee, a group responsible for overseeing U.S. covert operations, to discuss Chile.[43] Kissinger himself was chairman of this committee, which also comprised a wide selection of administration officials, including the U.S. attorney general, deputy defense secretary, chairman of the Joint Chiefs of Staff, deputy under secretary of state, and the director of central intelligence. When, on 8 September, this committee first met to discuss Allende's victory, Charles Meyer, Kissinger's assistant for Latin American affairs, and members of the CIA's Western Hemisphere Division were also present. Meanwhile, the U.S. ambassador in Santiago's alarmist telegrams—considered "frenetic and somewhat irrational" by Secretary of State William Rogers, but "excellent" by Kissinger—shaped the discussion that ensued.[44]

Despite blame being heaped back and forth about whether anything could have been done to stop Allende's victory, the majority of those present at the 8 September meeting managed to agree on two things. First, Washington could not intervene overtly for fear of exacerbating hemispheric hostility, damaging the United States' credibility as protector of democracy worldwide, and bolstering Chile's left wing.[45] Second, all agreed that Allende would sooner or later abandon constitutional democracy and establish an authoritarian Marxist regime.[46] Those in the State Department and the National Security Council (NSC) who argued against significant covert intervention did so not because they believed in Allende's commitment to democracy but because they worried he might be the "lesser of two evils" in the short term—better than provoking civil war in Chile by forcing the Left to turn to violence and better than the fallout in Latin America that would follow a Dominican Republic–type invasion or Bay of Pigs–style debacle.[47] In any event, they were overruled by Kissinger,

U.S. attorney general John Mitchell, and Pentagon officials who insisted the United States had to intervene urgently.[48]

The two options for overturning Allende's election that the 40 Committee subsequently examined on 8 September, and henceforth implemented, were political efforts to get the Chilean congress to vote against Allende and the possibility of persuading Chile's armed forces to intervene.[49] Although Track II would take the latter of these two options to the extreme of precipitating Schneider's murder, both options were also components of Track I. Indeed, the focus on Schneider as an obstacle to military intervention was starkly revealed as a result of broader efforts to persuade him to intervene in the political process.

In all cases, the Nixon administration focused first and foremost on supporting Chilean initiatives rather than inventing its own.[50] As Rogers warned Kissinger ten days after Allende's election, the key was "encouraging the Chileans to do what they should. If it's our project as distinguished from Chile it's going to be bad."[51] There was also no lack of anti-Allende Chileans lining up to secure Washington's support. Augustín Edwards, an influential right-wing Chilean businessman and owner of the newspaper *El Mercurio*, departed from Chile in early September and contacted Kissinger and Nixon through his friend, Donald Kendall, as soon as he arrived in Washington.[52] Meanwhile, President Eduardo Frei, who regarded Allende's election as cataclysmic, approached the U.S. ambassador in Santiago, Edward Korry, in the hope of securing "direct private access to the highest levels" of the United States government.[53] Once political ploys in Congress to stop Allende's victory being confirmed appeared to have failed, the 40 Committee then welcomed Chilean politicians' efforts to involve the armed forces in an "in-house coup." The idea behind this was simple: claiming that the country faced a threat to stability, Frei would let military leaders take over the government and then call new elections in which he would stand. Ultimately, however, the Chileans on whom these operations relied—specifically Frei and the Chilean military high command—vacillated and refused to act, angering Washington's policy makers in the process.[54]

Faced with hesitancy, the 40 Committee thus began sanctioning riskier unilateral action in late September. The CIA ordered its Santiago station to "employ every stratagem, every ploy, however bizarre, to create internal resistance." And its agents were instructed to use "all resources in terms of human contact, propaganda or denigration" to persuade Frei to move.[55] In advocating such operations, the United States thus pursued precisely the type of U.S.—as opposed to Chilean—operation that Rogers had warned against. As Kissinger explained to the 40 Committee on 6 October, Nixon wanted "no stone unturned."[56]

By this date, the president's acute sense of urgency had also already led him to instigate Track II. Having listened to Edwards's pleas upon his arrival in Washington in early September, the president had met with the director of central intelligence, Richard Helms, on 15 September and ordered the CIA to "save Chile!" using the "best men we have," working "full time," without concern for the "risks involved." Helms was told he could spend $10 million or more but that he was to avoid embassy involvement.[57] The following day, Kissinger incorporated the CIA's Western Hemisphere division, its deputy director of plans, Thomas Karamessines, and selected Pentagon officials into a Special Task Force to ensure faster, more secretive action. Track II was therefore distinct from Track I in that it sidestepped Washington's bureaucracy. As Kissinger told Nixon, overturning Allende's victory was "a long-shot" as it was, without the "handicaps of well-meaning but unprofessional activism, of lack of coordination and of bureaucratic resistance."[58] Track II also avoided depending on the cooperation of Chilean political elites and focused instead on a handful of paramilitaries and on some retired officers who were plotting to instigate a coup. By late September, as already noted, the CIA's headquarters in Langley was quite simply on guard, in the CIA's own words, for any "target-of-opportunity situations fraught with promise."[59]

Why were the president and his national security adviser so frantic about Chilean events? As noted, Nixon and Kissinger sanctioned Tracks I and II because they feared the regional consequences of an Allende government. Speaking in Chicago in mid-September, Kissinger argued that a communist Chile, adjoining Argentina ("deeply divided"), Peru ("already . . . heading in directions that have been difficult to deal with"), and Bolivia ("also gone in a more leftist, anti-US direction"), would be hugely detrimental to the Western Hemisphere.[60] Or as Nixon later recalled, with Castro in the Caribbean and Allende in the Southern Cone, he had feared that the continent would be squeezed between a "Red Sandwich."[61] Economic concerns were less of a worry to Nixon; as Kissinger explained to the 40 Committee, "if higher authority had a choice of risking expropriation or Allende accession, he would risk the dangers of expropriations."[62] Chile was far away, relatively poor, and tiny compared to the world's biggest superpower. But its size and location were disproportionate to the impact that

Nixon and Kissinger feared Allende's democratic road to socialism could have on Latin America. Of secondary importance was also the worry that Chile might serve as a model for left-wing parties in Europe, particularly in France and Italy.

With these fears in mind, and in spite of the State Department's instructions to assume a position of "painstaking non-involvement" when it came to Chile, Nixon eagerly lobbied other governments about Allende's threat.[63] During his European tour in late September 1970, he agreed with the Italian president, Giuseppe Saragat, that Allende was merely a smokescreen for communist control of Chile.[64] In conversation with Pope Paul VI, Nixon also explained the Chilean situation was "serious, but not lost," promised that the United States was doing its best to stop Allende, and asked the pope to "discreetly influence the situation." (The pope said he would try.) Then, in Britain, Nixon personally urged Prime Minister Edward Heath to suspend the United Kingdom's credits to Allende. (Kissinger had also already expressed concern to the Foreign Office that the British ambassador in Chile was not taking Allende's threat seriously enough.)[65]

By mid-October, however, it was becoming clear that these international appeals, together with Tracks I and II, might not be enough. The 40 Committee's efforts to create a "coup climate" were acknowledged to have failed.[66] Kissinger was also informed that the chances of Track II succeeding in this context were "one-in-twenty-perhaps less." But he did not give up. On 16 October, under Kissinger's instructions, the CIA informed its Santiago station that efforts to provoke a coup should "continue vigorously."[67] Paul Wimert, Washington's military attaché in Santiago, accordingly delivered $50,000 and three weapons to one group of officers who aimed to kidnap Schneider as a means of provoking a full-scale coup on 20 October. As Wimert later recalled, the money "wasn't guided. It was like a Xmas party—throwing some here, some there."[68] Then, on 22 October, two days before the Chilean Congress met, another group of plotters the CIA was in contact with mortally wounded Schneider in a botched kidnapping attempt. Kissinger would later claim that the United States should be exonerated from all responsibility for this plot precisely because a different group eventually carried out the deed, obscuring the fact that the United States had been in contact with both, that they were both connected, and that their strategy was the same.[69] However, both he and the president were well informed about the plot and its purpose. When Nixon called Kissinger on 23 October to see what was happening in Chile, he heard that, contrary to plans, it had not "triggered anything else." "The next step," Kissinger explained, "should have been a government take-over," but the Chileans involved were "pretty incompetent."[70]

Meanwhile, even before the Schneider assassination, Kissinger had already begun preparing a longer-term strategy to "save" Chile from the Chileans he so clearly disdained.[71] Realizing that an effective anti-Allende operation would require unity and direction, he called a National Security Council meeting, which finally took place on 6 November 1970.[72] But first, as his assistant for Latin American affairs, Pete Vaky, advised him to do, Kissinger brought the administration together to define Allende's threat by arranging two meetings of the NSC's new preparatory Senior Review Group (SRG), which comprised the same individuals as the 40 Committee.[73]

When the SRG had met on 14 October 1970, its members had all concluded that Allende posed a psychological, ideological, and potentially geostrategic threat to the United States, Latin America, and the world. Doom followed gloom. As the group's members agreed, Allende would work against the United States in regional affairs, would forge ties with the Soviet Union and Cuba, and would turn Chile into an international sanctuary for subversives. Deputy Secretary of Defense David Packard warned that appearing to do nothing would also damage Washington's prestige in Latin America, and the chairman of the Joint Chiefs of Staff, Admiral Thomas Moorer, argued that Allende could threaten hemispheric defense, causing "extreme gas pains" by giving the USSR access to the southern Pacific. As Kissinger argued, concluding that "no vital interests" were at stake, as NSSM 97 had done, depended on how "vital interests" were defined.[74] In the overall balance of power in the world, he later recalled that any "subtle change in the psychological balance of power could be decisive," and it was his priority to ensure that the United States remained a credible world leader.[75]

When the SRG met for the second time, five days after the Chilean Congress had overwhelmingly confirmed Allende as president by 153 to 42 (partly, it has to be said, as a result of Schneider's assassination and the shock that this created), its members were in complete agreement about the need to intervene in Chile. Under Secretary of State John Irwin II expressed the whole group's hope when he said that Allende would not fulfill his six-year mandate. He also spelled out that détente did not apply to Chile because it was in the United States' backyard, but he conceded that Washington had to be careful that its approach to Latin America did not contradict its dealings with Eastern Europe too much. As he stated, the State Department "would be happy to see . . . action, covert or otherwise, that would hasten his [Allende's] departure."[76]

Having pulled the administration together to formulate policy toward Chile, Kissinger then targeted Nixon, who was distracted by the Republican Party's congressional election campaign in late October and early November. Arguing that Chile could have severe domestic political consequences by being "the worst failure of our administration—Our Cuba by 1972," Kissinger managed to get Nixon's attention and to delay the forthcoming NSC meeting scheduled for 5 November so that he could ensure the president was fully briefed.[77] It was a shrewd move, and it gave him an extra twenty-four hours to make his case. Indeed, Nixon was highly receptive to arguments regarding Chile's potential impact on his domestic political standing, especially as he believed the Cuban revolution had cost him the 1960 presidential election. Having got the president's ear in this way, Kissinger then outlined the international consequences of Chilean events in a memorandum to the president designed to prepare him for the forthcoming NSC meeting. As he stressed, Allende's victory via the ballot box made Chile "more dangerous" than Castro's Cuba because it posed an "insidious" model that Latin American, Italian, or French communists could follow.[78]

Pivotally, Kissinger also forwarded Nixon a copy of a memorandum he had received from General Vernon Walters, "Future Courses in Latin America," which, in Kissinger's words, was "directly related to the Chile problem."[79] Although Walters was the U.S. defense attaché in Paris, he was considered something of an expert on Latin American affairs and had advised Kissinger on regional developments during the transition period between Nixon's election and his inauguration.[80] He also had a close, personal relationship with the president, having accompanied Nixon on his disastrous vice presidential visit to Latin America in 1958 and his presidential tour of Europe in September and October 1970. In between, in 1964, he had played a key role in the Brazilian military's coup plotting and had been an adviser on Latin America to successive U.S. presidents. There is also strong evidence to suggest that Walters visited Rio de Janeiro, Buenos Aires, Santiago, and Lima in late October around the very time of Schneider's murder, although the details of this particular mission are not known.[81]

What is clear is that Walters's memorandum to Kissinger was a report on his trip and the conclusions that he had reached on the situation in the Southern Cone. In it, Walters warned Kissinger that Latin America's situation was "deteriorating steadily" and that the Alliance for Progress's "coddling of leftists" had conclusively failed in Chile. It was also Walters who described the United States as being "engaged in a mortal struggle to determine the shape of the future of the world" in which there was "no acceptable alternative to holding Latin America." As he saw it, the region's "resources, the social and economic problems of its population, its proximity to the U.S." all made it "a priority target" for Washington's Cold War enemies.[82] Nixon wholeheartedly and enthusiastically agreed with Walters's conclusions: "K," he scribbled to Kissinger, "read the Walters memo again + see that it is implemented in *every* respect."[83]

To a large degree, Allende's election was therefore a watershed that compelled the White House to pay attention to Latin America and to seize control of U.S. policies there. Like Castro, the Nixon administration had been unprepared for Allende's election, but unlike the Cubans, Washington pursued immediate, risky, long-shot operations in Chile before stopping to evaluate the significance of Chilean events. When the Nixon administration finally paused to discuss the consequences of an Allende presidency, decision makers from the State Department to the Pentagon and from the White House to the CIA agreed that "saving" Chile and U.S. influence in Latin America were two sides of the same coin. Intragovernmental squabbles about how and what to do about Allende in no way detracted from the sense that the United States had just suffered a profound regional defeat, and one that would have a significant impact on the global contest for influence and power. And although the White House's conclusions were more apocalyptic than those of other branches of government, the *whole* administration broadly shared fears of the possible international significance of Allende's election. Indeed, like the Cubans, U.S. policy makers now believed that La Vía Chilena's potential success or failure could significantly alter Latin America's destiny.

Packaged Policies

U.S. and Cuban approaches toward Chile's new government were being rapidly refined when delegations from both countries touched down in Chile to attend Allende's inauguration. Primarily, both Havana and Washington continued to monitor how their Chilean policies were tailored to suit international, domestic, and Chilean audiences and feared that their ultimate objectives could succeed only if they were perceived as acting "correctly." As such, leaders in both capitals opted for double-sided public and private strategies. Allende and Cuban representatives were therefore simultaneously discussing how to facilitate Cuban assistance to Allende's bodyguard even as they were laying the groundwork for reestablishing more formal diplomatic ties. Meanwhile, back in Washington, members of the Nixon administration were arguing over the difference between packaging and substance while feigning a "correct" response to the incoming government. The main difference of opinion in Washington lay between the State Department, which advocated covert and overt caution as a means of limiting Allende's ability to rally support based on anti-Americanism, and Kissinger, who strongly urged Nixon to prevent a "steady shift toward the *modus vivendi* approach."[84] But in essence the long-term policy goal was the same across all branches of government: to bring down Allende.

Although Fidel Castro had wanted to attend Allende's inauguration in person, he stopped himself from going so as not to provoke Allende's enemies. Instead, Cuba was well represented by a high-level delegation led by Deputy Prime Minister Carlos Rafael Rodríguez. It also officially included the three Cubans who had been clandestine in Chile for more than a month and Cuba's future ambassador to Chile, Mario García Incháustegui, a former Cuban delegate to the UN and an old school friend of Castro's.[85]

In spite of this high-level presence, Havana issued words of caution to the new Chilean government that reflected the general shift in the Cuban revolution's domestic and foreign policies since 1968. Rodríguez, for example, advised the Chileans not to be impatient to meet people's needs but rather to concentrate on acquiring the technical, political, and economic resources to be able to do so.[86] And as one journalist for the Havana-based news agency Prensa Latina recalled, Cuban news agencies intentionally avoided classifying La Vía Chilena or Allende in ideological terms.[87] Fidel Castro also privately advised Allende not to "ignite" continental revolution or be "too revolutionary." As he had told Beatriz when she visited Havana in mid-September, instead of Allende receiving the blame for "all the conflict situations in Latin America," he was happy to continue assuming responsibility.[88] And he had urged Allende to wait ("not to worry if he had to wait six months, a year, or two") before establishing formal ties with Cuba.[89]

However, the incoming Chilean administration did not wait. On 12 November 1970, Allende formally announced the reestablishment of diplomatic relations with Havana, using the Cuban delegation's presence in Chile to finalize arrangements. The move was hardly surprising, given

Allende's election promises and national support for such a move. But by giving Havana its first diplomatic opening in Latin America since 1964, it was a major turning point. After the reestablishment of relations was announced, the three Cuban officials who had been so constrained previously also had a legitimate reason to be in Chile and to move around freely. For the time being, Luis Fernández Oña was named as Havana's chargé d'affaires, and decades later he would remember his amazement when other diplomatic missions in Santiago began sending him flowers and congratulatory messages. However, he also found himself in a tricky position, having never been trained as a diplomat or knowing fully what one did.[90]

Oña's transition from years of work as a covert agent to accredited chargé d'affaires was far from unique. To the contrary, the Cuban officials who began arriving in Santiago after November 1970 and handling the nuts and bolts of different party-to-party and governmental strands of the new Cuban-Chilean relationship were predominantly intelligence officers or members of the Tropas Especiales. After all, as a result of OAS sanctions imposed in 1964, Cuba had had little call for diplomats in Latin America. At the party-to-party level, eight or nine intelligence officers from DGLN including Oña and Juan Carretero, who had played a key role in coordinating Che Guevara's Bolivian campaign, therefore took up posts as political counselors at the Cuban embassy in Santiago and began handling Cuba's relationships with Chilean left-wing leaders.[91] Ulises Estrada, the DGLN's desk officer for Chile and Che Guevara's companion in Tanzania and Prague prior to his Bolivia venture, also traveled to Santiago twice a month to oversee operations and deliver or collect sensitive communications. Meanwhile, at the governmental level, Foreign Minister Raúl Roa, Cuba's Ministry for External Trade, Ambassador García Incháustegui, and Cultural Attaché Lisandro Otero were responsible for rapidly developing commercial, scientific, technological, and cultural exchanges between both countries at a state level.[92] And, of course, above them, Allende, Castro, and Piñeiro oversaw all strands of this new relationship.

As the Chilean-Cuban relationship leaped into a new era, the United States' representatives at Allende's inauguration waited in the wings. The United States had sent a low-key delegation to Allende's inauguration headed by Assistant Secretary Charles Meyer. As Nixon, Kissinger, and Rogers had calculated, by sending Meyer with an oral message of congratulations as opposed to a formal written letter, Washington could be as "cool as possible and still polite."[93] And Allende appears to have been encouraged by the assistant secretary's visit. When the new president met Meyer on 4 November, the latter promised to convey his impressions of the president's "sincerity" and "cordiality" to Nixon when he returned to the United States. Afterward, one Chilean diplomat present at the meeting also observed that Meyer had "acquired a far more rational and well informed impression" of Chile than other U.S. officials he had spoken to.[94]

However, this was an optimistic reading of the situation. On his return to Washington, Meyer did not stand up for Allende as the Chileans had hoped, but instead told the 40 Committee that "very few Chileans accurately evaluate the Allende threat to Chile—they believe the 'Chilean character' will somehow miraculously preclude a Marxist take-over of the country."[95] Moreover, by the time Meyer returned on 6 November, the decision had already been made not to leave the situation to chance. As Kissinger warned Nixon during the twenty-four hours he had been given to make his case to the president, the "dangers of doing nothing" were bigger than the risks of doing "something." It is true that Kissinger seems to have appreciated certain parameters for action. "We clearly do *not* have the capacity to engineer his overthrow ourselves in the present circumstances," he gracefully acknowledged. However, Kissinger also raised the possibility of examining feasible actions that the United States could take "to intensify Allende's problems so that at a minimum he may fail or be forced to limit his aims, and at a maximum might create conditions in which a collapse or overthrow may be feasible."[96] As Kissinger informed Nixon, it was "a question of priorities and nuance" between those who wanted to limit the damage Allende's election had caused and those who wished to "prevent" it altogether.[97]

The State Department was the main advocate of "damage limitation" through flexible engagement and suggested seizing on Allende's future challenges when they arose as opposed to creating them directly. In this respect, its recommendations closely reflected U.S. diplomatic consultations with Latin American leaders between September and November. As the State Department's Bureau of Intelligence and Research noted, although the region was clearly divided on the subject of Allende's likely alignment with Moscow and export of revolution, the majority's view was that obvious U.S. intervention would encourage such a trend. Meanwhile, the Peruvian Foreign Ministry counseled "patience and restraint," Venezuelan president Rafael Caldera Rodríguez warned Washington to be "careful," and Mexico's foreign minister, Antonio Carrillo Flores, urged a "posture of courage, serenity and confidence." Overall, then, the State

Cuban DGLN officers at a school in Chile. Men in suits, left to right: Juan Carretero, Manuel Piñeiro, Luis Fernández Oña, and Ulises Estrada. Courtesy of Luis Fernández Oña private collection.

Department's analysts concluded that U.S. "over-reaction" could "push Chile away from the inter-American system," as it had done in the case of Castro's Cuba.[98] Three days before the NSC meeting on Chile, the State Department's Latin American Bureau had therefore advised Secretary Rogers that the United States' approach to a democratically elected president in a continent where U.S. hegemony was a key concern could "incur even more serious losses" than Allende's victory represented.[99] Subsequently, at the NSC meeting, Rogers advocated "bringing him [Allende] down . . . without being counterproductive."[100]

Kissinger "basically" ended up agreeing on the need to be publicly "correct" when it came to opposing Allende.[101] As he advised Nixon, the United States had to "package" its approach "in a style that . . . [gave] the appearance of reacting to his moves."[102] In contrast to the State Department's concern for heeding Mexican, Peruvian, and Venezuelan advice, however, Kissinger, Nixon, and the Pentagon were focused on other Latin American dynamics. Their primary preoccupation was to assure conservative regional forces that Washington was not lying back and accepting Allende's government. "If [the] idea gets around in Brazil and Argentina that we are playing along with All[ende] we will be in trouble," Kissinger warned Nixon; the United States risked "appearing indifferent or impotent to the rest of the world."[103]

Nixon's strong endorsement of Vernon Walters's memorandum a day before the NSC meeting is the clearest indication we have of the president's own views on this question and, more broadly, on Latin American affairs as a whole at this point. By instructing Kissinger to implement Walters's recommendations "in *every* respect," Nixon accepted that the United States had to draw Latin Americans' focus away from purely internal security concerns and provide them with "a sense of participation in the defense of freedom" worldwide. In his view, the United States also had to do a better job of demonstrating its dedication to help regional leaders reach their objectives, and "increase, not reduce" military sales, assistance, and friendly understanding toward Latin America. Finally, Walters stressed that the United States should "move actively (not necessarily openly) against . . . opponents."[104]

When the NSC addressed Chile on 6 November, Nixon translated this advice and his own personal instincts into a call for reinvigorated attention to Latin America:

> Let's not think about what the really democratic countries in Latin America say—the game is in Brazil and Argentina. . . . I will never agree with the policy of downgrading the military in Latin America. They are power centers subject to our influence. . . . We want to give them some help. Brazil and Argentina particularly. Build them up with consultation. I want Defense to move on this. We'll go for more in the budget if necessary. . . . Privately we must get the message to Allende and others that we oppose him. . . . Brazil has more people than France or England combined. If we let the potential leaders in South America think they can move like Chile . . . we will be in trouble. . . . We'll be very cool and very correct, but doing those things which will be a real message to Allende and others. This is not the same as Europe—with Tito and Ceausescu—where we have to get along and no change is possible. Latin America is not gone, and we want to keep it.[105]

On 9 November Nixon's rambling instructions were articulated in National Security Decision Memorandum 93 (NSDM 93), which ordered maximum pressure on Chile's new government to "prevent its consolidation and limit its ability to implement policies contrary to the United States and hemisphere interests." Pivotally, it also outlined a framework for a new regional strategy to contain Allende's Chile and build up U.S. influence in Latin America. "Vigorous efforts," NSDM 93 instructed, should be undertaken "to assure that other governments in Latin America understand fully that the United States opposes consolidation of a communist state in Chile hostile to the interests of the United States and other hemisphere nations, and to . . . encourage them to adopt a similar posture." Toward this end, the directive explicitly instructed the administration to collaborate and forge closer relations with military leaders in the Americas and to consult "key" Latin American governments in Brazil and Argentina.[106]

While Nixon was clarifying and imposing a new regional policy in the wake of Allende's inauguration, he also articulated his views on nationalism and anti-Americanism in the hemisphere. The issue at stake was not the investments that the United States stood to lose, Nixon implied, but rather Washington's credibility, prestige, and influence. What is more, Nixon reaffirmed the very conditional and paternalistic approach that the ARA's "mature partnership" had dismissed only a year before: "No impression should be permitted in Latin America that they can get away with this, that it's safe to go this way," he instructed. "All over the world it's too much the fashion to kick us around. We are not sensitive but our reaction must be coldly proper. We cannot fail to show our displeasure. We can't put up with 'Give the Americans hell but pray they don't go away.' There must be times when we should and must react, not because we want to hurt them but to show we can't be kicked around. The new Latin politicians are a new breed. They use anti-Americanism to get power and then they try to cozy up. Maybe it would be different if they thought we wouldn't be there."[107]

Clearly, the United States would not be there for Allende, and Nixon personally outlined the kind of punishment he wished to see unleashed on Chile: economic "cold Turkey."[108] A Covert Action Program annexed to NSDM 93 also provided an overarching framework for intervening in Chilean domestic politics. Specifically, the program aimed to maintain and enlarge contacts with the Chilean military, support Allende's non-Marxist opposition, assist the anti-Allende Chilean media outlets, launch black operations to divide and weaken the Unidad Popular coalition, and disseminate propaganda against Allende throughout Latin America, the United States, and Europe. Notably, this included instructions to "play up" Cuban and Soviet involvement in Chile.[109] And, finally, given the haphazard response to Allende's unexpected election, NSDM 93 also established a new decision-making structure to oversee policy toward Chile: the

SRG would meet monthly "or more frequently" and would monitor operations together with an Ad Hoc Interagency Working Group on Chile.[110]

As the tension of the election period diminished in Santiago, the internationalization of Chilean politics was therefore just beginning. On the one side, the Cubans proceeded with cautious enthusiasm, conscious that closer association could burden Allende with counterrevolutionary hostility. On the other side, the Nixon administration chose a delicate double-edged "cool but correct" policy to guard against provoking anti-Americanism in Latin America or bolstering Allende's position in Chile. In this respect, Washington's policies were not determined by the fact that Chile was one democracy in a Southern Cone dominated by military regimes. It did, however, have an impact on the means that the world's self-proclaimed champion of "freedom and democracy" would use to undo Allende's free and democratic victory.

Conclusion

When Allende challenged the foundations of the Cold War order in the hemisphere by reestablishing diplomatic relations with Castro's Cuba, he reinforced the impression that his presidency signaled a watershed in Latin America. As he told Radio Habana Cuba, the Cuban revolution had taught him a lot, and the Chilean people were now ready to "begin to advance along their own path, different from that of Cuba, but with the same goal."[111] In fact, for Chile's left wing—including the PCCh, which had been so opposed to Castro's Latin American policies in the 1960s—the decision had been urgent, automatic, and nonnegotiable. As the Chilean Communist senator Volodia Teitelboim proclaimed, the UP's victory was "absolutely inconceivable" without the Cuban revolution.[112] For the political parties that now made up Chile's coalition government, it was also a move destined to underline Chile's independence in accordance with long-standing aims. For Havana, meanwhile, the new relationship exemplified broad possibilities for progressive (and possibly even revolutionary) change in the region. And for Washington—caught out by the speed of Allende's decision despite his election promises—this was a further warning of how precarious U.S. influence in the hemisphere had become.

Although Latin America had been awash with bubbling nationalism before this moment, Allende's victory brought a changing situation into focus, initiating a reinvigorated struggle for influence in the Southern Cone. To be sure, the Cubans did not consider Allende's democratic road to socialism as applicable to any other Latin American country, but Chile nevertheless became the best example of progressive change in the region and what Cuba's foreign minister called "the strengthening of solidarity in Latin America."[113] It therefore promised to improve Cuba's hemispheric position and to encourage regional social and economic transformation in the direction of socialism. Henceforth, when it came to Chile itself, Havana opted for a mature partnership with Allende rather than imposing its own agenda in the belief that this was the best way of helping him survive and succeed. Cuba's own shift toward a slower, safer path to socialism at home also underpinned the advice that the Cubans delivered to Chile's newly elected government. As Havana's leaders were acknowledging, it was not as easy to skip stages of revolutionary progress as they had previously thought.

Beneath this new "maturity," the Cubans nevertheless continued to ardently believe in the inevitability of revolution. What changed was their analysis of how and how fast this would occur, not that it would occur in the first place. Speaking privately to Polish leaders in Warsaw in June 1971, for example, Cuba's foreign minister, Raúl Roa, would report that Latin America was on the verge of "erupting" and had all the "objective" conditions for revolution. In his view, what was missing for the moment were "subjective" factors such as a revolutionary awareness on the part of the masses.[114] These temporary limitations notwithstanding, Castro expressed total certainty in public. As he later told a Chilean journalist, Latin America "has a child in its womb and its name is revolution; it's on its way and it has to be born, inexorably, in accordance with biological law, social law, the laws of history. And it shall be born one way or the other. The birth shall be institutional, in a hospital, or it will be in a house; it will either be illustrious doctors or the midwife who will deliver the child. Whatever the case, there will be a birth."[115]

Of course, the natural corollary of this rising nationalist and revolutionary wave in the Southern Cone was the growth of counterrevolutionary forces. As events were to prove, Allende did not signify the United States' "defeat" but merely the beginning of its resurgent influence in the Southern Cone. For now, Washington's "correct" tolerance of Allende's new government masked the true sense of the alarm felt by the White House. But behind rhetoric about a new "mature partnership" and a "cool but correct" posture toward Chile, Washington was simultaneously embarking on a new mission in Latin America to "bring Allende down" and to redirect the region's future.

3 REBELLION

In Pursuit of Radical Transformation, November 1970–July 1971

Salvador Allende embraced the idea that his election represented a turning point for inter-American affairs. On the night of his election victory, he had spoken elatedly to thousands of supporters in downtown Santiago and declared that countries around the world were looking at Chile.[1] And they were, but not necessarily with the admiration that Allende implied. Beyond Cuba, and across the Americas, his election simultaneously sparked jubilation, terror, respect and apprehension. While the majority of Latin America's leaders adopted moderate postures toward Chilean events, others were far more alarmist. Brazilian military leaders, in particular, began referring to Chile as "yet another country on the other side of the Iron Curtain," only more dangerous because it was so close.[2] Or, as one Brazilian Air Force general put it just over a month after Allende was elected, "the international communist offensive, planned a little more than two years ago in Cuba, through OLAS [the Organization of Latin American Solidarity], finds itself in marked development in this continent. . . . Taking advantage of the painful state of underdevelopment or disagreements from some and the most pure democratic idealism from others, international communism comes demonstrating its flexibility . . . in the conquest of power, using either violence and coup d'états, or legal electoral processes. . . . We will be, without doubt, overtaken by the ideological struggle that we face, [which is] now more present, more palpable and more aggressive."[3] Indeed, to seasoned Brazilian Cold Warriors—far more so even than their contemporaries in Washington—Allende's victory was not merely a Chilean phenomenon but the embodiment of something more ominous and antagonistic. So much so, that the Brazilians even briefly considered breaking off diplomatic relations with Santiago before they decided this might offer Allende a convenient enemy around which he could rally support.[4]

As we have seen, the Nixon administration had similar concerns about boosting Allende's chances through overt hostility. Although it could not completely hide its coolness toward Chile's new government, from early 1971 onward the Nixon administration increasingly played a clever game when it came to hiding its hand. In this respect, the contrast with the period immediately after Allende's election could not have been starker. From a frantic and chaotic series of failed efforts to try and prevent Allende assuming power, the United States' policy toward Chile now assumed an aura of confidence. Reaching out to the Brazilians and focusing on what it—and they—could do to turn back the tide in the ideological struggle that engulfed the Southern Cone was one astute way to reassert influence in the region. And in Brazil, Washington found a useful and fanatically anti-Allende ally that was already pursuing its own regional strategy to uphold ideological frontiers against revolutionary influences.

Although the incoming Chilean government was not prepared for the degree of enmity it would have to deal with, it nevertheless recognized that La Vía Chilena would probably face some kind of hostility in the Americas. Yet, as regional players jostled to reassert their positions in a changed inter-American setting after Allende's election, Santiago's new leaders were somewhat belatedly debating how to approach the outside world. The Unidad Popular's election manifesto had pledged to assert Chile's economic and political independence and to show "effective" solidarity with both those fighting for their liberation and those constructing socialism.[5] But when Allende entered La Moneda, and his ministers, diplomats, and advisers moved into their new offices, what this would mean in practice was unclear.

The Unidad Popular coalition's leaders faced a myriad of opportunities and challenges as they began formulating Chile's international policy. On the one hand, as we saw in the introduction, the evolution of superpower détente, the United States' ongoing difficulties in Vietnam, frustrated development in Latin America, and Washington's failure to address this, all suggested that the early 1970s would be an opportune moment to pursue radical transformation at a domestic, regional, and international level. On the other hand, Allende had limited room for maneuver on account of receiving only 36.4 percent of the popular vote, which left his position at home relatively weak and potentially unstable, especially in the shadow of Schneider's murder. In this context, Allende and the UP's leaders therefore feared that external intervention in Chilean affairs could magnify domestic difficulties. Consequently, they needed time, space, and continuing credit flows to continue on their peaceful democratic road to socialism. As Allende warned his supporters, winning the presidency had been hard, but consolidating his victory and building socialism were going to be far harder.[6] Indeed, overall, Chile's political and economic weakness, its distance from alternative sources of support from the Soviet bloc, and historic tensions with its neighbors (all of whom had military governments in 1970) made its international position particularly delicate.

During the UP's first nine months in power, the government therefore grappled first and foremost with how it should deal with its most obvious potential enemies, the United States and its neighbors in the Southern Cone. In this respect, Allende's policies did not always evolve in a straight line but rather responded to mixed signals Santiago received about the likelihood of confrontation and opportunities for pushing through its core agenda. One of the key issues concerning the new government was how to nationalize its copper mines without facing reprisals. Another was how to read between the lines of the Nixon administration's diplomacy to determine precisely what U.S. aims and objectives were vis-à-vis Chile. Last, but by no means least, Chile's Foreign Ministry paid particular attention to reaching a degree of mutual understanding with military governments in Argentina and Peru to counteract what was considered to be the very real possibility that the United States would rekindle Chile's border disputes with them. With reports reaching Santiago in early 1971 of deep Brazilian hostility to the new Chilean government, along with the news that the United States was keen to work with Brasilia in regional affairs, establishing a good relationship with Buenos Aires and Lima appeared all the more important.

Indeed, Allende's foreign minister later recalled that a proactive foreign policy had been "obligatory" for the UP.[7] The key to avoiding isolation and foreign intervention, as Allende's foreign policy team increasingly saw it, was to tear down the notion that Chile had realigned itself behind the Iron Curtain or that it had to be contained behind ideological frontiers. Instead, the UP emphasized a foreign policy of "ideological pluralism," while pursuing active diplomacy aimed at forging the best relations with as many countries as possible. The UP also sought an ever greater role for Chile within international organizations and Third World forums while it established new state-level relations across the globe and quietly began seeking assistance and support from the socialist bloc.

As it turned out, these policies were only partly successful. They did not stop Washington courting the Chilean armed forces or prevent the extensive U.S. Covert Action Program in Chile, which focused on boosting the UP's political opponents. They also failed to curtail Washington's efforts to improve its relations with military leaders in the Southern Cone or prevent the Brazilians from appealing to Washington about the seriousness of the threat that Allende posed. To be sure, the United States neither controlled the complexity of the multisided Cold War conflict in the region nor fully understood the depth of ideological hostilities it embodied in late 1970 and early 1971. But this did not mean that the Nixon administration was intent to let the situation drift now that Allende was in power.

From the Inside Looking Out

Like many new presidents, Allende had not fully decided on a precise or coherent foreign policy strategy when he was inaugurated. True, he had a two-month transition period in which to plan an overall framework and appoint key foreign policy advisers. He also had clear, long-standing ideals about what was wrong with the world and what position he wanted Chile to assume within it. Yet the fraught period between his election and his inauguration had not helped smooth his transition to power. The international situation that his new government confronted was also highly complex, as were the varying—and often contradictory—ideas that the UP parties brought to government on international affairs. As a friend of Allende's, the senior Chilean diplomat Hernán Santa Cruz, privately warned him a week after his election, the world was scrutinizing everything the president-elect said, so he had to think carefully about what he wanted his message to the outside world to be. Santa Cruz also privately wrote to Allende about the heterodox nature of the Unidad Popular coalition and his concerns regarding its organizational and foreign policy planning capabilities. Improvisation was not an option, he insisted, because governments that improvised "paid a hard price."[8]

In seeking to give his foreign policy clearer definition and focus, Allende faced a basic choice: to confront potential enemies or to seek accommodation with them. Both choices had drawbacks. Confrontation with the United States and conservative regional powers—à la Cuba—ran the risk of isolation and external intervention, which was particularly problematic given that the new Chilean government had no assurances about obtaining economic support from elsewhere and certainly no detailed plans for closer ties with the Soviet bloc at this stage. The other choice, that of seeking a meaningful modus vivendi with Washington, entailed the prospect of sacrificing election promises.

So, which was it to be? By reestablishing diplomatic relations with Havana just over a week after taking power, Allende signaled that he was not prepared to bow to Washington on certain issues. Yet, how far he would go when it came to showing solidarity with revolutionary movements, leaving the Organization of American States (OAS), or nationalizing Chile's large copper mines was more ambiguous. The reason for this was that such actions carried the risk of U.S. intervention. As an internal Chilean Foreign Ministry memorandum would note, both U.S. governmental and nongovernmental sectors were bound to react to the new Chilean government's "struggle against imperialism."[9] Allende also considered Peru's nationalization dispute with Washington beginning in 1969 as clear evidence of the United States' continuing "imperial" design on Latin America.[10] Yet the nationalization of Chile's copper mines, in particular, had been a nonnegotiable cornerstone of Allende's presidential campaigns between 1952 and 1970.[11] As Allende told Debray shortly after taking office, "economic independence" was a necessary precursor to political independence and "unquestionable power" for the majority of Chile's population.[12]

The big question was therefore how to square the circle—how to acquire this "unquestionable power" without provoking reprisals. Decisively choosing confrontation or accommodation not only risked pitfalls but also required an accurate reading of international affairs and U.S. intentions, neither of which the new Unidad Popular government had. In a few cases, paranoia clouded analysts' judgment when it came to identifying U.S. malice toward Chile. For example, some warned that the Cienfuegos crisis that had erupted in September 1970 regarding Soviet submarine bases in Cuba had been a mere "*fantasmagórico*" designed by the Pentagon to coincide with Allende's election, reemphasize the dangers of communism in the hemisphere, and warn Moscow not to intervene.[13] In reality, however, the events were unrelated, despite Henry Kissinger's later attempt to link them in his memoirs. Not only did Kissinger confuse the chronology of events (the crisis occurred *after* Allende was elected, not before), but the Cienfuegos crisis was also instantly perceived in Washington as a U.S.-Soviet issue that was resolved bilaterally without any reference to Latin America. Unbeknownst to the Chileans, it was also never discussed when Washington's policy makers were formulating their policies toward Chile.[14] Even so, there were other signs of U.S. hostility that are still difficult to disprove. Santa Cruz's allegation that the CIA broke into the Foreign Ministry and stole a personal letter he had written to Allende is a case in point.[15]

These episodes notwithstanding, other confidants were advising the president-elect to act cautiously. As we saw in chapter 2, Allende's most intimate international ally, Fidel Castro, was one of those who urged the new president to avoid conflict with Washington. (Among other things, he specifically advised remaining in the dollar area, maintaining traditional copper markets, and staying in the OAS.)[16] Another of those who suggested that Allende should try and avoid a clash was Orlando Letelier, a Chilean Socialist Party member working at the Inter-American Development Bank (IDB). A month before Allende's inauguration, he had written to his party to urge it, Allende, and the UP as a whole to devote time and resources to formulating a coherent international strategy. In a long letter to the Socialist Party's general secretary, Aniceto Rodríguez, he stressed that confrontation with the United States was not inevitable. As he put it, the Nixon administration had various "internal problems" as well as difficulties in the Middle East and Vietnam. Moreover, because of "the tremendous criticism that Nixon's international policy is receiving daily in the North American congress, its attitude toward the Chilean situation will not be able to be of an openly aggressive character. . . . I think that faced with what is occurring in Peru and what is occurring in Bolivia, the [United States'] position in respect to Chile will be to find a level of understanding and to avoid a situation of crisis. All this favors us."[17]

Letelier nevertheless recognized that U.S. policy could make or break Allende's presidency, particularly when it came to financial considerations. Chile's international economic policy and its relationship with the United States would be the pivotal determinant of the UP's political success, he argued. And in this context, he urged Allende to pay close attention to who might take on the pivotal role of being Chile's ambassador in Washington (he then offered to take up the position himself).[18]

Allende appears to have taken this advice seriously. He demurred when far Left members of the UP coalition adopted what Allende's foreign minister, Clodomiro Almeyda, later recalled as having been a "primitive battle instinct" toward the United States. As Almeyda remembered, the individuals concerned saw confrontation as a source of internal strength and a decisive means of challenging imperialism. Instead, the president sided with those who favored a more pragmatic, tactical, approach. In December 1970 the new Chilean government subsequently announced that it had decided to follow a policy of "healthy realism" in foreign affairs—an optimistic and ambitious option between confrontation and accommodation that would allow Allende to survive *and* succeed.[19] As his confidants remembered years later, Allende quite simply recognized that Chile could not yet "fight the giant."[20]

The foreign policy team that the incoming president assembled reflected this understanding. Although Allende retained close ties to more radical individuals, such as his daughter, Beatriz, members of his own party, the PS, and the MIR, in the veritable scramble for positions in the new UP government, who got what job mattered. And, pivotally, Allende tended to surround himself officially with a group that favored careful negotiation over hasty confrontation. After some in the UP rejected Allende's first choice of ambassador to Washington, the IDB's first president, Felipe Herrera, on the grounds that he was too centrist, for example, Allende offered the position to Letelier.[21] The latter would then become an increasingly important and trusted figure within Allende's foreign policy team over the next three years. He had risen in the ranks of international organizations and was also part of the so-called elegant Left, one of the many groups that made up the Chilean Left with which the new president worked particularly well.[22]

Allende also had strong and long-standing links with established Chilean diplomats. He respected their advice, and largely kept the Foreign Ministry's traditional structure intact.[23] He even offered to let ex-president Eduardo Frei's foreign minister, Gabriel Valdés (who was a friend of his), remain in his post.[24] Although Valdés refused on account of his allegiance to Chile's Christian Democrat Party (PDC), his assistance and that of confidants such as the career diplomat Ramon Huidobro helped smooth the transition of governments. Before Allende's inauguration, for example, Valdés took his successor to the United Nations to meet key personalities in international politics.[25] In this context, Almeyda, a Socialist on the left wing of his party and an old political rival of Allende's, had been rather a surprising second choice for foreign minister. Yet, in the years that followed, Almeyda steadfastly joined Letelier, Huidobro, Santa Cruz, and others in arguing for a nonconfrontational line. "The only way to restrain our adversaries," Almeyda later explained, "was to try and neutralize them, divide them, negotiate with them; to compromise and even retreat tactically in order to avoid collision or confrontation, which could only have a negative outcome for Chile."[26]

If he wanted to survive, Allende did not have any real alternative. When it came to formulating foreign policy, he certainly did not have the means or the desire to realign Chile decisively with the East as Cuba had done a decade before. Not only were pro-Soviet Chilean Communist Party (PCCh) officials kept from key foreign policy posts, but the evidence available also suggests that very little preplanning to improve governmental trade relations with Moscow took place either immediately before or after the election.[27] Instead, Allende appears to have believed that Chile's relations with the USSR could be conducted through the PCCh's existing party-to-party ties with the Communist Party of the Soviet Union. The PCCh certainly had intimate party links with Moscow, receiving $400,000 from it in 1970 (as opposed to $50,000 ten years earlier).[28] It also remained the Soviet bloc countries' primary source of inside information throughout the three years of Allende's government. However, beyond this, Almeyda later recalled that Chileans generally believed that Moscow had tacitly recognized Latin America as a U.S. sphere of influence after the Cuban Missile Crisis and that socialist countries would have limited logistical capacities to assist Chile even if they wanted to.[29]

Interestingly, the message from Soviet-sponsored Cuba echoed concerns about the limitations of Soviet bloc support. Not long after Allende assumed the presidency, Cuban foreign minister Raúl Roa advised the Chileans not to rush into reestablishing relations with East Germany at the cost of beneficial trade and technical assistance from West Germany.[30] As it turned out, the UP held out on recognizing East Germany for far longer than it had originally planned, while simultaneously making successful overtures to Bonn in the hope of avoiding a break.[31] Indeed, Almeyda would privately explain during a high-level visit to Poland in May 1971 that the Chileans had acted in a "balanced way" when it came to Berlin precisely because continued trade with West Germany was considered so important.[32] Clearly, Allende wanted to maintain ties with the West, and he hoped that the evolution of détente would allow him to do so, while also gradually improving relations with the Soviet Union, East Europe, and China.

This caution was evident in Allende's contacts with foreign leaders in November and December 1970. When the Organization of American States' secretary-general, Galo Plaza, met Allende just before his inauguration, the president-elect had taken pains to differentiate himself from ideological Cold War foes. Asked how he would describe his government to the outside world, Plaza recorded Allende as explaining that "his ideological principles were firmly grounded in Marxism, but not as untouchable dogma." Allende denied his government would be "Marxist or Communist" on the grounds that not even the USSR had established communism and not all the parties in the UP were Marxist. Instead, in Plaza's words, Allende portrayed his government as "a Chilean-style reformist regime, not patterned after Cuba, Russia or Czechoslovakia. He cited, as the best proof of the direction that his government would take, his impeccable democratic credentials . . . he was not a khaki-clad guerrilla coming down from the mountains with rifle in hand. Fidel Castro was a close personal friend of his and he admired him in many respects, but he did not intend to be a Fidel Castro, and Chile was not Cuba . . . he pointed out that Chile had a solid political structure that was lacking in Cuba, and that he was democratically elected as a constitutional president, while Castro was a dictator who took power by force." The new president also explained that while he wanted to expand Chile's foreign relations worldwide, he wanted it to remain firmly within the Western Hemisphere and maintain good relations with the United States.[33]

But, of course, placating the giant in this way was quite clearly a tactical acceptance of reality rather than an abandonment of long-held principles. Just before Allende had begun explaining to Plaza how he wanted the world to picture his government, he had issued a private "tirade against the OAS." And although Allende now announced that he would not leave the organization as he had promised during his election campaign, he proclaimed that Chile would work from inside it in a "constructive, but uncompromising" manner. This was also essentially the message that Almeyda later conveyed to leaders of the socialist bloc. To be sure, he acknowledged that the OAS was a "reactionary" organization. But he also privately reasoned that Cuba's experience had shown Chile had to conduct "a very careful policy" in Latin America so as not to "give a pretext to the accusation of 'exporting the Chilean Road.'"[34]

Allende therefore sacrificed his pledge to leave the OAS but committed Chile to influencing other countries within it.[35] He also publicly maintained that the "ideological" differences separating Latin America from the United States had to be addressed. Whereas the United States was "interested in maintaining the current world situation, which [had] allowed it to attain and strengthen its hegemony," he proclaimed shortly after becoming president, Latin Americans had to shed themselves of dependency and underdevelopment by adopting "progressive, reformist or revolutionary" ideologies of change.[36] Allende may well have decided to opt for "healthy realism," but as was becoming clear in early 1971, his emphasis was on rejecting the unhealthy status quo that had gone before it. Realism, in this sense, was conditional and did not mean relinquishing sovereignty or submitting to U.S. threats on key issues.

Indeed, when it came to Cuba, relations evolved rapidly after November 1970 at a political party level and along state-to-state lines. In late January 1971, a delegation led by Cuba's vice-minister for external trade, Raul León, arrived in Chile to expand commercial relations that had been in place for a year before Allende came to power. Then, two weeks later, he signed a three-year trade agreement, which was followed by a "Basic Agreement on Scientific and Technological Cooperation." At a governmental level, Santiago's new leaders viewed their growing economic relationship with Havana as part of something new and conceptually significant, even if it hardly transformed either country's trading patterns. Those at the Foreign Ministry involved in negotiations emphasized the symbolic value of these ties as an example of a different type of economic relations rather than radically significant commercial ventures. Traditionally, international scientific and technological cooperation had been "vertical"— between more developed and less developed nations. Now, they noted that Santiago wanted to establish more "horizontal" ties with other developing countries, such as Cuba, which would not be clouded by ulterior motives of profit and control.[37]

At the same time, Chile also eagerly expanded its involvement in the Third World and international forums, joining the Non-Aligned Movement as a full member in 1971. Although Frei's government had set the wheels in motion to join the grouping, the acceleration of this process during Allende's first months in office significantly underscored Chile's new international role. Apart from Cuba, no other Latin American country had formally joined the Non-Aligned Movement despite many having sent observers to the group's conference in Lusaka in 1970. At the beginning of 1971, the Chilean Foreign Ministry also opportunely put Santiago forward to hold the third United Nations Conference on Trade and Development (UNCTAD) when African and Asian countries suddenly rejected Geneva in the final stages of preparations. The decision to do so was not without cost. As Hernán Santa Cruz warned from Geneva, changing UNCTAD III's location at such short notice would involve not only extensive diplomacy to win support for Santiago's candidacy but also logistical planning and massive building works to host delegates from 136 countries.[38] Yet, the benefits seemingly outweighed these warnings, and Chilean diplomats went ahead with successfully getting the necessary support from other countries to host the conference.

Positive as all this seemed, and despite having taken the decision to avoid confrontation with Washington within the parameters of a realistic but redefined relationship, Santiago nevertheless began accumulating persuasive evidence of U.S. hostility during the first few months of Allende's presidency.[39] As well as Nixon failing to send a customary written message of congratulations to Allende and conveying it orally through Meyer instead, the United States unilaterally dismantled meteorological observation installations on Easter Island weeks before Allende's inauguration, the Export-Import Bank dropped Chile to its lowest credit rating, and at the end of February 1971 Washington abruptly canceled the U.S. nuclear aircraft carrier *Enterprise*'s visit to Chile a day after Allende publicly announced it.[40] Chileans also received warnings from the United States that Washington's "correct" approach to Santiago's government was contingent on Allende's foreign policy. In early January, during a televised press conference, Nixon stated that although Chilean events were not something the United States was happy about, it would respect the principle of nonintervention and continue U.S. aid programs "as long as Chile's foreign policy is not antagonistic to our interests."[41] A month later, when Nixon said he was only "prepared to have the kind of relationship" with Allende that the latter was "prepared to have" with the United States, Santiago's embassy in Washington took note. Although diplomats concluded that these warnings were less "severe" than they could have been, analysts nevertheless acknowledged that they were not a hopeful sign for accommodation either.[42]

Meanwhile, Allende's public response to Nixon's comment was defiant: good U.S.-Chilean relations depended on the United States recognizing Chile's sovereignty and its right "to differ, dissent and negotiate from different points of view," he insisted.[43] But behind the scenes, Chile's new policy makers began adjusting their hope for a realistic dialogue to the potential for a deteriorating relationship with Washington in early 1971. Specifically, the UP now adopted seven specific measures to ensure that if U.S.-Chilean relations broke down—as the Chileans expected they eventually would when Allende nationalized copper later that year—this occurred in favorable circumstances. First, Santiago would try to "minimize" areas of potential conflict so as not to offer the United States a "pretext" for hardening its position (the Chileans regarded their relatively calm reaction to the cancellation of the *Enterprise* visit as a calculated example of this approach). Next, the ministry vowed to try and improve the image that diverse sectors of the U.S. public had of Allende and the UP. Third and fourth, the UP would coordinate its actions with relevant Chilean institutions and financial sectors to ensure that the United States did not suspend military credits to Chile's armed forces. Fifth, the Chileans focused on improving their country's relations with other Latin American nations as a means of forming a "front" vis-à-vis the United States. Sixth, the Chilean Foreign Ministry began seriously exploring the possibility of funding from the socialist bloc. And, seventh, the UP set up a high-level working group to examine the implications of its plan to nationalize Chile's biggest copper mines.[44]

The creation of this working group in February 1971 reflected the Chilean government's growing preoccupation with the issue of copper. Not "fighting the giant" had never meant renouncing nationalization promises, just as it did not mean abandoning Third Worldist, Latin Americanist, and anti-imperialist principles. But it did mean finding ways to achieve them without causing conflict. At the start of his presidency, Allende had publicly proclaimed that Chileans had "always preferred solving social conflicts by means of persuasion and political action"; the nation's coat of arms "By Reason or Force" put "Reason first," he underlined.[45] For someone who had witnessed, and so vehemently denounced, Washington's "imperialist" policies toward Latin America in the past, relying on "reason" to redefine relations with the United States in this instance took a monumental leap of faith. And, in essence, this was based on the lessening of Cold War tensions, the Nixon administration's difficulties at home and abroad, the power of Chile's unique democratic experiment to win U.S. policy makers over, and Allende's sincere belief that he had the *right* to "dissent." The question ahead was obviously whether Nixon was ready to let him do so.

Deceptive Dialogue

Early Chilean efforts to alleviate the danger the United States posed met with mixed success. Primarily this was because the Allende government found it difficult to accurately gauge the subtleties of Washington's policies and the precise danger the United States posed. On the one hand, this is testimony to the way in which the Nixon administration pulled itself together when it came to its policy toward Chile at the beginning of 1971.

Yet, on the other, it was also the result of Chileans' misreading of U.S. priorities. Ultimately, Almeyda's strategy of "healthy realism" would work only if the United States reciprocated, and although Allende, Almeyda, and Chilean diplomats in Washington urged U.S. officials to avoid a global Cold War framework when dealing with Chile—very consciously framing disagreements in legalistic as opposed to ideological terms—this failed to alter the guiding principles behind the Nixon administration's policies. Ignoring the Cold War framework that still determined U.S. policy, the Chileans continued to focus on Allende's nationalization plans as the key determinant of future U.S.-Chilean relations, not knowing that this issue was only just coming to the forefront of U.S. policy makers' agenda.

At the end of 1970, the UP had sent a constitutional amendment to the Chilean Congress to establish state control of the country's largest copper mines and enable expropriation of foreign companies working them. Henceforth, at the beginning of February 1971, the Nixon administration began sending Santiago soft but direct threats regarding the future of the UP's nationalization program. In a démarche that the U.S. ambassador in Santiago, Edward Korry, delivered to Almeyda, Washington urged the Chilean government to have early conversations with North American businessmen and emphasized the U.S. government's responsibility to safeguard U.S. investments.[46] Meanwhile, the ambassador was also privately lobbying "influential Chilean politicians" and, in his words, "spelling out possible international consequences of confiscatory nationalization and what consequent radicalization of Chilean politics would mean."[47]

Days after the U.S. démarche was delivered, Almeyda privately approached Korry at an embassy reception to express hope that the United States would avoid the issue of copper being "inflated by ideological or global considerations." In particular, he stressed that the deterioration of U.S.-Cuban relations after 1959 should not be repeated. Yet, for someone trying to limit associations with a worldwide ideological struggle, Almeyda then incredibly told Korry that he "followed Mao's advice in separating short-term tactics from longer-term strategy" and urged U.S. policy makers to deal with one specific problem at a time.[48] Korry seems to have been rather unsurprised and unfazed by the wider implications of this message. What he did note was a "kind of pragmatism . . . when confronted with the possibility of firm confrontation." There was "a chance of a deal" for the copper companies, he advised, if—and he underlined that this was the "essential question"—the United States wanted to encourage one.[49]

While the Nixon administration was privately deliberating the pros and cons of a deal over the next month, the Chileans began feeling the pressure to modify their nationalization program. As the Chilean Embassy in Washington warned, the Nixon administration could quite easily use this issue to justify a hard-line policy toward Chile if they did not.[50] In the meantime, U.S. pressure was becoming "serious and unsatisfactory," principally because threats were so ambiguous.[51]

In an effort to ascertain exactly what the nature of an eventual clash with Washington would look like, the ministry asked Chilean diplomats in Washington to investigate the legal and political implications of nationalizing Chile's mining industry.[52] And in early 1971, the UP also received two Foreign Ministry commissioned reports from U.S. law firms on Washington's previous responses to nationalization programs in Mexico, Iran, Guatemala, Brazil, and Cuba. These spelt out that U.S. law required "adequate, prompt and effective compensation" for expropriated U.S. companies (within six months). Yet the lawyers also underlined Washington's proclivity to deal on a "case-by-case" basis, advising Santiago it was "impossible to predict the precise moves" the United States would take.[53] As late as July, Letelier was also reporting that State Department officials were exhibiting "extreme caution" when discussing nationalization, making it difficult to come to any firm conclusions.[54] Indeed, the Nixon administration's diplomacy during these months was particularly effective in not giving away the United States' position on Allende's nationalization plans. It was also cleverly throwing the Chileans off the scent when it came to U.S. objectives in Chile. As Chilean Embassy reports from Washington surmised, the United States' policy toward Allende seemed to be "a rough draft," if that.[55]

As we know, although it is true that Washington's officials had not yet formulated a coherent plan regarding the stance they would take in the event of Chilean expropriations, they *were* clear about wanting to bring Allende down while pretending that they were not intervening in Chile. In conversation after conversation with Chilean diplomats during the first months of 1971, senior members of the administration therefore tried to deflect Chilean questions by underlining the possibility of establishing a working U.S.-Chilean relationship. In one such conversation, Deputy Assistant Secretary for Latin American Affairs John Crimmins told Letelier that "there was a major disposition on the part of the U.S. government . . . to resolve [any future] problems."[56] And when Letelier underlined Chile's proud constitutional history as he presented his diplomatic credentials to Richard Nixon, the president offered his own reassurances about respecting Chilean democratic politics:

The beliefs of the American people regarding democracy, cherished and vigorously defended in the almost two hundred years of this nation's independence are also well known. It is, inevitably, our hope that the blessings we perceive in free and democratic processes will be preserved where they now exist and will flow to an ever greater number of the peoples of the world. We do not, however, seek to impose our beliefs on others, recognizing that perhaps the most important freedom of all is that of selecting one's own path, of determining one's own destiny. The path represented by the program of your government is not the path chosen by the people of this country, but we recognize the right of any country to order its affairs.[57]

Henry Kissinger then added his own gushing guarantees to the Chileans when he met with Letelier at the end of March. As the ambassador optimistically wrote to Almeyda, the meeting had been "much more positive . . . than hoped." Kissinger promised that the U.S. government "did not wish in any way to interfere with the internal affairs of Chile" and had even stated twice in a forty-minute meeting that the way Allende was leading the new Chilean process was "worthy of great admiration."[58] Considering Kissinger's pivotal position in Washington's foreign policy establishment, Letelier believed this assurance to be highly significant. Indeed, together with the results of the embassy's public relations campaigns in the United States, he concluded that the "stridency" of anti-Allende factions was "melting" along with the snow in Washington.[59]

There were two key problems with Letelier's analysis besides the fact that he had been misled by Kissinger's duplicitous diplomacy and was therefore essentially wrong. First, the Chileans' inability to get an exact indication of U.S. reprisals undermined their already limited ability to avert them or confront them head on. Second, focusing on nationalization policies to determine Washington's approach to Chile diverted the UP's attention away from understanding the Nixon administration's fundamental concerns. To be sure, Nixon believed private investment was the answer to development, faced aggressive lobbying from multinationals, and was eager to protect investments in Chile.[60] But, as already indicated, from the moment Allende was elected, the U.S. president's predominant concerns had been Allende's impact on Latin American instability and the United States' influence in the region, not Chile's potential impact on U.S. finances.

Having largely ignored the nationalization question in the immediate aftermath of Allende's election, Nixon administration officials had only in early 1971 begun to decide whether to become directly involved in negotiations or to let private U.S. copper companies go it alone. Washington officials clearly distrusted the Chileans, and Kissinger questioned whether Allende was really adopting a nonconfrontational position or merely hoping to postpone a clash while he consolidated his position. Was Allende trying "to suck the U.S. government into the negotiations" so that he could use them to "bargain for leverage in other areas," he asked.[61] When Kissinger's NSC staff had examined these issues in February 1971, it had outlined three major concerns regarding direct governmental involvement in negotiations: first, the effect these negotiations would have on the companies' chances of getting compensation; second, the implications of failure for the administration's ability to sustain a "correct but cool" policy toward Allende; and, third, the extent to which they might undermine U.S. economic sanctions against Allende that were already being put in place.[62] Ultimately, the National Security Council's Senior Review Group (SRG) had postponed making a final decision on copper, having agreed only to try to influence the character of Chilean nationalization programs through dialogue.[63] At the end of March, Kissinger had then personally told Letelier that the administration did not consider this to be a political or governmental issue. Washington "already had a sufficient amount of enemies abroad" without making Chile into a new one, he had insisted.[64]

Notwithstanding Kissinger's platitudes, the Nixon administration had simultaneously been pursuing a comprehensive destabilization campaign in Chile in line with NSDM 93 since November 1970. As the acting chairman of the NSC's Ad Hoc Interagency Working Group on Chile concluded, "restraint" did not mean "passivity or inaction."[65] Already, during Allende's first two months as president, the administration had instructed U.S. representatives at the Inter-American Development Bank and the World Bank to work behind the scenes to delay Chilean loans and pose awkward questions about the UP's economic programs, business and labor leaders were informed of the U.S. government's "discouraging view" of Chilean developments, and the State Department Agency for International Development (AID) and the Export-Import Bank were explicitly told to "withhold" loans and investment guarantees "until further notice."[66] Compared to the $110 million AID administered in Chile between 1968 and 1970, Chile would receive approximately $3 million during Allende's presidency. Similarly, between his election and his overthrow in 1973, IDB loans totaled $2 million compared to $46 million in 1970, and the World Bank approved no loans at all compared to the $31 million it had granted in the two years before Allende assumed power.[67]

Meanwhile, as part of the Nixon administration's Covert Action Program inside Chile, Washington had been boosting Allende's political opposition parties. Primarily, U.S. covert operations focused on the biggest of these, Chile's Christian Democrat Party (PDC) and its prospects in Chile's forthcoming municipal elections in April 1971, but it also delivered funds to the right-wing National Party (PN) and the conservative wing of the Radical Party. Intervening in municipal elections was nothing new for the United States; in 1969 Washington had expended $350,000 to help the PDC.[68] However, two years later, denying the UP a majority in an election that was widely regarded to be a "plebiscite" on Allende's mandate was considered well worth quadruple that amount. According to a memorandum drafted for the purpose of persuading 40 Committee members to support the allocation of substantial funds, the United States' financial contribution was necessary to "slow down Allende's progress in establishing a totalitarian Marxist state in Chile." In January the 40 Committee heeded such warnings, granting $1.24 million for improving media capabilities and ensuring that the opposition was able to conduct a "vigorous electoral effort to maintain the morale." As far as U.S. government officials were concerned, supporting Chile's opposition parties had widespread benefits — "any opposition voice will be helpful," Kissinger's new assistant for Latin American Affairs, Arnold Nachmanoff, had written to him ahead of the 40 Committee meeting in January. With extra support, it would be "more difficult for the [Chilean] Government to pressure or squeeze out opposition. . . . The parties do not have sufficient resources nor access to other sources of funds." Nachmanoff also warned that "a massive UP electoral victory would have significant psychological repercussions not only in Chile but throughout Latin America." Given this threat, the United States was concerned about the opposition's lack of unity and its failure to launch a coordinated attack against him. As Nachmanoff had informed his boss in January, the CIA was "urging cooperation." However, just over two weeks before the election the situation had not improved. Indeed, the director of the CIA reported to the 40 Committee that "factionalism" continued and that the PDC was "urgently seeking" more support from the United States in the context of the Allende government's "impressive election effort" and a lack of anticipated funds from industrial and commercial sectors. The Nixon administration was only too happy to fill the gap; it responded positively to this request, granting an additional $185,000 to the PDC on 22 March.[69]

In the end, however, this financial investment fell short of denying the UP victory. When Chileans went to the polls on 4 April 1971, the UP's parties gained 49.7 percent of the vote, a sizable share compared to the 36.4 percent that Allende had received six months earlier. To a large extent, the results indicated the success of the UP's domestic program that, by April, had achieved a partial redistribution of income, a modest decrease in unemployment and inflation, and support for its nationalization and agrarian reform programs.

However, the municipal results were by no means decisive when it came to the balance of power between the UP and its opposition. In spite of the increased support for parties on the Left, the CIA also claimed success, concluding that denying the UP an outright majority and restoring the Chilean opposition's confidence were the "fruits of U.S. government financial assistance." Furthermore, the CIA congratulated itself on achieving this without significantly raising Allende's suspicion. As U.S. intelligence analysts concluded, the UP's opposition was "buying time and remaining viable," even if they were pessimistic about Allende's future revolutionary programs.[70]

Washington was concurrently focusing on courting the Chilean military, which it believed would be pivotal in any "potential future action" against Allende.[71] In 1971 there were 146 Chileans being trained to fight communism at the U.S. Army School of the Americas in the Panama Canal Zone (the number would rise to 257 by 1973). There, they took courses on counterguerrilla operations, the use of informants, counterintelligence, subversion, countersubversion, espionage, counterespionage, interrogation of prisoners and suspects, handling mass rallies, populace and resources control, psychological operations, raids and searches, riots, surveillance, and terror and undercover operations.[72] When the issue of Chilean requests to the Foreign Military Assistance program had come up in February 1971, the Pentagon had also indicated its predisposition to help. As a paper drawn up by the Defense Department noted, assistance would "1) strengthen our influence in the Chilean military services and thus attempt to harden resistance to communist domination of Chile; 2) increase Chilean dependence on U.S. sources of supply for spares; and 3) pre-empt communist suppliers of equipment from an association with Chilean military services."[73]

Back in late February, the SRG had therefore decided to grant $5 million in Foreign Military Sales credits to Chile for the year ahead. Although not the maximum amount requested, this had been the best the administration felt it could offer without causing undue suspicion. As Kissinger commented to Secretary of State Rogers, the United States was going "out of [its] way to be nice to the Chilean military."[74] Interestingly, the Chilean Foreign Ministry recognized this, but what is rather surprising is that it noted that this was positive. According to analysts in Santiago, the continued flow of military credits had helped "project an image of normality" in U.S.-Chilean relations, a factor that was considered especially important when it came to Chile's standing vis-à-vis its neighbors in Latin America.[75]

More than thirty years later, details of Washington's covert policies and diplomatic maneuvers make something of a mockery of the Allende government's optimistic hopes of being able to redefine U.S.-Chilean relations along healthier but realistic lines. An internal Chilean Foreign Ministry review of policy toward the United States in mid-1971 repeated the supposition that Vietnam, the antiwar movement, and opposition to the Nixon administration at home all favored Allende's Chile.[76] And to a certain extent, these issues did circumscribe Washington's ability to maneuver. However, with the UP acting cautiously, rather than changing U.S. aims, they merely persuaded the Nixon administration to act covertly, while offering assurances of neutrality. As things stood in early 1971, because its warnings about nationalization procedures were frustratingly vague, Washington continued to hold all the cards. In fact, Deputy Assistant Secretary of State for Latin American Affairs John Crimmins was later surprised to hear how effective and unified the Nixon administration's message had been, especially considering the animosity between the State Department and the NSC that plagued Nixon's administration.[77] Even when the Chileans expressed suspicions that U.S. actions in Latin America seemed to be aimed at isolating Chile, Washington officials held their own and maintained the United States was doing nothing unusual.

Ideological Pluralism versus Ideological Frontiers

Santiago and Washington had good reason to be mutually suspicious about each other's policies in Latin America after Allende assumed the presidency. Both wanted to readjust the inter-American system to suit their own aims and were worried that, if they made the wrong moves or alienated potential allies, the other side might gain. As the Chilean Foreign Ministry acknowledged in June 1971, Allende's policy toward Latin

America was likely to determine the United States' approach to Chile.[78] For other states in the region, the months after Allende's election were also a moment of change. Although Washington and Santiago wanted to get these countries on their side, Southern American leaders had their own sovereign agendas and regional strategies to pursue. In early 1971, for example, Brazil launched a highly ambitious diplomatic regional offensive designed to boost its own position in Latin America, while upholding ideological frontiers against the likes of Chile and Cuba. Although U.S. policy makers appear to have been largely oblivious to the extent of Brasília's new regional diplomacy, Latin American responses to it revealed a wary sense of upheaval in the Southern Cone. This was especially so amid rumors that the United States was using Brazil in inter-American affairs, and ironically these fears did a great deal to ensure Chile's ability to break down some of the ideological barriers it might otherwise have confronted. Be that as it may, in reality outsiders knew very little about the nature and scope of growing U.S.-Brazilian communication on regional affairs or the lead that Brazil was taking in this dialogue.

From November 1970 onward, the United States had combined its efforts to undermine Allende's presidency with the bigger goal of containing the Left and salvaging U.S. influence in the inter-American system. The news that Peru and Bolivia had been interested in emulating Chile's reestablishment of relations with Cuba and that Castro's "new maturity" in the hemisphere was beginning to bear fruit magnified Washington's sense of vulnerability.[79] At the end of November, the State Department's Bureau of Intelligence and Research (INR) had noted that Chile's reestablishment of relations with Castro would become contagious unless Havana and Santiago increased their efforts to export revolution, a prospect that it judged to be "unlikely." As the INR observed, OAS members appeared "impressed" by Cuba's reduced support for revolutionaries in the region since Che Guevara's death.[80]

Although the Nixon administration had concluded it could do nothing to reverse Chile's decision, it moved quickly to contain it.[81] When Latin American leaders took advantage of Mexican president Luis Echeverría's inauguration in December to discuss the possibility of reviewing their position toward Cuba in the light of Allende's move, for example, U.S. and Brazilian representatives had effectively resisted any serious debate.[82] But in January 1971, Washington had remained uneasy. The State Department had thus instructed all U.S. ambassadors in Latin America to contact host governments and reaffirm Washington's opposition to any change. Ambassadors were also told to underline the dangers of not upholding collective security by "gratuitously" offering Castro "a badly needed and prestigious political and psychological victory over the OAS," or giving Cuba economic relief that would allow it to revive its continental subversion.[83]

Meanwhile, the Nixon administration had also begun collecting information to use against Chile in Latin America.[84] In the months after Allende came to power, CIA station chiefs were instructed to pass on information to U.S. ambassadors that could be disseminated to journalists and politicians. In particular, Washington wanted to undermine Allende's independence and democratic credentials and therefore sought to "play up" the notion that Chile was awash with subversive Cuban and Soviet agents.[85] U.S. policy makers had little concrete information about Cuban involvement in Chile at this stage, relying instead on what NSC staffer Pete Vaky recalled as supposition rather than fact.[86] Yet, by calling attention to Cuban involvement in Allende's Chile, U.S. officials were squarely able to attack two birds with one stone. And certainly, when Brazil's ambassador in Santiago sent an alarmist telegram back home detailing stories of ominous Cuban intervention in Chile, he relied purely on spurious press reports.[87]

All the while, the Allende government was clearly aware of the United States' hostile reaction to the new Chilean-Cuban relationship. Chilean diplomats heard from the OAS secretary-general that the State Department had "paralyzed" a Colombian initiative to review Cuba's position within the inter-American system. Another source provided information about a private conversation Nixon had had with a Bolivian diplomat in which the president presented himself as being highly interested in working with regional countries in the context of Latin America's "new political configuration."[88] As the Chilean Embassy in Washington had concluded in February 1971, there was a strong feeling that the Nixon administration was trying to isolate Chile "as the black sheep of the [inter-American] family."[89]

Henceforth, rumors about Washington's diplomacy within inter-American forums exacerbated Santiago's fears of being isolated.[90] In early 1971 the Chilean Embassy in Lima warned that the Nixon administration was paying new attention to Chile's traditional rival, Peru.[91] Numerous conjectures followed: Was the United States trying to drive a wedge between neighbors? Was Washington behind what was reported as being a resurgence of anti-Chilean feeling in Peru? Did rumors that the United States was supplying weapons to Peruvians hidden in earthquake aid have any substance? In reality, these fears actually exaggerated the United States attention to Peru in early 1971. But Allende's ambassador in Lima, Luís Jerez Ramirez, was worried enough to keep asking. As he surmised, Peru would be a crucial part of any attempt by Washington to win back its "past hegemony" in South America.[92]

What the Chileans had to work out was whether this U.S. attempt to win back influence in Latin America was squarely aimed against Chile or not. When Chilean press articles falsely alleged that Allende possessed a U.S. document outlining Washington's plans to isolate it, the Chilean Foreign Ministry immediately issued denials and downplayed the "cloudy" possibility that Chile could be isolated in the first place.[93] Privately, however, diplomats continued to speculate about "consultations to blockade Chile," especially after news of a meeting of U.S. diplomats working in Latin America in Panama in March.[94]

The Chilean Foreign Ministry also paid "special attention" to evidence of growing ties between Washington and Brasilia and the prospect that Brazil itself could be a serious and immediate threat to Chilean sovereignty in early 1971.[95] As the Chilean ambassador in Brasilia, Raul Rettig, noted, "It is not a mystery to anyone that the current Brazilian regime constitutes a potential enemy for progressive and revolutionary governments in the continent. Chile is, in these moments, the object of attack that the military government and the dominant classes that control nearly all mediums of mass communication use most frequently. This is perhaps the most important and combative front of reactionary forces that act at the international level. Behind the press, there exists a real sustained war [against Chile] that is expressed in repeated editorials and distorting information aimed at damaging the prestige of President Allende's government."[96]

Among the editorials Ambassador Rettig referred to were repeated references to the "tragedy" that had befallen Chile, a traditionally friendly nation where, according to the Brazilian press, nothing very important ever happened.[97] Like the Nixon administration, Brazil's military leaders had clearly not been prepared for Allende's victory, but in its aftermath news coverage of Chilean affairs had tripled. In one instance, a press report cited a Brazilian official warning that Russian flotillas were on their way to the Chilean port of Valparaiso.[98] In another, the anticommunist Brazilian daily *O Estado do São Paulo* claimed that "socialist loyalty and submission to Fidel Castro's continental revolutionary leadership were absolute priorities for Allende's Government."[99] Of course, it is quite possible that the CIA planted these alarmist reports. But it would also be a historical error to attribute all ideologically driven hostility toward Allende's Chile to

Washington. Certainly, the Chileans noticed a new and ominous attitude toward their country growing within Brazil itself.

In early 1971, for example, the Chilean Embassy in Brasilia had begun receiving information that this hostility was being translated into action. When Chile's Consular Division moved from Rio de Janeiro to Brasilia at the beginning of the year, the Brazilian Foreign Ministry had launched an investigation into its activities. More ominously, the Chileans learned that a Brazilian general had offered to help establish a resistance movement in Chile. Although this news appears to have been relayed to the embassy only once, it did not seem to be an isolated show of support for anti-Allende groups; in São Paulo, senior military officials were said to be recruiting Chileans living in Brazil for belligerent action against the Unidad Popular. At the beginning of March, a trusted embassy informant also passed on news that Brazilian military leaders had gone so far as to establish situation rooms at the army's headquarters in Rio to study Chile's threat. According to this informant, these rooms were filled with scaled models of the Andes stretching along Chile's borders with Argentina, Bolivia, and Peru. During meetings between senior military officials, they were then used to determine which zones might become locations for future guerrilla struggles (anti-Allende Chileans and other Latin American civilians were mentioned as being the ones who would fight antiguerrilla battles). Furthermore, news that Brazilian secret agents had been sent to Chile to find out more about such zones coincided with other information reaching the Chileans that the Brazilian government had dispatched intelligence operatives along with seventy prisoners Santiago had reluctantly taken as part of a hostage exchange.[100] Last but not least, the Chilean Embassy in Brasilia reported that the Brazilian army had staged military exercises specifically designed around the premise of fighting guerrilla forces residing in Chile.[101]

Unsurprisingly, this information sparked alarm in Chile, especially when coupled with indications that U.S.-Brazilian relations had suddenly improved and that Brasilia was launching a major new diplomatic offensive in Latin America. After U.S. assistant secretary Charles Meyer's visit to Brazil in March, Brazilian newspapers reported that he and Foreign Minister Mario Gibson Barbosa had discussed "Cuban infiltration in Chilean internal affairs" and the future "transformation of that country into a base of support for the export of terrorism and subversion."[102] Only a year before, Brasilia's relations with Washington had suffered serious tensions on account of U.S. congressional investigations into allegations of torture in Brazil.[103] Now, the two Latin American countries' situations seemed to have been reversed. Moreover, the Chileans feared that Brazil's new diplomatic offensive was aimed at isolating Chile and assuming a dominant position in South America. As Almeyda would later explain to Polish leaders, not only was Brazil the United States' "most loyal collaborator," but there was evidence to suggest Brazil's foreign minister had gathered together all his friends from Latin America to organize an anti-Chilean campaign in early 1971.[104] In view of these apparent maneuvers, Santiago had ordered its diplomats throughout Latin America to report on Brazilian activity in their host countries.[105] Was the United States "distributing different geographic regions of the world?" Chile's ambassador in Buenos Aires asked.[106] Ambassador Rettig echoed this possibility, concluding that because the United States wanted to rescue its faltering position in Latin America and was reluctant to be the one to intervene directly in regional affairs, it was taking advantage of Brazil's diplomatic offensive to prevent "another Cuba." He urged Santiago to build the best possible relations with Latin American countries as an "antidote."[107]

It was in this context that Chile launched its very own diplomatic offensive in Latin America in 1971. From the start of Allende's presidency, the UP had emphasized its attachment to the "Andean Pact," a group dedicated to subregional development and economic integration that was established in 1969 by Chile, Peru, Colombia, Ecuador, and Bolivia. At the end of 1970, the UP had then signed the group's "Decision 24," an agreement to regulate foreign investment and decrease external control of the members' industrial production. Foreign Minister Almeyda later admitted that Chile's main purpose in doing so was political rather than economic and that Chile had "no illusions" about the prospects for economic collaboration. Member states did not have a history of commercial relations; in fact, when the pact was signed, their exports to and imports from each other amounted only to just under 3 percent and less than 5 percent of their total trade respectively. As Almeyda recalled, some in the UP believed that trying to transform this unfavorable balance of trade was economically unwise, but it was increasingly considered politically important to show "an active and visible Chilean loyalty to the process."[108]

Beyond the Andean Pact, Chilean diplomats campaigned widely in early 1971 to spread information about the democratic, peaceful, noninterventionist character of Allende's government and its commitment to "ideological pluralism" in foreign affairs. As Mexico's foreign minister told Santiago's ambassador in Mexico City, this type of diplomacy was pivotal, given the way in which foreign news services had taken to attaching "political or ideological surnames" to all things Chilean. His advice was to launch an "open and extensive campaign" as the only means of defending the truth, which is exactly what the Chileans were already doing.[109] Allende publicly challenged the idea that he planned to export La Vía Chilena in the Southern Cone, noting that it was "difficult to conceive" how this would happen in countries with no political parties, workers organizations, or a parliament.[110] In April, Almeyda then emphasized Chile's "sober" approach to foreign affairs and rejected the idea that Allende had any regional leadership pretensions when he addressed the OAS General Assembly. And with regard to Chile's decision to reestablish relations with Cuba, Almeyda not only defended his government's actions by pointing out that Chile was not the only one that had relations with the island—Mexico also had them— but argued that the nature of Cuba's isolation was becoming ever more "artificial."[111]

Yet, in practice, the UP's regional policies were far more ambiguous to outsiders than the Chilean Foreign Ministry and Allende proclaimed. Partly, this was the consequence of the heterogeneous nature of the UP. At the PS Congress in January 1971, the party's newly elected general secretary, Carlos Altamirano, publicly declared that Uruguayan and Brazilian revolutionaries would "always" receive asylum and support from "comrades in arms" in Chile.[112] Allende's own position also raised doubts about conflicting allegiances abroad. When in mid-1971, the British ambassador in Montevideo, Geoffrey Jackson, was kidnapped by the Uruguayan revolutionary movement, the Tupamaros, London discreetly asked Allende to appeal for his release, which he did. As Britain's ambassador in Santiago, who was rather sympathetic to La Vía Chilena, noted after he met the Chilean president, Allende was "very good at making those with whom he talks feel that he is fundamentally on their side."[113] Moreover, in helping out on this occasion he surmised that Allende had wanted "the best of both worlds." "He has hoped for a great boost for himself as president of Chile and as leader of the Latin American left," the ambassador noted; "he would not do anything to embarrass the Tupamaros and he might indeed be able to help them both by facilitating a satisfactory arrangement over Jackson and by presenting them and the left wing in general in a relatively good light. He also wants to gain credit with us: he is anxious to be on good terms with the Europeans, and we are particularly important as Europeans and also as an influence on the US."[114]

Despite this rather ambiguous image, and while engaging in active diplomacy elsewhere, the Chileans began questioning officials in Washington directly about their Latin American policies. Unsurprisingly, Deputy Assistant Secretary of State Crimmins "absolutely, totally and categorically" denied the existence of a plan to isolate Chile.[115] And Kissinger predictably told Ambassador Letelier the idea was "absolutely absurd . . . with no foundation."[116] In fact, so persuasive was Kissinger that as a result of these conversations Letelier was once more taken in. Certainly, he advised the Chilean Foreign Ministry to avoid making the mistake of reading too much into U.S. visits to Latin American countries. And he also urged Almeyda again not to underestimate the value of the high-level personal assurances he had been given.[117]

But of course, as in the case of U.S.-Chilean bilateral relations, the Chileans had *every* reason to be suspicious. Although there were differences in Washington regarding the extent to which the United States should rally Latin American counterrevolutionary forces against Chile, the whole administration wanted to curtail Allende's regional influence.[118] As Crimmins told one Latin American diplomat, "U.S. policy toward Chile is to act with prudence and restraint, reacting to Chile rather than taking initiatives. We want to avoid any confrontation; if any untoward difficulties arise, they will be Chile's fault. We are not happy or optimistic; but we don't believe it is good to assume that all is lost."[119] The Ad Hoc Interagency Group on Chile also recommended that although anti-Americanism in the region meant that the United States had to tread gently, it could still play a "behind-the-scenes" role, "encouraging Latin Americans to take the initiative but, if necessary, feeding suggested initiatives to them."[120]

In fact, U.S. leaders were once more heavily engaged in building up Latin America's military institutions and antidemocratic strongmen. As Rettig had feared, the Nixon administration was making a concerted effort to improve Washington's relations with Brazil's military regime. And, already, by the beginning of 1971, Nixon's orders to pay special attention to the country as a response to Allende's election had significantly changed the results of a yearlong Program Analysis at the eleventh hour. Before this, Nixon's and Kissinger's attention to Brazil as an emerging Third World power had been resisted by the State Department, which called for distance from General Emílio Garrastazu Médici's authoritarian regime.[121] Moreover, those at the State Department who had been mainly responsible for compiling the Program Analysis on Brazil (NSSM 67) had stressed Brazil's relatively unimportant strategic significance. Brazil's military use, they argued, was only in "UN and OAS peacekeeping operations" and did not justify substantive military assistance.[122]

However, when the NSC's Senior Review Group met to discuss NSSM 67 back in December 1970, these conclusions had effectively been thrown out the window. On the surface, the SRG had approved a "Selective Support" option.[123] But discussion had inevitably drifted to the impact Allende's election had on the inter-American system. In this climate, those who argued that U.S.-Brazilian relations should not be determined by Allende's arrival on the scene lost out.[124] For one, Kissinger had already preempted the SRG meeting's conclusions by asking Nachmanoff how U.S.-Brazilian relations could be improved.[125] And echoing General Vernon Walters's advice to Kissinger a month earlier, Nachmanoff had suggested that although Washington would have to respond as favorably as possible to military equipment requests, and even address the problems of economic development "if necessary," it also had "to try to lift their sights to bigger concepts and historical problems." He recommended that a way to do this was to concentrate on improving "matters of style and consultation," and shortly afterward Nixon instructed Kissinger that he wanted President Médici invited to the United States by July 1971.[126] Indeed, in late 1970 the White House effected a decisive priority shift when it came to U.S.-Brazilian relations. By January 1971 the American Embassy in Brasilia had prepared a Country Analysis and Strategy Paper (CASP) underlining what had changed:

> The fundamentally most important U.S. interest in Brazil is the protection of U.S. national security through the cooperation of Brazil as a hemispheric ally against the contingencies of: an intra-continental threat, such as a serious deterioration in the Chilean situation (example—Chile adopting a Cuba-style "export of revolution" policy) or the formation of an Andean bloc which turned anti-US; or an admittedly more remote extra-continental threat, such as Soviet penetration of the South Atlantic. The danger posed by recent events in Chile and Bolivia establishes a hemispheric security threat which did not exist at anywhere near the same level as this time last year. The maintenance, therefore, of Brazil as a potential ally in hemispheric security affairs could be of critical interest to the U.S.[127]

Nixon was especially insistent on improving and strengthening the U.S.-Brazilian alliance. As he later privately told Kissinger and Haldeman, he wanted the Brazilians to know that "we are just about the best friend Brazil has had in this office [the Oval office]." There may have been sectors of Congress and the State Department that were opposed to strengthening relations with the military regime, but, as Nixon instructed on this occasion, he wanted Brasilia to know they were being ignored.[128]

At the same time as the U.S. administration was reviewing policy toward Brazil, the Pentagon had also taken advantage of this priority shift to stop scheduled reductions of Military Group personnel in Latin America.[129] As Deputy Assistant Secretary Crimmins noted, the Pentagon tended "to be uneasy with the restraints imposed by the risks of playing into Allende's hands through becoming too overt. Against these risks they set those of appearing to Latin America and the opposition to Allende in Chile to be weak and indecisive."[130] Indeed, Secretary of Defense Melvin Laird had written directly to Nixon at the end of November, arguing that reductions were "inconsonant" with the president's instructions to improve ties with the region's military leaders. Instead, he called for a joint interagency plan to increase Military Groups "on a selective basis . . . as quickly as possible."[131] When Laird informed Kissinger of progress toward upgrading military assistance a month later, Kissinger welcomed the news. As far as the latter was concerned, it was essential that the Latin Americans understood they should go only to the United States in search of security and military supplies.[132]

By this point, Kissinger had also already ordered an interagency review of the U.S. military presence in Latin America.[133] The conclusion he received in response was bold: aside from having security and military value, the Interdepartmental Group on Inter-American Affairs found that "military missions, attaché staffs, training, and other programs" were highly effective for diplomatic and political purposes. To clear up any ambiguity, the Interdepartmental Group recommended sending "definitive guidance removing any doubts about the permissibility, propriety and desirability of utilizing mission personnel and attaches for purposes of influencing host governments' military leaders toward U.S. foreign policy objectives." In addition, it advised overcoming legislative restrictions on military sales and according Latin America a "high priority" over other regions.[134] In April 1971 the president also took a direct interest in ensuring a strong U.S. military presence in Latin America when he intervened to stop plans to phase out the U.S. Armed Forces' Southern Command (SOUTHCOM).[135]

Brazil's military regime was either unaware of or unimpressed by this resurgent U.S. interest in hemispheric affairs. Indeed, throughout early

1971, the Brazilians believed the United States was not doing *enough* to combat the communist threat in the Southern Cone. Brazil's ambassador in Santiago, Antonio Castro da Câmara Canto, certainly doubted the United States' ability to counter Allende's impact in the hemisphere effectively. He regretted that, together with Washington's difficulties in Vietnam and tensions with a number of Latin American countries, Chilean "able diplomacy" was limiting its impact. Not only did the UP's legal, constitutional approach give the United States nothing to "protest," but the United States had been too wary of repeating the same mistakes it had made in 1959. By contrast, Câmara Canto suggested that Santiago had absorbed the lessons of Castro's experience well.[136]

In view of these concerns, the Brazilians tried to persuade Washington to do more about Chile and, beyond that, about what they perceived to be threatening trends in South America. One Brazilian vice admiral spoke to the U.S. ambassador in Brasilia, William Rountree, "at length and almost emotionally" about the prospects for U.S.-Brazilian military cooperation and "dangerous potentialities in Latin America" (he highlighted Chile, other Andean states, and Uruguay for particular attention).[137] In November 1970 Brazilian foreign minister Gibson Barbosa had also told Rountree, that "he realized that [the] U.S. was far more important to Brazil than Brazil was to [the] U.S. Nevertheless he regarded Brazil's success as [a] large, dynamic, and successful country with [an] economy based on [a] free enterprise system, and serving as an important counter [weight] to trends in certain other Latin American countries, to be important to [the] U.S. and [the] free world."[138] Then, in early February, Gibson Barbosa stressed the potential for U.S. cooperation when he raised further concerns about "trends" in the Southern Cone region directly with U.S. Secretary of State William Rogers in Washington. Specifically, he underlined Allende's impact on nationalist military governments in Peru and Bolivia and also on Uruguay, where Brazil was particularly concerned about "marked leftist gains." Although Gibson acknowledged that direct intervention in Chile would be "counterproductive," he urged the United States to work with Brazil "to meet the threats posed by these developments . . . (1) to counter the Chilean situation; (2) to help rebuild friendship for the United States which has waned in certain sectors in Brazil and (3) to reinforce trends in Brazil toward a return to responsive political institutions." (The latter was presumably for domestic U.S. consumption.)[139]

Overall, these efforts to attract Washington's attention would be highly effective. Yet in the short term they actually had a somewhat negative impact on Brazil's standing in the region. Immediately after Allende's election, Brazilian military leaders had made obvious attempts to work with their traditional regional rivals, the Argentines, to combat leftist threats in the Southern Cone.[140] Yet in the months that followed, Argentina's leaders had increasingly become more worried about Brasilia than Santiago and were highly suspicious that, by reaching out to the United States, Brazil was seeking to bolster its position vis-à-vis its southern neighbor.[141]

Ultimately, Chile benefited. At first, Argentina's right-wing military leaders had been concerned about Allende's election due to their fears about left-wing insurgency at home. In view of potential hostility with the Argentines, Allende and the Chilean Foreign Ministry had consequently placed special emphasis on improving Chile's relations with Buenos Aires.[142] Indeed, in a battle against isolation, Chile's long vulnerable border with Argentina and an annual trading relationship worth $200 million made establishing amicable relations with Argentina's military leaders a key priority.[143] After making contacts with leaders of the PCCh and diplomats from the Soviet bloc, the Polish Embassy in Santiago also reported home to Warsaw in May 1971 that there was a real possibility of Argentine intervention in Chilean affairs.[144] And as Chile's ambassador in Buenos Aires, Ramon Huidobro, later recalled, the Chileans were worried that Washington could exacerbate outstanding border disputes to provoke conflict.[145]

The Chilean Foreign Ministry therefore expended considerable effort to persuade Argentina that the new Chilean government posed no threat and that it wanted good relations with its neighbor. As Almeyda privately explained to leaders from the socialist bloc in May 1971, the Chileans were also exploring the idea of exchanges between certain sectors of both countries' military forces in the hope of isolating the pro-American right-wing members of Argentina's armed forces. Moreover, Almeyda noted that the Chileans were underlining to the Argentines that Chile was "not a rival and would not be a rival." Brazil was the rival that Buenos Aires had to look out for, the Chileans stressed.[146]

Allende's visit to Argentina in July 1971 and, before that, Buenos Aires's support for Santiago's candidacy to host UNCTAD III, were thus the combined outcome of Argentine fears regarding Brazil and intense Chilean diplomacy (Brazil and the United States had backed Santiago's rival Mexico City to host the conference).[147] However, there is reason to suggest that the Argentines had been inclined to tactically appease Allende early on.

As Argentina's ambassador in Washington had told State Department officials back in December 1970, Allende should not "automatically [be] presumed to be a total loss. His attitude toward other Latin American states and the United States will depend in part on how we act toward him. Closing all doors will surely drive him to other more hospitable arms."[148] Subsequently, when Argentina's foreign minister, Pablo Pardo, had met with Allende in June, it seems that he had warmed to the president and passed on his approval to President Alejandro Lanusse Gelly.[149] Then, when Lanusse and Allende met at Salta on 24 July, they declared their agreement to principles of nonintervention, peaceful resolution of bilateral disputes, and the importance of "friendship and co-operation."[150] As the *Washington Post* noted, the meeting was an "important blow to Latin Americans who [sought] to quarantine newly socializing states."[151]

Chile therefore avoided isolation. But as Brazil stepped up its diplomatic offensive, the Nixon administration was also getting up to speed on developments in the Southern Cone. In particular, with Brazil's prodding, Washington began to focus on the unstable situation in Bolivia and Uruguay. And it was this multisided combination of actors and fluid developments in the Southern Cone that would shape the inter-American Cold War struggle ahead. The Chileans understood that these regional dynamics made it imperative to win over friends. The suggestion that the Nixon administration was lacking a clear regional policy or that it had been contained in South America, as Chilean Embassy staff in Washington concluded, was also quite perceptive. However, the idea put forward by Chilean diplomats in Washington that economic difficulties or problems dealing with Peru, Bolivia, Chile, and Vietnam had forced the United States toward a position of "wisdom and maturity" in the hemisphere was wrong insofar as this meant lessening levels of U.S. intervention in the hemisphere.[152]

This error reflected a more general misplaced understanding of the inter-American balance of forces. In July 1971 Fidel Castro proclaimed that the United States was "a lot more fragile, and . . . much more limited, in its possibilities for intervention in and crushing of revolutionary Latin American processes."[153] Yet this analysis was clearly premature and overly simplistic. As later events proved, counterrevolutionary forces within Chile, the Southern Cone, and Latin America stood ready to resist radical transformation with or without the United States and were just as ideologically driven in their motives as Castro or Allende.

Conclusion

In many respects, Allende's first nine months as president were character-ized by relative hope and optimism. Among the reasons that Santiago's leaders had to be cheerful were the resounding successes of Allende's visit to Argentina, the UP's impressive showing in Chile's municipal elections, and repeated U.S. reassurances that the United States wanted to avoid conflict. As Chilean foreign policy analysts surmised, their diplomatic campaigns had already strengthened Chile's position in the United States by improving the way the U.S. public viewed Allende, ensuring continued flows of military equipment, and nurturing bilateral relations with key Latin American states.

Indeed, Chile's international standing had risen dramatically, and the UP's nationalization projects, Santiago's appeal to ideological pluralism in international affairs, and Allende's message of wealth distribution and emancipation resonated especially well in the Third World. For the time being, in fact, La Vía Chilena seemed to epitomize the possibility that an era of Cold War confrontation and hostility was over and that the global South was in ascendance. President Houari Boumedienne of Algeria was one of those to express his sincere support for both Chile's nationalization project and its proposal to hold UNCTAD III in Santiago.[154] Chilean diplo-mats also increasingly found common cause with Peru's president, Juan Velasco Alvarado, when the latter publicly attacked the way international financial institutions were used to put pressure on countries that pursued nationalization. As the Chilean ambassador in Lima noted, Velasco Alvara-do's anti-imperialism was "poorly defined," but it was "useful and posi-tive" for Chile.[155]

The Cubans were also hopeful. As CIA analysts observed, "Chile, Peru, Uruguay, Bolivia and Guatemala, in that order" were now "the most im-portant Latin American countries in Havana's foreign policy scheme. . . . Fidel Castro has issued instructions to maintain complete cooperation with Chile at all costs."[156] In a handwritten letter to Allende at the end of May, Fidel Castro summed up his own exuberant optimism. "We're amazed at your extraordinary efforts and the limitless energies you've poured into maintaining and consolidating your victory," he wrote. "Here, we can appreciate that the people are gaining ground, in spite of the dif-ficult and complex mission they shoulder. . . . The April 4 elections were a splendid and encouraging victory. . . . Your courage and resolve, your mental and physical energy and ability to carry the revolutionary process forward, have been of the essence. . . . Great and different challenges are surely in store for you, and you must face these in conditions which are not precisely ideal, but a just policy, with the support of the people and applied with determination, cannot be defeated."[157] And yet, as Castro's letter implied, Chile's position had been readjusted rather than redefined. In conversation with his Polish counterpart during an official visit to Warsaw in June 1971, Cuba's foreign minister, Raúl Roa, similarly described Allende as "intelligent . . . experienced and measured" but stressed that the president's position was "extremely difficult." As Roa told his hosts, Chile's left-wing parties had assumed the government, but they did not yet hold power.[158]

Meanwhile, Allende emphasized that persuasion could still be used as a tool for transforming Chile's foreign relations. Looking ahead, the Chilean Foreign Ministry acknowledged that in the next phase of Chile's nationalization process, "the reactions of the forces of imperialism" would be "more aggressive." The ministry therefore underlined the imperative of a carefully coordinated international strategy, something that would prove increasingly difficult as Chile's external pressures escalated.[159]

Indeed, Allende's first nine months would turn out to be the calm before the storm. Although reason—rather than force—had worked for Allende when it came to gaining power, it would not be enough to achieve his goals and persuade Washington of the legitimacy of his cause. Partly, of course, this is because U.S. officials were simply not predisposed to sustain warm relations with dissenting Latin American leaders; Nixon did not believe he should have to negotiate his foreign policy with "ungrateful" "Latins." And Allende was not just any Latin American leader. Inescapably, Chile was first and foremost an ideological Cold War problem for the United States despite hopeful Chilean readings of world affairs, and skeptics in Washington (and Brasilia) viewed the UP's "healthy realism" with incredulity and fear.

After all, Allende's lifelong campaign against U.S. "imperialism" and the UP's manifesto pledge to rid Chile of capitalist exploitation, not to mention the new president's identification with Cuba, did not disappear overnight when Allende took office. Keeping Cuba at a distance or denouncing left-wing movements in Latin America would also have involved betraying his ideology and abandoning the past. Consequently, like the United States and Cuba, the UP tried to downplay its real intentions while members of the coalition and the MIR unhelpfully refused to be tied to prescriptions of "caution" in their support for armed revolutionaries. And, meanwhile, there were many who continued to think that Chile would ultimately come under Cuba's influence, especially when Allende invited Cubans to assist in matters of intelligence and security, thereby exacerbating these fears in the process.

For their part, Nixon and Kissinger hoped that regional allies could help defend against these threats and make up for self-perceived U.S. weakness. However, in mid-1971 the application of the "Nixon Doctrine" in Latin America was not yet fully developed. True, the United States had found a willing and impatient ally in Brazil, but at this stage Washington neither delegated responsibility to Brasilia nor informed it of its own aggressive covert operations and psychological warfare against Allende. To the contrary, it neglected to share information with Brazil to such an extent that in July 1971 U.S. diplomats had to reassure the Brazilians that the United States was in no way poised to accommodate Allende.[160]

4 DISPUTES

Copper, *Compañeros*, and Counterrevolution, July–December 1971

On 17 November 1971 Fidel Castro visited the southern Chilean city of Concepción and told crowds that a brilliant revolutionary future lay ahead. "The road that revolutionaries propose for humanity is rose colored!" he proclaimed. Yet, he also urged his audience to be realistic about the present. "In a revolution not everything is rose colored," he warned. "We revolutionaries cannot speak of any rose-colored present . . . we revolutionaries can speak of a present of self-denial, a present of work, a heroic, sacrificial and glorious present."[1] Castro's visit to Concepción was just one stop on a gargantuan tour that took him from Chile's arid deserts in the north to its frozen glaciers in the south. However, this twenty-five-day visit was monumental not only in its duration and diversity; it also coincided with—and contributed toward—mounting political tension in Chile. As Castro observed for himself, the optimism that had characterized Salvador Allende's first months as president was disappearing as nationalization disputes, complex political alliances, and counterrevolutionary forces began impeding his progress.

The stakes at play in implementing La Vía Chilena had been rising long before Castro's plane touched down in Santiago in November 1971. In June, the murder of Chile's former interior minister, Edmundo Pérez Zujovic, by a small extremist group had intensified fear of radicalism in the country, leading more than one foreign observer to warn that "sharp conflict" was on the horizon.[2] Meanwhile, as the Unidad Popular pushed ahead with redistributing Chile's wealth and nationalizing the country's copper industry, it ran up against domestic and international hostility. At home, parliamentary opposition, paramilitary violence, rumors about military intervention in politics, and divisions within Allende's own cabinet considerably undermined the chances of a peaceful democratic road to socialism. Abroad, Santiago's relations with Washington also deteriorated, and left-wing hopes for revolutionary change in Latin America were eclipsed by right-wing counterrevolutionary victories in the Southern Cone.

Overall, in fact, it seemed as if Allende's domestic and international fortunes were increasingly intertwined. On the one hand, Allende's external relations had a significant bearing on internal politics, most obviously in the shape of Fidel Castro's extended visit to Chile and Washington's reaction to the expropriation of private U.S. copper companies. On the other hand, domestic developments affected Chile's international standing and foreign policy priorities more and more. Pivotally, by late 1971, the UP was keenly looking abroad to solve mounting economic difficulties. With dwindling foreign exchange reserves and a crippling external debt, Santiago's leaders publicized their objectives and challenges worldwide in the hope of changing their enemies' behavior and expanding their own trade relations. Privately, this meant reaching out—rather unsuccessfully—to the socialist bloc. Publicly, Chilean leaders sought moral support in the global South, arguing that what was occurring in their country was relevant to all Third World nations seeking independence and development, either by reflecting their aspirations or as a direct example. To this end, Allende personally traveled to Ecuador, Colombia, and Peru in August and September 1971, while his foreign minister, Clodomiro Almeyda, spoke at the United Nations General Assembly and a G77 summit in Lima, visited European capitals from East to West, and journeyed to Washington, Moscow, Algiers, and Havana.

The ideological scope of these journeys seemed to match the times. In July 1971 President Nixon sent shock waves around the world by announcing that he planned to visit Beijing the following year. Indeed, crossing ideological divides through summit diplomacy would be such a part of the United States' pursuit of détente that two historians have described "the frequency with which he negotiated with communists" as Nixon's "signature achievement."[3] But, of course, the way that Nixon and Kissinger dealt with their enemies (and their allies) depended on who they were and where they were. True, they were preparing to initiate "triangular diplomacy" through high-level summit meetings in the Soviet Union and the People's Republic of China. But when it came to smaller, less powerful countries in the Third World, the White House was unprepared to put ideology aside, focusing instead on fighting the Cold War rather than negotiating a modus vivendi with governments it considered to be ideologically repellent.

In an ever more interconnected world, the manner in which nations confronted each other nonetheless continued to be highly important. As far as Kissinger was concerned, image, prestige, and reputation were not only adjuncts to balance-of-power politics but also integral components of a country's efforts to protect its national interests. His interlocutors and enemies agreed. Nixon, Allende, and Castro all certainly operated on a world stage, for domestic and world audiences and in search of approval. Fidel Castro would state that he hoped Nixon was watching the impressive welcome he received in Chile, that the United States seized on Chile's nationalization program as a convenient pretext for the deterioration of U.S.-Chilean relations, and that the Chileans accused the United States of pursuing precisely the type of outdated ideological hostility toward Allende that U.S. officials professed to have abandoned.[4] Indeed, while Washington and Santiago tried to project a fashionable nonideological image of themselves—emphasizing international law, economic imperatives, and pragmatism as the determinants of foreign relations—they pointed the finger at each other as being the one that threatened stability and mutual understanding.

It was for this reason that the Nixon administration was on the defensive in late 1971. U.S. officials were particularly worried that the UP might be able to blame its domestic difficulties on "U.S. imperialism" and undermine Washington's already diminishing influence throughout Latin America and the Third World. At the same time, analysts were concerned that the Soviet Union might come to Allende's aid, as it had for Castro a decade before. For the Nixon administration, then, Chile appeared to embody the fusion of snowballing Third World nationalism and falling Cold War dominoes. The big question was how the United States could undermine Allende's presidency without doing so too obviously and alienating world opinion. As evidence of U.S. intervention in Chile surfaced and circumscribed Washington's room for maneuver, the U.S. government therefore opted for tempering a more instinctual desire for confrontation, and Kissinger engaged in ever more skillful dialogue with the Chileans to distract them from the continuing U.S. destabilization measures against Allende. However, these tactics evolved gradually, responding as they did to the changing character of Chilean diplomacy and domestic politics, U.S. foreign policy priorities, inter-American affairs, global superpower relations, and the North-South divide in international politics.

Reasoned Rebellion

In his own rose-colored view of the world, Salvador Allende hoped reason and the power of Chile's democratic example would persuade outsiders to accept La Vía Chilena. At the beginning of September 1971, he consequently wrote a three-page letter to Richard Nixon appealing for understanding. The timing of his letter was important, seeing as it was sent amid growing evidence of the United States' hostility toward his country and on the eve of Chile's ruling on the compensation it owed to recently expropriated U.S. copper companies. Essentially, the letter appealed to Nixon's moral conscience by underlining Chile's legalistic and constitutional tradition and asking the president to stop interfering in Chilean affairs by means of "economic and financial coercion." Allende wrote that "the greatest defense of the legitimate rights and aspirations of small countries such as mine lies in the moral strength of their convictions and actions.... The harsh reality of our country—the hunger, the poverty, and the almost complete hopelessness—has convinced our people that we are in need of profound changes. We have chosen to carry these changes out by means of democracy, pluralism, and freedom; with friendship toward all peoples of the world. Such an internal process is only possible if its external aspects are based on the sound principles of non-intervention, self-determination, and an open dialogue among nations. We have adhered strictly to this line."[5]

No amount of democracy and "friendship toward all peoples," however, could hide the fact that the UP's nationalization of Chilean copper mines in July 1971 had been a direct attack on U.S. economic interests in Chile. Rather than shying away from or apologizing for such a move, Allende had called it a "definitive" moment in Chile's quest for "economic independence."[6] Responding to U.S. calls for "just" compensation for expropriated U.S. companies, Chile's foreign minister also replied that it depended on what one understood to be "just."[7] As one Cuban intelligence officer put it years later, Allende's nationalization of Chile's copper mines was "a kick in the United States' balls."[8]

Even so, the Chileans were acutely aware that the prospect of deducting "excess profits" from the compensation it offered U.S. companies— the "Allende Doctrine" as it was later known—was an act of rebellion that carried substantial risks. The move was riskier still considering the Chileans' growing recognition that the Nixon administration was not adhering to its own promises of nonintervention and open dialogue. Santiago's leaders had begun to acknowledge that U.S. reassurances masked a deeper hostility toward them in mid-1971. In May, the UP had applied for an Export-Import Bank (Eximbank) loan to purchase three Boeing airplanes for Chile's state airline, LAN-Chile, worth $21 million. When Santiago received no response to its application after two months, Santiago's leaders became suspicious. Allende was "personally preoccupied" about the issue from the start, instructing Chile's ambassador in Washington, Orlando Letelier, to raise Chile's "restlessness" with U.S. government and Eximbank officials. Yet no progress was made, despite State Department reassurances that this was not a "political issue."[9] Then, on 7 July, four days before the Chilean Congress passed Allende's copper nationalization bill, Eximbank's president, Henry Kearns, informed Chilean representatives that a decision depended on Chile's future nationalization program. As the Chileans noted, this tied the Nixon administration irrefutably to protecting business interests.[10] What is more, Letelier had concluded there was "no doubt . . . Eximbank was backed at a high political level" after his meetings with the bank's officials—Kearns was "evidently nervous, repeatedly consulting a document . . . by his side."[11] On the basis of these observations, Letelier warned Kissinger that if the U.S. government continued to hold its position on this issue, it would harm U.S.-Chilean relations.[12]

In private, the ambassador was less assertive and more concerned that the UP's nationalization program had "clouded" Chile's position in Washington.[13] Allende was also personally nervous about the repercussions a deterioration of relations with the United States could have on Chile's armed forces. Indeed, to counteract the possibility of a U.S. embargo on military assistance and equipment, he dispatched an ultrasecret military mission—one that was to have no contact with Chilean embassies abroad—to the Soviet Union, Poland, Czechoslovakia, Romania, Yugoslavia, and France to reconnoiter the prospect of arms supplies from these countries in the form of either aid or purchases. The idea behind the mission was not to discuss details—that would be done later. Rather, as Allende told Poland's ambassador when he summoned him to La Moneda to discuss the visit, Chile had to "take into account all eventualities" and plan for U.S. sources drying up despite doing everything possible to avoid this happening.[14]

In early August and September, the Chileans had also launched an impressive international campaign to clarify and justify the UP's nationalization program.[15] As Letelier wrote to Foreign Minister Almeyda, Chile's strategy was to promote "the most support possible for Chile, not only in Latin America, but also among important sectors of this country [the United States], for the most difficult moment in our relations with the U.S., which will be without doubt President Allende's decision regarding . . . excess profits."[16] As Chilean diplomats in Washington reminded their superiors back home, their country was now receiving new attention in the United States—second only to Cuba in Latin America—and, as such, the Chilean Embassy was in a good position to publicize its cause. It had therefore begun holding press briefings and sending information to influential journalists and Democrats about underlying U.S.-Chilean tensions. And Letelier had proposed that by leaking information about Eximbank, in particular, the Chileans could prove the United States had thrown the "first stone" and could use it to "cushion" announcements regarding compensation.[17]

Would it not have been easier to abandon the "Allende Doctrine"? Perhaps, but only if the Chileans' goal was simply to get on with the United States, which, of course, it was not. Challenging "U.S. imperialism" and asserting Chilean economic sovereignty were fundamental pillars of Allende's mandate. It was on this platform, rather than capitulation to U.S. pressure, that he had fought and won the presidential election. Being defiant was also politically useful as it ensured support from the far Left members of his ruling coalition whom he both needed and admired. Parts of the Socialist Party—and Allende's daughter Beatriz, in particular—had strongly encouraged him not to offer the U.S. companies compensation— so much so, that Beatriz and the president had made a deal whereby she promised Allende a painting of hers that he had often admired by the Cuban artist René Portocarrero on the condition he found a way to nationalize copper without paying "a *centavo*." When he announced his "excess profits" ruling, he happily collected the painting.[18]

Publicly, at least, "Decree 92," which created the UP's constitutional amendment on excess profits, underlined Chile's right to "rebel" against an "unjust" system that benefited hegemonic powers and contributed to "underdevelopment and backwardness."[19] Eventually enshrined on 28 September, this decree classified "excess profits" as those above 12 percent of a company's book value between 1955 and 1970. And this obviously affected two U.S. mining companies, Kennecott and Anaconda, which had reaped average annual profits of 56.8 percent and 21.5 percent respectively.[20] Then, on 11 October 1971, as widely expected, Chile's controller general confirmed that when "excess profits" were deducted from compensation deemed payable, these companies *owed* his country money rather than the other way round.[21]

By the time the "Allende Doctrine" came into force, Chile's diplomatic campaign outside the United States to attract support and sympathy in the Americas, the Third World, and the international communist movement was already well under way. The UP still lacked financial means to confront the United States and had not yet secured alternative sources of credits or supplies. Even so, it did have legalistic armor to legitimize its actions and was able to identify with a broader Third World struggle for economic justice. In fact, to many leaders in the global South, the Chileans were valiantly putting widespread demands for compensation of past exploitation into practice.

When it came to attracting support, Santiago had focused first and foremost on the inter-American community. In August and September, Allende had toured Andean Pact countries, depicting Chile's struggle for "economic independence" as an example to follow. When he described his message as "rebellious but reasoned" in Ecuador, he received understanding from a government already at odds with Washington over the sovereignty of territorial waters.[22] Foreign Minister Almeyda also recalled that Colombia's conservative foreign minister, Alfredo Vásquez Carrisoza, showed surprising comprehension, interest, and sympathy.[23] Indeed, formal communiqués at the end of all of Allende's visits also underlined every country's rightful sovereignty over its natural resources and included public denunciations of foreign intervention.[24] Subsequently, days after Allende's return to Chile, Fidel Castro sent him enthusiastic praise. "We were very pleased with the extraordinary success you had in your trip," Castro wrote. As he observed, the Chilean president had encountered "heartfelt emotion and the warmth" in all three countries he visited.[25]

Beyond purely defensive aims, the trip had also been a good opportunity for Allende to advance his more ambitious goal of challenging U.S. hegemony in the Americas. Promoting the need for a "second Latin American independence," he had repeatedly called on Latin Americans to unite and speak with "one voice." In Quito, he had told the press he believed in socialism and that if others did not, Chile would "convince them" through its example.[26] At a presidential banquet to welcome him to Colombia, Allende then urged Latin Americans to reject U.S. "diktats" on how to conduct their economic affairs. In his words, Latin America was "a dynamic reality," edging along a predetermined historical road of "liberation—

social, political and economic."[27] As the U.S. ambassador in Bogotá noted, even if Allende professed Chile's revolutionary road was "not exportable," his speeches suggested otherwise.[28] Certainly, Allende was convinced that Chile's experience was highly significant for Latin America and the Third World. As he later explained to one Chilean journalist, "The exploited peoples of the world are conscious of their right to life. And this is why the confrontation [between revolution and counterrevolution] goes beyond our own frontiers and acquires universal meaning. Latin America will one day be free from subjugation and have its rightful voice, the voice of a free continent."[29]

Foreign Minister Almeyda echoed Allende's identification with this struggle against "exploitation" when he addressed the UN General Assembly and a G77 conference in Lima in October.[30] In response to the U.S. State Department's explicit warnings that Chilean policies could have "adverse effects" on other developing countries by affecting private investment, Almeyda contended that Third World aspirations were not threatened by Chilean moves but were rather "intimately linked and complemented" by separate countries' efforts to harness "natural, human, and financial resources" for developmental purposes.[31] Chilean spokesmen also made abundant reference to their compliance with constitutional procedures and internationally recognized principles such as those enshrined in the G77 "Charter of Algiers on the Economic Rights of the Third World" (1967) and promoted by the Non-Aligned Movement. Rather than being against international law, Almeyda insisted, Chilean actions were *justified* by it.[32] And in this respect, the Unidad Popular pointed to UN resolution 1803 (December 1962), which recognized the "inalienable right of all states to dispose freely of their wealth and natural resources" and stipulated that expropriating countries should determine what compensation they offered.[33]

The UN General Assembly and the G77 were logical forums in which for Chile to seek collective support by calling for systemic change of international economic and political relations. At least at this point, Santiago's timing also appeared advantageous. As Almeyda noted, there was already a "growing feeling of frustration and impotence" in Latin America and "grotesque evidence" of the difference "between words and deeds" in the battle against underdevelopment.[34] Nixon's imposition of a 10 percent surcharge on all imports to the United States in August 1971 had added to the Third World's perception of a "crisis" and the likelihood that Chile would find a receptive audience. When leaders of the G77 met in Lima to formulate a united position to present at the forthcoming UNCTAD III conference in Santiago, Almeyda therefore used the occasion to call upon delegates to "define . . . points of attack," emphasizing that

> the fundamental task of developing countries is to work to modify the international political and economic structure that has assigned them the role of servitude. . . . If this structure does not change this could result in stagnation and violence. Nothing is obtained through postulating, or even by achieving partial solutions . . . if we do not comprehend that it is the nature of the system of international relations itself that needs to be reformed . . . the struggle of backward and dependent countries to reach their emancipation and full economic, political and social development . . . [is] defined by the battle between the forces that sustain and defend the current social and international structure of the world, and those that strive to destroy it.[35]

However, Almeyda's call to action did not scare the United States into accepting Allende's "excess profits" ruling or unite the G77 as a vehicle for providing Santiago with meaningful support. To the contrary, Chile's senior diplomat, Hernán Santa Cruz, later reported on serious divisions within the G77 between Africans and Latin Americans. Ostensibly, these revolved around the Africans' desire to "catch up" with Latin American development and the question of how countries were ranked within the group. The Africans refused to accept that Uruguay, Paraguay, and Central American countries were as underdeveloped as sub-Saharan nations, for example, while Brazil, Central America, and Colombia were, in his words, "almost hysterical" in their refusal to grant African nations bigger quotas for producing coffee that had previously been agreed at UNCTAD II. While the Chileans worked hard to bridge the gap, with Algeria's help, the conference dragged on an extra two days and closed on what Santa Cruz reported to have been a "solemn" note. As he warned Foreign Minister Almeyda, the G77's platform at UNCTAD depended on "the unity of action and force within proposals," and he feared that as things stood, the United States and Western powers were in a position to "pulverize" them.[36]

Chile's role within the group also appears to have caused problems. Rather than uniting the G77 to "define points of attack," the tenor of Chilean (and Peruvian) demands seemed to widen Third World divisions regarding how to deal with the global North. When Almeyda demanded equal measures of "negotiation, confrontation, and denunciation," others therefore shied away.[37] As the British ambassador in Lima observed, the meeting illustrated the polarization between what he termed "extreme," "aggressive" countries such as Peru and Chile, and more cautious, conservative African and Asian nations. Consequently, in the ambassador's words, "drawing up a 'shopping list'" for UNCTAD III had become "arduous and unexpectedly time-consuming." He also concluded that the "wild men" had been restrained—an outcome that did not bode well for Allende's chances of rallying the global South to join Chile and take a collective stance vis-à-vis the United States.[38] As another British diplomat surmised around the same time, poorer African nations "[appreciated] the no nonsense mood of President Nixon's administration."[39]

Like Chile's efforts to mobilize the Third World, the results of its foreign policy outreach toward communist countries were mixed. Ideological pluralism—the cornerstone of Allende's foreign policy—had certainly taken off rapidly. Within a year, it had found expression in Chile's courtship of conservative regional powers such as Argentina and Colombia, its new commercial relations with North Korea and North Vietnam, and new diplomatic relationships with countries as geographically diverse as China, East Germany, Libya, Tanzania, Guyana, Albania, Hungary, and Equatorial Guinea.[40] Allende had also sent delegations to Europe, the Soviet Union, and China in search of trade and economic assistance; Almeyda had spent six weeks touring East and West European capitals in May and June; the Chilean Central Bank's president spent two and a half months in Eastern Europe; and Soviet, East German, and Romanian trade missions arrived in Santiago. As Almeyda had told Polish leaders when he met them at the end of May, Chile was seeking "dynamic development and diversification of trade" with socialist countries. This was by no means just rhetoric. During his trip, Almeyda explicitly raised the possibility of Chile joining the Soviet bloc's Council of Mutual Economic Assistance (COMECON).[41]

Although much still remains to be known about the details of Chile's economic relationships with the countries of the Soviet bloc, the Chileans clearly achieved far less than they had hoped for (and certainly never joined COMECON). The reason, in part, was that the Soviet bloc was wary about backing a project that had not yet proved itself as being viable. During consultations between representatives of COMECON countries in Santiago in April 1971, general "disquiet" had been voiced about the UP's record. To be sure, these diplomats recognized that Allende's government had been focusing on gaining political control and doing well in the April elections and that it had been in power for only five months when they met. But they also observed "organizational paralysis" within government ministries when it came to economic policy. As a Polish report sent back to Warsaw at the time had stressed, the UP's parties had still not mapped out the basic principles of how to go about institutionalizing control of the economy and ensure growth of the government sector.[42]

The other major problem with Santiago's outreach to the East was that the Chileans overestimated what they could hope to gain when they approached socialist bloc countries for assistance. In October and November 1971, the UP made a new request for assistance from Soviet bloc countries. Specifically, UP representatives said that Chile wanted raw materials and food supplies, that it wished to sell its copper to Eastern Europe (as long as this would not then be sold off to make a profit), and that it needed credits for consumer goods on the basis of deferred repayment. Chilean representatives also appear to have battled to bring down interest rates on hypothetical future credits (from 4 percent to 2.5 percent), something that the Polish ambassador in Santiago warned Warsaw about on the eve of a visiting Polish delegation to Chile led by Minister of Foreign Trade Olczewski. As Poland's ambassador wrote home to Warsaw in late October, the Chileans' proposals were "unacceptable" and the list of goods that the Chileans had asked for to cover 1972 and 1973 was "premature." At the same time, he privately did his best to explain Poland's own economic difficulties to Allende in person.[43]

Even so, by the end of 1971, Poland, Hungary, Bulgaria, and Romania had pledged credits for industrial projects and Allende had secured Soviet credits amounting to $95 million—just under $40 million more than those granted to Frei but never taken up—for machinery, equipment, and industrial development.[44] Building on an initial arrangement made by Frei's government to export 1,000 tons of unrefined copper to East Germany, Berlin had also agreed to a new deal worth $2.2 million to raise this amount to 2,400 tons in 1971.[45] Chile's economic ties with the People's Republic of China (PRC) also grew, ending in a three-year agreement for copper exports worth $70 million annually until 1975, a $2 million loan after Chile's earthquake in July 1971, and an arrangement for Beijing to import nitrates.[46]

Overall, however, the Chileans faced the logistical problems of swapping U.S.-modeled industry, transportation, and supply routes for Chinese and Soviet bloc alternatives. When the secret military delegation that Allende had sent to Eastern Europe and France returned to Santiago, its members advised against purchasing military equipment from the Soviet bloc for this reason as well as warning that there were "implicit psycholog-ical" implications involved in such a shift to the East.[47] And yet beyond the Soviet bloc there were no obvious alternatives. In late October 1971, Javier Urrutia, Chile's financial representative in New York, firmly concluded that European banks would not be able to satisfy Chile's needs if the United States banking sector closed its doors. As he explained in a lengthy memorandum to the Chilean Foreign Ministry, Chile's historic economic relationship with European banks had been modest and the Europeans were not usually predisposed to granting credits unless they were linked to specific purchases.[48]

Given the limitations of substituting European and Soviet bloc credits for disappearing U.S. assistance, Allende clung to the hope that he might be able to avoid a confrontation with the United States. For the time being, the international environment remained a positive sign that this might be possible notwithstanding evidence of hostility. Certainly, when the White House had announced Nixon's trip to China, Letelier wrote of a definitive "end of the Cold War."[49] As a result of a "new world reality," a new "Latin American reality," and the United States' declining position in the region, Letelier suggested, the Nixon administration was "playing a policy of equi-librium" and shying away from "excessively hard actions" that could make the United States' position more "fragile."[50] He also again suggested that the United States lacked a "coherent" policy toward Latin America and that the Nixon administration's attitude toward Chile was still relatively undefined.[51] Moreover, Allende told a visiting U.S. academic that Nixon's dealings with China, the Soviet Union, and Yugoslavia were clear indica-tions that the United States could work with Chile. Unlike those commu-nist states, Allende insisted, Chile's brand of socialism was constitutional, and it was in these circumstances that Allende had appealed to Nixon's moral conscience in the letter he wrote to his U.S. counterpart in Septem-ber 1971.[52]

Would U.S. policy makers be swayed by Chile's ambitious diplomacy and Allende's constitutional methods at home to give up their hostility toward his government? The Chileans' effort to redefine their country's international position and assert its independence worldwide in late 1971 was ambitious and far-reaching. Increasingly, however, it was evolving out of necessity rather than design. Overcoming the constraints of traditional economic dependency on the United States meant expanding Chile's for-eign contacts and working out how they might be able to help defend La

Vía Chilena either through direct assistance or by putting pressure on the United States to accept Allende's road to socialism. In this respect, Santiago's leaders now realized that they faced an uphill struggle and predicted that what they defined as Allende's anti-imperialistic policies would make it steeper. Even so, the Chileans were still relatively optimistic that they would at least be able to keep climbing, especially given indications that the Nixon administration did not want a confrontation.[53]

Crime and Punishment

While it is easy to dismiss this optimism as naive, Chile's foreign policy tactics did present Washington with a very real challenge in late 1971. In fact, what Santiago had regarded as U.S. evasion on the Eximbank affair turns out to have been the result of indecision and disagreement within the Nixon administration when it came to dealing with Allende. The issue at stake was not the United States' overall objective toward Chile; at no stage did Washington try to "understand" Chilean reasoning, contemplate abandoning its destabilization policies in Chile, or forgo its counterrevolutionary offensive in the Southern Cone, especially given Santiago's overtures to the Soviet bloc, Chile's relationship with Cuba, and Allende's Third World appeal. However, U.S. tactics toward Chile were increasingly called into question as the Nixon administration adapted to what some within Washington saw as an evolving popularity contest between the United States and Chile at a domestic, regional, and international level.

In this context, the relative consensus that had characterized policy toward Chile between late 1970 and mid-1971 broke down internally as a growing impetus to punish Allende overtly for the temerity of his nationalization policies clashed with continuing fears that doing so would bolster his chances of success and undermine Nixon's foreign policy reputation. During three strategy review meetings Kissinger called between June and November 1971, therefore, administration officials primarily discussed who would be blamed for Allende's growing economic difficulties. While Treasury officials lobbied Nixon to stand up and be counted—to defend economic interests at all costs—Kissinger joined the State Department and CIA analysts in arguing that this would be too risky for the United States' prestige in Latin America and the Third World. To this latter group, the U.S.-Chilean relationship was increasingly presenting itself as a test case of Washington's commitment to development, democracy, and détente that it could not fail—or at least not publicly. And once the Exim-bank affair had undermined Washington's "correctness" and had given Allende a basis on which to rally support, Kissinger's priority was to recre-ate the impression of meaningful cooperation.

After Allende nationalized copper, the White House had faced increas-ing pressure from business leaders to retaliate.[54] Within the Nixon admin-istration, Treasury Secretary John Connally had also begun challenging Nixon's "correct but cool" policy toward Chile and lobbying the president to take a harder line in the context of an overhaul of U.S. policy toward the Third World. Specifically, Connally argued that Chilean nationaliza-tion projects formed part of a "snowballing" trend of expropriations in Latin America and the Caribbean, which could no longer be dealt with "in a piecemeal fashion."[55] To stop expropriations by Third World nation-alists—and especially Allende—he therefore demanded that the United States make an example out of Chile by issuing severe and overt reprisals.[56] Initially, at least, Nixon, who was impressed by Connally, had responded sympathetically by personally being the one to instruct Eximbank to with-hold credits while an in-depth study of U.S. policy toward expropriation (NSSM 131) was conducted.[57]

Although Kissinger sanctioned this study, he nevertheless tended to side with the State Department in opposing the Connally-Nixon line. As Deputy Assistant Secretary of State for Latin American Affairs John Crim-mins argued at the time, Connally's demand to punish *all* expropriat-ing states on an immediate and automatic basis was a "frontal attack on the basic concepts" of the Nixon administration's Latin American policy, which emphasized political flexibility rather than economic interests.[58] Kissinger surprisingly agreed with the State Department on this occasion and, as far as the Eximbank loan was concerned, believed that it was better to appease the Chileans than provoke open confrontation over the issue.[59] Then, when Chilean economic difficulties grew in the latter half of 1971 and people began accusing the United States of being responsible, Kis-singer joined the majority of the administration's foreign policy team in urging tactical caution. As Ambassador Korry and intelligence analysts argued, the United States had to avoid giving the UP a "scapegoat" to blame for the deterioration of the Chilean economy.[60]

This was essentially the position that the NSC's Senior Review Group adopted when it met in September 1971. As the Ad Hoc Interagency Work-ing Group on Chile reported to it, there was little chance of forcing the Allende government to pay U.S. copper companies compensation and thus no obvious gains in pursuing more overt credit freezes. While the Working Group dismissed direct negotiation on the assumption that this would boost "Chile's image as a new model of a 'democratic' Marxist state," it also cautioned against open confrontation on the grounds this would enhance Chile's stance as a "popular cause in Latin America and elsewhere in the underdeveloped world, with corresponding disadvantage" to Washington.[61]

In this respect, the formal adoption of Allende's "excess profits" ruling came at just the right time. With it, the United States had a more obvious pretext for economic pressure on Chile's democratically elected Socialist president in the supposedly nonideological era of détente. The result of the administration's review of U.S. policy toward Third World expropriations, which was enshrined in National Security Decision Memorandum 136 on 8 October 1971, also helped. In reality, NSDM 136 was a compromise rather than a victory for Connally, as it prescribed only the "presumption" that Washington would punish any state that expropriated private U.S. companies without "reasonable steps to provide compensation" rather than giving a concrete order, and ironically it excluded Eximbank operations. Even so, the United States' tougher overall stance on expropriation, elaborated in public by Treasury Department officials, was now used retrospectively to justify Washington's obvious economic pressure on Chile to domestic and international audiences.[62]

Privately, U.S. administration officials also used it to explain why more credits were not being granted to Chile when they met with Allende's representatives, and all the while indicated that they wanted to avoid escalating tension between Washington and Santiago. Kissinger played a key role in this respect. During back-channel discussions with Letelier, he even went so far as to offer to visit Chile in search of a modus operandi.[63] In early October 1971, Kissinger then met with Foreign Minister Almeyda while the latter was in Washington, and according to a Chilean record of the conversation, he bent over backward to give the impression that the United States was not hostile to the Chilean government:

> Referring to the Chilean revolutionary process, Kissinger indicated
> to Minister Almeyda that . . . he profoundly admired the way in
> which President Allende was leading the Chilean political phenom-
> enon. He signaled . . . his interest in Chile and in maintaining the
> most constructive relations possible. . . . He also indicated that if at
> any moment the Chilean government wanted to present his gov-
> ernment with a proposal of a confidential character with respect

to the relationship between both countries . . . this could be managed through him at a presidential level in the assurance that there existed [in the Nixon administration] an attitude of understanding and orientation toward facilitating constructive links between both countries. . . . as far as his country was concerned, Chile had a great importance within Latin America, and he indicated that it would be very incongruous if, while the United States was able to seek a form of understanding with the PRC from which it had been separated for so many years, it could not find positive solutions to problems with Chile. . . . In this respect, he alluded to the tendency toward ideological pluralism in international relations.[64]

Two months later Kissinger was still insistent. Pulling Letelier to one side at a private dinner party in December 1971, he underlined once again that the United States was "not intervening in Chile." Eximbank's position had not been a question of politics but a "natural reaction" to questions of nationalization and compensation, as he put it. The Chilean ambassador replied warily but acknowledged, yet again, that it was difficult to ignore such a "categorical" assertion.[65]

Because there are still no available U.S. records of Kissinger's back-channel approaches to Letelier, they have been unexamined to date. But they are particularly intriguing, given how effective they were. In his correspondence back to Santiago, the Chilean ambassador continued to believe Kissinger's word carried weight and should not be dismissed. To be sure, he was not totally fooled by the national security adviser's silver tongue, but Santiago's leaders were interested enough to devote considerable time throughout 1971 and 1972 to exploring whether they should take Kissinger up on his offer of private negotiations.[66]

While Kissinger was trying to convince the Chileans that Washington meant no harm, U.S. policy makers simultaneously contented themselves that Chile's economic difficulties had already begun taking their toll on Allende's government.[67] In November, Allende had announced a moratorium on debt payments and applied to reschedule them. Although Washington deemed Allende's financial difficulties not "exclusively" the result of U.S. efforts, the Ad Hoc Working Group on Chile concluded that U.S. policy had been a "fairly good success": Allende's victory did not seem "irreversible," and financial measures had begun to "take their effect."[68] The question was whether the Chileans could do anything to reverse this deterioration or whether the Soviet Union would step into the breach.

The Nixon administration had been receiving indications that the Chileans were cozying up to the East throughout the second half of 1971. True, observers noted that Soviet credits were "not always immediately or fully implemented" and that both the Chileans and the Soviets had shown immense caution in forging closer relations with each other. But the State Department was also cynical about the UP's professed nonalignment.[69] By August, U.S. intelligence analysts had concluded that closer ties between Santiago and Moscow were inevitable, that the Soviet bloc would "probably help Allende in an economic crisis," and that the Soviets would "continue to cultivate channels of influence" in Chile.[70] In Ambassador Korry's words, Allende was attempting "to enjoy all worlds, capitalist, nationalist and revolutionary, populist and ideological." "Almeyda can in Moscow seek association with COMECON at the same time that Chile pursues uninterrupted flows from the IDB, IBRD and the EXIM," he complained. "Allende can call for the best possible relations with the U.S. while stating that his foreign policy is based on creating a special relationship with . . . the socialist world. He can invite Castro to Chile while arranging for a prior journey to Colombia . . . Perhaps it was a slip of the lip . . . when he referred to his government once . . . as representing the 'Popular Democratic Republic of Chile.'"[71]

Certainly, President Nixon viewed Chile's government as a "communist dictatorship—elected, but communist."[72] And it is also now clear that the Pentagon had its own Cold War concerns, having been particularly worried that any Boeings Chile purchased would furnish a new route between Santiago and Havana and thus help spread Cuban subversion in Latin America. (In fact, Washington had warned UP officials of these concerns in early 1971 and had received no reassurances, but a bigger issue was not made of it because the State Department had been reticent about inciting Chilean charges of undue political pressure, and in the end, the Chileans had offered little reassurance on the issue.)[73] The Chilean government had also played on Washington's Cold War fears to extract concessions by exaggerating Chile's ability, and desire, to turn to the East.[74] In this respect, Letelier's private insinuation that Allende would turn to the Soviet Union if the UP could not buy Boeings in the United States had not only been jumping the gun in regard to Chile's exploration of the options it had but must surely have added to the feeling that the Chileans were trying to blackmail Washington.[75]

Allende's efforts to get Latin Americans to unite and speak with "one voice" had also encouraged U.S. intolerance for regional "disobedience."

In October 1971, Nixon privately talked of instituting a "program of reward and punishment—not openly but just quietly" rewarding Latin American countries "when they start acting properly!"[76] This was hardly the "mature partnership" that Nixon had announced two years earlier. But it did reflect the disdain for regional politics that characterized much of the United States' foreign-policy-making community at the time. Looking back on nationalist and revolutionary ferment during the early 1970s, Nixon's ambassador at the OAS, Joseph Jova, recalled that Secretary of State William Rogers "didn't understand Latins." According to Jova, Rogers "felt there was too much hot air, and . . . anti-Americanism." "I remember," Jova continued, "I used to say, 'Remember what Don Quixote said . . . when they were attacked by dogs, or unfriendly villages, or something of that sort of thing.' . . . [He] rode off quietly without even replying. . . . So some of these things you have to realize were just part of the game."[77]

The problem was that when Allende challenged this "game" in late 1971, U.S. officials began worrying about what would happen if they rode off into the sunset. When Kissinger had ordered a study of U.S. policy toward Latin America (NSSM 108) after Allende's election, State Department officials reported that regional threats to U.S. interests were, overall, not "serious." However, Kissinger's assistant for Latin American affairs at the NSC, Arnold Nachmanoff, had vehemently disagreed. As he had advised his boss, Latin America's situation by itself was "tolerable," but the decline of Washington's regional influence was "excessive and more rapid" than NSSM 108's authors acknowledged. He also argued that the State Department had inadequately considered "where Latin America fits into our global policy." "The loss of U.S. influence in Latin America and an increase of Soviet influence in what is perceived throughout the world as our backyard," he warned, "will affect the global balance of power in political and psychological terms, if not necessarily in strategic terms." He had then gone on to suggest a reranking of U.S. foreign policy priorities: "If Southeast Asia is the most imminent test of the Nixon doctrine," he contended, Latin America could "well be its most serious test in time. The pressures for intervention should there be two or three Chiles or Cubas in our backyard would undoubtedly be high."[78]

In many respects, the Nixon administration seemed to be searching for a more coherent policy toward the hemisphere. When the SRG had met to discuss NSSM 108 in August 1971, its members had pinpointed various vague objectives: the United States had to "ameliorate" anti-Americanism ("or at least eliminate its negative effects"), assist Latin Americans' quest for economic progress (but "encourage more realistic expectations of such progress"), boost the idea that the United States and Latin America shared a set of common interests, and "limit or protect against the increasing Soviet diplomatic, trade and military presence in the region."[79] Together, these aims then translated into concrete action as evidenced by the jump in the total U.S. military assistance to Latin America and the Caribbean from $26.1 million in fiscal year 1970 to $96.9 million and $86.9 million in 1972 and 1973 respectively.[80] Kissinger also requested that the bureaucracy reexamine its previous conclusions about the United States' position in Latin America and ordered more "intensive utilization of different bilateral approaches."[81]

By the end of 1971 the burgeoning bilateral relationship between Washington and Brasilia, in particular, was already beginning to bear fruit. At the very least, Nixon acknowledged Brazil's "help" in turning back left-wing advances in Bolivia and Uruguay.[82] In late August 1971 Bolivia's nationalist military leader since October 1970, Juan José Torres, had been overthrown by a right-wing coup. Only a few months before, the White House had begun paying close attention to his government. Back then, Nachmanoff had warned Kissinger of a "highly unstable and deteriorating situation" in the country.[83] Torres had closed a U.S. satellite tracking station in the country, expelled U.S. labor organizations, and sent the Peace Corps home, while Bolivian students seized U.S. properties, causing $36,000 worth of damage.[84] Although these actions were often the result of local factors, American officials perceived them as part of a Cold War zero-sum game.[85] Indeed, the U.S. ambassador in La Paz, Ernest Siracusa, warned that, having gone from being "unimportant," Bolivia was on the verge of becoming a "Soviet satellite."[86] And by June 1971 Kissinger had regarded the Bolivian situation as "urgent."[87]

Available evidence suggests more than a coincidental link between this concern and the events that followed. Along with indications that CIA and Pentagon officials were involved in plotting, the U.S. Air Force is reported to have allowed coup leaders to use its communications system on day one of their offensive.[88] After the coup took place, Kissinger also personally pushed for improving ties with the coup's leader, Colonel Hugo Banzer, who had close links to the Pentagon.[89] Even so, by getting involved, Washington joined—rather than directed—Brazilian and Argentine interventions. Certainly, Brazil had been plotting against Torres since 1970, when Brazilian intelligence services had furnished Banzer with a plane and weapons to escape Bolivia after a previous failed coup attempt.[90]

To Cuba's foreign minister, who was visiting Chile when Torres was overthrown, the Bolivian coup was clearly a continental "American battle" and an "objective lesson for revolutionaries throughout the hemisphere" rather than an isolated incident that concerned only Bolivia.[91] Only two months earlier, Foreign Minister Raúl Roa had privately described Torres as a positive pillar in a new Latin American configuration of forces. As the Cubans saw it, Torres had secured the support of Bolivia's peasant masses, and the country had a higher degree of social radicalization than even Chile or Peru.[92] Yet the Cubans' hopes for Torres now lay in tatters. Moreover, Havana's leaders interpreted the Bolivian coup as a signal that a "counteroffensive" aimed at putting the "breaks on growing revolutionary processes" in Latin America had begun.[93]

If Nixon was grateful for Brazil's "help" in Bolivia, he also recognized that Brazil had "helped" Washington in Uruguay. There, it had helped forestall the victory of Uruguay's left-wing coalition, the Frente Amplio (or Broad Front), in elections widely feared as a possible repeat of Chile's 1970 race. While advocating U.S. operations to "blunt" the Frente Amplio's chances, the U.S. Embassy in Montevideo had welcomed cooperation between Uruguay's security forces and Brazil and Argentina.[94] Before the election, Brazil had also stationed military units on Uruguay's border and formulated plans to invade should sabotage fail.[95] As it turned out, extensive reports that the Brazilians planned to intervene may well have been exaggerated (the units on the border actually withdrew before the election in the face of widespread condemnation), but Brazil's shadow had a psychological effect on internal Uruguayan developments. And when Uruguayans went to the polls on 28 November, the ruling Colorado Party and its candidate, Juan María Bordaberry, overwhelmingly defeated the Frente Amplio. In Nixon's words, Brazil had helped "rig" the elections.[96]

Less than a week later, the Washington-Brasilia axis was consolidated when Brazil's president, General Emílio Garrastazu Médici, arrived in the United States. The visit had not been without its procedural difficulties, given that the Brazilian leader had asked for a greater public fanfare upon arrival than he received. However, once in Washington, Médici was privately accorded deference and special treatment. As he told Nixon at the end of his visit, he could not have been "more pleased with the way things had gone."[97] The general not only shared the U.S. president's view of unsettling and potentially dangerous trends in Latin America but was also able to inform Nixon about Brazil's initiatives and "assistance" to counter such developments, particularly when it came to Uruguay and Bolivia. Sitting in the Oval Office during two summit meetings, Médici nevertheless noted "the future of Latin America looked pretty bleak." As he stated, "it was true that the 'Broad Front' had been defeated [in Uruguay] and the traditional parties had led the election, but if one looked at the other side of that coin one would see that the Communists and their friends, who had polled 5% of the votes in the preceding election, had polled 20% this time. . . . [Meanwhile] Bolivia was in desperate straits. . . . if the present Bolivian government did not succeed it would be the last moderate government in Bolivia, which would then fall into the arms of the Communists and become another Cuba or Chile."[98]

Nixon, who seems to have been more aware of the situation in Uruguay and less up to date on the Bolivian developments, appreciated his guest's analysis and said he was "very happy to hear about" Brasilia's efforts to combat these dangerous trends. And in this respect, Médici specifically mentioned his efforts to persuade Paraguay's dictator, Alfredo Stroessner, to give Bolivia access to power supplies from the hydroelectric dam Brazil was financing on the Paraná River. Médici also raised the problems related to funding Brazil's armed forces in the light of their new requirements for dealing with developments in neighboring countries. As Médici lamented, the Brazilian armed forces were a third the size of Italy's, despite Brazil having double Italy's population. When Nixon then asked if military contacts should continue between U.S. forces and their Latin American counterparts, Médici replied affirmatively, arguing that it was "the only way to ensure the stability that was essential to economic development." In both meetings, the presidents also agreed unequivocally not to change their policies toward Cuba, which they regarded as representing a threat to the hemisphere. "We should not lose sight of the situation in Latin America which could blow up at any time," Médici warned.[99]

While exchanging views on this explosive situation and the general's opinion of the "desperate" situation in Bolivia, Nixon appears to have been very taken by Médici's insistence that Brasilia and Washington coordinate their efforts to improve the balance of forces in the region. As the CIA noted afterward, "President Nixon took great interest in this proposal and promised to assist Brazil when and wherever possible."[100] General Vernon Walters, who had returned to Washington to serve as an interpreter for these meetings between two presidents he also counted as his personal friends, later wrote up memorandums of their conversations. He recorded the Brazilian president as saying that "both the U.S. and Brazil should do everything in their power to assist the other countries of South America. [Médici] did not believe that the Soviets or the Chinese were interested in giving any assistance to these countries' Communist Movements; they felt that Communism would come all by itself because of the misery and poverty in these countries."

When Nixon asked Médici what he thought of Chile, he must have been thrilled with the reply he received, for the general not only underlined similar concerns about Allende's government but also stressed the prospects for cooperation. As Walters noted, Médici told his host that Brasilia was *already* intervening in Chilean affairs.

> President Médici said that Allende would be overthrown for very much the same reasons that Goulart had been overthrown in Brazil. The President then asked whether President Médici thought that the Chilean Armed Forces were capable of overthrowing Allende. President Médici replied that he felt that they were, adding that Brazil was exchanging many officers with the Chileans, and made clear that Brazil was working towards this end. The President said that it was very important that Brazil and the United States work closely in this field. We could not take direction but if the Brazilians felt that there was something we could do to be helpful in this area, he would like President Médici to let him know. If money were required or other discreet aid, we might be able to make it available. This should be held in the greatest confidence. But we must try and prevent new Allendes and Castros and try where possible to reverse these trends. President Médici said that he was happy to see that the Brazilian and American positions and views were so close.[101]

Médici's acknowledgment of Brazilian intervention in Chile and the prospect of a U.S.-Brazilian partnership against Allende were perfect examples of the Nixon Doctrine's regional potential. Nixon appears to have been ready to intervene unilaterally in Latin America if need be, but Brazil's growing role in boosting counterrevolutionary forces in South America perfectly suited U.S. attempts to share its Cold War burden with key regional allies and lessen its own exposure. In a separate meeting with Médici, Kissinger followed up on this idea of cooperation and coordination. He explained that the United States needed the "advice and cooperation of the largest and most important nation in South America. In areas of mutual concern such as the situations in Uruguay and Bolivia, close cooperation and parallel approaches can be very helpful for our common objectives. He felt it was important for the U.S. and Brazil to coordinate, so that Brazil does some things and we do others for the common good."[102]

To facilitate such coordination, Nixon offered Médici a direct channel of communication to the White House, "outside the normal diplomatic channels."[103] As it turns out, Kissinger had actually raised the idea of a "special consultation arrangement" with Brazil six months earlier when he and the president had been discussing their fears that congressional investigations on torture in Brazil and misguided liberals in the State Department might undermine the United States' relationship with Brasilia.[104] But the success of the Brazilian president's visit—or, as Nixon put it, because he and Médici had "gotten along so well"—added impetus to the idea. Subsequently, when Nixon named Kissinger as the U.S. contact for this channel, Médici happily reciprocated, nominating his foreign minister, Gibson Barbosa, as his respective interlocutor (he explained that he already handled selected private matters outside the Brazilian Foreign Ministry with Gibson Barbosa). For "extremely private matters," Médici also recommended that the White House could contact the Brazilian colonel Manso Netto. Having agreed on who would be involved in this special channel, the next step was to decide what it would accomplish. Médici, for one, suggested it could be used as a way of discussing how Brazil and the United States might help the "million" Cuban exiles throughout the Americas to overthrow Castro. Nixon agreed to look into this. On a more general note, he then again conveyed his hopes for the special channel and the new U.S.-Brazilian axis, particularly as "there were many things that Brazil as a South American country could do that the U.S. could not."[105]

It is hard to imagine a more successful summit or a more gratifying follow-up to Nixon's orders to build up relations with Brazil in the immediate aftermath of Allende's election . During his meeting with the general, Kissinger had underscored the "paramount importance" Washington attached to relations with Brasilia and had listened as his interlocutor referred to the two countries as "lovers."[106] Even more so than Kissinger, Nixon was eager to ensure that Médici enjoyed his visit, and Kissinger later assured the president that Médici had been "really very impressed" by Nixon.[107] And to crown this mutual affection at the end of the visit, Nixon publicly toasted Médici by saying "where Brazil goes, Latin America will follow."

Although the State Department regarded this as highly embarrassing given domestic sensitivities to the Brazilian regime and Latin American suspicions about Brasilia's hegemonic pretensions, Nixon's public faux pas revealed a private reality.[108] Certainly, after his own meetings with Médici, Nixon privately told Rogers that he wished the general was "running the whole continent," and the secretary concurred.[109] By the end of 1971, Brazil was experiencing its third year of 9 percent economic growth. And despite its unequal distribution (Brazil's poorest 80 percent received 27.5 percent of its GNP), Nixon held this growth up as proof that private investment and political authoritarianism paid off.[110] Beyond the State Department's reaction to Nixon's speech, the impact of the White House's decisive pro-Brazil policy, initiated as a direct consequence of Allende's election, was becoming all the more obvious to outsiders. As the *Washington Post* observed shortly after Médici's visit, "after years" of what appeared to be no U.S. policy toward Latin America, one seemed to be evolving.[111] Observantly, Castro also acknowledged that "partial imperialist victories" in Bolivia and Uruguay demonstrated a mobilized and strengthened "imperialist intention" to "restrain" new revolutionary trends in Latin America.[112]

Nowhere was this more so than in Chile. Throughout late 1971, the 40 Committee had kept up its financing of Allende's opposition parties and their media outlets while the CIA launched black operations to discredit La Vía Chilena and divide the Chilean Left. "Where possible," the CIA station in Santiago had informed Langley, it was playing up Allende's links to the far Left party, the MIR, implying that it was the president's "covert action arm" and very useful "when he has to step outside the constitution to accomplish his objectives."[113] Meanwhile, U.S. officials in Santiago kept a close eye on the military. In conversation with ex-president Eduardo Frei, Ambassador Korry had voiced his concerns that the Chilean armed forces were "a rather hermaphroditic body which Allende massaged seductively."[114] Frei then implored the U.S. assistant secretary of state for Latin American affairs, Charles Meyer, to maintain "the closest possible relationship" with them, noting that "the Chilean people and their neighbors would understand this even if all other relationships were to be cut off."[115] And in this context State Department officials agreed.[116]

Yet amid rumors of military plotting against Allende in late 1971, the CIA got cold feet. True, U.S. intelligence had drastically improved and could now count on a collection of agents within the armed forces along with daily information on plots against Allende.[117] But when CIA station officers proposed encouraging such plotting by working "consciously and deliberately in the direction of a coup" and establishing a "covert operational relationship" to discuss the "mechanics of a coup" with "key units," they received a negative response.[118] With no approval from higher authorities,

Emílio Garrastazu Médici and Richard Nixon in Washington, December 1971. Courtesy of Richard Nixon Presidential Library and Museum.

and fearing the negative implications of a botched coup attempt both in Chile and beyond, the chief of the CIA's Western Hemisphere Division, William Broe, definitively curtailed the station's actions. "We recognize the difficulties involved in your maintaining interest and developing the confidence of military officers when we are only seeking information and have little or nothing concrete to offer in return," he wrote. "There is, of course, a rather fine dividing line here between merely 'listening' and 'talking frankly about the mechanics of a coup' which in the long run must be left to the discretion and good judgment of the individual case officer. Please err on the side of giving the possibly indiscreet and probably uncontrolled contact little tangible material with which to accuse us."[119] It was this fear of being accused of intervention—a particularly sensitive concept in late 1971 U.S. domestic and international contexts—that led the United States to hesitate. As Under Secretary Irwin summarized, the key was "to allow dynamics of Chile's economic failures to achieve their full effect while contributing to their momentum in ways which do not permit [the] onus to fall on us."[120]

Crucially, Chilean diplomacy in late 1971 had made this task more difficult as it made U.S. actions against Allende more visible. While Letelier's suggestion that the United States was merely "playing a policy of equilibrium" was clearly misguided, he was right in suggesting that the weakness of Nixon's position in Latin America, U.S. domestic politics, and the Third World continued to limit the United States' flexibility when it came to opposing La Vía Chilena. Chilean policies also bolstered Kissinger's predilection for interpreting the global balance of power in broad conceptual, as opposed to material, terms. Together with the majority of Nixon's foreign policy team, he consequently believed that the United States had to restrain its impulse to fight openly against Allende and to speed up efforts to "bring him down." Given the international environment of late 1971, a divided administration therefore proceeded with cautious determination to transform the direction of Chilean and inter-American politics and to warn Third World nationalists not to follow Allende's path. As it turned out, and for reasons not exclusively connected to the United States or its destabilization campaign, the dynamics of Chilean domestic developments were actually moving in the United States' favor. By the end of 1971, U.S. policy makers could point to a range of factors causing Allende trouble at home and threatening to undermine his peaceful democratic road to socialism. From November onward, these included not only the cost of the UP's economic policies and the growing polarization of political forces but also the impact of Castro's extended tour of Chile.

"A Symbolic Meeting of Two Historical Processes"

Fidel Castro had received a clamorous welcome when he landed in Santiago on 10 November 1971. One Chilean Communist Party member recalled her "heart nearly ripped in two" as she watched Fidel drive by, and even unsympathetic bystanders came out onto the streets to catch a glimpse of Latin America's most famous living revolutionary.[121] The visit was not only a clear affirmation of the evolving ties between Havana and Santiago but also an obvious turning point in hemispheric affairs. Cuba seemed to have formally returned to the inter-American system, and Castro described his trip as "a symbolic meeting between two historical processes."[122] As Allende proclaimed, Chile and Cuba stood on the "front lines" of Latin America's struggle for independence, constituting "the vanguard of a process that all Latin American countries" and "exploited peoples of the world" would eventually follow.[123] Before Fidel's arrival, he had also proudly noted that in one year the Chileans had done "more than the Cubans did during their first year of the Cuban Revolution." While his comment was "not intended to the detriment of the Cubans," he did say that when Fidel arrived he would "ask him" what he thought. "I know what the answer will be," Allende had confidently predicted. "Let it be known for the record that we made our revolution at no social cost."[124]

When indeed asked to comment on whether Chileans had done more than Cubans in their first year, however, Castro had demurred, arguing it was "completely inadmissible" to make such comparisons. Instead, he said that in Chile the process was much more "tiresome and laborious," pointing out that whereas the whole Cuban system had collapsed in 1959, the revolutionary process in Chile was still developing and faced more obstacles.[125] Indeed, if Castro was hopeful when he arrived in Chile, he left preoccupied, and Cuba's Chilean policy underwent a considerable shift as a result. Instead of confirming Allende's achievements, the visit also seems to have magnified his difficulties. During his stay in Chile, Castro openly indicated that he thought revolutionary transformation needed speeding up, that there were merits to using violence to advance this transformation, and that Allende bestowed too much freedom on his opposition. In Fidel's view, a confrontation between "Socialism and Fascism" loomed on the horizon and if Chile's left-wing leaders did not take his advice, they would not survive it.

By the time Castro touched down in Chile, governmental and extragovernmental ties between Havana and Santiago had grown substantially. At a ceremony to commemorate the tenth anniversary of the Bay of Pigs in April 1971, the Chilean Embassy in Havana had reported that Castro and his audience seemed to be celebrating Chilean developments rather than Cuba's revolutionary victory.[126] On this occasion, the Cuban leader also meaningfully pledged Cuban "sugar . . . blood, and . . . lives" to help Chile's revolutionary process.[127] Chile had clearly become a celebrated cause in Cuba and the focal point for cultural, economic, and social exchange projects to such an extent that by the end of 1971 state-approved collaborative projects had been established in the fields of cinema, agriculture, fishing, housing, mining, energy, health provision, sport, and publishing. In addition, the University of Havana now had formal links with five separate Chilean universities.[128]

Bilateral trade between Cuba and Chile had also grown. Whereas the UP had spent $13 million on Cuban imports in 1971, it proposed to import $44 million worth of sugar in 1972. Cuba also agreed to increase the value of its Chilean imports to just over $9 million (which would include 100,000 cases of wine despite the Cuban population's preference for rum).[129] What is more, in June 1971, Cuba's national airline had begun direct flights between Santiago and Havana, and around the same time the Cubans had also approached the Chileans enthusiastically regarding the possibility of joint mining projects. (Cuba's minister for mining, Pedro Miret, had explained that the Soviet bloc lacked expertise and had not been very forthcoming with technical assistance but that Cuba was interested in increasing mining production.)[130] However, trade figures demonstrated a stark imbalance and the incompatibility of the two countries' economies. The UP's growing financial difficulties were also increasingly limiting the scope of this blossoming economic relationship. Indeed, at the end of 1971, earlier optimistic estimates for Chilean exports were already being scaled back. For example, the Chileans had to acknowledge that they would be able to provide only 150 of the 2,000 tons of garlic that they had offered months before.[131]

Irrespective of these trade difficulties, Havana and Santiago had already reaped tangible benefits from the evolving diplomatic relationship between them. Foreign Minister Almeyda had abandoned relative caution at the UN General Assembly when he proclaimed that Chile would work tirelessly to overturn Cuba's isolation.[132] Havana had also been able to reestablish better links with Latin America through its embassy in Santiago. Not only did Havana's communication with Latin American revolutionary movements in the Southern Cone improve, but the Cubans also began developing economic relationships in Argentina and Peru. From 1971 onward, for example, Cuban representatives began making secret trips across Chile's borders into these countries with Allende's knowledge and with tacit support from Argentine and Peruvian authorities. Private Chilean companies also provided a channel for Cuban purchases in the outside world (Castro's Cuba even managed to purchase Californian strawberry seeds through a surrogate Chilean business whose crops were eventually destined to serve Cuban "Copelia" ice creams).[133]

Allende's government also benefited from the more covert side of its relationship with the Cubans. At the beginning of 1971, the UP had begun to discuss how it would respond to a coup if one were launched against it. Although the government was divided on the issue of military preparation, testimonies of those involved indicate that basic contingency plans were revised both by those who supported some form of armed struggle and by those, such as the Communist Party's leader, Luis Corvalán, who dismissed its relevance for Chile. Allende's constitutional commander in chief of the army, General Carlos Prats, also appears to have seen the plans, and his participation in any effort to thwart a coup was considered pivotal. Beyond these tentative moves, the Socialist Party had approved the creation of an organizational "Internal Front," a "Commission of Defense" with a military apparatus and intelligence wing, and a commitment to strengthen the president's bodyguard at the beginning of the year. Together, members of this new defensive structure concluded that a peaceful democratic transition to socialism was unlikely and that confrontation was probable. They also observed that the armed forces increasingly believed they had a political role to play in the country and that, as a result of all these factors combined, it was unlikely the UP would complete its six-year mandate.[134]

Ever since Allende's direct request for Cuban security assistance in September 1970, the Cubans had been helping the Chileans by collaborating with their intelligence services and arming Allende's bodyguard, the GAP.[135] As one of the MIR's leaders later recalled, the Cubans helped turn the GAP into an "organized military structure" with "schools of instruction," and he admitted that the MIR took advantage of these schools to train its own cadres surreptitiously.[136] Beyond the GAP, the Cubans would also separately train and arm sectors of the MIR, the PS, the PCCh, and MAPU during Allende's time in office. Although the numbers of those trained varied considerably when it came to the different parties (with the PCCh's and MAPU's numbers being considerably smaller), this support was offered with Allende's knowledge.[137] The president's private cardiologist would later recall that the Cubans also gave him a Browning pistol so that he could step in for the GAP in times of need. (During Allende's trip to Colombia, for example, he had smuggled the gun nervously into a presidential banquet when the GAP was refused entry.)[138]

Although the CIA did not know the precise quantity of arms delivered to Chile, it knew enough by November 1971 to be able to inform Langley that the GAP's "Cuban-provided" pistols had completely replaced what had been a "haphazard collection of sidearms."[139] The CIA also reported that thirty Chileans were already receiving training in Cuba "at the Cuban department of state security school," with another thirty being recruited to join them. And, overall, the CIA concluded that this evidence suggested the Cubans were helping to create a "substantial guerrilla force" in Chile.[140] Indeed, the new information that the CIA had on Cuban operations by late 1971 meant that it abandoned its policy of fabricating stories of Cuba's role in the country and began passing "verifiable" information to Chilean military leaders.[141]

Besides indications that the Cubans were delivering weapons to the Chileans, Allende's relationship with the MIR came under scrutiny, just as the CIA had hoped it would. In August the brief rapprochement between the MIR and the PCCh had begun disintegrating.[142] The MIR was also excluded from the GAP after its members were found to be stealing the bodyguards' arsenal for its own purposes.[143] The GAP's principal Cuban instructor, a member of Cuba's Tropas Especiales by the name of José Rivero, seems to have precipitated this crisis. By secretly colluding with the MIR, which he was especially and personally sympathetic to, Rivero had also gone against the instructions he had been given by his Cuban superiors to work first and foremost for the Chilean president and the GAP. Understandably, Allende was not happy when he learned about his duplicitous role. Upon hearing about Rivero helping the MIR to take arms from the GAP for its own purposes, he summoned Cuba's ambassador, Mario García Incháu-stegui, to complain and demand that Rivero be removed from his position. As one of the MIR's leaders recalled decades later, Rivero was not only removed because Allende requested it but also personally reprimanded by Fidel Castro for having sided with the MIR over the interests of Allende's personal escort and the maintenance of harmony between the MIR and the PS.[144] Indeed, despite not having any idea what was behind it, CIA sources noted that Havana supported the restructuring of the GAP, which now comprised PS militants only.[145]

Even if the Cubans acted to alleviate the crisis, a U.S. informant nevertheless reported that Allende was "very depressed feeling that the MIR would soon get out of hand, that the Armed Forces would have to be brought in to control them, and that the country may be on the brink of a civil war."[146] On the first anniversary of Allende's election, when the president referred to his opposition as "troglodytes and cavemen of an anti-communism called upon to defend the advantages of minority groups," he therefore warned his supporters to unite. "Let us not permit extremism," he warned, demanding that the Left find a common "language" to use in its fight against powerful enemies.[147]

The Cubans echoed this message. In August, the Chilean press had printed Castro's call for "true revolutionaries" to "abandon romanticism for [the] more humdrum tasks of building [the] revolution's economic and social foundations."[148] Even so, Castro's association with Allende and Cuba's not-so-secret involvement in forming the GAP was increasingly used against the president. Chile's opposition press had falsely accused Cubans of assassinating Frei's minister of the interior, Pérez Zujovic, in June 1971, and this event had radicalized sectors of the Christian Demo-

La Tribuna, 11 November 1971.

crat Party and the armed forces against Allende.[149] Chilean senators also denounced the size of Cuba's embassy. Even the British Embassy, which had a rather measured approach to Allende's government, considered the Cuban diplomatic representation in Santiago "sinister" and "heavily weighted" toward "subversive and intelligence operations."[150] And the right-wing tabloids began a propaganda campaign denouncing the GAP as violent assassins and warning of Cuban intervention in Chile. Indeed, it was in this context that, on the eve of Castro's visit, the right-wing tabloid *La Tribuna* ran front-page news that warned "Santiago Plagued with Armed Cubans" and paid homage to Fulgencio Batista.[151]

Castro thus arrived in Chile as Allende's first anniversary celebrations were turning sour. The timing of his visit had been discussed since September 1970 but had been postponed as a result of both Cuba's domestic situation and the Cuban leader's hope that the UP would consolidate its position before he arrived.[152] (In fact, it was six months after Allende had sent the Communist senator Volodia Teitelboim to Havana specifically to invite Castro before he arrived.)[153] Once he did, there was uncertainty and speculation regarding the visit's length and scope within government as well as outside it.[154] Fidel's revelations years later suggest that the trip's duration was never his prime concern. In fact, Castro had sent Allende a proposed itinerary two months before he arrived. "You may add, remove, or introduce whatever modifications you deem appropriate," Castro wrote, "I have focused exclusively on what might prove of political interest and have not concerned myself much about the pace or intensity of the work, but we await your opinions and considerations on absolutely everything."[155] Of course, it is entirely possible that he quite simply never received a reply. If we judge from Castro's subsequent stay in Chile, Allende wanted Castro's support and approval rather than the authority to dictate the length of his stay. At a Cuban Embassy reception, Allende told the assembled guests that there were only two things he could not tolerate in life. One was a look of displeasure from his daughter, Beatriz. The other was a scolding from Fidel.[156] Even the moderate director of Chile's Foreign Ministry conveyed his hope to the British ambassador that Castro would "be impressed both by Chilean democracy and institutions and also by the Chilean balance between the various power groups in the world."[157]

Castro used his visit to Chile as an opportunity for extensive field research, but initially he offered neither wholehearted praise nor disapproval. As a means of deepening his understanding of the Chilean revolutionary process, he spoke to government ministers, military leaders, students, miners, trade unionists, the clergy, and members of Allende's parliamentary opposition. He visited the Chuquicamata copper mine, paying detailed attention to copper production, and spent hours discussing the Sierra Maestra campaign with fascinated naval officers while on route to Punta Arenas in the south.[158] Jorge Timossi, who worked for Prensa Latina and accompanied Castro throughout his visit, recalled that they would also meet each night to discuss the day's events until three or four in the morning before getting up a few hours later.[159] As Fidel insisted, he had come to "learn" rather than to teach. The Polish ambassador in Santiago also reported home after Castro's first week in Chile that the visit was proof of Cuba's new approach to revolution in Latin America: the Cuban leader's relations with the Chilean Communist Party had improved; he was showing moderation and had expressed acceptance of different revolutionary processes in the region.[160] As Castro described himself to Chilean audiences, he was a "visitor who comes from a country in different conditions, who might as well be from a different world."[161]

During his visit Castro certainly encountered stark differences between Cuban and Chilean revolutionary processes. In particular, the space the UP gave to the opposition bothered him. The free press launched open and vicious attacks against Castro that included labeling him a homosexual.[162] And the unusual length of Castro's visit also exacerbated accusations about Cuban intervention in Chilean affairs by giving criticism the space to grow. On 1 December 1971, Chilean women, together with members from the right-wing paramilitary group, Patria y Libertad, staged the first of what would be known as "Empty Pots" demonstrations, where wealthy women protested incredulously about their limited access to food supplies by hitting empty saucepans. When violence ensued, Allende called a state of emergency and a weeklong curfew in Santiago. He could not deny that Castro's presence in Chile had fueled counterrevolutionary hostility. As he told his friend, the Chilean journalist Augusto Olivares, it was only "logical" because Castro's visit had "[revitalized] the Latin American revolutionary process."[163]

Even if it was "logical," the Cuban leader increasingly concluded that the UP had not adequately mobilized its supporters to push that process forward. In conversation with Czechoslovakia's ambassador in Havana after his Chilean visit, he described his lengthy meetings with students and the working class as something Chile's left-wing parties should have been doing more of on their own. And toward the end of his stay, he gave up earlier moderation and circumspection, took on a more instructive tone, and issued stern warnings to the Left about the future. Would "fascist elements" stand back and allow revolutionary progress? Castro asked. In his view, the answer was no, and he implored the Chileans to be prepared.[164] This did not mean that he supported the MIR's increasingly public criticism of the UP and the pace of its reforms. To the contrary, during his stay in Chile, he convened an important meeting with the MIR's leaders in which he urged the party to cooperate more effectively with Allende's government. As Armando Hart, a member of the Cuban Party's Politburo who was present at this meeting, later recounted, Fidel very clearly told the MIR's leader, Miguel Enríquez, that the revolution in Chile "would be made either by Allende or by no one" and that the MIR therefore had to unite behind him.[165]

At the same time, Castro covertly urged parties within the Unidad Popular to equip themselves to fight against any future counterrevolutionary attack. During a meeting at the Cuban Embassy with leaders of the Communist Party—a party that had been traditionally skeptical and opposed to armed struggle in Chile—Castro showcased and explained the merits of various different armaments that the Cubans could acquire for the PCCh. Tell us what you need, and we will get it for you, was the message that he delivered as he showed off the weapons that were available, with Cuba's senior general, Arnaldo Ochoa, sitting by his side. When the secretary-general of the party, Luis Corvalán, responded cautiously and conservatively about a few of the arms that the PCCh might be interested in acquiring, rumor has it that Ochoa threw his chair back and stormed out of the meeting, furious that the Chilean Communists had failed to grasp the importance and scale of what was needed.[166] Reports also reached the CIA that Castro had gone as far as privately urging UP leaders to meet the opposition's violence with revolutionary violence (within universities and against the women's marches). According to this source, Castro insisted that "confrontation" was "the true road of revolution" and told UP leaders not to worry about possible injuries or deaths.[167]

Whether he specifically offered this advice, Fidel's encounter with the PCCh and public speeches increasingly conveyed a similar message. He repeatedly reminded crowds of nineteenth-century Chilean nationalists who had pledged to "live with honor or die with glory."[168] While the Chileans argued their country's unique situation allowed them to embark on a new route to socialism without armed struggle, he insisted they could not avoid historical laws.[169] Instead, emphasizing the importance of unity with heartfelt urgency, Castro instructed Chileans to "arm the spirit" and unite behind Allende.[170] Moreover, Castro appeared throughout to be saying that as a result of Cuba's experiences, he knew how to play by the rules of revolution in Chile better than the Chileans he spoke to. As he put it, Cuba had survived mud "higher than the Andes" being thrown at it.[171] And in contrast to the vulnerable Chileans, Castro explained that Cubans were safe from intervention because "imperialists" knew and respected the fact that "men and women are willing to fight until the last drop of blood."[172] Certainly, during the Cuban Missile Crisis, he recalled, Cubans had "all decided to die if necessary, rather than return to being slaves."[173]

While the Chileans were still absorbing Castro's advice, the Cubans began preparing *themselves* for the Chilean battle they saw on the horizon. One night, toward the end of his stay, Castro went to Cuba's embassy in Santiago despite the curfew. There, he spoke about his concerns until dawn with Cuban personnel congregated in a darkened patio.[174] Surveying the embassy at 2:00 A.M., Fidel Castro was appalled by the building's defensive capabilities. "I could take this embassy alone in two hours!" he exclaimed. He therefore instructed the embassy to make sure it could withstand a direct attack, and during a secret visit the following year, Piñeiro oversaw planning toward this end. Henceforth, Cuban diplomats undertook construction work to make space for medical facilities and provisions so the embassy could survive a battle. Indeed, Cuba's cultural attaché, commercial attaché, and the latter's wife remember arriving at work in the morning dressed in diplomatic clothing and then changing into "work clothes." They would then spend days or nights digging beneath the embassy to create a sizable cellar.[175]

Meanwhile, the day Castro left Chile he told a group of journalists that he departed more of a "revolutionary" than when he had arrived on account of what he had seen.[176] Was Castro "disappointed" with the UP government, as the CIA concluded?[177] Looking back on events over thirty years later, Luis Fernández Oña disputed this assessment, arguing instead that Castro was "preoccupied" rather than disappointed. As he put it, "Anyone who has ever traveled to see a friend and discovered he was sick would return worried about that friend's health."[178] In private, Castro's comments to socialist bloc leaders were nonetheless rather critical. "Allende lacked decisiveness," the Czechoslovakian ambassador in Havana reported him as saying.[179] Fidel Castro also summed up his own views in a private letter to Allende that offered both praise and a pointed call for the Chilean president to take up a more combative position. "I can appreciate the magnificent state of mind, serenity and courage with which you are determined to confront the challenges ahead," he wrote.

> That is of the essence in any revolutionary process, particularly one undertaken in the highly complex and difficult conditions of a country like Chile. I took away with me a very strong impression of

the moral, cultural and human virtues of the Chilean people and of its notable patriotic and revolutionary sentiment. You have the singular privilege of being its guide at this decisive point in the history of Chile and America, the culmination of an entire life devoted to the struggle, as you said at the stadium, devoted to the cause of the revolution and socialism. There are no obstacles that cannot be surmounted. Someone once said that, in a revolution, one moves forward "with audacity, audacity and more audacity." I am convinced of the profound truth of that axiom.[180]

Whether or not Allende would proceed with "audacity, audacity and more audacity," he had generally accepted Castro's analysis of his difficulties. When he had delivered a farewell address to the Cuban leader at Chile's national stadium, he warned Chileans that a "fascist germ" was infecting women and a younger generation of Chileans. He, too, compared his own experience with that of Brazil's ex-president, João Goulart, a decade before. And he also spoke of Cuba and Chile facing "identical enemies, foreign and domestic," the "hand of imperialism."[181] When it came to following Castro's advice to "arm the spirit," Allende had then prophetically staked his life on fulfilling La Vía Chilena: "Let those who want to turn back history," he promised, "those who want to ignore the will of the people, know that I am not a martyr, but I will not retreat one step. Let them know that I will leave La Moneda only when I have fulfilled the task entrusted to me by the people . . . only by riddling me with bullets can they stop me from fulfilling the people's programs."[182]

However, beyond his own future, Allende left the question of revolutionary violence "hanging in the air," as the United States' new ambassador in Santiago, Nathaniel Davis, observed.[183] The president was far more explicit about prescribing constitutional means of combating his opposition, and warned that preemptive violence would only provoke the enemy. He also spent much of his farewell speech to Castro actually emphasizing the *differences* between Cuba and Chile, arguing the UP's opposition was a minority, underlining Chile's democratic freedoms, and pledging his faith in the constitutionalism of Chile's armed forces.[184]

Beyond Allende, the UP coalition was divided on how to respond to Castro's advice. Castro's arms fair at the embassy for the PCCh notwithstanding, the Communist Party called for keeping Chile's revolutionary process within legal bounds, for consolidating the UP's position rather than overextending its aims, and for dialogue with the Christian

Democratic Party. Meanwhile, Socialist Party militants regarded legality and dialogue as overly restrictive. According to them, the right-wing demonstrations against Castro's presence had justified the need for armed preparation, and they now called for accelerated training in operational tactics and explosives.[185] Indeed, the divergence between the Socialists and the Communists had been growing for some time and PCCh leaders had been bemoaning the PS's "excessive radicalism" in their conversations with diplomats from the socialist bloc for some months already. As the Polish ambassador in Santiago had warned back in August 1971, there was "a multiplicity of conflict" within Chile's political parties, and fissures were already weakening the UP coalition. Now, just over four months after he had made this observation, the fissures were becoming increasingly public.[186]

Which side would Allende take in this context? The president offered no explicit answers, even if he warned a rally of thousands of the threat of a growing "international conspiracy" against his presidency, something underlined by the government's "December Declaration."[187] In December, when Nixon's personal envoy to Latin America, Robert Finch, had publicly predicted that Allende's government "wouldn't last long," Foreign Minister Almeyda had complained that it was not "international practice" to talk about the overthrow of a government one had "good" relations with.[188] But, privately, doubts within government regarding the UP's survivability were beginning to spread.

On the other side of Chile's political divide, the PDC's new leader, Renán Fuentealba, had spoken at an opposition rally, describing the president as subservient to Castro, denouncing Fidel's "interference" in Chilean affairs, attacking the UP for stoking class hatred, and condemning the government for tolerating illegal armed groups such as the MIR and the GAP. With reference to the United States, Fuentealba also berated the UP's "increasing sick attitude," arguing that Allende sought "gradually to insert Chile within the orbit of those socialist countries commanded by [the] USSR."[189] In keeping with how Allende's domestic aims transcended Chile's borders, his international alliances and the way he dealt with his enemies abroad were having increasingly significant political implications within Chile.

Certainly, Fidel Castro had added an extra—and particularly powerful— voice to the growing debate regarding Chile's revolutionary future during his stay. Although the Cuban leader emphasized his respect for Chile's sovereignty, the sheer length of Fidel's visit and the instructive tone of his advice suggested otherwise. On a positive note, Castro's support had given Allende heightened revolutionary credibility in Chile and throughout the socialist world, as well as a powerful ally in the quest for Latin America's definitive second independence. Castro was also clearly focused on working *with* the president rather than *around* him. As his advice to the MIR, his public speeches, and his subsequent letter to Allende demonstrate, he seemed to believe that the president's democratic mandate and his position at the head of the UP coalition were pivotal for the success of Chile's revolution. But on the negative side, Castro worried that Allende was not decisive enough, while the contradictions between Cuba's partnership with the president and the country's simultaneous support for the far Left—whether as a result of a pro-MIR maverick like Rivero or not—were beginning to surface. Allende clearly valued his links with Havana, sought Cuba's support, and hoped for Castro's approval. But so did the MIR and increasingly radical sectors of the PS. And as their positions diverged, Castro would not be able to satisfy both.

In this regard, Castro's trip did not cause either the growing strain within the UP or the opposition's rising confidence. But his extended presence in Chile did boost antigovernment forces and leave the government arguing over his advice. Moreover, the intimate relationship between Santiago and Havana, and Allende's suggestion that he and Castro stood together at the vanguard of a new revolutionary era in Latin America, did not guarantee that the two leaders shared the same vision for Chile's future. On the contrary, many on the Chilean Left—not least the PCCh and Allende—did not regard Cuba as an appropriate model for Chile to follow, regardless of Castro's numerous attempts to impart the wisdom of Cuba's experience. Instead, they argued that Chile was different, that its constitutional traditions were robust, and that it could still reach socialism peacefully and democratically. Whether it was or could nevertheless remained to be seen.

Conclusion

Allende's position at the end of 1971 was far more fragile than it had been six months earlier, but it was far from hopeless. Even U.S. observers had to agree that his foreign policy had been a "major achievement": the UP had sensitively managed its external image, avoiding isolation and ensuring that it would receive "support and sympathy" if its relationship with the United States ended in confrontation. Crucially, as Ambassador Davis noted, Chile had "neutralized hemisphere qualms about its Marxist credentials" with the "exception of Brazil's conspicuous coolness, and the new government in Bolivia."[190] Similarly, an East German report on Chile at the end of 1971 proclaimed that "ideological pluralism" had "decidedly trumped the thesis put forward by the United States which assumed that there were 'ideological frontiers' in Latin America."[191]

The UP had also made considerable progress during its first year in redistributing wealth within Chile. On the first anniversary of his inauguration, Allende announced 2.4 million hectares of land had been expropriated and 900,000 extra Chileans received benefits.[192] The government had increased spending by 30 percent; Chile's GNP had risen by just over 8 percent; industrial production was up by more than 12 percent; employment had grown by 45 percent; and wages had increased.[193]

The problem was sustaining such progress. The UP already faced significant financial difficulties. First, it had to deal with a drop in foreign exchange reserves (from $345 million in November 1970 to $200 million in August the following year) and, second, it had to cope with disappearing U.S. credits without any others secured to replace them. Its spending increases, the disruption to agricultural production caused by land reform, and an unpredictable drop in copper prices (from eighty-four cents during Frei's administration to forty-nine cents in 1971) also limited Allende's options.[194] More important, class conflict was gathering pace, and in the opinion of those inside and outside the UP, the government was struggling to respond to growing opposition. As the East German Embassy reported back to Berlin, Corvalán had privately acknowledged that the situation was even more difficult because the left wing had not yet "fully grasped the complexity of the situation, the immensity and the importance of our fight," which in turn diminished its chances of "properly reacting to oncoming problems." The rising intensity of "reactionary forces" toward the end of the year, the embassy's report continued, had "destroyed some of the illusions the UP may have had."[195]

Moreover, the kind of socialism the UP was aiming for and exactly how its peaceful democratic road would achieve it were far more confused at the end of the year than they had been at its start. While the far Left— inside and outside the UP—encouraged land seizures, and miners went on strike for even higher wages, the president's authority to control the pace of change was directly challenged. As such, La Vía Chilena became an increasingly fragile new model of development even as it began its second year. By December 1971 Washington's embassy in Santiago was also reporting that sectors of Allende's opposition were attempting "to prod [the] military into taking sides," something that the East German Embassy was particularly concerned about, noting that Chile's armed forces remained a "source of insecurity" for Allende.[196] What is more, now that rumors of prospective armed conflict were rife, the UP's leaders increasingly disagreed about not only what they were hoping to achieve at home and abroad but *how* they would get there, and how they would react in the event of a coup. With such big questions about the future hanging heavily over Chile, the country's rose-colored future was therefore looking decidedly more distant.

Of course, at the center of Chile's foreign policy challenges lay the United States. Although the Chileans now had a clearer idea of the Nixon administration's agenda, they were still receiving mixed signals in Washington and appreciated that there were also divisions within the U.S. government that affected how Chile would be treated. On the one hand, Kissinger said the White House was disposed to finding a modus operandi. On the other hand, Letelier observed that Nixon's treasury secretary, John Connally, was likely to try to make Chile's life more difficult in the future.[197]

More important, however, the UP did not have a clearly defined notion of what it actually *wanted* from the United States. To date, the Chileans' emphasis had been on avoiding confrontation—and launching an international campaign to win support—rather than designing the way in which they wanted future relations to be conducted. Letelier was one of those who noted that this was now becoming a problem. At the end of 1971, he called on UP leaders to conduct a serious review of how Chile should deal with Kissinger's openings, the mounting fallout from Chile's nationalization program, and its application to reschedule its external debt.[198] Yet his call for rethinking the art of conflict avoidance met with muted enthusiasm in Santiago. During his farewell speech to Castro, Allende merely insisted that "threats . . . pressures . . . restricting our credits or . . . thwarting our possibilities of refinancing our foreign debt" would not work. As he proclaimed, Chile was "not a no-man's land. Chile belongs to the Chileans. Its people after years and years of suffering, duty and hope, have come to power."[199]

But how could he consolidate that power? And to *which* Chileans did Chile belong? Clearly, different sectors of Chile's population wanted different kinds of society and sought different external sponsors to help them. While the Cubans began delivering limited caches of arms to the Chilean Left, Washington's funds and economic sanctions fueled political confrontation within Chile. And in the latter case, one of Washington's principal Chilean partners was happy with the way things were going. As Eduardo Frei put it when he spoke to the United States' ambassador in Santiago, he was grateful to U.S. officials for the "sophistication" of their policy toward Chile.[200]

This sophistication rested on maintaining a "correct but cool" approach so as not to offer Allende an enemy against which to rally support. Although a U.S. priority since 1970, when the Chilean government had begun vocalizing its fears that all was not as it appeared, this had led to ever-greater U.S. efforts to prove that it was not intervening in Chile. In fact, instead of opting for tougher sanctions against Allende, Washington stepped shrewdly away from greater confrontation. And despite divisions between policy makers, the Nixon administration would largely follow this path through 11 September 1973. As far as Washington was concerned at the end of 1971, the time was not yet ripe for pushing for accelerated military plotting—at least until it could find partners and a situation which guaranteed success. Thus, for the time being, the United States would wait, all the while turning the screws on Chile's economy and fueling political opposition to Allende's government.

Where Latin America was concerned, the Nixon administration was also more content now that it had Brazil on its side as a firm ally and fellow conspirator. As a National Intelligence Estimate concluded at the beginning of 1972: "Brazil will be playing a bigger role in hemispheric affairs and seeking to fill whatever vacuum the U.S. leaves behind. It is unlikely that Brazil will intervene openly in its neighbors' internal affairs, but the regime will not be above using the threat of intervention or tools of diplomacy and covert action to oppose leftist regimes, to keep friendly governments in office, or to help place them there in countries such as Bolivia and Uruguay."[201]

This emerging role for Brazil notwithstanding, President Médici's comments to Nixon in December 1971 illustrate that the battle for control of South America was far from won. The revolutionary tide may have been paused, but Fidel Castro's visit to Chile had equally been a major step toward Cuba's formal reintegration into continental affairs that proved Washington's efforts to isolate the island had failed. In mid-December, Peru (backed by Chile) officially proposed that the OAS reassess its policy toward Castro. Pointing to changing Latin American dynamics, they argued that ostracizing Cuba was becoming increasingly senseless, something that Brazil and the United States stood poised to resist.[202] Although the Peruvian initiative failed on this occasion, friends and foes considered

Cuba's return to the inter-American "family" only a matter of time—Cuba's isolation in the hemisphere was "crumbling," as one sympathetic observer noted.[203] Crucially, however, the precise character of the inter-American family and who controlled its destiny were increasingly being fought over. And although multiple actors were involved, Chile more than ever seemed to be an indicator of what the future would hold.

5 BATTLE LINES
Détente Unmasked, January–October 1972

A year after Allende's presidency began, he spoke enthusiastically about signs that the world was undergoing some sort of profound transformation. "The American empire is showing signs of crisis," he proclaimed. "The dollar has become nonconvertible. Apparently, the definitive victory of the Vietnamese people is drawing near." More important, "The countries of Latin America [were] speaking the same language and using the same words to defend their rights."[1] Yet the transformative trends in international affairs in the early 1970s were obviously far more complicated than Allende suggested.

In many ways, the world was changing dramatically but not necessarily in the manner in which he implied. In Latin America, Allende's notion of "one" voice that seemingly excluded Brazil and Bolivia and unsatisfactorily lumped the immensely different economic and political nations of Chile, Peru, Colombia, Argentina, and Cuba together was a discordant one at best. President Médici had noted Brazil's own peculiar position in Latin America when he met Nixon in Washington. Suggesting that Brazil and the United States were in the same boat when it came to being non-Spanish speakers in the Americas, he admitted that he had problems "dealing with and understanding the Spanish-American mentality."[2] Beyond questions of unity and language, it was also not just the United States that was in crisis. In 1970, Fidel Castro had had to acknowledge publicly that the pace of socialist revolution in Cuba would be slower than first thought, and Havana's leaders had henceforth been undergoing a decisive transition toward a Soviet-style institutional and economic reform as a means of shoring up past failures. Meanwhile, the Soviet Union's own economic strains led it to eagerly embrace superpower détente. Indeed, despite Washington's financial difficulties and the United States' role in Vietnam, Moscow was actually looking to improve trade with the West as a viable solution for its own shortages.

So where did Chile's revolutionary process fit within this picture? Could it avoid ideological differences from determining U.S.-Chilean relations? Did détente and global economic upheavals in the early 1970s offer Santiago the opportunity that Allende and many of his closest foreign policy advisers hoped? The short answer to these latter two questions is no. It was in 1972—the very year that Nixon visited Moscow and Beijing—that the Chileans came to realize this and to acknowledge that détente actually closed doors instead of opening them. Pivotally, the Soviet Union was increasingly reluctant to let a Latin American revolutionary process spoil its new understanding with the United States, especially given indications of the UP's growing economic and political difficulties at home. And where the United States was concerned, there remained little chance of any meaningful compromise with the Chileans or the Cubans. Indeed, on his return from Beijing, Nixon sent Secretary of the Treasury John Connally to Latin America for private "post-summit consultations" with six of the region's presidents in which he explicitly delivered the message that détente with Beijing and Moscow would *not* extend to Havana.[3] When it came to publicly affirming that Latin America was an exception to the new rules of the game, however, Washington officials appeared more reticent. While the United States' ambassador to the OAS, Joseph Jova, succinctly explained that "Cuba is not China," State Department officials obfuscated when answering broader questions about the double standards Nixon was applying to Mao or Brezhnev and Castro. According to the State Department's Robert Hurwitch, "consistency" was "a simplistic basis for addressing this complex question."[4]

Of course, a more accurate answer would have been to admit that beyond superpower relations and Nixon's opening to China, the inter-American Cold War—and the ideological battle at the heart of it—was still very much alive. As Allende's ambassador in Beijing noted at the beginning of the year, détente "arbitrarily de-ideologized" the language of international politics but did not fundamentally change the substance of world affairs.[5] Although détente would take years to unravel at a superpower level, its failures as a framework for solving a global ideological struggle between communism and capitalism—or even pausing it—were also already unmasked in Latin America when Nixon was touching down in China. As Letelier would acknowledge in mid-1972, the so-called "end of the Cold War" that he himself had championed only a few months before did not seem to apply to Chile; it merely changed the way U.S. interventionism occurred.[6]

Letelier was right in the sense that the Nixon administration adopted flexible tactics to destabilize Allende's presidency in an effort to avoid criticism for doing so. Yet, in 1972, this flexibility continued to be tested as the costs of its interference against Allende mounted. Key to Washington's worries was the Chilean president's growing prestige within a Third World chorus that demanded changes to the global economy and assurances that the United States would not intervene in other countries' internal affairs. As Chile and the United States assumed diametrically opposed positions in the North-South battles of the early 1970s, Allende told thousands of delegates who gathered in Santiago for UNCTAD III in April and May that the Chileans were not only supporting the quest for restructuring the international economic and political order but practicing it with "deep conviction."[7] And, in this respect, the increasingly obvious battle against private U.S. companies and Washington over questions central to the North-South debate, such as economic sovereignty and its external debt burden, was tarnishing the United States' already beleaguered Third World reputation.

The coincidence of Chile's rising position in the Third World and the United States' Cold War ideological antipathy toward Allende's government led Washington to speed up its reappraisal of its position in Latin America. By early 1972, the United States and Brazil were making considerable headway in their new offensive in the Southern Cone and, as a result, the inter-American Cold War was now increasingly being channeled into Chile as counterrevolutionary trends gained on neighboring states. But as far as the Nixon administration was concerned, this still left the prospect that regional powers outside the Southern Cone such as Peru and Mexico could be tempted toward a Chilean model. Signs that the Cubans—and to a lesser extent, the Soviets—were interested in working with these non-Marxist nationalist states also pushed U.S. policy makers toward efforts to win them back. As Nixon had said in November 1970, he wanted to "save" Latin America and, in the end, it was agreed that to do this, it did not matter that Mexico or Peru traded with Moscow or befriended Castro and were vociferous *tercermundistas*. As long as they were not Marxist, could be divided from Chile, ultimately depended economically on the United States, and were open to capitalist investment, Washington would try to win back its influence and improve bilateral relations with them. In Nixon's language, this was what it meant to act "properly." It was also the type of "attitude" that he had advocated back in 1967 when he visited South American countries. Five years later, his administration now saw its task as being to segregate the global South and inoculate nationalists against the temptation of adopting "improper" revolutionary solutions to their development needs.

In reality, the Nixon administration had little to worry about when it came to the prospect that Allende's efforts to build a Latin American or Third World coalition would challenge the United States' influence and power. Aside from Latin America's discordant voices, ninety-six nations within the G77 continued to disagree about how to approach developed countries and what they wanted to achieve. For most of them—including Chile—the absence of obvious alternatives to dependency on the United States still made American credits and developmental assistance ultimately necessary and desirable. However, as 1972 began, and as the UP continued to explore means of diversifying Chile's economy, Allende had not yet reconciled himself to this fact. Indeed, at least at the very beginning of the year, the shape of détente and what it meant for Latin America were still mysterious, and the global economy's durability looked shaky enough to suggest it could be reformed to give the Third World a more representative position within it.

Options

In the wake of Fidel Castro's visit to Chile and the state of emergency Allende had been forced to call in December 1971, the UP found it increasingly difficult to reconcile its election promises of a better future with evidence of a mounting economic crisis and growing political chaos. In early 1972, East German diplomats in Havana reported back to Berlin with information that the Cubans had decided to refrain from too much open discussion about Castro's Chilean trip because of their "reservations and doubts" about Chile's revolutionary process. According to these reports, the Cuban leadership was especially concerned about three specific issues: the extent to which strategic goals could be accomplished by democratic means alone, the appropriateness and relative success of Allende's tactics for dealing with the growing power of the extreme Right, and the prospect that Chile's armed forces might end up being referees in a future conflict between the UP and its opposition.[8] Indeed, the news of the Cubans' "great anxiety" when it came to Chile appears to have filtered through the socialist bloc—as Polish Foreign Ministry analysts noted in early 1972, their Cuban comrades were giving all the help and support to the Chileans they could, but they had also begun to criticize the Allende government's indecision.[9]

On the other side of the political spectrum, ex-president Eduardo Frei was describing Chilean democracy as walking along a "razor's edge." As he told the U.S. ambassador in Santiago, he not only doubted that Allende desired to govern democratically but also now believed the president would be unable to do so.[10] The far Left's growing calls to overthrow constitutional restraints and right-wing paramilitary violence certainly threatened the very concept of a peaceful transition to socialism, and throughout 1972 the UP's political opponents also blocked government proposals in Congress, impeached government ministers, and launched vigorous media campaigns to denounce Allende's growing economic failings.[11] True, these financial difficulties were partly the result of the UP's policies. But Allende now also faced what Ambassador Orlando Letelier regarded as a "true economic war" with Washington.[12] Time to carry out La Vía Chilena did not seem to be on Allende's side.

As the UP's leaders argued over what to do, Allende had to cast a deciding vote. In some areas, such as his approach to the MIR's provocative stance outside the government and Cuba's increasingly controversial role in Chile, he took a firmer line. But when it came to dealing with the United States, he failed to impose a clear direction to solve the inner wrangling within his government, preferring instead to wait and see what Chile could achieve through international forums. At least at the beginning of 1972, policy makers still generally had the impression that the global correlation of forces was relatively favorable and that this offered opportunities for promoting worldwide systemic change as a means of neutralizing the United States' threat. It was in this context that the president placed his hopes on what might be achieved at UNCTAD III, which met in Santiago in April and May 1972. However, Allende's depiction of his domestic battles as a reflection of a broader international Third World struggle for emancipation did not hide the fact that the foundations he needed to propel both his foreign and domestic goals forward were steadily eroding.

In February 1972, government leaders had met for the Unidad Popular's national convention in El Arrayán. There, they called for unity and what the Communist Party termed "intensified political and ideological warfare against the enemy."[13] Essentially, however, the Arrayán declaration failed to solve underlying differences that had emerged within the coalition about how to explain or overcome mounting opposition. On the one hand, the PCCh blamed "ultra leftist . . . excesses" for provoking the enemy, by implication pointing to the PS and the MIR.[14] On the other hand, the PS increasingly regarded the immediate overthrow of Chile's bourgeois capitalist system as being the only way to construct socialism.[15] It therefore fell to Allende to decide between the two, and he tended to side with the Communists rather than his own party. Indeed, at the PS's National Plenum at the beachside resort of Algarrobo the same month, Allende insisted that "the shortest road to qualitative transformations" did not involve "the destruction of constitutionality" but rather an effort to work though it to convince Chile's majority that socialism was desirable, in his words, "through revolutionary action, example, effectiveness."[16]

However, Allende did not convince the far Left within the government or outside it. Although he maintained personal—and in the case of his nephew, Andres Pascal Allende, familial—contacts with the MIR's leaders, his relationship with the party as a whole reached a crisis point in early 1972. By this stage, the party had already been excluded from the GAP and was increasingly open in its denunciation of government vacillation.[17] But when it publicly opposed the Communist governor of Concepción and a student died during intra-Left clashes in May, the UP as a whole publicly vowed to distance itself from the MIR's divisive tactics.[18] Unsurprisingly, antigovernment forces ridiculed the notion that the UP and the MIR could be divided. *El Mercurio*, which was still receiving significant covert funds from the United States, pointedly asked "what authority . . . the defenders of continental armed subversion and those who admire Fidel Castro's regime without any reservations" had to criticize others who had "taken up the same revolutionary flags."[19] As opposition leaders informed U.S. Embassy staff, they planned to launch a "campaign of intensive scandal-mongering" to attack Allende's vulnerable "image and credibility" as a democrat.[20]

A key way of doing so was to emphasize Allende's Cuban ties. Castro's speeches in Chile had clearly demonstrated that the Cubans sympathized with the PS and the MIR. Indeed, the Cuban leader would openly explain to one visiting French politician that "the Chileans would not be able to stay where they were" if they wished to make a socialist revolution and would have to abandon the "swamp of institutions" that bogged them down.[21] More than that, however, the opposition was effectively turning what the U.S. ambassador called "minor occurrences" into breaking stories of Cuban arms transfers.[22] When packages on board a Cubana aircraft had been unloaded at Santiago's airport without passing through customs in early 1972, this had caused a public outcry. Furthermore, because government officials were at the airport on the day the airplane had arrived, the opposition was able to use the incident to impeach Allende's minister of the interior, Hernán del Canto, and the head of Chile's Police Investigations Branch, Eduardo "Coco" Paredes.[23] In their campaign of "scaremongering," the opposition also had ample means of dissemination; it controlled 115 out of 155 radio stations, four out of six national newspapers, and fifty out of sixty-one regional newspapers.[24]

Meanwhile, intense scrutiny of Cuban activities in Chile, and the crisis between the government and Miristas, led to significant tensions between Allende and the Cubans. In May 1972 this escalated when Allende asked Cuba to suspend its military assistance to the MIR. The DGLN's desk officer for Chile, Ulises Estrada, remembers hearing this news while he was in Romania accompanying Castro on his tour of Eastern Europe, but he was instantly sent to Santiago in an effort to try and persuade the president to change his mind. When he arrived, he put forward the Cuban leadership's view that the MIR's preparations for armed insurgency could play an essential role in defending the government from opposition attacks or military intervention. Indeed, Havana was so convinced that the MIR should be involved that when Estrada arrived in Santiago, the message he delivered to Allende was that, if Cuba could not arm the MIR, it would suspend training to *all* parties in what turned out to be "a very long conversation."[25]

Ultimately, Estrada remembered that a compromise was reached with Allende whereby Cuba would continue offering armed training to the MIR (in Pinar del Río, Cuba's western province, and in Chile) but would provide it with no new arms until or unless there was a coup, at which point the Cubans would hand over a stockpile that they would now begin assembling in Santiago. The Cubans also urged the MIR's leader, Miguel Enríquez, to be "careful" about attacking the government.[26] Even so, for Cuba as well as Allende, the task of juggling between different left-wing factions in Chile was becoming increasingly problematic as the gap between them widened.

Meanwhile, when it came to the United States, the UP had yet to respond to the appeal Letelier had made in November 1971 to define a new cohesive strategy of compromise. On that occasion, Letelier had warned that the lack of a carefully defined strategy vis-à-vis Washington could well lead to a situation in which the Chileans "lost control" of U.S.-Chilean relations and ended up being controlled by others.[27] Only a couple of months later, his prediction had appeared to be coming true. As 1972 began, so, too, did a barrage of lawsuits and credit freezes in the United States supposedly in response to Chilean expropriations, which left Santiago playing a game of catch-up.[28] Although Chilean legal experts had replaced political representatives in negotiations with Allende's blessing, their technical approach to resolving Chile's financial battles failed to override the fundamental clash between Nixon's new, tougher stance on expropriation and Allende's refusal to overturn his "excess profits" ruling on the compensation Chile would offer to private U.S. copper companies.[29]

Capitulation to U.S. pressure was still not an attractive prospect for Allende, in terms of either his ideals or his domestic political standing. When, in November 1971, Letelier had personally urged the UP to consider entering into bilateral negotiations with the United States to discuss questions of compensation, debt negotiations, arbitration, and the status of North American investments in Chile, his proposals met with little enthusiasm.[30] Then, in February 1972, when Allende had decided to pay compensation to Kennecott's subsidiary, the Braden Copper Company, after strong U.S. State Department warnings that this would ease Chile's chances of renegotiating its debt, this was heavily criticized.[31] As the U.S. ambassador in Santiago, Nathaniel Davis, observed, the decision had been taken with "extreme difficulty by an ill-coordinated Chilean leadership."[32] Indeed, while Cuban advisers in Chile urged Allende to pay up and reach some kind of modus vivendi in this instance, some of the president's closest advisers were unhappy. After hearing the president was paying, Allende's daughter Beatriz vowed to take back the Portocarrero painting she had given him when he nationalized copper without offering any compensation, believing that he had gone back on his word.[33]

Beyond the issue of dealing with U.S. copper companies and lawsuits, preparing for multilateral debt negotiations in Paris scheduled in April was increasingly taking over the Chilean Foreign Ministry's time. As the United States was the holder of the largest portion of Chile's debt—48 percent of it—the ministry wanted to bring it on board or at least prevent Washington from sabotaging its chances of a favorable multilateral settlement.[34] As Chilean diplomats prepared to meet with their creditors in Paris, they thus spent much of their time contacting Europeans and trying to "prevent U.S. maneuvers" to undermine Santiago's position.[35] By this stage, the Chileans had at least some evidence to suggest either that Washington would not attend or that it would pressure its European allies into adopting a tougher stance. They were also conscious that U.S. Treasury officials were pressuring the State Department to adopt a hard line and had basically taken over the United States' approach to debt negotiations. In addition, growing U.S. congressional support for punishing expropriation without compensation worried Santiago's policy makers. With Chile and Peru clearly in mind, for example, the U.S. Congress had passed the González Amendment that required U.S. representatives in international financial institutions to vote against loans to countries where expropriation occurred without "adequate compensation." The United States, it seemed to Letelier, had very obviously substituted "Dominican gunboat-diplomacy" for "credit diplomacy" as a means of intervention.[36]

By this stage, Allende's government was particularly susceptible to such economic pressure. In the first four months of 1972, the cost of living had risen 10 percent, Chile had less than $100 million in foreign exchange reserves left, and opposition leaders were pointing to a predicted budget deficit of $600–$700 million by the end of the year, of which external debt repayments that the UP was trying to reschedule accounted for only $300 million.[37] At the grass-roots level, opposition spokesmen remarked with some surprise that "the poor and humble voter never talked about food but always about liberty."[38] But as U.S. ambassador Davis observed, food shortages were becoming a "significant psychological (but not nutritional) problem" among wealthier sectors of Chilean society—the core of Allende's opposition—serving as a useful excuse for antigovernment demonstrations.[39]

Given this deteriorating political and economic situation at home, the Chilean Foreign Ministry continued to court the idea of easing the country's financial situation by establishing a healthier balance of trade and aid between what it saw to be the four power blocs in global affairs, the United States, Western Europe, China, and the Soviet Union.[40] In January, Allende had written to Leonid Brezhnev vaguely accepting an invitation to visit the Soviet Union but strongly emphasizing his hopes that the imminent arrival of a high-level Soviet delegation in Chile would increase Soviet-Chilean economic ties.[41] However, subsequent bilateral talks did not go well, not least because the Soviets had regarded the Chileans as having been wildly optimistic about what the Soviet Union could provide. Specifically, the UP had proposed increasing annual trade between Chile and the USSR from 7.8 million rubles (approximately $5 million) in 1971, achieved mainly as a result of Soviet wheat and tractor exports, to $300 million by 1975. Moreover, although the Chileans suggested that they would pay for immediate Soviet imports *after* presidential elections in 1976, they also hoped to sell Chilean products to Moscow in the meantime and demanded immediate payment in hard currency. In a specially commissioned report for the Soviet Politburo, the Latin American Institute at the USSR's Academy of Social Sciences thus noted that the Chilean plan implied the USSR would have to comply with conditions it had not granted any other developing country. Considering the USSR was desperate for grain itself in 1972, the authors of this report noted, Soviet leaders were not attracted by the prospect of providing long-term credits or exporting great quantities of items that were already in short supply in the USSR.[42]

Meanwhile, the UP's leaders could not agree on the Soviet Union as an alternative source of economic support. Sectors of the coalition—often the very ones that opposed making a deal with Washington—regarded the prospect of becoming increasingly dependent on the Soviet Union skeptically. Carlos Altamirano, general secretary of the Socialist Party, exhibited "nothing but scorn for the Russians and their system" when he met Britain's ambassador in Santiago. According to Altamirano, Fidel Castro had privately lamented Cuba's dependency on the USSR to him while in Chile. The Cuban leader had apparently bemoaned that "he had no alternative but to turn to the Russians" and found them "extraordinarily slow-moving and rigid"—"Every time he asked for urgently needed equipment," Altamirano recounted, "he was told that he could not have it for several years because all supplies had been allocated well in advance and changes could not be made without wrecking the current plans. Castro wanted to build up trade with Western Europe and also said that he would like to restore relations, particularly in the economic field, with the United States, though of course the Americans would have to accept him . . . [and] this would [not] be possible as long as Mr Nixon was President."[43] Although Castro's objections to the USSR may have been astute, Altamirano does not appear to have offered any alternatives to seeking support from the Soviets. And while Nixon remained president, and the Soviets stalled, the UP's economic difficulties continued to mount.

In this context, many Chileans—and Allende in particular—hoped that the Third World would collectively act to change the international balance of power and give Chile greater leeway to attract support. UNCTAD III was to be the largest conference on trade and development ever held, comprising 141 delegations and giving the UP an opportunity to show the world Chile's democratic character while negotiating a better deal for the Third World.[44] Chilean diplomats insisted that transforming the system of global trade and creating a better situation for worldwide economic development was "a similar and parallel fight" to the one going on in Chile, and even the Brazilian ambassador in Santiago was forced to acknowledge that the conference offered the UP international "recognition."[45] The East German Embassy in Santiago reached a similar conclusion, optimistically noting that the conference would give Chile a positive "opportunity to strengthen its position in the 'Third World.'"[46]

Even so, before the conference, it had been unclear precisely what the Chileans were hoping to gain from UNCTAD III beyond recognition and prestige. Six months earlier, Foreign Minister Almeyda had publicly stated that, as well as embarking on "conventional" negotiations, the global South should use its "moral authority" to confront and denounce "the incongruence and irrationality" of an unjust international system.[47] After the disappointments of the G77 meeting in Lima in October 1971, Chile's representative in Geneva, Hernán Santa Cruz, had nevertheless become highly skeptical of the conference's potential. In keeping with his own proposals of what could be done to improve the G77's chances before the conference opened, he visited European capitals, where he emphasized constructive negotiation rather than confrontation, and thirteen African countries, where he tried to mobilize a unified Third World coalition.[48] But as he had warned Almeyda before taking off on these trips, within the Third World it had become clear that there was a group of members that were wary of pushing for too much from developed countries at UNCTAD III. There were also other obstacles. As Santa Cruz wrote, not only were poorer African countries more concerned with how they could catch up with other countries *within* the G77 itself, but the Soviet bloc and the People's Republic of China were not as involved as they could be in supporting the G77's efforts. Meanwhile, North Korea and North Vietnam were absent from UNCTAD, Arab countries were distracted by their own problems, and India, the Philippines, Pakistan, Malaysia, Indonesia, Iran, Burma, South Vietnam, Thailand, and Cambodia were all either satellites of the United States or playing a "game of equilibrium." Santa Cruz consequently warned Almeyda that the G77 was unlikely to adopt a united radical posture and forcefully exert its demands on developed countries.[49]

Then, at the last moment a possible silver lining appeared. On the eve of UNCTAD III and Chile's external debt renegotiations in Paris, the *Washington Post* published documents pertaining to the International Telephone and Telegraph Corporation (ITT) that detailed Washington's efforts to prevent Allende's inauguration and create economic chaos in Chile.[50] Immediately, Chile's economic ills were attributed to Washington, and the United States was put on the defensive. Certainly, the disclosures provided Chile with immense sympathy abroad, and their fortuitous timing appeared to strengthen Santiago's position as its representatives headed to Paris for debt negotiations. Overall, however, Letelier urged Allende to be restrained, privately suggesting that holding back would give the Chileans "cards in their hand to play later on."[51]

At the grand-opening session of UNCTAD III, Allende chose a characteristic in-between stance by denouncing multinational companies' actions in the Third World while conspicuously neglecting to mention the United States by name. As he proclaimed, he subscribed to a "Third World philosophy," which stood for recuperating national resources from foreign ownership and sustainable development against cultural and economic imperialism.[52] But as the spotlight hovered over Chile, the question was whether Allende could capitalize on UNCTAD III to undermine his enemies' ability to hurt him. Within the G77, Allende was one of only a few leaders that decisively challenged the international economic system in words as well as deeds. Now, Chile's deteriorating economic and political situation weakened the effectiveness of its challenge, especially as the possibility of rescheduling Chile's external debt burden was still being negotiated in Paris. There were also some within Chile who did not agree with the prospect of sitting down to negotiate with the global North and demanded that the South should squarely confront and overthrow the world's already tottering economic system. Certainly, as delegates sat down to discuss the finer points of international economic relations at UNCTAD, Miristas burned U.S. flags outside the conference hall and demanded that a "revolutionary wave" engulf Chile and expel the U.S. delegation.[53]

Overall, then, there was no Chilean left-wing consensus on how to deal with the United States, the USSR, or the Third World, let alone any agreement on what the ultimate shape of Chilean socialism should be. Even if Allende restrained the MIR by curtailing Cuba's support for the party, he could not eradicate its influence altogether or impose unity on his coalition government. Internationally, Santiago also found itself reacting as fast as it could to mounting financial pressures while looking to multilateral forums for support. In this situation, what could UNCTAD III achieve? Letelier, for one, was highly dubious that it would resolve anything. Just before delegates arrived in Santiago from around the world, he had warned Almeyda that the conference would be of only "secondary value." It was unlikely to significantly change Washington's posture toward the Third World, he argued, and would not have any substantial impact on the United States' approach to Chile.[54]

Tactics

Letelier would have been surprised to learn that U.S. policy makers were actually rather worried about UNCTAD III and that they would change the way they dealt with Chile partly as a result of it. What made the conference a daunting prospect for Washington's policy makers was not that it would force the Nixon administration to substantially alter its policies toward Chile given the country's new standing in the Third World. Rather, it was the other way around: administration officials feared that the conference would unfavorably change the power dynamics between the United States and Chile and that this would consequently have negative implications for Washington's standing in Latin America and other areas of the global South. Rather than merely being concerned about UNCTAD, however, it was the coincidence of this event, the ITT revelations, an imminent OAS General Assembly meeting, and forthcoming debt negotiations in Paris that concerned U.S. officials as they believed that they all provided Allende with sympathetic platforms from which to rally support. As the State Department and Kissinger's new assistant on Latin American Affairs, William Jorden, warned, the ITT leaks had been a "setback" and Allende was "increasingly positioning himself as leader of [the] Third World."[55] In what was commonly regarded as a balance between "him and us," administration officials were now concerned that they were about to lose ground to "him" in Chile, Latin America, and the global South overall.[56] These fears were clearly exaggerated, but they were taken seriously enough to precipitate a number of actions to prevent a loss of worldwide prestige. Henceforth, the Nixon administration appeased the Chileans at Paris at the last minute and also began working more effectively with frustrated Latin American nationalists in order to undercut Chilean, Cuban, and Soviet influence in the hemisphere.

As had been the case since Allende's election, the majority of Washington's foreign policy team still believed that the United States could not overtly bring Allende down without bolstering the latter's chances of success and harming Washington's reputation in the process. As the State Department explained at the beginning of April, "combining independence from U.S. influence and sweeping social change carried out with a show of legalistic deference to pluralism, has inherent appeal in Latin America. The extent to which this appeal is manifested in political developments in other countries will depend on the evident success or failure of the Allende regime, and whether Allende can persuasively attribute his difficulties to external factors. The implications for U.S. strategy are clear."[57]

Making sure that the United States did not receive the blame was also a priority for Kissinger and his staffers at the NSC, the U.S. ambassador in Santiago, and leading opposition figures in Chile. And in April, this most obviously meant suggesting that the United States accept Chile's petition to reschedule debt repayments. Ex-president Eduardo Frei privately also urged Washington not to "torpedo" negotiations, and Ambassador Davis warned his superiors in Washington not to give Allende a "credible and emotionally overwhelming foreign threat" by doing so. As Davis saw it, a U.S.-Chilean confrontation coupled with the deterioration of Chile's economy would only lead Allende to "press harder for larger-scale [Soviet] bloc aid . . . in desperation."[58] In Davis's words, ITT revelations had offered the UP persuasive evidence it could use to argue that the United States was "attempting to deny Chile necessities of life."[59]

Even so, this majority still faced the task of winning over Nixon, who had been more inclined to punish Allende overtly for having expropriated U.S. copper companies without compensation. In early 1972, Washington insiders were referring to the deterrence of future Third World expropriations as "one of the cardinal objectives" of Nixon's foreign policy.[60] Thus, when Treasury Secretary John Connally had complained to Nixon that the State Department was poised to renegotiate Chile's debt at the beginning of the year, the president had reacted by swiftly placing the Treasury Department in charge of negotiations and instructing it that he was firmly against any rescheduling.[61]

Essentially, it was the growing prospect that Allende would effectively use UNCTAD III, Paris, and the OAS to boost his chances that altered this hard-line posture and led the White House to contemplate a more flexible position. As Jorden warned Kissinger three days before UNCTAD III, it was time to get Washington's "ducks in a row" and to make sure Treasury officials understood that "strictly financial objectives" would be pursued only in the context of Washington's *overall relations* with Chile."[62] As things were, State Department analysts warned that European creditors appeared to be on the verge of rescheduling Chile's debt independently, placing Washington's position in "serious danger."[63] Others were also suggesting that by actually joining in and rescheduling Chile's debt, the United States would not be in danger of solving Allende's economic problems anyway. In fact, Ambassador Davis, the State Department, and Jorden argued that the United States would be in a far more favorable position to undermine

Allende's government further down the line if it gave ground on this issue. They therefore advocated appearing cooperative while simultaneously gaining a lever to use against Chile in the future in the shape of a clause linking future debt renegotiation with evidence of compensation for copper companies.[64] As Jorden advised, Chile would still have to renegotiate future debts and, if Allende had not abided by agreements by then, the United States would be "in a much stronger international position" to take a "tougher line."[65]

Although it is unclear what Nixon thought of this argument, he did nothing to oppose it. On 20 April 1972 the United States signed the Paris Agreement, which gave Chile a three-year deferral on 70 percent of its external debt between November 1971 and December 1972, as well as the opportunity to reschedule debts for 1973 at the end of the year. Crucially, the agreement also stipulated that Chile was to reschedule remaining repayments with individual creditors, which tied Santiago down to bilaterally negotiating its repayments with Washington. As per U.S. designs, the Paris Agreement also included a clause regarding Chile's commitment "to grant just compensation in accordance with Chilean legislation and international law" for expropriations. This reference to "just compensation" in Article 4, as it was subsequently known, was clearly open to conflicting interpretations, and it would become a frustrating impediment to Chile's efforts to resolve its issues bilaterally with the United States.[66] Washington's decision to go along with a framework for debt rescheduling therefore turned out to be a shrewd move. Although it offered the Chileans some respite, it allowed the Nixon administration to regain much of the initiative vis-à-vis Chile that it had lost in the previous few months.

In the end, things also went well for the United States at UNCTAD III, which ultimately failed to change either the U.S.-Chilean relationship or the balance of international economic relations. One participant later went so far as to describe the conference as a "gigantic farce," and Venezuelan leaders would later explicitly label it as having "failed" to do anything about the rising debt problem in Latin America.[67] The North managed to defend its position and the South managed only to get hazy commitments on aid. So much so, in fact, that after the conference, Algeria's foreign minister, Abdelaziz Bouteflika, lamented that "the road of Third World economic emancipation . . . does not run through UNCTAD" but rather through the South's own efforts to forcibly change its relations with the developed world.[68]

However, it was not only the North that was intransigent. To be sure, where Chile was concerned, delegates pledged their support for its economic battles. But as far as the British ambassador in Santiago was concerned, Allende's opening address—which the ambassador labeled as "extreme" and "demagogic"—had "probably divided rather than helped the developing world."[69] Although the ambassador's labels may have been somewhat shrill, his observations regarding the problems the developing world faced in uniting behind a common cause led by Chile were astute. As Hernán Santa Cruz had forewarned, the Third World's leaders who had gathered in Santiago to change the world economic system and their position within it had been vulnerably divided when they arrived. Or, as Ambassador Letelier observed from Washington, all that UNCTAD III had done was to show the Third World's task of transforming the world economic system was going to be long, with "scarce" prospects of success and with little immediate impact on Chile's situation. He therefore advocated the promotion of "more limited, solid, stable and also more realistic nuclei, at regional and sub-regional levels, like the Andean Pact."[70]

Chile's chances of benefiting from the Andean subregional grouping were nevertheless also increasingly tenuous. By 1972, investors abroad were welcoming the pact's apparent new "flexibility" regarding the restrictive rules it had previously placed on foreign investment. After an initial year of activity, international observers also noted a "depressing . . . lull" had overtaken the group. True, by the end of 1971, trade within the pact had increased by $100 million, reaching a total of $160 million. Yet foreign observers were unimpressed, especially as Peru's exports to member states were decreasing. Chile and Peru were also rumored to be resisting new imports that competed with local industries.[71] Although the UP was politically committed to the pact, Chile's economic situation was clearly affecting its participation. With Chile increasingly forced to focus on essential imports to save its shrinking foreign exchange reserves, it was growing apparent that the UP could not comply with the pact's stipulations for economic integration.[72] Beyond this, when Andean foreign ministers met in Lima in June 1972, they could confirm commitment to "ideological pluralism" and an "Andean Spirit" on "political, economic, cultural and social issues," but little more.[73]

Ends and Means

What did this mean for the Nixon administration's approach to Latin America? Having joined forces with Brazil the previous year, and having more than survived UNCTAD III, the United States now began paying far more attention to this "lull" and to calculating how it could take advantage of regional divisions. As we have seen, Nixon's Latin American policy was still rather ill-defined beyond its general anticommunist offensive in the Southern Cone. And, officially at least, the United States was supposed to be pursuing a "low profile" in Latin America. However, as Kissinger had privately remarked at the beginning of 1972, there was a "major revolution" going on in Latin America and "not being domineering, is not an end in itself. We have to say what we are for."[74]

Gradually, Kissinger opted *for* pragmatically pursuing rapprochement with certain nationalists but only as long as they were not Marxist inspired. Although this excluded clear-cut ideological foes, this matched the State Department's much earlier inclinations to deal with regional leaders in a more flexible, "mature" fashion and was an idea that had been around since before Allende's election. Moreover, when the administration more meaningfully embraced this flexible stance in mid-1972, the character of its "maturity" had changed. Now, as a result of Chilean developments, Cuba's expanding influence in the inter-American system, and signs of Soviet interest in courting nationalists, this more flexible approach was not a rearguard action to prevent further decline in the United States' regional standing but an offensive effort to isolate Allende and Castro and to actually win back regional influence.

This new approach to Latin American affairs centered on U.S. analyses of the balance of forces within the region. By mid-1972 the State Department understood Latin America as being divided between three different models of development: Chile's, Brazil's, or an "indecisive mix" of the two. When the State Department asked U.S. ambassadors to define which model their host country most resembled, it underlined the drawbacks of Santiago's example. "We doubt that the Chilean economic model can be followed for very long without authoritarianism, if only because of the need under it for forced restriction of consumption to achieve capital formation in combination with rapid and forced redistribution of wealth. The Brazilian model is also probably more likely to entail authoritarianism than is the indecisive mixture of the two . . . dissatisfaction with the results of any one of the three models could lead to a move to one of the others. But movement from the Chilean model back to one of the others is more difficult than movement the other way."[75] As the State Department rather simplistically saw it, the key was therefore to court countries in the middle, to prevent them from veering toward Allende's example, and to hold Brazil up as the model to choose if need be. In mid-1972, even the White House and the Treasury Department appear to have become convinced of the merits of conjoining efforts to win over nationalists with more straightforward anticommunist offensives.

When, in June 1972, Connally was sent to Latin America after Nixon's visits to Beijing and Moscow for "post-summit consultations," he stopped in Brazil, where he once again underlined the Nixon administration's admiration for the country. "Brazil's political stability and economic growth provided a superb example for other developing nations," Connally marveled. Following Nixon's instructions, he also sought his host's views on a number of international issues ranging from Vietnam to the Middle East and, crucially, U.S.–Latin American relations. Should the United States pursue a regional "Latin American" policy, Connally asked, or focus on bilateral relationships with individual countries? Pandering to his host's sense of importance and recognizing a mutual antipathy toward left-wing trends in the hemisphere, he acknowledged that Brazil was obviously different from Uruguay and Chile but noted there were general issues that were of importance to the whole region which might warrant a broader approach. Unsurprisingly, Médici rejected the idea of a blanket policy, preferring the strengthening of bilateral ties, and responding emphatically that it would be an "injustice to equate . . . small countries with Brazil, which was far larger in area and population and was making heroic efforts to transform itself into a developed country."[76]

This did not prevent Connally and his Brazilian hosts from discussing broader regional problems. To the contrary, representing a country they saw as being above and distinct from other Latin American states, the Brazilians interpreted their role as engaging the United States more in regional affairs, all the while advising and informing Washington's representatives about what was needed to combat the Left in the Southern Cone. When it came to Chile, for example, Connally encountered affirmation of the United States' new nuanced approach to Chile. As Brazil's foreign minister, Gibson Barbosa, counseled, more direct intervention in Chile at this point would only "strengthen Allende's position." President Médici also repeated the general thrust of his comments to Nixon—the United States had to act, albeit "very discreetly and very carefully."[77]

However, when it came to Bolivia the Brazilians continued to urge greater U.S. action. Following his meetings in Washington, President Médici had written to Nixon in March 1972 warning: "Political chaos, or the establishment of a Marxist-Leninist regime in Bolivia, would entail—I would not hesitate to say—for South America as a whole, consequences far more serious, dangerous and explosive than the Cuban problem, due to the geo-strategic position of Bolivia." He had also urged Nixon to help support General Hugo Banzer's regime against Bolivian exiles stationed in Chile.[78] The U.S. Embassy had echoed this message. "The rapid and efficient Brazilian assistance to [the] Banzer government in its early days reflected not only concern over [an] active security threat GOB felt Torres government posed, but also genuine enthusiasm for and sense of affinity with Banzer government," it reported. Even so, the Brazilians now expected the United States to step up to the mark and carry the "bulk of the load" when it came to economic and budgetary assistance.[79] And by the time Connally met Médici in Brasilia, the latter was able to tell his guest that he had heard back from Nixon and was pleased to learn that the United States was now helping Bolivia in a "very substantial manner." Although Connally reaffirmed Washington's commitment, Médici nevertheless took the opportunity to have Nixon's envoy in Brasilia underscore once more that "Bolivia was a permanent worry to Brazil, that Brazil was assisting Bolivia as best she could but that the U.S. must play a major role in supporting Bolivia or else that nation would fall to the 'other' side." He also expressed his certainty that Cuba and Chile were aiding subversion in Bolivia.[80]

When Connally landed in La Paz, he then received direct and repetitive pleas from President Banzer himself for more assistance. As a memorandum of the long conversation between them records, the Bolivian president stressed emphatically that his government was "anticommunist" but had to

> make economic and social progress in order to immunize Bolivians from the appeal of Communists and extremists . . . the needs, ambitions and aspirations of Bolivians are really modest and it does not take much to satisfy them. At the present time, however, these modest ambitions are unsatisfied and it is necessary to keep many political prisoners as a means of preventing these people from taking advantage of the situation of Bolivia in general. But if his administration is able to make progress, then the Bolivians will be naturally immunized from the appeal of the extremists. To make this progress . . . Bolivia desperately needs help from the United States. Bolivia also felt entitled to this because the revolution of last August represented an important defeat for communists, and as

such, an important victory for the United States and its objectives in Latin America. He noted in this exposition the strategic location of Bolivia in the heartland of South America.[81]

Even before Banzer's pleas, the United States had already committed itself to loaning Bolivia's new government $20 million and Connally now emphasized this point, making clear that Washington would prefer La Paz to first use this loan wisely—and follow advice on devaluing the Bolivian peso—before the Nixon administration handed out yet more assistance. Assuring Banzer that the United States was committed to helping him, he also promised to see what he could do to limit conditions on U.S. loans to Bolivia so as to make the Bolivian government's task of consolidating its hold over the country easier. And despite not giving Banzer all that he desired, U.S. aid to Bolivia did increase by 600 percent in the new government's first year in power. Kissinger had also intervened to do what he could to ensure economic aid would not be conditional on La Paz's fiscal performance.[82] As William Jorden argued, Banzer's "heart [was] in the right place" and his regime had "progressed nicely" by expelling Soviet personnel and cracking down "hard" on "leftists."[83]

To Santiago's horror, U.S. defense secretary Melvin Laird also publicly used the prospect of Chilean support of anti-Banzer forces to justify increased U.S. military assistance to Bolivia.[84] Although this was a convenient justification for increased spending, Washington actually had no precise or compelling intelligence on this issue. Instead, the State Department noted that "some extra-legal support, principally from the Socialist Party, has already been given, and aid to subversives from Castro or other sources will almost certainly transit through Chile" but acknowledged there was "no known direct GOC support for subversives against other neighboring countries," a view that is supported by available evidence from Chile and Cuba when it comes to Bolivia after the coup in 1971.[85] Even Brazilians privately acknowledged that Cuba's support for revolutionary movements in the hemisphere had diminished.[86]

In this context, it seemed increasingly clear to Santiago that the United States' approach to Latin America was ideologically driven and that Chile was singled out as a special target of hostility. And while the Chileans had no information about Connally's private conversations or the details of increased U.S. spending in Bolivia, they were clearly wary about the purposes of his trip and the implications it had for inter-American affairs. Seen from their perspective, the treasury secretary appeared to be laying down what Letelier referred to as the "rules of the game" by visiting Venezuela, Colombia, Peru, Bolivia, Brazil, and Argentina but skipping Chile. Why was Chile the exception? Lima had nationalization disputes with Washington, had improved relations with the Soviet bloc and Cuba, and had vociferously called for international economic reform in Third World forums. Yet it clearly faced less hostility.[87] Furthermore, the Chileans were curious about what lay at the heart of Nixon's relationship with the Mexican president, especially in the light of the latter's visit to Washington in June 1972.[88]

Mexico's president, Luis Echeverría, was ostensibly one of Allende's principal allies in the North-South debates of the early 1970s. As Mexico's ambassador to Chile recalled, Echeverría also faced considerable domestic pressure to support the UP in whatever way he could.[89] During the president's visit to Santiago for UNCTAD III, Echeverría had also been invited to a private convivial family dinner at Allende's residency, Tomás Moro, where his wife, Maria Esther, had established what would later be highly significant personal ties with Allende's wife, Hortensia.[90] Yet, although Echeverría publicly defended Allende's sovereign right to determine compensation, he also disagreed with the Chilean president's socialist goals, an opinion he had shared privately with Allende in Santiago.[91] In fact, the Chileans had been wary of Mexico's position for some time before the two presidents met. In Almeyda's opinion, expressed privately a year earlier, the Mexicans were acting under the "guise of progress and an attachment to a revolutionary tradition" but were in reality closely tied to U.S. interests. Or, to put it another way, Echeverría wanted to appear "progressive" among his own people, which is why he was reaching out to Allende, but as far as Chile's foreign minister was concerned, this was merely a "facade."[92]

Declassified records of the Mexican president's summit with Nixon in Washington demonstrate that U.S. officials certainly had nothing to worry about when it came to the prospect of Mexico's government being infected by Chilean ideas. On the contrary, when Nixon told Echeverría that "it would be very detrimental . . . to have the Chilean experiment spread through the rest of the continent"—that the hemisphere would be "very unhealthy" as a result—his guest agreed. During the Mexican president's visit to Washington, the two of them had then discussed their mutual fears of the Soviet Union and China. While congratulating Nixon on his trips to Beijing and Moscow, Echeverría perceived a continuing Chinese and Soviet menace in Latin America. He had "observed it in Mexico and . . . directly in Chile, and in every Latin American country in one form or another," he told his counterpart. Echeverría also underlined the dangers of Cuba and of Castro's alternative model for economic and social development in Latin America. By contrast, the Mexican president seemed receptive to Nixon's emphasis on the advantages of private U.S. investment and the need for Latin Americans to responsibly protect that investment, so much so that the U.S. president urged his guest to "let the voice of Echeverría rather than the voice of Castro be the voice of Latin America." In Nixon's words, "If the poison of communist dictatorship spreads through Latin America, or the poison of unrest and . . . revolution spreads through Latin America, it inevitably will infect the United States."[93]

While Mexico was essentially on board, or at least willing to play the game of being on board, the United States government was still worried about Lima's leaders. Despite traditional frontier animosity between Chile and Peru, President Velasco Alvarado had worked surprisingly closely with the Chileans within the OAS, in the G77, and at UNCTAD III to push for a review of Cuba's status in the inter-American system and to regulate foreign investment in the region. Partly as a result of its nonideological character, Peru was also now attracting considerable attention as a new focus of the inter-American Cold War.

Indeed, even before Allende was elected, Peru had become a key pillar of Cuba's shifting approach to the inter-American system. Now, compared to Allende's increasingly beleaguered and ideologically driven revolution, Velasco Alvarado's position looked more secure and more promising to the Cubans. In mid-1971 Cuban foreign minister Raúl Roa had told his Polish counterpart that Peru's government was a decidedly "revolutionary government." To be sure, it did not have a clear political doctrine, and Peru's military leaders were divided. But as Roa insisted, what was important was the "progressive character" of Velasco Alvarado's reforms and the course of development he had initiated, which the Cubans believed would eventually lead to "socialist transformation."[94] The Soviets seemed to agree with this. According to one Cuban Embassy employee in Santiago, Soviet Ambassador Aleksandr Alekseyev privately confided to her that he believed Peru would be socialist before Chile.[95] Given these views, Cuba's DGLN had been pursuing what one of its members described as an "ad hoc" program since mid-1970. Specifically, this brought together the Cuban Ministry of Public Health and Cuba's Ministry of Construction to deliver assistance after an earthquake struck the Peruvian fishing port of Chimbote, north of Lima, on 31 May 1970 and, simultaneously, to develop closer relationships with Lima's leaders.[96] Then, on 8 July 1972, Peru had followed Chile's example by unilaterally reestablishing diplomatic relations with Cuba regardless of OAS sanctions. From the very beginning, the Cuban leadership clearly nurtured this relationship, looking after visiting Peruvian delegations and working with what Chilean diplomats jealously called "surprising speed" to help Lima set up a new embassy in Havana. Indeed, within a few months Santiago's ambassador in Cuba was speculating that if the Chilean and Peruvian embassies competed for attention, the Cubans would help the latter over the former.[97]

Seen from a Cuban perspective, this growing attention to Peru had not *replaced* Havana's focus on Chile, but it does appear to have been a welcome distraction from mounting difficulties in supporting La Vía Chilena (one need only compare the number of articles on Chile and Peru that appeared in *Granma*). By mid-1972, the Cubans were feeling increasingly constrained in their ability to defend Allende not only owing to the Chilean president's curtailment of their role in arming the MIR but also because Cuban involvement in Santiago was being so scrutinized that it was more and more difficult to move around the city freely. Chile's inability to fulfill previous trade agreements was also undermining trust between both countries in a way for which there did not seem to be any easy solution. And in this context, Cuba's relationship with Peru offered Havana a new, and potentially less complex, opening in Latin America that underlined the shift that had taken place in Castro's regional policy since 1968. Indeed, as a reflection of imminent diplomatic openings, Cuba's Foreign Ministry (MINREX) reopened its Latin America Department in mid-1972 for the first time in eight years. Manuel Piñeiro's department, the DGLN, still retained overall control of policy toward the region, and Cuba's armed forces were actually central to a burgeoning relationship with Peru's military leaders, but by reopening this department at MINREX, Cuba's leaders signaled they were adapting their foreign policy to match changing opportunities in the region.[98] As Cuban foreign minister Raúl Roa publicly proclaimed, Cuba was no longer isolated in the hemisphere—there were now three types of revolution in Latin America: Cuba's, Chile's, and Peru's.[99]

Although the combination of these three revolutionary processes was positive for Cuba, Havana's leaders were nevertheless increasingly aware that one plus two did not a Latin American revolution make, especially given recent counterrevolutionary gains in the Southern Cone. To the contrary, behind the scenes, Piñeiro told DGLN officers in August 1972 that regardless of "new dynamics" in the hemisphere,

The prospects for Latin American liberation now appear to be medium- or long-term. We must prepare ourselves to wait—to wait as long as necessary: 10, 15, 20 or even 30 years. We must prepare to repulse the enemy in all fields. . . . And, of course, we must prepare to help to speed this process of revolutionary transformation as much as possible . . . keeping in mind that the struggle will be a particularly long one in the ideological field and that imperialism is giving ever-greater importance to the subtle weapons of penetration and domination. This means that we must continue delving into the principles of Marxism-Leninism, revolutionary ideas, the study of great problems of history and political problems of the present day.[100]

As Havana settled for dealing with countries on a case-by-case basis and prepared itself for a longer-haul struggle than its leaders had predicted only a couple of years before, Castro increasingly focused on the Third World beyond Latin America and on the Soviet bloc. In mid-1972, Roa led a large delegation to UNCTAD III despite Havana's cynicism regarding the global South's chances for negotiated transformation, and Castro traveled to Guinea, Sierra Leone, and Algeria on his way to visit Eastern Europe and the Soviet Union.[101]

Although Castro clearly wanted to strengthen ties with the socialist bloc, his visit to Eastern Europe was not without its difficulties. Primarily, his sharp critique of détente, the notion of peaceful coexistence, and the Soviet Union's role in the Third World brought him into direct conflict with the international direction of Communist Party policies in Eastern Europe and the Soviet Union. As a Polish report of his stay in Warsaw lamented, Castro's views on the Vietnam War and his arrival so soon after Nixon's visit largely spoiled what could have been a celebratory visit to consolidate the vastly improved relations between Cuba and Poland over the past year and a half. Not only did Castro privately exhibit profound suspicion of peaceful coexistence and superpower agreements, but he also placed excessive emphasis on the "correctness" of fighting imperialism while cloaking his "dogmatic" opinions in "revolutionary phraseology." On the Third World, for example, he lambasted the Soviet bloc's role in encouraging an Arab-Israeli armistice after the June 1967 war and argued that it would have been better for the aggressor to occupy Cairo, Damascus, and Beirut so as to give birth to a people's uprising in the future (he mentioned that he had since sent Cuban instructors to train Fatah). As Polish ministers reflected after his visit, when Castro spoke of Vietnam, he was clearly thinking of Cuba and its ongoing battle against the United States. Moreover, Warsaw's leaders concluded that their guest may have wanted to get these views off his chest in a socialist bloc country where he felt able to do so before journeying on to Moscow, where it would be more difficult to speak candidly. Clearly, the Cuban leader hoped that the Poles would relay his views to the Soviet Union so that he did not have to make them known directly when he met Brezhnev in the USSR. As it turned out, however, the Poles decided to be "balanced" and cautious about how they conveyed their opinions of the trip to their comrades in Berlin and Moscow. The burgeoning dialogue between Poland and Cuba should continue, they reasoned, but the socialist bloc countries would have to exercise influence over Fidel Castro on the important matters of détente and peaceful coexistence in the future.[102]

It seems that Castro managed to hold back when he continued his journey in the USSR, or at the very least hold back enough not to anger his hosts, who subsequently helped Castro consolidate his four-year rapprochement with the Soviet Union. Despite the frustrations he had aired to Altamirano about how "slow moving" the Soviets were, Castro's June visit produced concrete results, in the shape of membership in the Soviet bloc's Council for Mutual Economic Assistance and five new major treaties deferring debt repayments, increasing trade, and establishing a new flow of economic assistance to the island.[103] As Castro insisted, this did not mean Cuba was turning its back on economic development through Latin American integration, but rather that the inadequacies of regional integration gave him no choice. As he put it, Latin America's "hour of the revolution" had not yet arrived.[104]

Cuba's archrivals in the hemisphere, Brazil and the United States, happily tended to agree with this appraisal and were now looking for ways to ensure Latin America's "hour" *never* arrived. And toward the end of the year they began detecting positive signs. By September, for example, Brazil's foreign minister remarked to U.S. secretary of state William Rogers that the Southern Cone's revolutionary "snowball had been reversed." Chile's road to socialism looked increasingly as if it was nearing its end and, as Médici had earlier, he commented that Chile in 1972 resembled João Goulart's final days in 1964. By this stage, the Brazilians were also far calmer about the situation in Bolivia, where increasing U.S. assistance had been effective in helping to consolidate Banzer's position. In addition, Gibson Barbosa reflected on the "much improved" situation in Uruguay. At their meeting in June, the Brazilian president had already indicated to Connally that Juan María Bordaberry's government "had taken hold very well and was manifesting a strong hand with respect to the terrorist problem."[105] Now, three months later, Barbosa celebrated the fact that the Tupamaros' leadership had "virtually disappeared" following a government crackdown with Brazilian and Argentine help (in just three months, Uruguay's civilian-military regime took 2,600 prisoners, while a considerable number of Tupamaros sought exile in Chile).[106]

With more obvious Cold War battles in the Southern Cone going well, the Nixon administration finally began reappraising its policy toward Peru in September 1972. In June, Connally had told Peruvian foreign minister Miguel Angel de la Flor that there was a "tremendous reservoir of good will" toward Peru in the United States. However, given Connally's intransigent position on expropriation and the Peruvians' continued insistence that as far as they were concerned the International Petroleum Company case was settled, there had been no significant improvement of relations during this visit. As Foreign Minister de la Flor had told Connally, Peru also had the "best of good will" when it came to resolving issues with the United States, as long as this was in keeping with the "concept of [the] revolutionary government's standards of sovereignty, independence and the humanist goals of its programs." In expressing his hope that the United States would see fit to help Peruvians achieve their "new goal of social justice for all," he had also underlined socialist countries were "interested and cooperating through new and generous credits."[107] Indeed, on the surface, the prognosis for winning back U.S. influence in the country had not been good. Moreover, analysts in the United States observed that Moscow was trying to expand its role and undermine Washington's ties to the region through the "creation of an atmosphere of hostility" vis-à-vis the United States and Peru.[108]

And yet when U.S. policy makers studied how they might be able to reduce the Soviets' chances of success in late 1972, they found that Lima's leaders were actually very interested in repairing relations with the United States. And in the United States, the Interdepartmental Group for Latin America noted a number of very good reasons for reciprocating. Specifically, National Security Study Memorandum 158, completed at the end of September 1972, listed the Nixon administration's goals as including the "enhancement of the U.S. image as a power prepared to support responsible reform and to accept diverse approaches to achieving such reform," "limitation of Chile's influence as a model for other countries," and "stemming the growth of Soviet, Cuban and PRC influence in the Hemisphere."

In pursuit of these objectives, its authors advocated reducing economic sanctions that Washington had applied against Peru since IPC's expropriation three years earlier on the grounds that this had made Peru more independent and anti-American rather than less so.[109] Intelligence analysts also suggested that it was a good time to act because the Peruvians had gained only limited assistance from socialist countries and were therefore looking more favorably on private investment. Lima "needs and wants more from the U.S.," they concluded.[110]

In considering the prospect of trying to improve relations with Lima, Washington officials homed in on the negative impact this would have on Allende's Chile. As the Interdepartmental Group noted, there were clear benefits to approaching Peru and Chile differently. "The threat to all our interests, including the investment interest," NSSM 158's authors argued, "is manifestly greater in Marxist Chile than it is in non-Marxist Peru. . . . Differentiation would deprive the Allende Government of the politically useful 'protective cover' that being lumped with Peru would provide, thus making a hard line on Chile more readily accepted elsewhere." Moreover, U.S. analysts concluded that the "prospects for limiting Chile's influence on Peru" were "good," on account of a historic rivalry between both countries and the Peruvian military's inherent suspicion of Chile's Marxist policies.[111] Thus, when the SRG met at the end of 1972, Nixon deferred ending all sanctions on Lima but agreed to new initiatives to resolve the IPC case with a view to being able to ease pressure against Peru. Military assistance to Peru consequently jumped from $0.7 million in fiscal year 1973 to $15.9 million the following year. Furthermore, in 1973 Nixon would send to Lima a special representative, Jim Greene, who successfully negotiated a full settlement of the IPC crisis the following year worth $150 million, thereby paving the way for Washington to end all economic sanctions on Peru.[112]

Overall, U.S. policy toward Latin America had therefore shifted in late 1972 as a result of Washington's efforts to isolate Chilean, Cuban, and Soviet influence in the hemisphere. When U.S.-Chilean relations had begun attracting worldwide attention and got entangled in a North-South struggle, the Nixon administration had tactically retreated and had altered its approach to Latin American Third Worldists. This reorientation dovetailed with changes in the region that took place around the same time. Following UNCTAD III's disappointments and in the context of the USSR's failure to meet their development needs, regional leaders became increasingly accommodating. Washington did not actually have to deliver any significant assistance in this context—as Letelier argued, Nixon's record of helping developing nations revealed "serious transgressions" from his promises of "action for progress."[113] Yet with no satisfactory alternatives, countries such as Mexico and Peru ultimately opted for a special relationship with the United States instead of relying on collective confrontation through slow-moving international forums. Indeed, having wobbled for the past few years, the inter-American balance of power seemed to be moving decidedly back in the United States' favor.

What is more, although the prospect of revolutionary change within Chile was still alive, it was faltering and increasingly isolated in the Southern Cone. While the inter-American Cold War that had expanded beyond Chile appeared to have been largely won, it was now closing in and gathering force within the country itself. Compared to Peru, Santiago faced far greater obstacles when it came to straddling Cold War divides in an effort to get outside help. Indeed, despite Chilean initiatives, there would be no presidential summit between Nixon and Allende, as there had been with Echeverría and Médici; no high-level visit along the lines of Connally's trips to Venezuela, Colombia, Peru, Bolivia, and Brazil; and no policy review like the one conducted with regard to Peru. As one U.S. banker quite plainly told one of Allende's representatives in New York, Chile could not possibly hope to receive help from the capitalist world to attain what he referred to as its "ideological aspirations."[114] Astute as this advice may have been, it had not necessarily filtered through to Allende's inner foreign policy circle as the UP faced painful choices about how to assert Chile's independence toward the end of the year.

What Now?

In August 1972 Allende had asked Letelier to draw up recommendations about how to deal with the United States and how to resolve the government's financial problems. The analysis of Chile's international position that Letelier drew up was far more pessimistic than anything he had submitted before. As the ambassador saw it, if the UP could not avoid a confrontation with the United States, it would simply not survive. The UP's political future, he insisted, depended on resolving Chile's financial difficulties by seeking international assistance. Specifically, he calculated that Chile needed an immediate injection of approximately $300 million and would have to try and scrape the amount together from a variety of sources simultaneously (capitalist, socialist, European, Japanese, South and North American) to get it. Without a doubt, the key to success was unfortunately the United Sates. As Letelier stressed, 25 percent of Chile's overall supplies, 50 percent of its industrial supplies, and most of its military supplies came from the United States. He also highlighted the socialist countries' reticence about undermining détente to help Chile and suggested that instead of using the United States as a scapegoat, Allende's only hope was to enter into serious bilateral negotiations with it.[115] As he put it on 6 September in a personal letter to Foreign Minister Almeyda, he did not foresee how Chile could "confront . . . serious financial problems with any success and simultaneously face an economic and financial confrontation with the United States." At a moment when things were becoming far tougher "on all sides" for the Chileans, he urged the UP to consider more tactical efforts at compromise to postpone an overt U.S.-Chilean conflict.[116]

Despite its sense of urgency, Letelier's advice, which was laid out in full in two lengthy memorandums he sent back home in August and September 1972, was not all that dissimilar to his earlier recommendations.[117] But it did seem to underscore an increasingly obvious failure: Chile now appeared to be *more* dependent on the United States than it had been before Allende's election. Because of this, the far Left within the UP was especially angered by what Letelier was proposing, namely that the Chileans put all their energies into negotiating a way out of its difficulties by making a deal with Washington and therefore tying their future to the United States.

A few months earlier, Allende had tried to improve the UP's economic strategies by dismissing his controversial minister of the economy and appointing the more pragmatic Communist, Orlando Millas.[118] In part, the move had been an effort to placate the Soviets, to show the socialist bloc countries that Chile now had a grasp of the economy, and to persuade them to offer Chile more assistance. By August, however, Allende was warning supporters about the inadequacies of Soviet bloc aid to meet Chile's economic needs. As he had lamented, socialist credits for industrial investment and future economic development would take "two or three years" to be effective.[119] Indeed, Moscow's relationship with Santiago was evolving too slowly when it came to the rapidly changing situation within Chile.

Unbeknownst to the Chileans, the Soviet leadership was also increasingly disdainful of the UP's performance. A report written by the Latin American Institute at Moscow's Academy of Sciences in mid-1972 had described the Chilean situation as "uncertain and unstable" and had predicted the months ahead would be "agitated and tense." The UP had only partial political power, its authors argued, and Chilean parties had no fixed ideas or immediate means or potentials for launching Chile on a road to socialism.[120] In fact, in the context of disturbances between left-wing supporters in Concepción back in May, the Soviet Union's ambassador in Santiago had called all Soviet bloc ambassadors in the capital together to discuss the "deep crisis" developing within the UP. A month later, the East German ambassador had reported back to Berlin that left-wing Chilean unity remained a problem and was likely to remain one for the foreseeable future. To be sure, he noted that the UP's composition had changed and that the PCCh was making concerted efforts to curb "adventurism." But, overall, he lamented the growing divergence between the Communist and Socialist parties, caused by the "outright lack of maturity" and discipline within the PS itself.[121] Then, in October 1972, the Soviets downgraded their definition of Chile from a country "building socialism" to a Third World nation seeking "free and independent development on the path of democracy and progress."[122]

For their part, however, Allende's inner circle tended to concentrate on global developments rather than internal developments when explaining the Soviets' lack of interest in offering more meaningful assistance. As Letelier pointed out, Chile's timing in seeking more assistance from the East was bad. One only had to recognize that for "tactical and strategic reasons on both sides," the world was "living through a moment of convergence and understanding between the United States and socialist countries," which meant that Chile could not expect to receive the same type and amount of financial help from the Soviet bloc that it might otherwise have.[123] Allende's curious decision to send the anti-Soviet Socialist, Carlos Altamirano, to the USSR just one month after Nixon's summit with Brezhnev must also not have helped win over the Soviet leadership, suspicious as it was of far Left "extremists" hijacking the Chilean revolutionary process.[124]

Even so, as the Soviets dragged their feet, Chile was in ever greater need of hard-currency loans to cover its balance-of-payments deficit. In conversation with a U.S. Embassy official, a Chilean lawyer with contacts in the UP government described Orlando Millas as an "astute and able man" who recognized the USSR would not necessarily be as forthcoming as hoped: "[Millas] realizes that Chile's economic problems are grave and that a solution will require credit from abroad. The extent to which this help will be provided by the Soviet Union is limited . . . the only alternative, therefore, is for Chile to restore its financial relations with the West, particularly the U.S. Millas, who like most Chilean Communists is above all a pragmatist, will have no ideological difficulty in moving in this direction . . . [and] realizes that the kind of financial relations he desires will not be possible unless there is progress in solving outstanding bilateral economic problems between Chile and the U.S."[125] Although himself a Socialist, Letelier offered a similar assessment, reasoning that given the state of world politics, socialist countries would be more likely to increase their assistance to the UP if Chile first repaired relations with developed countries in the West. As he saw things in August and September 1972, hopes of seeking benefits from contradictions between capitalist countries were futile because of the growing interdependency between them. He thus urged the Chileans to transcend the deadlock in U.S.-Chilean relations by pushing for a meaningful compromise.[126]

The three obvious questions Letelier's proposals raised were, first, whether the Nixon administration would be at all receptive to the idea of meaningful bilateral negotiations; second, what exactly the Chileans could ask for in return for certain compromises; and, finally, whether he could persuade the whole of the fractious UP coalition—and particularly the Socialist Party—that this was the best course forward. By late 1972, it seemed clear to Chilean diplomats that the United States was "playing dirty." Chilean properties in the United States had been ransacked, and its diplomats were so worried about being under surveillance that they were using voice distorters during telephone conversations or conducting conversations outdoors.[127] The Chilean Embassy in Washington had also been burgled in May, and although intruders had ignored valuables, they had stolen a list of subscriptions to embassy publications and four radios that staff had been using to muffle sensitive conversations. Indeed, the Chileans suspected the U.S. government and/or multinationals were behind the robbery, especially when a similar burglary took place at the Watergate complex a month later.[128]

Even so, Letelier was now insisting that the UP still had a slight window of opportunity before things got even worse. To some extent, his appreciation of the severe deterioration of Chile's position was conditioned by his exaggerated faith in Kissinger's reassurances the previous year. Yet, it was also clear that Allende was running out of options when it came to avoiding confrontation with the United States over compensation claims. Looking ahead to what they expected would be the Chilean Special Copper Tribunal's rejection of Anaconda's appeal on the "excess profits" ruling, Chilean diplomats had been trying to keep Chile's international options open by rescheduling debt repayments with other Paris Club creditors as quickly as possible (and not always as satisfactorily as more time might have allowed).[129] As Letelier forewarned, the tribunal's pronouncement was likely to undercut the Chileans' chances of receiving credits from international organizations, U.S. government organizations, and private banks. He also observed that those in Washington who were happy to wait until Chile's economic problems overtook the UP—those who, in Letelier's words, appeared happy to wait until "fruit ripened and fell from the tree"—were also a growing minority in Washington. And because Letelier predicted that Nixon's widely expected reelection would allow him to pursue a harder line toward Chile, the ambassador called on his government to seize the moment before U.S. presidential elections on 7 November to improve relations with the United States. The Nixon administration would not want to appear to be intervening in Chile before this date, and he also had indications from Washington officials that the United States wanted to sit down and talk.[130]

So what did Letelier propose that the Chileans should talk *about*? What is particularly interesting—and surprising—about the proposals that he sent to Almeyda is the sheer scope of issues that he suggested his government could negotiate. Not only did he propose asking for understanding, but he now also suggested Santiago might request *assistance* from the United States to help Chile's ailing economy and, by implication, La Vía Chilena. In concrete terms, this involved ensuring that Washington cooperated in debt negotiations and modified existing U.S. policy (e.g., by securing agreement from the administration that it would not apply sanctions as stipulated by the González Amendment and that it would normalize trade as well as AID and Eximbank credits). It also involved requesting a $50 million credit to help Chile's balance-of-payments problem and a further $50 million for foodstuffs under the United States' PL-480 credits. Moreover, Letelier indicated that the Chileans could not hope to receive this assistance for nothing. Instead, he proposed that the Chilean government should consider international arbitration to resolve the gridlock with private copper companies, that it should be prepared to pay off the Cerro copper corporation and examine a way of paying Anaconda, that it could offer a moratorium on nationalizing further U.S. investments in Chile, that it could review ITT's case, and that it would commit itself to not accentuating ideological differences with the United States by ensuring that the media under its control did not harden its anti-American posture.[131] These were hardly small concessions. In no uncertain terms, Letelier was proposing taking considerable steps backward when it came to asserting

Chile's independence vis-à-vis the United States as a means of helping the UP survive.

Unsurprisingly, Letelier's proposals caused immense controversy even when presented to the government in a watered-down and most basic form by Foreign Minister Almeyda. After three long and arduous meetings in September 1972 between the UP's Economic Committee of Ministers and the UP's party leaders, Almeyda wrote to Letelier that the matter was a difficult one and that its "result would at worst end up making conflict [with the United States] even more difficult to resolve." Both the ambassador and Almeyda had always recognized that the task of persuading certain members of the government coalition would be difficult. Furthermore, the PS's leader, Carlos Altamirano, had already voiced opposition to a similar suggestion only months before Letelier formally re-proposed negotiating with the United States in September 1972.[132] Now, even though Almeyda had refrained from suggesting that the UP be prepared to compromise on ITT and despite promising that the issue of compensation would be non-negotiable, Altamirano expressed palpable contempt for negotiations. He vehemently criticized what he called the UP's "bland" policy toward the United States, its failure to denounce Washington, and its lack of preparation when it came to mobilizing Chile's population to face a confrontation with the United States.

Indeed, when it came to Chile's relations with the United States, the government was clearly severed in two. On one side the Communist Party; the Radical Party; Chile's newest economics minister, Carlos Matus; and Gonzalo Martner were among those who agreed that Chile should negotiate meaningfully in good faith even though they were rather pessimistic about what could be achieved. On the other side, ex–economics minister Pedro Vuskovic, MAPU, and Altamirano were unsympathetic and opposed to negotiations, fearing that they would force Chile to relinquish its stance on compensation. Allende had to break the deadlock, which he did when he voted to approve negotiations.[133]

In October 1972 the UP approached talks with the United States through gritted teeth. Need rather than desire pushed it toward such an approach. And rather than Santiago setting the agenda for bilateral discussions as Letelier had hoped, troublesome intragovernmental divisions were holding the Chileans back and attaching heavy weights to the process. As UP officials deliberated, they stalled, and as they did, U.S.-Chilean relations deteriorated even further.[134] As predicted, a major reason for this was the Special Copper Tribunal's final decision to uphold Allende's "excess profits" ruling. With it, the atmosphere of crisis in Chile got worse, and Allende's negotiating position weakened as Kennecott halted copper shipments to Europe.

In contrast to the Chileans, the U.S. administration was in a highly advantageous position. Washington did not need the negotiations in the same way as the Chileans did, instead regarding them as being a useful alternative to confrontation—a way of tying Chilean officials into a drawn-out process with no promises of concessions. In September and October, as Letelier had predicted, U.S. officials presented themselves as being highly amenable to starting talks, albeit under their own terms and conditions and safe in the knowledge that their interlocutors needed them more than the United States needed Chile.

Discussions about how to even begin negotiations were slow and tense. In early October, Chile's Foreign Ministry responded to a U.S. note that insisted compensation be a prerequisite for opening bilateral talks by delivering an angry reply filled with frustration and recrimination, more characteristic of Altamirano's stance than Letelier's proposals. Specifically, it underlined Allende's strict adherence to constitutional procedures, rejected any prospect of overturning Allende's "excess profits" ruling (and hence Chilean diplomatic procedures), and accused the Nixon administration explicitly of "economic aggression" and "incomprehension and hostility."[135] Indeed, Davis was so worried that the note's language could lead to open confrontation, he secretly (and successfully) begged UP representatives to consider rewording it.[136]

Ultimately, both Allende and the Nixon administration wanted to avoid open conflict.[137] On the U.S. side, this meant lessening the prospect of angering domestic audiences on the eve of an election or alienating international public opinion and Allende's Latin American and Third World sympathizers at the very moment that Washington was trying to extricate itself from the Vietnam War. On the Chilean side, it was about the very survival of La Vía Chilena as both an economic and political project. And despite intense opposition to even the prospect of sitting down and opening discussions with the Americans, not to mention growing fears of U.S. intervention in Chile, Allende had fewer and fewer alternatives.

At home, the Chilean government was urgently struggling to retain control of La Vía Chilena as a three-week truckers' strike in October paralyzed the country. Although the UP blamed U.S. imperialism for fueling the strike, Washington does not seem to have directed the campaign, which was heterogeneous and, at least initially, not led by the parties the CIA was funding.[138] However, the financial support it offered to the private sector (to give it "confidence") *was* undoubtedly channeled to strikers. Certainly, Santiago became flooded with dollars, and the 40 Committee acknowledged that its assistance to the private sector was helping to "dramatize" Allende's challenges.[139]

The strike aside, U.S. diplomats were particularly keen to "reduce friction" between the UP's two leading opposition parties, the National Party and Christian Democrat Party, with a view to improving their chances in Chile's forthcoming congressional elections scheduled for March 1973.[140] In this respect, they received promising signs of an evolving two-sided antigovernment front; as one CIA official called it, Chile faced a "good-guys-versus-bad-guys" battle.[141] Washington also kept an eye on the military balance of power and escalating violence in the country, although it by no means controlled it. As a member of the Nationalist Party confided to a CIA officer, although it—and, by association and funds, the United States—had "financed and created" the right-wing Patria y Libertad, the paramilitary group had gotten "too big for its britches" and was out of control.[142]

Meanwhile, as far as the armed forces were concerned, the CIA continued to monitor plotters and had penetrated a group of them but refrained from pushing it toward any action.[143] But it was not just the United States that was monitoring the escalating probability of some sort of violent confrontation in the country. In September, the PCCh's leader, Luis Corvalán, had warned the Soviet ambassador in Santiago that a coup was a "real danger."[144] In fact, leaders of all political persuasions had been warning of civil war or a military coup for months.[145] Speaking to university students at the end of August 1972, Allende had described himself as "horrified" by both prospects. "Although we would win . . . and we would have to win" a civil war, he ambiguously proclaimed, the president warned that "generations" would be scarred and Chile's "economy, human coexistence and human respect" would be destroyed.[146] Yet students, women, and paramilitary groups had continued to mobilize while sabotage attacks on the country's infrastructure had multiplied.[147] Then, during the October strike, factory workers formed what became known as *cordones industriales* (industrial belts) around cities to maintain Chile's industrial output, to secure control of state-owned properties, and, crucially, to organize their military defense.

Overall, the October strike demonstrated very well how intertwined the UP's economic, political, and military challenges were becoming, even if

Allende refused to accept the prospect of armed struggle. The battle to secure international economic assistance, which Letelier was so preoccupied with as a result of his vantage point in Washington, was also only one of two key factors that would determine Chile's future. And with respect to the second—the ability to resist a violent confrontation with counter-revolutionary forces—the UP was even more divided as to what to do. The Cubans were particularly frustrated with the ill-defined nature of preparations for what they considered to be an inevitable armed confrontation. In a handwritten letter to Allende in September 1972, Castro underscored Cuba's disposition to increase its assistance and its "willingness to help in any way." "Though we are conscious of the current difficulties faced by Chile's revolutionary process," he wrote, "we are confident you will find the way to overcome these. . . . You can rely on our full cooperation." Trying to evoke the image of Allende as a military commander, Castro signed off by sending the Chilean president a "fraternal and revolutionary salute."[148]

When Allende ended the truckers' strike by bringing the armed forces into government, he also took a huge risk in politicizing military leaders and making their cooperation central to La Vía Chilena's survival. As the general secretary of the PCCh would later tell East Germany's leader, Erich Honecker, the decision was first and foremost Allende's although the Communist Party had to help him resist strong criticism of such a move from the PS. As a result of the move, however, Corvalán recounted Allende as being "optimistic" about the future and the prospect that the UP's parties would do well in the March 1973 elections.[149] In many respects, this move nevertheless ended the Chilean road to socialism and began the road to militarism.[150]

By this stage, those within the PS's military apparatus had appreciated that coup-minded military leaders—*golpistas*—were influenced and inspired by their contemporaries in Brazil.[151] To be sure, the *golpistas* increasingly believed the military had a vital role to play in defending Chile against Marxism and that political parties could ultimately only slow down the installation of a Marxist dictatorship, whereas the military could stop it altogether. Certainly, the leader of coup plotting in mid-1972, General Alfredo Canales, also subscribed to this idea, which was enshrined in the National Security Doctrine that Brazil's military leaders adhered to. However, left-wing Chileans later admitted that the UP as a whole did not spend time studying the nature of thinking within military circles or the Chileanization of inter-American trends.[152] Moreover, far Left groups of Chileans and the Cubans, both of which were closely monitoring the growing threat of a possible coup, seem to have failed to grasp the extent—or even the relevance—of Brazil's direct interest in, symbolism for, or relations with Chile's armed forces.[153] Chile, after all, was different, with the majority of the armed forces still considered to be constitutionally minded defenders of Chilean democracy.

However, Chile's uniqueness was becoming increasingly blurred. Just as Chilean events had intensified the inter-American Cold War in the Southern Cone in 1970, regional developments were now spilling over into Chile. The UP's relationship with revolutionary movements beyond its borders was, on at least one occasion, diplomatically unhelpful. On 15 August 1972, Argentine political prisoners belonging to the Ejército Revolucionario del Pueblo (Revolutionary Army of the People, or ERP) broke out of the "Rawson" jail in Chubut, Argentina's southern province. Having made it to Trelew airport, they commandeered an Austral BAC 111 flight that had landed from Buenos Aires with ninety-two passengers on board and demanded that it fly them to Chile, where they then requested asylum.[154] This provided the UP's opposition with evidence of links to "foreign extremism" and, in addition, temporarily damaged Allende's working relationship with Argentina when he resolved the crisis by sending the prisoners to Cuba.[155]

More broadly, as the last remaining safe haven for the Left in the Southern Cone, Chile was increasingly becoming a destination of curiosity, refuge, and solidarity for revolutionaries around the region. Reliable evidence also suggests that, in some cases, Latin American revolutionaries received armed training in Chilean camps.[156] By the end of 1972, there were Uruguayan Tupamaros and approximately one thousand Brazilian left-wing exiles in Chile.[157] In late 1972, the MIR's leader, Miguel Enríquez, convened an ultrasecret meeting in southern Chile of the MIR, the Chilean branch of the ELN, the ERP, and the Tupamaros to discuss working together toward mutual revolutionary objectives. Primarily, the group, which would become known as the Junta Coordinadora Revolucionaria a year later, focused on how to respond to the counterrevolutionary offensive it faced so as to conserve forces for a future offensive of its own.[158] It is unclear whether Allende had any knowledge of this, and from what we know of his relationship with the MIR by this point, he certainly would not have approved of its role in acting outside the UP in this way. Yet he *did* personally know and meet Latin American revolutionary leaders while serving as president, including Tupamaro leaders who joined his intimate Chilean and Cuban friends for weekends at "El Cañaveral," La Paya's weekend home.[159]

Indeed, however exaggerated it might have been, the opposition's mantra that accused Allende of letting foreign revolutionaries into the country was not without some basis. Chile was increasingly becoming a theater of the inter-American Cold War on whose stage a whole cast of actors from the Southern Cone, the United States, Cuba, the Soviet Union (though far less so), and Europe (both East and West) assumed positions against each other and as sponsors of their divided Chilean allies. On one level, Frei warned the U.S. ambassador in Santiago about the "growth and arming of Socialist, Communist and Left extremist paramilitary brigades" and claimed that "Bolivian exiles, Cubans, Eastern Europeans and other leftist foreigners" were working for Chile's intelligence services.[160] On another level, the Cubans insisted that Allende had to take greater stock of the military balance of power within the country (and admit the necessity of bringing the militarily more prepared MIR on board to defend Allende's presidency) to counteract a foreign-backed plot to overthrow him.

Ultimately, as the Chilean documentary maker Patricio Guzmán noted in his film of the same name, the October strike was the start of a decisive "Battle for Chile" that would end on 11 September 1973. The international dimensions of that battle, to date not fully understood, helped determine how it would develop, complementing, sponsoring, or inspiring the Chileans at the center of the story. As the United States funneled covert support to Allende's opposition parties, Brazil's military regime provided a model for *golpistas* within the armed forces, the Soviet Union stood on the sidelines reluctant to help the Communist Party solve Chile's economic woes, and Havana continued to urge Allende to contemplate how he would militarily defend his government in the event of a coup. As he listened to this conflicting advice, Allende managed to regain control of the country by resolving the strike and relying on the military's institutional support. Yet, as his former economics minister Pedro Vuskovic remarked, "the problem of power" remained "unresolved."[161] This was not merely a question of the government's "power" vis-à-vis the opposition but rather of who was ultimately going to be in control of Chile's revolutionary process. And as the government's painstaking deliberations about how to approach the United States demonstrate, the UP coalition that had brought Allende to the presidency was unraveling. Given these circumstances, the president decided it was time for him to take matters into his own hands.

Conclusion

The international environment that Allende encountered two years after he assumed the presidency was unhelpful. By this point, the Chilean government acknowledged that détente did not apply to Latin America and that the United States still had ideological prejudices when it came to dealing with the region. As Letelier wrote to Almeyda, "It is . . . not a mystery that the White House's preferences lie with the governments that favor private investment and attack any 'Marxist' shoot. The cases of Brazil and Mexico . . . do not need more commentary." When asked for an analysis of the approach to Latin America that a second Nixon administration might take, Letelier concluded:

> The current administration has been characterized by the practical thaw regarding certain socialist nations. This could be interpreted as a favorable signal for Chile, if the White House's policies toward Yugoslavia or Romania were applicable to Latin America. However, the result of the election in Chile in September 1970 notably displeased Nixon. Dr Kissinger's declarations about the "domino theory" for Latin America (September 1970), the absence of a protocol greeting to President Allende and the president's own declarations that the new Chilean government "was not to his liking" but that "he accepted it" as a matter of respect for the Chilean people's will, reveal serious and profoundly different reservations from what can be found with other socialist nations located outside the continent.[162]

Although the Nixon administration was caught up in the high-level diplomacy of détente during 1972, this did not mean Washington ignored the hemisphere. The U.S. president was star-struck by his summit meetings with Mao and Brezhnev and, as we now know from the Nixon White House tapes, condescending toward Latin America's "importance" in this context.[163] Yet, he remained preoccupied with fighting the Cold War in the region, and U.S. policy makers continued to be concerned about how events south of their borders affected the United States' credibility as a superpower and the strength of its ideological convictions. As Connally had reported to Médici, Nixon "was hopeful that a long period of peace could be achieved as long as the United States remained strong and had the support of the countries of the free world such as Brazil."[164] Indeed, global politics may have been shifting away from the certainties of an earlier bipolar Cold War era, but this did not mean Nixon and Kissinger were willing to relinquish control. Thus, when Nixon urged the Mexican president to let his message triumph above Castro's in Latin America, he hoped not only that this would help ward off the "poison" of Chilean and Cuban influence but that his counterpart would contribute to spreading U.S. ideals of capitalist economic progress and its prescriptions of order in the hemisphere.

In return, Echeverría urged the U.S. president "for a whole new shaping or recasting of American policy vis-à-vis Latin America."[165] President Misael Pastrana of Colombia also urged the United States to "pay greater attention to [the] underdeveloped world and demonstrate less apathy toward Latin America" when he had met Connally in June.[166] In fact, beyond Allende and Castro, others clearly worried about the drift in the United States' commitment to regional development. What is more, by the late 1960s and early 1970s economic nationalists on the left and right viewed security not only in terms of external strategic threats but also increasingly in terms of economic stability. In this respect, many of the hemisphere's armed forces increasingly regarded themselves as needing to play a key role in politics because, for them, defending their countries was a geo-economic as well as a traditionally geostrategic question.[167] Within Chile, this was also the case, especially as there was an obvious contradiction between the claims of a government that purported to be bringing independence and sovereignty and the reality of growing indications that the UP was leading Chile to precarious dependency on external sources of funding.

Although Allende's message had inspired other nations in the global South, the UP's unique socialist democratic experiment therefore found itself increasingly out on a limb in late 1972. As UNCTAD's former secretary Gamani Corea noted, the organization's Third World members were ultimately more concerned with links to industrial nations in the East and West than with global bodies as a means of accelerating their countries' development.[168] And while other nationalists defaulted to traditional vertical patterns of trade and aid, reaping the benefits of the United States' growing efforts to work out bilateral solutions with key countries, this denied Allende the commonality of purpose and solidarity he sought in pursuit of his revolutionary aims.

Meanwhile, Chilean boldness in 1972 reaffirmed the Nixon administration's belief that Allende was anti-American, economically dangerous, and ideologically repellent. For Washington, then, bilateral U.S.-Chilean negotiations were purely pragmatic. Fighting for victory meant employing tactical retreat, and by this point Washington—as well as Santiago—was clear that it did not want a painful divorce that would undercut its ultimate objectives. For now, Allende stood at a crossroads of success, survival, failure, and disaster, and the UP had yet to prove that La Vía Chilena was a viable revolutionary process or adjust Chile's position more effectively to global realities.

Looking to the year ahead, Chile's population would have the chance to deliver its verdict on the government in congressional elections scheduled for March. If the UP's parties were going to do well, they had to improve the country's economic situation, but this was a tall order given the rapid nature of Chile's economic decline. In November it was expected that Chile's deficit would reach $430 million by the end of the year. And, by Letelier's calculations, if the economy was to function relatively normally, the UP needed to raise at least $100 million by January and a further $400 million or more during the course of 1973.[169] Would bilateral negotiations with the United States be enough? Clearly, Allende thought not. Indeed, in a dramatic gesture, he was preparing to leave Chile in search of an international cure for his beleaguered presidency.

6 CROSSROADS
Incomprehension and Dead Ends, November 1972–July 1973

In late November 1972 Salvador Allende set off on an international tour that took him from Mexico City to Havana via New York, Algiers, and Moscow. In many respects, the trip was a gamble—a somewhat uncoordinated effort both to improve Chile's position before its representatives sat down to bilateral negotiations with the United States in December and to boost the UP parties' chances in Chile's forthcoming congressional elections. The journey also encapsulated the different strands of Chilean foreign policy, which since 1970 had aimed to protect La Vía Chilena and to promote systemic change on behalf of the global South. During his trip, Allende simultaneously appealed to Latin Americans, the Third World, the UN, the Soviet Union, Cuban revolutionaries, and, at least indirectly, the Nixon administration. His country's experience, he told the United Nations General Assembly, was the epitome of a justified battle against imperialism for "social liberation, the struggle for well-being and intellectual progress, and the defense of national identity and dignity."[1]

The problem was that Allende was now clearly losing this battle. Nixon's anticipated and triumphant reelection as president of the United States offered no relief to U.S. pressure against his government. Two years after his inauguration, Chile also appeared to be an example of ineluctable dependency and an unworkable road to socialism rather than an alternative road to development or a shining beacon of independence and peaceful revolution. Given this predicament, the Chilean president was not running rings around Uncle Sam as depicted in a Cuban cartoon at the time; he and his divided government were struggling to prevent a net closing in on his presidency by acting on several different fronts at the same time. Chile's foreign policy, it seemed, was now increasingly subsumed in a struggle to acquire financial assistance.

The key questions were how, from whom, and how much. On the eve of Allende's international tour, the Chilean ambassador at the United Nations tried to warn his U.S. counterpart that the whole of Latin America was expectantly watching the evolution of relations between Washington and Santiago as a test of whether Nixon would work out a relationship with the region comparable to the "excellent" ones it now had with the Soviet Union, China, and Western Europe.[2] As far as the Nixon administration was concerned, however, Allende no longer posed the threat he had once appeared to. Since 1970, the revolutionary tide that had seemed poised to wash over the Southern Cone had ebbed and, with it, Chile's potential impact on the inter-American balance of power had diminished. Furthermore, Washington's intelligence analysts were relatively relaxed about Allende's trip in late 1972, believing that the Soviets were now rather unlikely to bail the UP out of its deteriorating economic predicament and that the Chilean president was unlikely to achieve any miracle cures for the economic and political crisis facing the UP.[3]

At least some within the UP nevertheless still held out hope that Moscow *would* substantially help solve their economic woes. And in an effort to try and persuade the Soviets to rethink their reticence to help Chile, Allende's tone changed. Acknowledging that efforts to avoid Cold War categorizations had failed to obtain more support from the superpowers in an age of détente, Santiago now tried a bit of reverse psychology: it tried to *play* a Cold War game at a global level to induce the Soviet bloc to help. In Washington Chilean diplomats therefore tried to suggest that Allende was on the verge of being pushed to the East, whereas in Moscow Allende explicitly depicted Chile's experience as a new Cold War battlefield. Indeed, borrowing Pablo Neruda's phrase at the time, he called his country a "silent Vietnam."[4] Yet his rhetoric did not fit the times. By the end of 1972, the Soviets' priority was reducing tensions with the United States as the Vietnam War drew to a close, not beginning another similar international conflict. Moscow's own economic problems and increasing financial commitment to Cuba after mid-1972 meant that it was also not prepared (or able) to bankroll the Chilean economy. Moreover, for at least six months, the USSR's leaders had increasingly been viewing La Vía Chilena as a lesson of what could go wrong in a revolutionary process rather than a good investment in a global battle against capitalism. In the end, Allende thus returned to Chile disappointed, becoming ever more reliant on negotiation with the United States as a means of solving his economic ills.

In fact, all the while that Allende was touring foreign capitals, the Chilean Foreign Ministry had been preparing for bilateral talks with the United

States, which began in December and dragged on without any decisive end in sight. And, as such, Washington was becoming far more central to Chile than Allende had ever hoped it would be. While the Nixon administration refused to countenance any financial settlement with Santiago to ease its balance-of-payments deficit, it also continued to exacerbate the UP's challenges back home, actively subverting the democratic process, encouraging Allende's parliamentary opposition, and sympathizing with military plotters.

Although in this respect, U.S.-Chilean bilateral negotiations seem to have been rather hopeless endeavors, they are intriguing insofar as they provided space for both sides to articulate the reasons why they opposed each other. As negotiators ostensibly fenced over questions of compensation and debt, the underlying obstacles to mutual understanding and progress surfaced. The Chilean government and the Nixon administration quite simply disagreed about the merits of capitalism and the world economic system. While U.S. officials plainly told Santiago's representatives that they had developed the best political and economic system worldwide, the Chileans told them that although they were committed democrats, they had this wrong. Consequently, although U.S. and Soviet or Chinese leaders had agreed to disagree across the Pacific, the Americans and the Chileans were still trying to explain their differences to each other.

Playing for Time and Sympathy

In the weeks before Allende left Chile, his forthcoming venture had divided his already splintered government. Exactly what the trip would achieve appeared uncertain. Chilean diplomats argued about the effect it could have on relations with the United States, where Nixon had now been emboldened by his recent reelection; they questioned which visits would reap the maximum benefit, East to West or West to East; and they debated what, if any, impact the trip would have on Chilean domestic politics. To a large degree, the answers to these questions depended on differing assessments of how Allende would get on in Moscow. There were some within the UP who clearly believed the president's mere presence in the USSR would cause the Soviets to leap into action and relieve Santiago of its dependency on resolving its problems with the United States. Yet Orlando Letelier, who unsurprisingly remained focused on the pivotal nature of Chile's relationship with the United States, was more skeptical. Even if the USSR suddenly offered Chile substantial assistance, he warned

Foreign Minister Almeyda, this would not be enough to cover the country's balance-of-payments deficits.

He also had good reason to doubt the Soviets' receptiveness to old-fashioned Cold War arguments. Writing to Foreign Minister Almeyda just over two weeks before Allende left Chile, the ambassador relayed an interesting two-hour conversation he had just had with his Soviet counterpart in Washington, Anatoly Dobrynin. The latter, it seems, had requested the meeting and then "insistently" conveyed the USSR's desire to avoid a confrontation with the United States in what was a "new era of international relations." As Letelier surmised, the message had not been "accidental," occurring as it did in the midst of Allende's preparations to visit Moscow.[5]

This was just one of the key issues that arose in a flurry of diplomatic correspondence between Santiago and the Chilean Embassy in Washington during early November. Indeed, the frantic arrangements and disagreements between Allende's advisers on the eve of his trip underlined the UP's ongoing lack of coordinated thinking on foreign policy matters (as well as the lack of presidential direction). As Letelier lamented, he simply did not understand the "philosophy" behind the president's trip and was unsure what purpose it would serve in terms of both Chile's foreign relations and its domestic political context. To be sure, he thought the UN would make a very good "tribunal," which could be used to put pressure on the United States. Yet without any firm consensus in Santiago about whether the UP wanted to confront the United States or negotiate with it, or, indeed, any indication of what the Soviets might offer, it was hard to decide what message Allende should convey. Would it not be easier for the president to go to the Soviet Union first, Letelier asked, so that he would then be able to "calibrate" his UN speech accordingly?

The other pressing issue dominating Chilean diplomatic preparations in the first few weeks of November was whether Allende should take advantage of his visit to New York to seek a meeting with Nixon. Clearly, the message from the Foreign Ministry in Santiago was to try and organize a summit, hoping that it would "impel" a new type of dialogue with the United States. But, as Letelier reminded Almeyda, the prospect was meaningless unless the UP agreed on precisely what the Chileans would bring to the table.[6] In the end, it seems that the foreign minister chose to ignore much of this advice when he instructed Letelier to meet with U.S. ambassador Davis during his brief visit to Chile later that month. Not only was Allende due to travel to Moscow *after* New York, but the Chileans had clearly also decided to gamble on trying to arrange a meeting with Nixon. When the

Chilean ambassador met Davis during his stay in Santiago, he thus told him that the United States and Chile had reached a "crossroads" and that a meeting between Nixon and Allende was a "last chance" to defuse bilateral tensions before relations soured further and Santiago turned East. If Letelier was privately unconvinced by the message he delivered, Davis was unimpressed. He wrote to Secretary of State Rogers that Chile appeared to be playing a misguided Cold War game and offering only "formulas of contact" — "The present Chilean effort has overtones of stage-setting for a repetition of the myth of Castro's 1959 visit to Washington," he argued. "We are already aware of the . . . concept of the 'the last chance' before Chile turns to the East. There is some truth in Letelier's allegation that this trip will be seen as a shift to the socialist camp. He also is probably right when he says it will make things harder. It is sad that the Chilean govt has structured it that way if not with care at least with weeks of tinkling cymbals."[7]

What Letelier did not know was that the State Department had already unequivocally rejected a summit two weeks before he even approached Davis on the grounds that such a meeting would only raise Allende's profile.[8] The department's Bureau of Intelligence and Research concluded that the Chilean president was most likely only trying to attract international sympathy as a "useful backdrop" to prescheduled bilateral talks in December rather than offering anything substantially new. Allende also apparently wanted to improve his chances of renegotiating Chile's debt by shifting "blame" for his economic performance onto "imperialist aggressors."[9] In this context, the administration therefore pressured news agencies to avoid interviewing him.[10]

Despite the Nixon administration's best efforts, however, Allende's speech to the UN General Assembly on 4 December resonated worldwide. According to U.S. news reports, he received a standing ovation similar to those received by the pope and President John Kennedy.[11] During a televised press conference in Mexico before arriving in New York, Allende had promised his speech would be a "call for moral force against injustice similar to the moral effect of calls to end [the] 'Vietnam genocide.'"[12] And once at the UN, he delivered a compelling performance, appealing to the "conscience of the world" and publicizing Chile's "financial strangulation." Allende also detailed the "perversion" of international agencies (being used as individual states' "tools") and denounced multinational corporations that drove "tentacles deep" into sovereign countries while earning obscene profits from the Third World ($1,013 million from Latin America,

$280 million from Africa, $366 million from the Far East, and $64 million from the Middle East). Chile's problems were part of "a long and ominous history in Latin America" of "imperialism and its cruelties," Allende insisted. "Ours is not an isolated or unique problem: it is simply the local manifestation of a reality that goes beyond our frontiers and takes in the Latin American continent and the whole Third World. In varying degrees of intensity and with individual differences, all the peripheral countries are exposed to something of this kind . . . imperialism exists because underdevelopment exists; underdevelopment exists because imperialism exists."[13]

In keeping with the idea of using the UN as a "tribunal," Allende also made a case for his defense. He explained that Chile had been "forced" to adopt a new development model to solve poverty, inequality, and dependency. And he justified his "excess profits" ruling by citing international law and detailing the profits private companies had accrued. He did not explicitly denounce the United States by name, although he proclaimed that Vietnam had "taught the world that the abuse of power saps the moral fiber of the county that misuses it . . . whereas a people defending its independence can be raised to heroic heights by its convictions."[14]

The Nixon administration was affronted by, and unsurprisingly unsympathetic to, Allende's speech. At a last-minute meeting at the Waldorf Hotel between Allende and the U.S. ambassador at the UN, George H. W. Bush, the latter tore Allende's arguments apart. "I told him that we did not consider ourselves 'imperialists' and that we still had a deep conviction that our free enterprise system was not selfish but was the best system—certainly for us, though we had no intention to insist on it for others," Bush recorded. He also told Allende that, although there had been "excesses from time to time," this system did not "bleed" people when it went abroad; "it was the best way to provide a better standard of living for all." Bush then rejected Chile's tactical attempts to distinguish between the U.S. government, U.S. companies, and U.S. people. Owing to a "deep conviction in the free enterprise system," he told Allende, "the people, the government and the system" were "interlocked."[15] If the Chilean president had any hopes of persuading U.S. officials of the merits of his argument or pressuring them into making concessions with his speech, he must have walked away with his hopes shattered.

After leaving New York, Allende stopped, on his way to Moscow, in Algeria, where he met President Houari Boumedienne. Yet, here too, Allende received warning signals. As well as exchanging views on Third World

Salvador Allende at the United Nations General Assembly, December 1972.
Courtesy of Fundación Salvador Allende.

issues, the Algerian president pointedly asked what the situation was inside Chile's armed forces. As Almeyda later recounted, Boumedienne was unconvinced by the notion of constitutionality among Chilean military leaders. Apologizing for his frankness, he ominously argued that the UP's political experiment would fail if it did not stamp out all counterrevolutionary vestiges in its military institutions.[16]

When Allende took off from Algiers for Moscow, he was still unsure what he would achieve. Two weeks earlier, the PCCh's secretary-general, Luis Corvalán, had traveled to East Germany and Moscow to discuss future assistance to the UP. On route, the president had sent this pro-Soviet leader with years of good relations with Moscow to Havana to consult the Cubans on how to deal with Moscow. One of the Cubans who attended the meeting recalls that Castro was concerned about the Chilean's lack of detailed technical knowledge to win over the Soviets. In fact, drawing on his own experience in dealing with Moscow, Castro quizzed Corvalán on his figures for hours and had concluded he knew more about Chile's economic situation than the Chilean sitting in front of him.[17]

Be that as it may, one of the essential problems that Corvalán encountered in Berlin and Moscow was that, as Dobrynin had indicated to Letelier, the Soviet Union did not want to risk a confrontation with the United

States by getting too involved in Chile. In Moscow, Corvalán had lengthy meetings with Brezhnev and other senior leaders of the Soviet Communist Party. Then, in a long meeting with East Germany's leader, Erich Honecker, on 24 November, Corvalán outlined Chile's problems, citing the growing strength of "united internal and reactionary forces," a deficit of $200 million, and the omnipresent threat of U.S. imperialism. As he stressed, Washington was challenging the UP in the form of the withdrawal of U.S. technicians and credits, the ITT conspiracy, and embargoes against Chilean copper sales. To be sure, the UP had survived the October strike, but 1973, in his words, was going to be "the most decisive year for Chile . . . the year when decisions will be carried out that will determine our path to socialism." Looking ahead, he also acknowledged that the Chileans would obviously have to make the biggest sacrifice to withstand challenges to La Vía Chilena (he mentioned butter and meat rationing as an example of savings already being made), but they could not do so successfully without "international assistance." In this respect, he recognized that his proposals for substantial increases in Soviet bloc aid were "not easy," but he said it was his "revolutionary duty to be open and honest" about what was needed.

After hearing the details of Corvalán's specific suggestions for Soviet bloc purchases of Chilean copper (that he recognized could not be sold on the international market owing to embargoes against it but which could be used for reserves), a $220 million investment in steel production, and large short-term credits to offset a predicted Chilean deficit until 1976, Honecker responded in a sympathetic but noncommittal manner. On the one hand, he pointed out that the German Democratic Republic already had to juggle previous commitments to aid other revolutionary processes, not least $100 million a year to North Vietnam. He also ignored Corvalán's efforts to single Chile out as a far better investment opportunity than Cuba. On the other hand, he also raised the issue of East Germany's own deficit and foreign debts, and the problematic nature of internal discussions about how to deal with these in the year ahead. Promising Corvalán he would look into how Berlin might be able to offer more help to the Chileans, he left specific answers to the Chilean's suggestions hanging in the air, noting only that he would send his views on to Moscow before Allende's arrival.[18]

Meanwhile, Soviet leaders were divided. The KGB had a grim view of the situation in Chile, while the Soviet Communist Party's ideologues were in favor of helping to consolidate the UP's revolutionary road. As the Russian

Salvador Allende in Moscow, December 1972. Front row, left to right:
Luis Corvalán, Alexei Kosygin, Allende, Leonid Brezhnev, and Nikolai Podgorny.
Courtesy of Fundación Salvador Allende.

historian Olga Ulianova has argued, it would seem that Moscow ultimately
declined to help more because it both lacked faith in Allende's project and
was financially unable to commit to a new Cuba.[19] However, the Chilean
president did not know this when he arrived in the USSR. In an effort to
raise the stakes of not helping Chile, Allende put forward the idea of his
country being a "silent Vietnam"—"without the roar of airplanes or grenade explosions"—at a Kremlin banquet thrown in his honor.[20] But despite
ample quantities of vodka to wash down disappointments, the visit fell
short of Chilean hopes. Allende's cardiologist, Oscar Soto, recalled that his
boss was "not happy at all." In his Kremlin suite, he commented loudly to
any of the walls that were listening that he would leave Moscow early if he
did not receive more positive signals of Soviet assistance soon; "the Soviet
compañeros don't understand us!" he complained to Soto.[21] He was right.
Moscow did not need Chilean copper and could not comprehend the UP's
chaotic management of its economy or its failure to use previous Soviet
credits granted to Chilean industrial development.[22]

Rather than receiving enough to counter Chile's foreign exchange deficit
for 1973, Allende left with advice to resolve conflicts with Washington and
promises of economic assistance that fell far short of hopes. Instead of

larger hard currency loans, for example, the Chileans received a new credit of $45 million and agreements using previously agreed credits to increase the USSR's technical assistance in developing Chile's copper, chemical, and fishing industries. Yet Santiago did not want Soviet technology, which it considered as being incompatible with Chile's U.S.-orientated industry.[23] And Allende also felt betrayed. "I never imagined that they would do this to me," he lamented to the Chilean diplomat Ramon Huidobro, who vividly recalled the Chilean president describing himself as having been stabbed in the back.[24]

The reception and mass adulation that Allende received when he arrived in Havana could not have been more different from the reception he had had in Moscow.[25] Castro had been pleading with Allende to visit for a whole year. Back in February 1972, shortly after his own visit to Chile, he had written to Allende about this idea:

> I can understand perfectly well that the intense work ahead of you and the tone of the political struggle in recent weeks have not allowed you to schedule the trip. . . . It is clear we had not taken these eventualities into account [when we talked about it]. That day, on the eve of my return to Cuba, when we dined in your house in the early morning hours, having little time and in the haste of the moment, it was reassuring for me to think that we would again meet in Cuba, where we would have the opportunity to converse at length. Nevertheless, I still harbor the hope that you can consider scheduling your visit for some time before May. I mention this month because, mid-May, at the latest, I must make a trip, which can no longer be postponed, to Algiers, Guinea, Bulgaria, other countries and the Soviet Union. This long tour will demand considerable time.[26]

Of course, Fidel had gone on his trip, and Allende's visit had been postponed yet again. However, when the two leaders finally met just over a year after Castro left Chile, they addressed what the Chilean chargé d'affaires in Havana enthusiastically recorded as an "incalculable magnitude" gathered at the Plaza de la Revolución.[27] Castro welcomed Allende as a leader who had shown Cuba the "most steadfast friendship" since 1959. He also likened the imperialist aggression Chile faced to the situation that Havana had encountered (even if he underscored that his country's experience had been far worse). "We [have] lived that experience and know about the reserves of energy, self-denial and heroism that exist in the people," Fidel knowingly explained. But he also warned that "revolutions do not emerge as a whim of men but as the result of historical processes," insinuating that Allende would not be able to dodge a class struggle and a confrontation with counterrevolutionaries. Castro finished with pledging Cuban "blood," "bread," and forty tons of the Cuban population's sugar rations to help Chile's revolution. "We must launch a gigantic wave of solidarity around the brother Chilean people," he instructed, explaining what the imperialists had "tried to accomplish with bombs in Vietnam they are trying to accomplish in Chile by economic asphyxia."[28]

Allende had finally got the recognition of his country's international significance that he desired, and thousands cheered in support.[29] Yet he was also uncomfortable. Before stepping up to the podium in his Cuban Guayabera shirt, his doctor observed his boss more nervous than he had ever seen him. The Chilean president, it seemed, was intimidated by speaking in this setting after Fidel.[30] When he did, Allende paid tribute to Cuba's revolutionary martyrs and the historic ties between Chile and Cuba. He thanked the Cuban people profusely, lambasted those who attacked his revolution, and expressed gratitude for the Order of José Martí President Dorticós had awarded him earlier that day.[31] As Chile's chargé d'affaires, Gonzalo Rojas Pizarro, proudly noted, the speech "showed the unquestionable personality of an American combatant and an authentic Marxist-Leninist."[32]

Even so, Cuba's understanding brought limited help. Moreover, sugar and blood could not solve the UP's immediate economic problems, which were even causing problems for Havana and Santiago's bilateral relationship. In November 1972 Castro had personally complained to Corvalán that he was unhappy with Chilean delays in fulfilling trade agreements.[33] While Cubans were insistent on moving the pace of negotiations forward, the UP lagged behind, and the Cubans also voiced concerns that Chilean firms were not selling products at a competitive rate to Havana.[34] Indeed, in this case the earlier celebrated idea that these two developing countries could work together to solve problems of development seemed increasingly untenable.[35]

Back in Santiago, there was no consensus about what Allende's trip had achieved. The main focus of press speculation was on whether the USSR might possibly help Chile more than official communiqués had suggested. As the U.S. ambassador in Santiago noted, the UP may have been "gratified at [the] warmth, enthusiasm and respectful hearing Allende's 'David and Goliath' portrayal seem[ed] to be eliciting abroad," but most of Allende's

Fidel Castro and Salvador Allende in Cuba, December 1972. Courtesy of Fundación Salvador Allende.

UN speech was "old hat to Chileans," and he reported that nothing "note-worthy" had come out of the president's visit to Havana.[36]

Allende was thus back to square one—namely, to working out his country's differences with the United States. Looking ahead to Chile's bilateral negotiations with the United States, the Chilean Foreign Ministry continued to define the country's overall strategy as being an effort to "win time" and "manage conflict," while simultaneously consolidating Chile's revolutionary process. If it could, diplomats also hoped to "induce a change" in the United States' rigid position on compensation by trying to move discussion toward broader political issues.[37] As the Chilean negotiators who arrived in Washington argued, Nixon's reelection in November 1972 meant they would have to "live with each other" at least until Chile's presidential elections in 1976, so it was time to reach some sort of understanding.[38]

By the end of 1972, the UP's odds of exerting enough leverage on Washington to induce it to change its credit restrictions nevertheless seemed slim. Although Allende had never wanted to ally himself wholeheartedly with the USSR, economic necessities had driven him to seek solutions to the UP's problems in Moscow. The advice he received to resolve Chile's dispute with the United States was consistent with the UP's own continuing efforts and thus offered nothing substantially new to hold on to. In fact, rather than increasing economic assistance to Chile, the Soviet Union would actually reduce it from a total of $144 million in 1972 to $63 million in 1973.[39] From the end of 1972 onward, Chilean approaches toward the United States therefore constituted an increasingly pivotal—albeit haphazard—process. Indeed, successive last-minute efforts to delay a showdown merely sought to "play for time" as Allende's options diminished.

"Slowing Down the Socialization of Chile"

The CIA defined its overall task in 1973 as "slowing down the socialization of Chile."[40] And while U.S. policy makers stalled negotiations, Washington subverted Chile's democratic process. Chile's forthcoming congressional elections were widely considered as having the power to decide whether Chile's future would be shaped by democracy, dictatorship (on the left or the right), or a civil war. But Allende's UN speech and international grandstanding had raised the profile of Washington's role in Chile, increasing the risks that intervention posed. Congressional investigations in Washington about ITT's relationship with Nixon's administration and the growing Watergate saga (with its possible link to the Chilean Embassy break-in) also raised awkward questions about the White House's covert operations. Therefore, when the outcome of the March elections led those who opposed Allende to desperate measures, the costs Washington faced by intervening rose. Henceforth, U.S. policy makers were unsure how to speed up Allende's downfall without offering the UP a pretext to hypothetically seize authoritarian control.

The Nixon administration obviously had no intention of making bilateral negotiations with Chile easy. After all, its hesitant agreement to enter into them in the first place had hinged on avoiding a confrontation with an internationally prominent Third World leader, denying Allende a role as a scapegoat, and gaining compensation for copper companies (considered to be a remote possibility). The Nixon administration also clearly doubted Chile's sincerity. As Rogers had advised Nixon in November 1972, he saw "no evidence" Allende was "prepared to offer meaningful concessions" or that hard-liners in his coalition would let him act on these if he did.[41] The United States therefore entered bilateral talks pessimistically, armed with "Article 4," the clause it had inserted into the Paris Club agreement explicitly linking compensation to any "normalization" of U.S.-Chilean economic relations.

When delegates met on 20 December, Assistant Secretary Charles Meyer opened proceedings by thanking the Chileans for having brought "spring to Washington" on account of Washington's unusually warm weather. Yet the temperature inside the negotiating room dropped over the next two days when both sides failed to map out a method of resolving disputes, let alone making progress toward solving them. Although each side promised to "leave ideology aside," this belied what the disagreements were about. As Letelier himself acknowledged, differences revolved around contradictory "conceptual" approaches to economic development and international relations. More specifically, the Chilean delegation assumed an uncompromising initial stance, insisting that the United States ease its discriminatory economic policies and underlining Allende's unwillingness to rewrite Chile's constitution to overturn his "excess profits" ruling. All the while, U.S. delegates nonetheless maintained that the "stone" blocking progress was Chile's refusal to pay compensation.[42] Then, on the last day of discussions, the Chileans proposed submitting all disputes to unbinding arbitration along the lines of an unearthed bilateral treaty from 1914. But with Christmas festivities looming, delegates suspended talks until the New Year.[43]

After these talks, Allende gathered Letelier, Almeyda, UP party leaders, and legal experts in Santiago to discuss options. In focusing on the 1914 treaty, policy makers reasoned that it offered an unbinding framework that could comprise a range of topics instead of compensation alone. They regarded such a framework as an unlikely means of "solving" the conflicts, but a useful means of ensuring disputes would not overshadow Chile's wider international relations, especially with a new round of Paris Club negotiations scheduled for January. Another advantage of the treaty, the Foreign Ministry noted, was that it placed the United States in the position of defendant, thus turning the tide on the balance of legal cases against Chile. By formulating arguments based on international law, Santiago thereby hoped to receive backing from Third World countries in similar situations.[44]

In the meantime, the abortive meeting in Washington offered Santiago short-term gains. When Chilean diplomats arrived in Paris for a new round of debt negotiations, they noted that it had produced a "positive climate" that helped disarm U.S. obstruction to a favorable deal. When the Paris

Club also decided to suspend any decision pending an International Monetary Fund report on Chile's economy, this eased immediate pressure on Chile to resolve its disputes with the United States or comply with Washington's demands.[45] In early February 1973, having previously worried about U.S. delaying tactics, Allende thus instructed Letelier to postpone a second round of talks until after Chile's congressional elections.[46]

In fact, as the U.S. ambassador in Santiago observed in early 1973, waiting for the elections had given Chilean politics a "brief Indian summer," placing a virtual "moratorium on political decisions." It was widely believed that this was going to be the country's most important election for "decades." Voters had a marked choice between socialism and capitalism broadly represented by a contest between the UP and the opposition's purpose-built coalition, Confederación Democrática (CODE), that comprised Chile's Christian Democrat and National parties.[47] As Ambassador Davis reported, "the feeling of 'it's now or never'" was growing daily among opposition ranks.[48] He also observed Chilean "society's deep attachment to electoral politics" and preference for solving Chile's political crisis "by constitutional means."[49] At the very least, CODE expected Chile's economic predicament would diminish the government's political strength, and U.S. analysts optimistically agreed.

Faced with economic and political upheaval, the Left acknowledged it would be difficult to match, let alone improve upon, the UP's 49.7 percent gained at municipal elections in 1971. But Allende clearly needed to avoid the opposition winning two-thirds of the vote that would enable it to block his congressional veto. In the months leading up to March, his prospects did not look good, especially as the UP coalition campaigned divided. At an informal lunch during this period, Allende reportedly criticized parties for being "parochial, pursuing their own individual and party interests instead of those of the Unidad Popular."[50] And less than two weeks before the election, the Soviet Foreign Ministry predicted that the UP would be defeated. Even if the opposition did not win two-thirds, it posited, "a political storm" would follow within forty-eight hours.[51] When a week before the election, an internal MAPU document leaked to the press exposed the extent of the split in government, this underscored the UP's weaknesses. MAPU joined the PS and the MIR in condemning the PCCh's "centrist" position and questioned the UP's ability to survive without external support. Limited loans from the Soviet Union and other East European countries would "keep the ship afloat" until the end of April 1973, it warned, but after that MAPU predicted Chile would be faced by an "explosive" situation and would be "unable to pay for debt servicing, necessary food-stuffs importation, or imported raw materials." Looking ahead, the party decided not to "abandon ship" but, instead, to "turn the wheel as far left" as possible, "to prevent the boat from sinking, but to learn how to swim just in case."[52]

For its part, the CIA felt unable to make any definitive predictions about the election's outcome and had suspended all covert operations planning beyond March at the beginning of 1973.[53] This did not signify inaction. To the contrary, during the five months leading up to the elections, the 40 Committee had committed $1,602,666 to help the opposition fight an "optimum campaign," while the CIA station in Santiago led what was internally judged as having been an "effective" and "outstanding" effort to help it do so.[54] Davis had also successfully argued against supporting unrealistic *golpista* plots that risked rallying voters around the UP.[55] Yet how 800,000 newly enfranchised (eighteen- to twenty-one-year-old and illiterate) voters would position themselves was ultimately unclear.[56] As the election neared, the CIA pessimistically saw "little prospect of a conclusive [election] outcome," suggesting instead that the UP would probably win 38 percent.[57]

U.S. officials were therefore shocked and "disappointed" when the UP won 43.39 percent of the vote, picking up two seats in the Senate and six seats in the Chamber of Deputies.[58] As foreign diplomats observed, this "psychological victory" enthused Allende with "a good quota of oxygen and legitimacy."[59] Contrary to predictions, Chilean opposition leaders and U.S. analysts also observed that ideological and class affiliations— *not* economic factors—had determined the outcome.[60] Ex-president Frei bitterly reasoned that the "poor had not yet felt the full effects of Chile's plight." They "never did eat much meat," he derided in private, "standing in lines was to some degree a 'social occasion' and not the frustration and annoyance it was for the middle class."[61] Ambassador Davis was a little more understanding. He wrote to Washington that the poorest half of the population was "materially better off" under the UP and "doubtless prepared to pay some economic price" for an "enhanced sense of dignity and satisfaction of putting down the upper classes."[62] As observers concluded, then, the UP's campaign of encouraging voter loyalty along class lines and equating a vote for CODE with a vote for civil war had been effective. "This government is shit but it is mine" ran one UP slogan painted across Chile's walls. And with newfound confidence after the results were announced, Altamirano demanded, "now more than ever, advance without compromising."[63] The problem was that in the immediate aftermath of the elections it was still not clear exactly *how* and *where* Chile's political future should or could advance to. Certainly, the divisions in Chilean society and the issues that political opponents fought over were ingrained as ever. Indeed, the Soviet Foreign Ministry described the outcome as merely prolonging an "unstable equilibrium."[64]

In these circumstances, Washington's enthusiasm for supporting Allende's democratic opposition waned. There were various reasons for this. Primarily, because the country's economic difficulties had brought seemingly limited political rewards, the Christian Democrat Party focused its subsequent campaign on wooing lower-income voters to undercut the UP's traditional support base.[65] As it did, U.S. intelligence officers warned of an inevitable leftward trend in Chilean politics and the implications this might have for Chile's 1976 presidential elections. And by April the CIA station noted that Frei had "reached the conclusion that throughout the so-called Third World the traditionalist capitalist system is not capable of realizing development goals and aspirations. Frei has also been impressed over relative success and rapidity in which Allende . . . has dismantled previously existing bastions of economic power. . . . Frei recognizes that he cannot reverse much of what the UP has done."[66]

Alongside the fear that the PDC might not be able to undo the socialization of Chile, Washington's decision makers had growing doubts about the party as a reliable ally. U.S. intelligence analysts regarded "socialist communitarianism," to which the majority of the PDC increasingly subscribed, as being "clear only in its rejection of free enterprise." As one CIA memorandum put it, a hypothetical PDC government after 1976 would ask the United States for "massive financial and economic support" without necessarily offering anything substantial in return.[67]

However, U.S. policy makers also had serious doubts about the military's ability to intervene against Allende and to stand as a viable alternative to the PDC. True, in the aftermath of the March elections, the CIA's station in Santiago continued to urge superiors to "keep all options open . . . including a possible future coup." As the station's chief, Ray Warren, argued, this would not mean abandoning support for Chile's political parties, private businesses, and the media but rather bringing these different elements together to create an "atmosphere of political unrest and controlled crisis" to "stimulate" military intervention. And, as far as he was concerned, the main obstacle to a successful coup lay within the military itself.[68] One of the problems was that Chile's armed forces were divided. Another was that given the UP's electoral success, U.S. ambassador Davis surmised that they were probably also preoccupied about the risks of the "large scale bloody action against elements of the civil population" that intervention in the political arena would entail.[69] To alleviate these problems, Warren therefore advocated establishing "a secure and meaningful relationship with a serious military plotting group" as a means of persuading "as much of the military as possible . . . to take over and displace the Allende government."[70]

However, Warren received a negative response from back home, where analysts were questioning "the risks involved in desperate remedies [i.e., supporting a coup]."[71] In Langley, doubts centered on an "abortive coup or bloody civil war" and the "objective" situation at hand. However much sympathy decision makers in the United States had for an increasingly "desperate" Chilean private sector, they were therefore unwilling to give Warren the green light. They insisted that, "unless it becomes clear that such a coup would have the support of most of the Armed Forces as well as the CODE parties," the station was to avoid backing a military coup and make this position clear to Chilean contacts.[72]

Overall, then, if the CIA regarded Chile's democratic future as "bleak," this was not, as one would assume, because the prospect of military intervention loomed ahead. Instead, CIA analysts warned danger lay in it *not* happening and the United States obtaining no "more than Pyrrhic victory" in 1976 if a PDC candidate won presidential elections.[73] Faced with deciding what the United States' role should be in this context, intelligence officials and members of the Nixon administration were keenly aware of Washington's limitations and excessively nervous about Allende's ability to resist his opponents. And there were obviously differences within the Nixon administration about how to ensure Allende's failure. To be sure, while Washington's leaders hesitated about taking the risks involved in accelerating coup plotting, the CIA continued collating information that might be valuable to military plotters in the event of a coup, such as arrest lists, intelligence of government installations, and the UP's contingency plans to resist military intervention.[74] But beyond this, the Nixon administration decided to wait and see how the situation in Chile evolved.

Waiting for Spring

For Allende, the brief Indian summer of the election period immediately gave way to a difficult Chilean autumn and winter and, with them, the return of political infighting, looming confrontation, and ever-greater economic crisis. Chilean military leaders who had joined Allende's cabinet in October 1972 left government after the elections as planned but remained on the sidelines of Allende's presidency. Questions about Chile's future also continued to grow and political tensions in the country were increasingly tense precisely because the stakes involved were so high. By early 1973, people in Chile and abroad were talking openly about imminent choices between democracy and bloody civil war, between socialism and fascism, or between a Marxist dictatorship and a liberal constitutional democracy, always of course, depending on where they stood politically.

A key problem underlying Allende's presidency and the UP's ability to survive in government was the lack of an obvious end goal and an agreed route by which to achieve it. After the government's electoral success, the PS received criticism for having lacked faith in the political-institutional road.[75] However, Allende's hopes of uniting his coalition behind the democratic process and reaching an alliance with the PDC, as the Communist Party in particular advocated, remained elusive. Differences on the left were so great that Chile's commander in chief, General Prats, had written to the coalition parties after the election, warning them that their divisions aggravated their problems and favored the opposition.[76] Similarly, at the end of March, Allende pleaded for "vertical discipline" to unite his government.[77]

The question of unity also concerned the UP's international allies. From Moscow, the Soviet Foreign Ministry concluded that the UP's future depended on it, together with progress in overcoming economic difficulties and attracting support from the widest sector of the population as possible.[78] And in all respects, *Pravda* blamed "ultra leftists" and "adventurers" for existing weaknesses.[79] Although the Cubans sympathized with the PS and MIR's analysis of what needed to be done, they were also increasingly concerned that the far Left's open attacks on Allende fundamentally undermined Chile's revolutionary process. Looking back on the period two years later, Armando Hart, a leading figure in Cuba's Communist Party, praised the MIR and acknowledged its links to Cuba but alluded to differences of opinion "regarding the ways in which it related with other forces on the Left" and the "methods, places, and moments" it had chosen to employ revolutionary violence.[80] What concerned the Cubans was not the MIR's call to arms but rather how to make this count in defending the government. Believing that Allende was absolutely pivotal to the task of uniting different strands of Chile's revolutionary process, Havana's leaders ultimately stood by the president. Attending the PS's fortieth anniversary celebrations in April 1973, Cuba's deputy prime minister, Carlos Rafael Rodríguez, was very explicit about this, reasoning that "if Cuba was able to defeat the most powerful imperialism in history, this was because our revolutionary forces—within which the differences were not few and the tradition of honorable rivalries was not small—overcame these and established unified control, discipline and a common program. . . . there is no revolutionary alternative to the Popular Unity government and President Allende. . . . To postulate policies that divide the working and popular forces that Socialists and Communists guide together is not to open a path toward a deeper revolution, but to open breaches where the enemy can penetrate."[81]

Privately, however, the Cubans continued to urge Allende to prepare more decisively for an armed confrontation. According to Carlos Chain, Cuba's deputy foreign minister, Castro responded angrily to a group of Chilean women—among them Allende's sister, Laura—who visited Havana around this time. When they spoke of being ready to fight until Santiago's river Mapocho flowed with revolutionaries' blood, the Cuban leader exploded—"this is not what we want!" he replied.[82] As the Cubans tried to persuade Allende to lead and accelerate defensive preparations, the message the Cubans delivered to the far Left was therefore to wait, to unite behind the president, and to prepare effectively for the oncoming conflict.[83]

In the aftermath of the March elections, the prospect of some sort of confrontation clearly appeared more likely.[84] Throughout the country, streets were barricaded, students clashed, Molotov cocktails were thrown, and smoke bombs were planted. Indeed, members of the president's bodyguard, the GAP, recalled being on the alert for "every noise, every car that passed."[85] In April the struggle to determine Chile's future was most obviously reflected in a struggle over the government's proposal for a new Unified National School System (ENU). Although some within the government tried to argue that the proposition had little to do with ideology and more to do with addressing a long-recognized crisis in Chile's educational system, its objectives were also explicitly ideological. Specifically, the ENU promised to replace an "authoritarian, competitive and traditionalist" education system with one dedicated to encouraging young Chileans to appreciate "the values of humanistic socialism" and fostering "skills, concepts, habits, opinions, attitudes and values favorable to collective labor."[86]

Indeed, to the opposition—and, crucially, to outspoken military leaders who publicly heckled the UP's education minister—the ENU epitomized the imposition of Marxist thought on a new generation of Chileans.[87]

Despite Allende's continued message that socialism would ultimately pay off, it also showed no signs of doing so.[88] In the first four months of 1973, inflation soared, the black market prospered, industrial production fell by more than 7 percent, car production was down 20 percent compared to the previous year, and, worse still, agricultural production had fallen by 25 percent. In April, striking miners then descended on Santiago to demand more pay, and commentators predicted that the cost of living in May would be considerably worse.[89]

In an effort to ease Chile's financial pressures, it seems that Allende was resigned to the process of trying to reach some sort of agreement with Washington. Among those who encouraged him was the Chilean army's constitutionally minded commander in chief, General Carlos Prats, who told the president not only that Chile was "not within the Soviet sphere of influence geopolitically" but that "further damage to U.S.-Chilean relations" would "seriously affect its national security." Stepping down from his temporary post in Allende's cabinet in March, he had pointedly also urged Allende to "decide on the government's future course so that the armed forces can determine their position."[90] Yet, from other quarters, Allende continued to receive criticism for continuing negotiations with the United States. Indeed, the far Left had begun to insist on a posture of "demand," not "compromise," and an end to what MAPU called "negotiated dependency."[91]

As seen from Washington, Allende's so-called compromise also rang hollow. U.S. officials regarded the offer of unbinding arbitration along the lines of the 1914 bilateral treaty that the Chileans had proposed in December 1972 unenthusiastically. As Davis argued, Chileans' purported "flexibility" was "an oasis shimmering in the distance."[92] In March, U.S. delegates also voiced their concerns that the Chileans' vague framework was "cosmetic," with no guarantees of compensation for the copper companies.[93] But the United States' position was by no means more conciliatory. As the Nixon administration had prepared for a second round of bilateral talks at the end of March, it had dodged either accepting or rejecting the Chileans' proposal. And when delegates finally met, U.S. representatives also disingenuously dangled Washington's rapprochement with China and the socialist bloc as an example of what could be achieved through direct bilateral negotiations as opposed to multilateral arbitration frameworks.[94]

Arguments over the process for resolving differences nevertheless hid the central issues at the heart of the U.S.-Chilean dispute. Letelier demanded to know why détente was not a viable option for Chile. Pointing to the UP's good relations with countries of different ideological persuasions (he mentioned Colombia), he called attention to a "positive" international climate for accommodation. As he noted, a "thaw in the Cold War and the elimination of ideological frontiers," a "ceasefire in Vietnam, the opening of links between the United States and socialist bloc countries, [and] the establishment of offices in China" all suggested that an understanding was possible if the United States would only reduce its intervention and economic pressure against Allende. After all, days before the talks got under way the U.S. Senate had begun hearings on ITT's role in Chile, unearthing what the Chilean Foreign Ministry labeled "irrefutable evidence" of Washington's meddling in Chile.[95] But, for their part, U.S. representatives continued to underline compensation as the only real sticking point between them. And, in the end, after two days of going round in circles and U.S. delegates refusing to accept the 1914 framework, the negotiations collapsed.[96]

Back in Chile, Allende found it hard to manage the fallout from this failure. When Chilean delegates (minus Letelier) returned from Washington, their public denunciations of the United States' responsibility for the gridlock surprised and angered the Nixon administration.[97] In April Secretary Rogers described Chilean comments as "major distortions" and a "semi-final" "calculated . . . decision to provoke a 'confrontation.'" In his view, the UP believed it was in a stronger position after the election and U.S. Senate hearings on ITT and was thus likely to use the forthcoming OAS General Assembly to denounce Washington. Given that the Chileans probably regarded their situation as being as good as it was ever going to be, he surmised that they had opted for open conflict.[98]

However, this assessment was only an approximation of one part of the UP coalition's position. Clearly, Allende and the Chilean Foreign Ministry remained keen to avoid further confrontation. Acknowledging that the impasse had "substantially limited" its strategy of playing for time and managing conflict without tying Santiago down to any type of decisions, the Foreign Ministry called for yet another "imperative" and "immediate" reexamination of policy toward Washington.[99] Allende also recalled Letelier urgently back to Santiago to hear his estimation of what might be done to salvage the situation. The ambassador's subsequent conversation with Davis revealed the importance the president placed on rescuing the talks. When he met Davis, Letelier argued that Washington's apparent "180 degree turn" toward a hard-line position had been a "bombshell" for the Chilean government. He pleaded with the United States to offer "understanding and flexibility." "Allende genuinely needs time to work it out," Davis reported. "Letelier understood that the president's deep internal difficulty was not the fault of the U.S., but it was nevertheless a reality."[100]

As a result of this conversation, Rogers and the White House agreed to pull away from the brink. In early April, Davis received authorization to approach UP government officials and emphasize that the United States had not categorically rejected arbitration but was merely studying options.[101] Later that month when Almeyda visited the OAS in Washington, U.S. representatives held informal talks with him that paved the way toward reopening negotiations. As Rogers noted, Letelier and Almeyda had become "more flexible" and were willing to hear U.S. counterproposals.[102] Indeed, back in Santiago, although Allende publicly accused the United States of "direct intervention in Chile," he also declared that, "in spite of everything, Chile is prepared for [more] dialogue." If new talks resulted in nothing, he added, it would not be Chile's responsibility. "It is obvious that we are right," he proclaimed, but he also underscored the need to show the world that Chileans were "prepared to talk."[103] In private, the Chileans also began to give way. Between April and June, when delegates met for a third round of negotiations in Lima, the UP tentatively began to explore the possibility of accepting some of the United States' demands, set forth in a counterproposal to the 1914 framework.[104]

In what turned out to be the last few months of Allende's presidency, these negotiations nevertheless remained slow and inadequate solutions to Chile's needs. Essentially, Santiago was locked in a process that its opponent controlled and which it regarded as a convenient vehicle for hiding ulterior motives rather than a priority in itself. As Letelier had candidly admitted during the tense bilateral negotiations between Chile and the United States in March, it was simply "vague and unrealistic to try and obtain solutions for which the objective conditions [did] not exist."[105]

Incomprehension

Washington's and Santiago's leaders certainly "objectively" failed to understand each other when it came to inter-American affairs. With some justification, the Chilean Foreign Ministry regarded U.S. citizens as being indifferent toward Latin America and lacking general "comprehension" of Third World nationalism, which they perceived as "anarchy" and "ingratitude."[106] Yet, in Latin America, Chile was now also failing to gain under-standing as the notion of constructing "one" regional voice to challenge Washington slipped away from its grasp. Indeed, in the first half of 1973, the Nixon administration enthusiastically observed that despite continued Chilean efforts to encourage systemic change, Santiago would not be able to significantly undermine U.S. influence throughout the hemisphere.

In April 1973 Almeyda had tried to initiate a radical review of the inter-American system when he addressed the OAS General Assembly. In what onlookers regarded as an "emotional speech," he vigorously denounced the inequality within the organization and the fictitious identity between Latin America and the United States. And he emphasized Latin American "frustrations" that Washington "lined up with the rich countries, not with [the] hemisphere."[107] He also urged the OAS to dismantle such "fossils of the Cold War" as the inter-American Defense College and continued sanc-tions against Cuba.[108] Yet, in doing so, Almeyda ignored the ongoing ideo-logical struggle in the Americas. Chilean proposals within the OAS also antagonized conservative members of the organization and were modified substantially. To Washington's delight, Santiago subsequently got only a relatively weak resolution on the principles governing relations between American states and the initiation of a review process to study the issue further. In one U.S. diplomat's opinion, this was "quite acceptable" and a much better outcome than anticipated.[109]

Indeed, by mid-1973 the Nixon administration calculated that regional counterrevolutionary victories, combined with the UP's mounting difficul-ties in Chile, made it unlikely Allende would open the floodgates of com-munism and revolution on the continent. The State Department was also largely in control of the administration's policy toward Latin America by this stage, indicating that it was not the urgent priority it had intermit-tently been since late 1970. The White House had designed Washington's overall thrust toward the region, which included embracing Brazil, fight-ing communism, and supporting military leaders as pillars of control and stability. But under this general rubric, and with Watergate consuming Nixon's time, State Department officials' earlier arguments for flexibility in the Americas increasingly held sway.

In the aftermath of Almeyda's OAS appearance, U.S. officials also made at least some effort to persuade critics that it had rejected paternalism. Before a follow-up meeting in Lima in July to discuss the inter-Amer-ican system, Secretary Rogers toured eight Latin American countries to deliver this message. As far as he could see, he wrote to Nixon, Washington's regional problems were now "either soluble or manageable, posing no dangerous threat."[110] The president was "very pleased" with this news and advised the secretary to shake off any angry demonstrations he might encounter—"as one who went through this in 1958 in Lima and Caracas," he said, "Welcome to the Club!"[111] As it turned out, however, Rogers did not face many hostile demonstrations because U.S. initiatives in South America since 1970 had smoothed his passage. Specifically, the secretary acknowledged that the recent adjustments Washington had made to its policy toward Peru—including a decision to waive previous suspensions of arms sales—had made the visit a "success."[112] And in Brazil, Rogers described U.S. relations with that country as "probably the best they [had] ever been."[113]

Rogers achieved far less pleasing—though by no means particularly worrying—results when he met Allende on 25 May in Argentina. The shifting balance of power in the hemisphere meant that the meeting was an aside—a bilateral matter with Chile and an appendage to a hemispheric policy no longer as concerned about the regional implications of Chilean developments. The meeting was solicited by Rogers and took advantage of their both being in Buenos Aires for the inauguration of Argentina's new democratically elected president, Hector Campora. But it was also unauthorized by the White House and accomplished little to ease the strained relationship between both countries. Moreover, Allende and Rogers pressed upon each other the merits of their own government's actions and the error of the other's ideals. While conveying platitudes about wanting good relations, both men talked past each other, detailing core disagreements on notions of independence, imperialism, and economic or political systems of government. True, both praised democracy and freedom, but it was clear that each of them had profoundly different concepts of the validity of the other's commitment to those principles.[114]

In seeking to bolster their respective claims, Allende and Rogers stressed their interpretations of the political, economic, and social upheaval in Latin America. In making his case against "economic imperialism" in Latin America, Allende insisted he was not alone in the region; a great many other countries throughout Latin America shared Chilean frustrations about the pace of economic development and U.S. interventionism and were seeking alternatives. Conversely, Rogers threw the blame for regional underdevelopment back on hemispheric nationalists. Despite eschewing notions of U.S. "paternalism" and directly challenging Latin Americans to "do things for themselves," he then laid down rules for this independence. "The U.S. welcomed nationalism," he said, but only "as long as it was constructive." Nixon's new assistant secretary of state for Latin American affairs, Jack Kubisch, was also present at this meeting and recorded Rogers as questioning the "purpose" of "negative" or "anti-U.S." nationalism — "The Secretary pointed out that in his travels to different parts of the world, particularly to countries such as Yugoslavia and Romania, the authorities consistently said that they wanted closer ties with the U.S.: they urged the U.S. to have closer relations and for the USA to encourage Americans to go to their countries. They seemed to trust us. They didn't make speeches against the U.S. — in fact, usually the opposite. But this was where problems came up in our desire to be friends with Latin America. We felt there had to be a change in climate . . . it was a mistake for developing countries to act as if profits were evil."[115]

Faced with incomprehension, the Chileans viewed Rogers's Latin American trip with impatience. The Chilean Foreign Ministry predicted that beyond a "thaw" in United States–Peruvian relations, Washington was likely to continue its "benign neglect, courting the continent with official visits and studies that allow it to gain time and not do anything positive."[116] And although some in Chile had considered Rogers's meeting with Allende to have been a useful opportunity to make progress on outstanding issues relating to U.S.–Chilean negotiations, Allende's advisers regarded it as generally pointless.[117] Rogers had certainly refused to concede any ground to the notion that Washington's position might be wrong; compared to Allende, "the U.S. had a system that worked" he argued.[118] And Chile's leaders had disagreed. In a June analysis of the United States' Latin American policy, Chilean Foreign Ministry officials lamented that by continuing to regard foreign investment as a generous way of "helping" regional states and safeguarding their profits, Washington missed a "central problem" at the heart of inter-American relations. Reflecting on Nixon's recent speech to the U.S. Congress, Chilean diplomats commented that the president sounded more and more like a "public relations" spokesman for private U.S. companies who disregarded hemispheric needs.[119]

By the time OAS delegates met in Lima in July 1973 to discuss the inter-American system's future, however, it was clear that Santiago was wary of obviously antagonizing the United States. When Chile's representative spoke out stridently against the United States and Davis complained to Letelier, for example, the United States instantly received an apology. Indeed, Letelier, who had recently been appointed Chile's new foreign minister, claimed that he had had no part in the speech and that Chile certainly did not want to "create additional difficulties" where the United States was concerned.[120] Two days later, when Chile's delegate addressed the meeting, he was notably more "restrained." As Washington's ambassador in Lima recorded, he now stated that Chile did not want the United States out of the OAS, but rather wanted an organization that engaged the United States and the Latin Americans together on "more equitable terms" and encouraged "positive, fruitful dialogue."[121]

In spite of these modifications, the main problem with Chilean hopes of impelling transformation of the inter-American system was the absence of any cohesive "Latin American bloc." At the Lima meetings, U.S. diplomats observed a "great many, sometimes contradictory, Latin ideas" and were unimpressed by the "concept of Latin American unity," either politically or in the approaches regional states adopted toward the "conceptual framework of the inter-American system itself." Although they acknowledged Peru's "concepts of economic security" were broadly supported, U.S. officials reported that Chilean efforts within a subcommittee on the OAS's structure "floundered . . . when great majority of delegates demurred."[122]

Of course, behind the scenes, the United States nevertheless continued to work through Latin American allies to undermine Chile's position. "We will need . . . cleared counter-proposals of our own . . . some of which can presumably be voiced by friendly governments," one U.S. diplomat advised the State Department in reference to follow-up talks on the OAS's future scheduled for later that year.[123] One such "friend" U.S. policy makers believed they could "count on" was Banzer's Bolivia.[124] Another was obviously Brazil, whose cooperation in the inter-American system was highly valued.[125] In fact, Peru's president, Velasco Alvarado, had told Rogers the United States put too much "faith" in Brazil when the secretary had visited Lima two months earlier.[126]

In reality, many Latin American nations shared the Chilean frustration with the United States' policies in the region. But Allende's ability to convert a general widespread restlessness into practicable systemic change was dependent both on Latin American unity and on Washington's willingness to negotiate the underlying principles of its foreign policy. And despite promises to end "paternalism" that the secretary of state had delivered throughout the region in May 1973, U.S. officials still plainly believed that they knew best. As Rogers had forcefully implied when he met Allende, the United States had a system that "worked" and this—or at least something similar—was also the best system for Latin America to follow. Words and personal attention from high-level U.S. officials could also not hide the fact that the United States tolerated only nationalism it judged to be "constructive" and relied on loyal states to "feed" its prescriptions for development throughout the hemisphere.

Conclusion

Sitting next to Ramon Huidobro's wife on his way home from a visit to Argentina in late May 1973, Allende voiced his concerns about surviving as president. "If I can get to spring [September]," he told her, "I can save myself."[127] At each political turn that Allende had taken in his last year in office, however, it had seemed as if he had run into a dead end. Certainly, in late 1972 and early 1973, Chile had found itself precariously drifting between East and West, powerless to influence systemic change, and losing face among those who had earlier shown Allende sympathy. Much of this stemmed from a lack of clear direction and agreement within government as to precisely what Chile's foreign policy should hope to achieve and how. Having gone from largely trying to avoid Cold War categorizations, it is true that a sector of Santiago's foreign policy team then earnestly tried to fight the Cold War on a global scale. But when Allende's much-anticipated trip to Moscow failed, Santiago's efforts to "induce a change" in U.S. behavior toward Chile remained stymied by the lack of consensus within the Chilean government as to what the best course ahead might be. As Allende avoided a painful choice of either backing down or embracing confrontation head on, Chile's U.S. strategy oscillated between managing conflict and avoiding it—privately appealing to Washington and publicly denouncing the United States at the same time. Ultimately, Allende did not compromise Chilean sovereignty by going back on the "excess profits" bill his country's Congress had unanimously passed. But, then again, faced with a soaring budget deficit crisis back home, he also failed to assert Chilean independence in the way he had initially promised. (In fact, during Allende's time in office, Chile's indebtedness had grown by a staggering $800,000 for each day of his government.)[128]

For its part, the United States was unimpressed with Allende's efforts to play Washington off against Moscow and impelled by profound certitude in its chosen path. When Nixon and Kissinger sought détente with the Soviet Union and China to solve their own problems in Vietnam and ease the costs of continued international tension, they had been impressed by indications that Moscow and Beijing were keen to work with them and awed by the power of those that they went to negotiate with. But in Santiago, they and Rogers saw ingratitude, weakness, and proof that social-ism was misguided. This was very much the attitude Nixon had had of even center-left politicians in South America when he visited the region six years earlier. Then, he had described a "battle of ideas" still very much up in the air in the region. But this battle was now moving much closer to being decided.

Even so, what surprised U.S. onlookers was the relative insignificance that Chile's economic difficulties had on the election results in March. When whole swathes of Chile's population appeared unlikely to recognize the error of their ways and Allende's democratic opponents seemed des-tined to move ever further to the left, Washington singled out a coup as the only way it could truly "save" Chile and ensure that the "battle of ideas" was decisively won in favor of capitalism and the United States. The question mark hanging over this prospect was whether the Chilean armed forces could shake off their divisions and decisively intervene against Allende.

Indeed, from a U.S. perspective, a successful coup was by no means pre-determined. Allende's maneuvers between different factions of the Left and his efforts to placate his opposition (particularly in the military) were certainly more and more difficult. However, U.S. intelligence analysts still concluded that there existed three possible Chilean futures over the next two or three years of which only one was military intervention in domestic affairs. The other two—a political standoff between Left and Right and consolidation of Allende's government—were respectively considered as "most likely" and "roughly equal" possibilities to that of a coup.[129] As they waited on the sidelines, U.S. observers therefore typically hedged their bets. Ambassador Davis wrote home that "*chance, blunder*, or the winter food riots that are widely predicted . . . could *conceivably* lead to ignition and the coup *possibility* has to be considered."[130]

For their part, the Cubans were more convinced than ever that the mili-tary would intervene and that the only way to resist an inevitable coup was to mobilize Chile's population and prepare it to resist. Yet faced with an inward spiraling circle, Allende refused to take a different nondemocratic or violent road. Ultimately, the question ahead was whether he would have a choice. The UP's ability to draw on class loyalty may have provided it with electoral strength and moral legitimacy, but it did not solve the question of power, let alone the basic necessities of a functioning state. As the govern-ment's economic policies faltered, the UP's parties argued, and the middle and upper classes in Chilean society took to hoarding food and bolstering the black market, Allende appealed for external economic support to meet his country's growing import needs. In this respect, his dynamic foreign policy toward Latin America, Europe, the Soviet bloc, and China began to pay dividends in the form of assembling a complex jigsaw puzzle of new credits and assistance. However, this took on the character of an increasingly desperate race against time rather than a long-term solution that would keep the government in power until presidential elections in 1976.

Simultaneously, Allende's position in the world, the manner in which his foreign friends responded to him, and the way he approached his external enemies all contributed to the arguments raging within Chile regarding the future of the government's revolutionary project. Stirred up by propaganda, Chile's right wing had certainly grown horrified by Cuba's involvement in the country. As one of the country's future military leaders wrote in his diary, Chile had become a "tragic" "laboratory" for "foreign ideologies, foreign personalities," and un-Chilean "theories" of revolution.[131] On the other hand, members of the armed forces feared Santiago's alienation of the United States. Even Allende's constitutionally minded commander in chief of the Chilean army, General Prats, had warned the president that the military was waiting for the government to define its international position so its leaders could decide where they stood.

The president had traveled to Mexico, New York, Moscow, Algiers, and Havana, leaving Prats in charge in Chile, serious conversations had taken place within the Chilean navy as to whether it should seize the opportunity to launch a coup d'état against the government. As one of those involved in these conversations remembered years later, it was Admiral José Toribio Merino—a key figure in the group that led the coup in September 1973— who had put a brake on this endeavor: "If we move now," he reportedly warned, "we are going to take over this chaos . . . [and] they are going to blame us for this situation. Because the truth is we do not have any alternative project that we can utilize to save the country. What is more, with the world propaganda that exists in favor of this government, we cannot risk adventuring alone on an unknown path."[132] And as coup plotters busied themselves trying to secure allies and formulate an "alternative project," Allende's government struggled to maintain a semblance of progress within the confines of constitutional democracy, limiting extralegal military preparations for a possible conflict. As it turned out, the opposition in Chile would not be so restrained.

7 CATACLYSM
The Chilean Coup and Its Fallout

In mid-August 1973 a retired Chilean admiral, Roberto Kelly, arrived in Brasilia on a highly secret and special mission. His goal was to inform the Brazilians that a group of Chilean plotters was poised to overthrow Allende's government and then to sound them out about the international repercussions this could have for Chile. The plotters' primary concern was that Peru might take advantage of a coup to seize disputed territory on the Chilean-Peruvian border. Kelly was therefore in town, waiting nervously at a hotel, to find out what Brazilian intelligence services knew about Lima's intentions. As Kelly recalled years later, fears of Peruvian intervention seemed real at the time, as its military regime was regarded as being sympathetic to Allende and had recently signed a new arms deal with the Soviets. The Brazilians were also the only ones that the plotters believed they could trust to deliver reliable intelligence on this front. It was therefore fortunate for Kelly, and for Admiral José Toribio Merino, who had sent him to Brasilia in the first place, that the Brazilians had enough information to offer definitive reassurance. Indeed, Kelly boarded a plane back to Santiago in good spirits. The *golpistas* now had a green light, if they could unite the majority of Chile's other military leaders behind their goal.[1]

Achieving unity and guaranteeing the success of a coup in Chile still remained a big "if" in mid-1973. In the months between May and September 1973, U.S. officials monitoring plotting in the country had been relatively unimpressed with the progress toward this goal. Although the Nixon administration was highly sympathetic to the prospect of a coup, its reading of the situation within Chile and its concern for its own image also meant that this did not translate into a precise policy to accelerate military intervention against Allende. Instead, as Kissinger himself admitted days after 11 September, the U.S. "created the conditions as great as possible."[2] Of course, this distinction did not stop finger-pointing at "U.S. imperialism" as having directed, planned, and organized the coup after the event, especially given worldwide attention to Washington's intervention in Chile while the UP was still in power. Few were also surprised—and everyone knew to whom he referred—when Allende, in his last ever radio address, blamed "foreign capital and imperialism, united with reactionary elements" for having "created the climate" for the coup.[3]

Yet, in trying to understand the international dimensions of Chile's coup and the seismic impact that it had on the country's international standing, the distinction between "creating the conditions" for a coup and "masterminding" it is important.[4] As we shall see, it was the Chilean military—not Washington—that ultimately decided to act, and despite Cuban preparations to face a coup, it was also Allende and the Chilean Left that were ultimately unable to defend the revolutionary process that they had initiated. Indeed, both the Nixon administration and Castro were deeply frustrated with their inability to manage Chilean events and were unprepared for the decisive role that General Augusto Pinochet would play in ensuring that the coup succeeded.

Even so, as Kelly's trip to Brasilia demonstrates, international considerations and relationships with foreign actors *did* play a decisive part in the way Chileans themselves made their choices and conceptualized their goals, their options, and their actions. Allende had reportedly been "enraged" when he heard that the Soviets had sold arms to Chile's traditional rival, not knowing that Peru's strength had been a key concern for the coup leaders that threatened to depose him. To him, Moscow's decision—made at the same time as Allende had been exploring the possibility of purchasing its own T-55 tanks from the Soviet Union in early 1973—put Chile in a vulnerable position and was yet one more example of Moscow's lack of support for La Vía Chilena.[5] While Allende held out for an agreement with the United States, he also thus turned to the Cubans to help him prepare for withstanding a coup, even if he was still unwilling to accept all of their suggestions. Meanwhile, coup plotters looked abroad for reassurance and inspiration while fantastically warning of a forthcoming battle with "15,000 foreign-armed extremists" allied with the Chilean Left.[6] The Cubans were obviously perceived to be the biggest threat in this regard. And, pivotally, it was because of the coup leaders' fear of the Cubans that they waged a battle against the Cuban Embassy on the day of the coup— without prior U.S. knowledge—and then chased the 120 Cubans stationed in Santiago out of Chile as quickly as they could.[7]

Although Chile's military leaders therefore greatly exaggerated the number of Cubans in Chile and the extent to which the Cubans could undermine the coup's success at this stage, their fears reflected the impact that non-Chileans and international concerns had on the escalating struggle within the country. At its heart, the coup was an explicit repudiation of socialism and revolution. And as the country had become a theater of an inter-American struggle over these ideas, an array of hemispheric actors had joined in the struggle for and against revolutionary change. Partly this was because Chileans of different political persuasions had asked them to, but it was also because their own ambitions had drawn them into the conflict. The question of where Chile fit in the world was also of key importance in the battle to define what Chile was going to be: a socialist democracy, a bourgeois democracy, a dictatorship of the proletariat, or a military dictatorship patterned on Brazil.

One of the junta's priorities, after overthrowing Allende, was consequently to seize control of Chile's international policy and radically reorient it. Henceforth, the dictatorship abandoned Allende's embrace of Cuba and the Third World, together with Allende's aspiration to become a worldwide beacon of peaceful socialist transformation, and instantly drew close to Washington and Brasilia. In its first declaration on the morning of the coup, Chile's military junta also claimed to be fulfilling a "patriotic" act to "recover *chilenidad*," proclaiming a month later that "Chile is now Chile again."[8] Of course, Allende had also come to power promising to recover "Chile for Chileans," to redefine Chile's place in the world and radically transform the international political and economic environment. He had also sought U.S. acquiescence and assistance for this project, and, in this respect, the government that took over did the same, albeit with vastly greater success. However, the Chileans whom they purported to be representing and the way they went about doing so were the key differences between the pre- and post-coup regimes. Assuming a different place in the world as a willing member of the United States' backyard, an implacable foe of international communism, an aspirant of capitalist prosperity, and an internationally condemned dictatorship, the Chile that emerged could hardly have been more different in terms of its foreign relations. As Chilean historian Joaquin Fermandois has noted, the "modern utopia" that some outsiders saw in Allende's Chile transformed itself into a celebrated "anti-utopia."[9]

Before examining this transformation, we must first turn back to the months preceding the coup. Right up until 11 September, Chile had remained something of a cause célèbre in the Third World even if it had lost much of its initial allure in the Soviet Union, Eastern and Western

Europe, and Latin America. On the eve of a meeting of Non-Aligned Movement leaders in Algiers at the beginning of September, Algeria's president had pleaded with Allende to attend, if only for twenty-four hours. Chilean diplomats were elected to chair the movement's Economic Council, and its Council of Ministers sent a strong message of support to Allende on the third anniversary of his election as president of Chile. Yet, on account of domestic tensions, the Chilean president stayed in Santiago, merely responding that this support showed "the growing unity of our countries in a common struggle against imperialism . . . dependency and underdevelopment."[10] As events turned out, his letter to Algeria's president was one of the last in a long line of hopeful statements of this kind. In mid-1973, one Chilean diplomat had also optimistically referred to "an irresistible avalanche" of Latin American and Third World demands that appeared ready to transform international affairs.[11] The stage was indeed set for an avalanche, but it was one that would have ominous implications for the Third World, would destroy Chilean democracy for two decades, and would demolish the chances of socialist revolution in the Southern Cone.

Hesitancy

After Chile's congressional elections in March 1973, preparations for an impending showdown by the Left and Right had become more urgent. As Ambassador Davis wrote in mid-May, "While Chilean politics is still by and large played under the old rules these rules are under new challenge."[12] Even so, U.S. policy makers were cautious not to pin too many hopes on news of accelerated coup plotting in Chile. The problem was that despite the Nixon administration's obvious sympathy for military intervention against Allende, it was unimpressed by its progress and therefore hesitant to get involved. Instead, in the months leading up to September, U.S. decision makers debated and disagreed on the issue of bankrolling the Chilean private sector's strikes to provoke a coup. As before, what concerned those who resisted more involvement was not only the consequences of exposure that could occur for the administration's domestic and international standing but also the prospect that failure would undermine its three-year campaign to bring Allende's government down.

In early May 1973 the CIA had reported that plotting was "probably" occurring in "all three branches of the services," with the air force and navy ready to "follow any Army move."[13] However, at this stage, analysts accurately acknowledged that the military was divided between constitu-

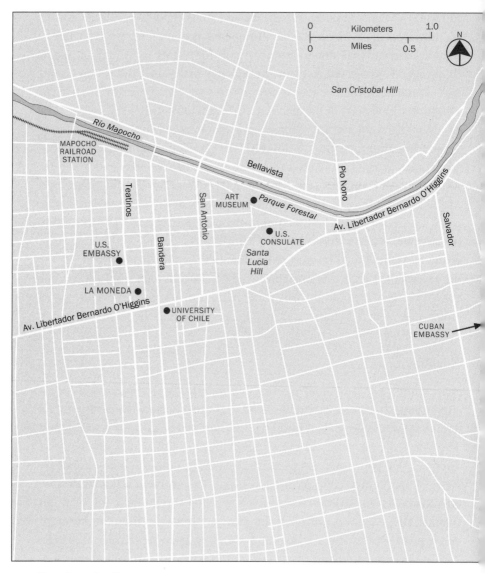

Downtown Santiago

tionalists and *golpistas* and that, as a member of the former group, Chile's
commander in chief of the army, General Carlos Prats, would block a coup.
Given these circumstances, the director of central intelligence instructed
the CIA's Santiago station on 1 May to "defer" action "designed to stimulate
military intervention."[14] Indeed, despite avid protest from the CIA's station
chief Ray Warren, the director of central intelligence categorically rejected

pleas to reverse his instructions, insisting that Washington needed "more solid evidence" that the military would move and that it had political support before acting.[15]

Back in Washington, government agencies—including the Pentagon—did not rate a coup's chances highly. When CIA and State Department officials discussed covert operations in early June, Assistant Secretary of State for Latin American Affairs Jack Kubisch concluded that "a military coup seemed to be a non-starter" owing to the lack of determination among plotters and a general Chilean predilection for "compromise." A CIA representative at the meeting concurred and those present also agreed that spiraling U.S. domestic criticism of the administration's covert operations enhanced the risks of greater involvement. Certainly, Harry Shlaudeman, recently appointed as deputy assistant secretary for Latin American affairs after being deputy chief of mission at the U.S. Embassy in Santiago, was recorded as arguing that "the Chileans were fighting Allende on their own initiative, the decisions were theirs. The little edge that we were giving them with our financial assistance was critical," but as Shlaudeman put it, the United States was "not and must not get into the position of saving them."[16]

The Nixon administration's fears of failed military intervention in Chile subsequently soared when, on 29 June, an attempted coup against Allende did not succeed in overthrowing the Chilean government. During this Tanquetazo, as it later became known, Chile's Second Armored Regiment advanced on Santiago's city center only to be confronted and overpowered by General Prats leading loyal sectors of Chile's armed forces and Chilean left-wing resistance.[17] To the Left's delight, and the Right's dismay, left-wing parties had also succeeded in distributing arms, silencing the opposition's radio stations, and maintaining communication between themselves and the population throughout the event.[18] However, by proving themselves capable and defiant, Chilean left-wing parties also gave away their evolving tactics for resisting military intervention.[19] Certainly, anti-Allende plotters analyzed their actions closely, and there is evidence to suggest that UP parties and the president's bodyguard, the GAP, were successfully infiltrated by the military after this failed coup.[20]

Meanwhile, U.S. analysts deliberated the future rather slowly. In a memorandum to the CIA's Western Hemisphere Division chief after the Tanquetazo entitled "What now?" one intelligence officer admitted it was hard to predict what would happen in the immediate future.[21] The Defense

Intelligence Agency (DIA) also reported that in spite of a Chilean governmental crisis, serious plotting had not "gone beyond the planning stage."[22] By contrast, U.S. intelligence operatives warned that left-wing parties were arming and that, if continued "for any length of time," the situation would favor the UP.[23] Over a month later, the situation remained unresolved. One CIA informant returning from Santiago explained that "none of our people has a clear solution to the Allende problem. . . . All feel a sense of frustration."[24] To be sure, the CIA already had contact with the group of plotters that would launch Chile's September coup, but U.S. intelligence agencies continued to fear that it would hesitate for too long or that its members would eventually compromise.[25]

As Washington tried to find a "solution," it avoided the UP's desperate pleas for financial respite and kept up international economic pressures against Allende.[26] In his new position as Chile's foreign minister, Orlando Letelier implored the United States to resolve financial disputes "rather than wait for . . . [a] hypothetical successor government."[27] Even the Chilean Christian Democrat Party's ex-presidential candidate, Radomiro Tomic, urged Davis to "come forward with some spectacular gesture" to put an end to Chile's political and economic crisis (he suggested tires or two thousand trucks for strikers).[28] When the World Bank considered issuing a loan to help Allende in July and August, however, the State Department launched a quick diplomatic campaign—providing "extra ammunition" where necessary—to block it.[29] And although Washington failed to convince all Paris Club members to back its obstruction of the loan, Chile's creditors refused to stand up for Chile, which meant that the World Bank ultimately deferred its decision.[30] Crucially, for Chile's international position, European creditors were also losing patience with Chile's inability to meet even rescheduled debt repayments.[31] At a Paris Club meeting in mid-July 1973, only Sweden (an observer to the talks) had defended Chile's request to defer 95 percent of repayments.[32]

Whether economic assistance at this stage would have significantly improved Allende's chances of saving his presidency is doubtful. As Allende faced crippling strikes and successive cabinet resignations at home, domestic observers and foreign commentators focused more and more on the political and military balance of power within Chile. Wary of backing action that did not have clear public support, the DIA still reported in early August that approximately 40 percent of the army and Chile's armed police service, the Carabineros, remained loyal to Allende, thus pointing to the prospect of a civil war if the other 60 percent took action.[33] Moreover,

David Atlee Philips, chief of the CIA's Western Hemisphere Division, noted that the "key piece in the puzzle" was the army, the branch of the armed forces that was least likely to act against Allende and in which the United States had the least influence.[34]

The army's position was, however, about to change. In late August, the opposition media, right-wing politicians, and army wives launched a vicious campaign against its commander in chief, General Prats, finally encircling his house, brandishing white feathers, and labeling him a "chicken" for not supporting military intervention.[35] When he finally resigned in response to this campaign on 23 August, U.S. analysts none-theless held out little hope that his replacement would join the plotters. Certainly, no one in Washington had any guarantees that this man, General Augusto Pinochet, would back a coup, or assume the position he later did. As late as 24 August 1973, a day after Pinochet assumed control of Chile's armed forces, the DIA described him as lacking in "prestige and influence" and "unlikely to wield . . . authority and control."[36]

Washington's decision makers also still disagreed about whether to offer assistance to strikers and right-wing paramilitary forces on top of the $6.5 million the United States had already delivered to Chile's opposition parties in its effort to destablize Allende's government.[37] On one side, Ambassador Davis strongly opposed such a course. Chilean left-wing accusations of CIA intervention had risen in July and August, thereby increasing the risks of counterproductive exposure, and in early August Davis had advised that "even more than previously" the United States had to "avoid giving the Allende regime possible pretexts for open confrontation."[38] On the other side, Kissinger had personally challenged the idea that the risks were "unacceptable" and asked for a cost estimate of increased support to the private sector. And it was only when Assistant Secretary Kubisch threatened to resign over the issue that Kissinger had backed down.[39] Then, on 20 August, an apparent compromise had been reached whereby the 40 Committee allocated an additional $1 million for Chile on the condition that Davis approved its precise allocation to different groups. In the end, however, no part of this fund was actually delivered despite the CIA's best efforts to circumvent such restrictions.[40]

By contrast, investors in Brazil, Argentina, and Bolivia actively supported Chile's private sector and Patria y Libertad in the months before September.[41] What turned out to be three weeks before the coup, UP officials also denounced suspicious military movements on the Bolivian border.[42] Since Hugo Banzer's coup in August 1971, the country had been effectively used by the Right to channel arms into Chile, and General Arturo Marshall, who had plotted against René Schneider in 1970, resided in Bolivia.[43] In mid-1973, Patria y Libertad's leader, Roberto Thieme, had also returned to Chile after having traveled to Bolivia, Paraguay, and Argentina in search of support. Once back home he had then vowed to initiate an urban guerrilla war against the government.[44] Military leaders throughout the Southern Cone were also believed to be actively conspiring with coup plotters, which is highly probable given what we now know about Brazil's interest in exchanging information with Chilean military leaders. The Brazilian ambassador in Santiago certainly made no secret of his antipathy for Allende. At a dinner party he hosted for Latin American diplomats in 1973, he very quickly took to criticizing Allende and making crude jokes about the president's wife in such a way that ten minutes after the Mexican ambassador and his wife had arrived, they broke protocol and left the party, shocked by the tone of the conversation and refusing to take any part in it.[45] The Brazilian ambassador also propositioned Davis about "cooperative planning, inter-embassy coordination, and joint efforts" to overthrow Allende. As the U.S. ambassador later concluded, he had "no real doubt" the Brazilians supported and coached Chilean coup plotters.[46]

Although there is no specific evidence to suggest the United States accepted the Brazilians' offer or encouraged them at this stage, there is also no indication that Washington was critical either. On the contrary, U.S. policy makers increasingly emphasized the potential benefits of Brazilian assistance to a future military government. Pivotally, the Nixon administration's Interagency Group on Chile was concerned that there did not seem to be an "indication of any widespread sense of 'mission' among the Chilean military to take over and run the country." To instill such a "mission" and to ensure that future Chilean leaders received the necessary equipment to carry it out, interagency contingency plans show that Washington wanted to encourage future collaboration with Brazil. This was also envisaged as a way to reduce future pressures on—and exposure of—U.S. assistance to any regime that succeeded Allende's. Three days before the coup actually took place, for example, U.S. policy makers were suggesting that if successful coup leaders asked for "easily identifiable U.S. equipment—i.e. helicopters etc.," Washington "would first seek to encourage support from other Latin American countries—Brazil."[47] Commentators also continued to insist on the parallels between an impending showdown in Chile and the Brazilian coup of 1964, pointing to private-sector-funded opposition parties, paramilitaries, women's groups aggravating antigovernment tension, and the specter of foreign subversion that was being vociferously played up.[48] Chile's politicians were also receptive to Brazil's example. As Washington's ambassador in Rio de Janeiro at the time of the 1964 coup later recalled, Chile's ex-president, Eduardo Frei, confided in him that Chile now needed "a Brazilian solution."[49]

As all these developments were gathering pace, Nixon was embroiled in the growing Watergate scandal, and Kissinger was busy concentrating on his new appointment as secretary of state. On 6 September, Kissinger called Ambassador Davis to the United States to offer him a new position in the State Department. Given reports from Chile suggesting a coup was imminent, Davis remembered being desperate to get back to Santiago but that Kissinger actually kept him waiting two days. "So there's going to be a coup in Chile!" the future secretary exclaimed when they finally met. Yet, despite expecting and welcoming such a development, both agreed only that obvious U.S. involvement should be avoided.[50]

Overall, the Nixon administration's imprecision and hesitancy to speed up the very goal it had sought for three years in these months is curious. It is conceivable that Davis was called back to Washington to remove him and the obstacles he placed on U.S. assistance to coup plotters, although the obvious results of this move, if indeed it was a sneaky move, are unclear. Instead, the administration seems to have held back amid fears U.S. government involvement could cause further damage to Nixon's domestic standing, speculation that the military might never move, and the chances of failure if it did.

The increasing politicization of Chile's armed forces and the growing pressure on its leaders to overthrow Allende nevertheless grew rapidly toward the end of August. Certainly, General Pinochet, who would be the key to the coup's success when it was eventually launched on 11 September, received pleas to take action days after he assumed the position of commander in chief of the army. Pointing to divisions within the UP, and between opposition leaders, members of the armed forces who urged him to take action lamented that the "political party had become more important than the country," that "respect for human life" had been lost, and that "the number of foreign extremists active in Chile" had reached "an unsupportable limit." As they insisted, the armed forces were "ideologically . . . antagonistic" to Marxism by their very nature, and it was now up to Pinochet to decide on Chile's fate.[51] Their message was increasingly echoed by a multitude of voices within the Navy. "Marxism intends to implant itself in Chile," a group of eighty-five lieutenants wrote to Admiral

Merino, "as citizens and Officials, we see the threat of Marxism closing in around our families, [a] threat, which as history demonstrates is not only intellectual but also physical." The solution, they insisted, was action to "eradicate Marxism in Chile, as the only way to return normality to our country."[52]

Impending Showdown

As Chile lurched toward confrontation, the ambitious domestic and international goals Allende had championed three years earlier dissolved. True, Chile continued to receive support and attention worldwide, but now, as Kissinger's assistant for Latin American affairs noted, "other governments that, at one time, were inclined to look on the Chilean experience as a likely model" were "disillusioned."[53] Among those deeply frustrated with the progress of La Vía Chilena were the Cubans. Although they continued to act as intimate advisers to Allende and Chile's left-wing parties, they had also now become prime targets of antigovernmental opposition themselves, which limited their scope of action. Moreover, Cuban strategies for defending Chile's revolutionary process were frustrated by Allende's guidelines, by the far Left's provocative actions, and, pivotally, by their failure to detect the coup until it was already under way.

The Cubans were not the only ones disillusioned. As far as Allende was concerned, the failure of the Tanquetazo had been a victory for institutionalism.[54] However, to the USSR's Foreign Ministry, it had shown both that an "open armed battle" was a serious possibility and that the UP had no united policy toward Chile's armed forces.[55] Proposing weekly meetings with other socialist bloc countries stationed in Santiago, the Soviet ambassador privately told staff at the East German Embassy that the Chilean government's problem had been to try and "implement a workable anti-imperialist democratic program in two years rather than waiting until 1976. Under pressure from reactionary elements, as well as petit bourgeois idealism, processes were accelerated and tasks were undertaken prematurely in conditions where the situation was not ripe. Instead of focusing efforts on consolidating and securing anti-imperial and democratic changes which were already under way . . . the 'road to socialism' was emphasized as the primary objective of the UP. Even our comrades from the Communist Party allowed themselves to be pulled in this direction. They now recognize the potential dangers."[56] The Chinese were also pessimistic. Earlier that year, Zhou Enlai had pointedly asked Foreign Minister Clodomiro Almeyda about the military when the latter visited China, asking if Allende had a "back-up plan." Almeyda had to admit that he did not.[57]

Meanwhile, within Chile, calls for expanding Poder Popular—"Popular Power," a loosely defined network of worker and neighborhood grass-roots organizations—mounted. However, the relationship between the government and Poder Popular was still ill-defined. Speaking to an Italian Communist Party member, the secretary of the Chilean Communist Party (PCCh), Luis Corvalán, openly remarked that the UP had "destroyed a rotten system . . . which worked" but was not yet in control of a system to replace it.[58]

In this context, Havana fast-forwarded arrangements for an impending conflict. On 30 June 1973 Castro had written to Allende congratulating him on putting down the Tanquetazo and urging him to have faith in his ability to lead armed resistance against coup plotters. "We are still under the impact of the great revolutionary victory of the 29th and your brilliant, personal role in the events," he wrote. "It is natural for many difficulties and obstacles to subsist [sic], but I am certain that this first trial, where you have come out successful, will encourage you and consolidate the people's confidence in you. . . . With actions like those of the 29th, the Chilean revolution shall come out victorious of any test, no matter how hard. Again, Cuba is at your side and you can rely on your faithful friends of always."[59]

Even so, after the Tanquetazo, all but a few Cuban women and children were evacuated from Chile.[60] By this stage, as Luis Fernández Oña later remembered, Havana was "super convinced" the military would launch another coup.[61] At the end of July, Manuel Piñeiro and Cuban deputy prime minister Carlos Rafael Rodríguez arrived in Chile to deliver another letter to Allende from Castro. Yet this one referred far more directly to the need for Allende to prepare for confrontation. Indeed, it is the beseeching tone of Castro's advice that is most revealing. He implored Allende to face a confrontation head on as the leader of mass resistance. "Do not for a minute forget the formidable strength of the Chilean working class," Castro insisted. He suggested that the workers could "paralyze" a coup, prevent vacillation and—if its actions were precise—decide Chile's fate. Rather than apologize for the Left's forces, Castro also argued that the enemy had to be made aware of its preparedness to fight a future confrontation. In this respect, Castro reminded Allende that his leadership was "above all . . . the key to the situation," and he signed off asking how Havana could help.[62]

It was around this time that Allende asked Cubans to prepare plans for defending the presidential palace and his residence, Tomás Moro. Allende had been clear for two years that in the event of a military attack he would go to La Moneda.[63] Yet Cuba's immediate concern was the strategic vulnerability of this location. La Moneda was (and is) a particularly vulnerable low-level building surrounded by taller ones. "From a military point of view, it was a disaster!" and "indefensible," Oña recalled.[64] If Havana had been in charge of strategic decisions, he and Estrada later explained, it would have sent Allende to the outskirts of the city, where workers had begun organizing themselves to resist an attack.[65] And from there the Cubans would have joined members of the Chilean Left in forming a defensive cordon around him to ensure he could survive, to consolidate his forces, and to begin preparing a counterattack.[66] In sum, Castro seems to have been in no doubt that Allende would "fight to his last breath," as he later told India's prime minister, Indira Gandhi, during his visit to New Delhi.[67] But he wanted the president's final battle to be prolonged and effective, and for that he needed to survive an initial assault.

Yet the Cubans could not alter Allende's determination to confront military intervention from the presidential palace as the democratically elected leader of his country. And, in the end, as Ulises Estrada recalled, "it was his country" and the Cubans "had to respect him."[68] When Allende showed the Cuban plans to Prats, then still commander in chief, and General José Maria Sepulveda, head of Chile's Carabineros, Estrada was nevertheless angry.[69] In his view, this clearly undermined Allende's defense and risked leaks to plotters. To date, it is not known whether Pinochet saw the plans when he succeeded Prats or what exactly they proposed. However, it is clear that the GAP began stockpiling weapons (including bazookas) at La Moneda and Tomás Moro with Cuban help in the months before the coup and that this was by no means a closely guarded secret.[70] Certainly, looking back, Estrada believes that this visible preparation contributed to the unexpected power and brutality of the military's coup. In his opinion, military plotters knew that the means and the will existed to resist any attack and that is why those who launched the coup used such ruthless force.[71]

When Allende had shown these plans to Prats and Sepulveda, the Cubans also bemoaned Allende's indiscretion because it further compromised Cuba's position in Chile. The antigovernment press was already stoking fears that Havana was preparing the government to launch a preemptive coup to seize dictatorial power. In the early hours of 27 July, when

Allende's naval aide, Captain Arturo Araya, was shot dead on his own balcony, the press instantly—and wrongly—pointed the finger at Oña and members of the GAP.[72] Havana's alleged smuggling of arms in boats of sugar that arrived after April 1973, Piñeiro and Rodríguez's trip, and the Cubans' supposed complicity in the escalation of violence in the country all helped fuel this propaganda and the increasing attacks against them. At least seven bombs targeted Cuban Embassy personnel, their business connections, and, on one occasion, a school for Cuban children in Santiago in the months before the coup.[73] Cuba's trade mission was a favorite target, and Havana's commercial attaché remembers that every night women surrounded his house beating saucepans.[74] Meanwhile, psychological warfare was employed. "Remember Jakarta," read one message posted to the Cuban Embassy and painted on walls throughout Chile, evoking the memory of the annihilation of more than 500,000 Indonesian Communist Party members in 1965.[75]

In this context, embassy personnel, including Cuba's cultural attaché, had received advanced arms training, carried pistols, changed houses at night to avoid vulnerability, and were assigned members of Cuba's elite Tropas Especiales to guard them.[76] And in late August, in preparation for the departure of one of the embassy's most senior political counselors, Juan Carretero, who was returning to Cuba to take up a new post within the DGLN, Castro sent Estrada to Santiago permanently to take over his post and manage preparations to withstand a coup.[77]

Meanwhile, although the opposition exaggerated the extent of Cuban involvement in Chile, Havana certainly facilitated Chilean left-wing military preparations. According to Chilean testimonies compiled almost thirty years later, the Socialist Party's military apparatus had received three arms deliveries "from the island" by September 1973, of which exactly half was given to the GAP. These deliveries comprised two hundred AK-47 assault rifles, four P-30 submachine guns, eight Uzi submachine guns, six Soviet RPG-7 anti-tank rocket propelled grenade weapons (each with nine rocket launchers), thirty-six P-38 automatic pistols, thirty-six Colt pistols, and two recoilless guns.[78] However, Estrada maintains that the number of weapons Cuba gave the Chilean Left overall was significantly higher. According to him, the Cubans had delivered a combined total of three thousand arms to the MIR (before May 1972), the PCCh and PS, and, to a far lesser extent, MAPU. He also remembered that they gave armed training to "hundreds" of Miristas and a total of nearly two thousand Chileans, in both Chile and Cuba.[79]

Even if these larger figures are more accurate, Castro later privately lamented that the Chileans took "far fewer" weapons than Havana had "wanted to give them." As well as his own personal efforts to persuade Corvalán to accept an array of weapons during his trip to Chile back in 1971, he later explained to East Germany's leader, Erich Honecker, that weeks before the coup the Cubans had stockpiled "enough weapons for a battalion" in the Cuban Embassy, comprising "automatic weapons, antitank weapons," but that when it asked the PCCh to collect them, "they never did."[80] Smaller collections of arms were also hidden around the city in locations specified by maps in key leaders' possession, meaning that the Left's ability to resist the coup was precariously reliant on these individuals. Finally, the Cubans also had weapons stored at the embassy and in a safe house nearby it for the MIR. But there was no clear strategy for distributing them in the event of a coup.[81]

Defying Cuban advice to unite behind Allende, the far Left also vociferously advocated confrontation with the opposition and fueled right-wing fears of subversion.[82] In August 1973 the collective group of far left Chilean, Uruguayan, Argentine, and Bolivian revolutionaries formed almost a year earlier under the MIR's leadership established a formal alliance aimed at launching armed revolution throughout the Southern Cone, the Junta Coordinadora Revolucionaria (Revolutionary Coordinating Junta, or JCR).[83] Estrada also recalled that by this stage all Chile's left-wing parties appeared to be "conspiring with the same General" within the Chilean armed forces.[84] Then, in early August, the Chilean navy announced that it had uncovered a left-wing conspiracy within its ranks involving the PS's Carlos Altamirano, the MIR's Miguel Enríquez, and MAPU's Oscar Garretón. The three leaders were subsequently put on trial, but they were unrepentant, insisting that it was the military itself that should stand in the dock. The MIR also claimed naval officers arrested on charges of subversion were being tortured (they probably were). Meanwhile, the Cubans' growing disillusion with the far Left led them to reportedly believe that it was merely "gambling" and "playing at revolution without any realism." As the East German Embassy in Santiago reported back to Berlin, "even the Cuban comrades" were "troubled by the adventurism and imprudence" of the Socialist Party and, in an "exhausting and long discussion" with its members, had pleaded with them to take a more "reasonable and responsible position."[85]

Devastatingly, provocative action by the far Left and the military's effective infiltration of left-wing parties made leftist preparations for armed

Cuban-Chilean strategy meeting in Havana, 1973. Left to right: Arnoldo Camú (PS),
Fidel Castro, Ulises Estrada, Manuel Piñeiro, Beatriz Allende, Luis Fernández Oña,
and Carlos Altamirano (PS). Also present, his hand barely visible to Castro's left, was
Rolando Calderon (PS). Courtesy of Luis Fernández Oña private collection.

confrontation transparent. Even before the Tanquetazo, U.S. intelligence
sources reported the PCCh had drawn up new plans for increasing its
military capabilities. "The intention is to create, as soon as possible, a
network of paramilitary units throughout Chile," the CIA concluded, noting that arms were being distributed between public buildings "for their
defense, or for attack purposes when necessary." It also knew the party was
coordinating its preparations for self-defense with other UP paramilitary
groups and that it had received Cuban training.[86] Later, in early August,
the CIA reported PS militants were on "alert 2 status," one step before an
"emergency." According to U.S. sources, this meant they were instructed to
remove "all files from PS offices at all levels" and each militant was given
a two-digit alias that only cell leaders could identify. Those with military
training were then instructed to choose sympathetic people close by for
possible training and incorporation into "neighborhood defense forces."
In the event of an emergency, cell leaders would "contact the militants
by telephone or messenger with further instructions."[87] This information
was largely correct; over a month before September, all left-wing centers
of potential resistance—factories, schools, and neighborhood groups—

jumped between alert statuses ranked from 1 to 3 while the majority of the parties' members awaited further instructions.[88]

On the far Right, preparations for an impending showdown were also visible. The Chilean government's intelligence sources reported that Patria y Libertad was receiving training from members of the armed forces and that meetings between PDC senators and military leaders were occurring in air force hangars. In August alone, right-wing paramilitaries launched 316 attacks, and members of the armed forces began assuming greater control in Santiago, Valparaiso, and Punta Arenas.[89] In particular, the military ruthlessly invoked an "Arms Control Law" that had been passed in October 1972 against the Left so that by the end of August, violent raids took place every day, hardly touching right-wing arsenals.[90] Chile's armed forces also patrolled the streets in Santiago and began registering workers and residents in slums across the country.[91] And, as they did, the tenor of the far Left's proclamations sharpened. Two days before it took place, Carlos Altamirano declared that revolutionaries had to "strike back." Referring to Allende and the PCCh's recent last-ditch efforts to reach an agreement with the PDC, he insisted that insurrection could not be fought "through dialogues." Instead he exaggeratedly proclaimed the Left had "a combative force which nothing and nobody can contain."[92]

In reality, the Left's combative force was of course far weaker than Altamirano suggested. Indeed, the Chilean situation was so tense, and the government's position so vulnerable, that members of Allende's bodyguard, the GAP, stopped carrying weapons just in case they were confiscated by the military under the Arms Control Law. According to the GAP's survivors, the group had sixty-eight members by this stage (spread out among Allende's escort and personnel at his home in Santiago, Tomás Moro, and his weekend retreat, El Cañaveral). However, this group believed it would have to shoulder the majority of the burden of any resistance to a coup.[93] Members of the GAP later testified that the PS also believed it could count on 45 men with armed training, 90 to 100 "special operatives," and between 15 and 20 intelligence agents.[94] But this was a relatively tiny force that would not be able to contain a coup and, in this situation, the GAP became openly critical of Allende for having failed to mobilize the population and prepare decisively for an attack. To be sure, the president had an anti-insurrection plan drawn up by the armed forces, "Plan Hercules," that would bring a thousand Carabineros to Santiago to restore order. But this did not count on revolutionary forces.[95] Rather, the idea was that the armed forces would divide in two in the event of a coup and that a sizable section would remain loyal to the government as it had done during the Tanquetazo. With faith in this idea, the president gathered all members of the GAP together on 26 August and promised that he would not compromise the people's mandate he had been given.[96]

Given the critical situation in Chile, Allende also canceled his much-anticipated trip to the Non-Aligned Movement Conference in Algiers and the possibility of visiting five additional African nations (Zambia, Tanzania, the Republic of Congo, Zaire, and Guinea) a few days after he met with the GAP.[97] Earlier, as noted, he had expressed enthusiasm about attending and his hope of combating Third World dependency. "We think that the Non-Aligned countries represent economic and political potentials of great significance," he had written to President Boumedienne of Algeria.[98] But Allende now informed him that Chile's situation was "serious" and that imperialism was helping those who attacked his government, making it impossible for him to attend.[99]

The position within the armed forces was certainly now serious. Having assumed the position of defense minister in the tenth (and last) of Allende's cabinet reshuffles on 28 August, Orlando Letelier found himself faced with intransigent opposition within the navy when he tried to prevent its commander in chief, Admiral Montero, from stepping aside in favor of Admiral Merino. At a meeting of the Naval Council on 1 September 1973, Letelier expressed his "surprise" when explicit fears of Marxism, infiltration in the armed forces, and the breakdown of cohesion within the navy were put to him. The armed forces were meant to be "professional and apolitical," he insisted, adding that while it was hard to remain on the margin of politics, the alternative meant rejecting the military's professional obligations. But the former ambassador failed to persuade Merino. As the latter stated categorically, parties aligned to the government had infiltrated the navy, and the institution did not want to be Marxist.[100]

In these circumstances, Allende feared the worst but was seemingly calm.[101] Nine days before the coup he told family members that he was prepared to die if need be.[102] A few days later, in conversation with a group of his closest loyal collaborators and speech writers that included his daughter Beatriz and her close friend and political ally, Felix Huerta, the president explained that he had lived a good, long life and that at sixty-five years old he was not worried about what happened to him. Although Allende worried that those younger than him would be left behind and would have to overcome the worst, Huerta vividly remembers that on this occasion the president described what he would do in the event of a coup:

he would kill himself using the AK-47 that Fidel Castro had given him.[103] Around this time, Allende also invited a Chilean historian to La Moneda to discuss the story of Chile's left-wing reformist president José Manuel Balmaceda, who had committed suicide in 1891 when his progressive reforms had failed.[104] Moreover, he gave cases of his private papers to his son-in-law, Luis Fernández Oña, so that he could send them back to Cuba for safekeeping or burn them in the event of a coup.[105] And, meanwhile, the president personally advised his doctors to make sure their families had contingency plans and passports prepared.[106] Then, on 8 September 1973, Allende's closest friends, including Estrada and Oña, gathered at El Cañaveral above Santiago to celebrate Beatriz's thirtieth birthday. But it was not much of a celebration. On this evening, Allende played a game of chess with Prensa Latina journalist Jorge Timossi, who recalled the president remarking that the situation was "ugly" and that he was "running out of pawns."[107]

Unbeknownst to Allende and the Cubans, on the day they assembled at El Cañaveral, Pinochet agreed not to oppose a coup. When the CIA received news on this day that military intervention was imminent, its station warned there was still a chance that Allende could maneuver his way out of the "most serious threat" he had faced. Yet it also surmised that Allende's "time could run out" if he did not know exactly what he faced and when, which crucially he did not.[108] On 9 September, Pinochet and Chile's commander in chief of the air force, Captain Gustavo Leigh, signed a note that Admiral Merino, by now commander in chief of the navy following Admiral Montero's resignation, sent them. By doing so, they agreed to unite their forces in staging a coup on the eleventh. "This is our last opportunity," Merino wrote, indicating to Pinochet specifically that if the latter did not rally all Santiago's forces to this cause from the first instance, they would "not live to see the future."[109] The next day, Monday, 10 September, the U.S. Embassy—having been told that the coup would now actually take place the next day—stood by, cautiously ready to help. Having returned to Santiago from Washington the day before, Davis sent news back to the United States that he had advised the Chilean navy that the embassy was "flexible and ready [to] satisfy any requirement" with regard to prescheduled U.S.-Chilean naval exercises due to take place the next day. "At this moment," Davis wrote, "our best posture is to continue about our business. . . . U.S. initiative would be difficult to explain and probably misinterpreted."[110]

All day on Monday, 10 September, plotters within Chile's armed forces successfully deflected government enquiries about troop movements.[111] On the basis of rumors Moscow had picked up in Western capitals about a coup, Corvalán made a number of phone calls. But he reassured the Soviet Embassy this was a "false alarm."[112] Meanwhile, although the Cubans were frustrated by the PCCh's belief in the constitutionalism and loyalty of the majority of Chile's armed forces, they had no information a coup would be launched on the eleventh. The stumbling block between expecting a coup and knowing it would happen was Pinochet. Like U.S. analysts, the Cubans and their Chilean allies had never suspected he would be one of the coup leaders.[113] Indeed, both PS and PCCh leaders had agreed he should succeed Prats and the Left trusted him.

As night fell over Santiago on 10 September, American Embassy staff were expectantly waiting to see what would happen next. That evening, an as yet unidentified "key officer . . . planning to overthrow President Allende" finally asked a U.S. official if Washington "would come to the aid of the Chilean military if the situation became difficult," but the official refused an on-the-spot commitment.[114] Meanwhile, across town, Allende and the Cubans were all unaware what was going on. When news of troop movements headed toward Santiago from Los Andes military base reached Allende and his closest advisers gathered at Tomás Moro at around 9:00 P.M., they made a number of calls to the very military leaders who were waiting in the wings to intervene and were assured nothing was abnormal. "We would not have slept for months if we had had to attend every rumor," Allende said, and having been placated with the story that troops were only mobilizing in case of disturbances at Altamirano and Garretón's naval conspiracy trial the next day, he went to bed at 2:30 A.M.[115]

The Avalanche

An hour before Allende retired to bed, Washington's defense attaché in Santiago had reported back home that a coup would *"apparently"* be launched in the morning but he speculated that Allende might survive it.[116] The question was how? The power potentially ranged against him was vast. Chile's combined armed forces numbered 87,000 in 1973.[117] And while counting on at least some of the military to remain loyal to the government, the contingency plans the Left had drawn up depended on forewarning so that advancing troops could be cut off before they reached La Moneda. By dismissing news of troop movements, Allende therefore missed an opportunity to preempt the somewhat nervous plotters. The

Cubans' logistical room for maneuver was also restricted given that their embassy was in a strategically vulnerable cul-de-sac and could easily be cut off. As the Cubans similarly had little forewarning of the coup, they also had no easy way of distributing the arms they had been stockpiling for the MIR. However, these setbacks did not alter Allende's plans to go to La Moneda in the event of an attack on his government. To the contrary, having been alerted to the coup at around 6:00 A.M., he went straight to the presidential palace to defend his presidential mandate and refused to leave the building alive. If what happened was not completely unexpected, the way it happened—the ferocity with which it took place—nevertheless shocked Allende's government and the world beyond.

Just before 6:00 A.M., Ulises Estrada received a telephone call informing him that the Chilean navy had begun seizing the port of Valparaiso. He immediately left for the embassy, where he set off a chain of phone calls around Santiago conveying the code word, *lapis [lazuli]*, after the precious blue Chilean stone. This meant that a military coup was under way and Cubans were to leave their houses immediately. There was not even enough time for Cuba's commercial attaché to collect sensitive documents or money from his office.[118] Estrada also alerted Carlos Altamirano and the Communist deputy chief of police investigations, Samuel Riquelme. And according to Estrada's recollection, both had some trouble grasping the magnitude of what was happening. In addition, Estrada spoke briefly to Miguel Enríquez, to inform him that the Cuban Embassy would not immediately be able to distribute the weapons it had been stockpiling for the MIR since mid-1972.[119]

By 7:30 A.M., just over one hundred Cubans had therefore arrived at their embassy. The building was sealed off, arms were distributed, and most embassy personnel assumed assigned defensive positions. In fact, by this date the embassy was a fortress awaiting siege. It was treated as Cuban territory, and hence, as its ambassador later recalled, it was to be defended "until the last man."[120] Although from the outside it looked like an unassuming adobe house dwarfed by taller buildings, inside staff had amassed food supplies, the building's swimming pool had been concreted over to conceal a tank of water, and in a recently dug cellar the Cubans had stored basic medical supplies to treat the wounded and quicklime to hide the smell of any decomposing dead. In all, they calculated they had provisions to last a month.[121] As the embassy's staff prepared to withstand a foreseeable attack, a group of Cubans (as yet, its size is unknown) also organized arms and transport to leave for Chile's presidential palace, where they planned to fight beside Allende.[122]

Meanwhile, across town, the president had arrived unscathed at La Moneda at 7:30 A.M., carrying the gun that Fidel Castro had given him. Twenty-three members of the GAP accompanied him, and between them, they carried a collection of arms, including AK-47 assault rifles, an indeterminable number of submachine guns, and two or three bazookas.[123] Having gradually gathered that all three branches of the armed forces were acting together and that he could not count on the Carabineros to defend him, Allende issued a radio broadcast at 8:45 A.M. explaining that the situation was "critical." To those who were listening, he proclaimed he had "no alternative" but to defend the Chilean revolutionary process and fulfill his mandate; that he would take no "step backward."[124] Inside the presidential palace, documents were simultaneously burned as a matter of almost obsessive priority, arms were distributed, and defensive positions were assumed.[125] Over the next hour and a half, a strange mix of the GAP, the president's closest advisers, government ministers, doctors, and journalists assembled, and just before 9:00 A.M., his daughter Beatriz arrived after driving her car determinedly through one of the first army blockades erected around La Moneda.[126]

Having entered the building, she was asked by her father to call the Cuban Embassy and instruct the Cubans not to go to La Moneda. In Allende's mind, this was to be a Chilean conflict, and aware that the world was watching, he did not want a battle between the Cubans and Chile's armed forces at the presidential palace.[127] Around this time, Miguel Enríquez also called Allende and offered to join him, but the president responded that the MIR should fight in the streets as it had been pledging to do.[128] And even if the MIR or a group of Cubans had set out at this point, it is uncertain whether they would have reached La Moneda without suffering substantial losses. One truck containing members of the GAP and arsenal never arrived.[129] Then, when the MIR offered to go to the palace and take Allende to lead a resistance from the outskirts of the city later that morning, Beatriz explained that Allende would never leave the palace.[130] Indeed, after the junta broadcast an ultimatum to Allende at 9:30 A.M. saying that if he did not leave by 11:00 A.M., the palace would be bombed, the president stood firm.[131] Reflecting on the tension that had built up in Chile before this day, Beatriz recalled that her father "felt a certain sense of relief that this moment had arrived." He felt "freed from the uncomfortable situation" of being "president of a popular government" while "the armed forces used the so-called Arms Control Law to oppress workers."[132]

Although Allende was clear about his own position, what he expected the workers to do was less obvious. In his last radio message, broadcast at 9:10 A.M., Allende had seemingly improvised an elegant farewell to the Chilean people conveying a vague message of restraint and resistance. "The people must be alert and vigilant," he instructed. "You must not let yourselves be provoked, not let yourselves be massacred, but you must also defend your conquests. You must defend the right to construct through your own effort a dignified and better life. . . . These are my last words and I am certain that my sacrifice will not be in vain, I am certain that, at the least, it will be a moral lesson that will punish felony, cowardice and treason."[133]

Inside La Moneda, Allende then donned a metal helmet and took personal charge of distributing weapons and ammunition. Those who accompanied him knew that they faced a battle that they were unlikely to win, but only as the morning progressed did they fully understand the extent of the situation they faced. At 9:15 A.M., there was an exchange of gunfire between soldiers stationed outside the palace and those inside, which grew fiercer when tanks arrived and began firing on La Moneda at 10:00 A.M.[134]

Around the same time, back at the Cuban Embassy—which kept abreast of developments via telephone contact with the palace and Prensa Latina offices opposite La Moneda—two unarmed members of the MIR, one of whom was the president's nephew, Andrés Pascal Allende, managed to reach the embassy. Upon arriving, they demanded to be given at least some of the MIR's arms. However, Estrada refused, believing this would have been "irresponsible." Between 10:00 and 11:00 A.M., approximately fifty members of Patria y Libertad had closed off the embassy's cul-de-sac with burning oil drums.[135] And, as such, Estrada's decision was based on his fear that the enemy would immediately seize arms given to these two Miristas. Only because others did not hold this view did the two members of the MIR leave the embassy with two donated pistols to defend themselves and somehow (it is not clear how) manage to survive.[136]

Before midday, two hundred soldiers from Chile's armed forces surrounded the embassy, occupying neighboring buildings and cutting it off completely.[137] In these circumstances, Estrada ordered the embassy's radio plant and its codes to be destroyed in case the building was overrun. Similarly, documents were burned (with candles) so that if and when the Cubans needed to leave Chile, they could use the thirty large crates these had been stored in to smuggle their weapons out of the country.[138] And, later, in the embassy's backyard, Oña also set fire to Allende's private papers as promised.[139]

Meanwhile, Chile's population listened to the junta's radio declarations to learn what was happening. U.S. Embassy personnel were also sitting by the radio, waiting for either Allende to resign or La Moneda to be bombed. Having arrived at the embassy diagonally opposite the palace, Davis sent regular reports to Washington detailing news he received from the junta's broadcasts but little more.[140] Meanwhile, at his residence, his wife and daughters were glued to the radio. Suddenly, just before midday, the Hawker Hunter jets everyone had been waiting for passed overhead. As Davis's wife later described, "It was an eerily beautiful sight as they came in from nowhere. The sun glinted on their wings. There were only two. Still in formation, they swung gracefully through the sky in a great circle, and then they tipped and dove . . . one bomb each . . . then, a gentle curve upwards."[141]

Of course, those inside the palace faced the grim reality of those "eerily beautiful" jets. Moments before the planes began bombing La Moneda, Allende had forced women to leave the building. The group that remained had then taken whatever cover it could, with a limited number of faulty gas masks. For the next twenty minutes, the palace was hit by at least eight bombs.[142] Over the next hour and a half, the resistance within the palace exchanged fire with the military, using two bazookas against the tanks. Pro-government snipers in the public works building next to the presidential palace also fired on the military.[143] Yet, together, these efforts were in vain. Just before two o'clock, the military stormed the building and found Allende dead.

Despite preparations over the course of three years to defend the government in the event of a coup, the Chilean Left also crumbled. The PCCh's newspaper, *El Siglo*, heard of the military's intervention just in time to order readers to their "combat position!" but many simply did not know where they should go.[144] Still uncertain of the nature of the situation they faced, leaders from the PCCh, the PS, and the MIR had finally met at 11:00 A.M. to decide on a course of action. But they could not agree, and the arms in their possession were limited. Enríquez, unable to access Cuban arms, for example, believed he could assemble four hundred militants by 4:00 P.M. but calculated that only fifty would be ready for combat, which was clearly not enough to withstand the military's onslaught.[145]

A key problem for the UP's parties was that communication broke down.[146] The Cubans explain this breakdown as the responsibility of party leaders and a consequence of the compartmentalization of trained militants. One key PS leader immediately sought asylum in a foreign embassy, for example, and another PCCh leader failed to alert militants to the location of stored armaments.[147] At 5:00 P.M., Estrada also fiercely rebuked Carlos Altamirano when he called the embassy to enquire where the MIR was fighting so that he could join them. Not only had Altamirano called on an open telephone line, but Estrada believed it was very late to be organizing the armed resistance that he had been recklessly boasting about.[148]

The Cubans were also too tied up with their own difficulties to be able to offer more assistance. At least two gun battles occurred between the Cuban Embassy and Chilean armed forces on 11 September.[149] The fiercest took place at midnight when Oña attempted to leave the embassy to escort Allende's wife and daughters to the ex-president's innocuous burial in Viña del Mar. Despite prior arrangements with the military and explicit instructions for him to leave the building specifically for this purpose, troops fired on Oña when he opened the door.[150] The Cubans returned fire so fiercely that a Vietnamese diplomat who witnessed the battle later told Timossi that he had never seen professional armed soldiers running backward as fast.[151] While bullets flew back and forth above them, Oña and the ambassador lay flat on the ground behind the embassy's wall. "It was probably a few minutes, but it felt like an eternity," Oña later remembered. Eventually, the military called a ceasefire, but not before it had suffered a number of (as yet unknown) losses. On the Cuban side, the ambassador and another person were wounded.[152]

The intensive targeting of Cubans by Chilean military and paramilitary forces is revealing in terms of their priorities and fears. Throughout 11 September, coup leaders threatened to send tanks and jets to bomb the embassy.[153] A Cuban merchant vessel, *Playa Larga*, was also heavily attacked by sea and air near the port of Valparaiso, and when the military forces raided factories and neighborhoods, they hunted down all foreigners as a matter of priority.[154] But no other embassy faced the same pressure as the Cuban Embassy. The Soviet Embassy, for example, was surrounded briefly a day after the coup but escaped the military's wrath.[155] Moreover, transcripts of Pinochet's conversations with the coup's other leaders on 11 September reveal that Allende's ties with Cuba were influential in determining the general's mind-set. He personally insisted on inserting a clause into the military's radio declaration pointing the finger at "foreigners who have assassinated our people," and at "foreigners who have intervened here on our territory."[156] And amid organizations for Allende's burial, he had commented that the body should be "put in a box and loaded onto an airplane, that the burial take place elsewhere, in Cuba."[157]

The junta also immediately broke off diplomatic relations with Havana and, seeming afraid of engaging in confrontation, urgently wanted all Cubans in Chile to leave the country.[158] Although the Cubans themselves now quite clearly also wanted to leave, they did not trust the military to guarantee their safety, and they wanted to safeguard their interests in Chile. Thus, while Cuban diplomats bombarded foreign embassies world-wide to demand "safe conduct" for their colleagues, frantic negotiations went on in Havana and Santiago to organize their departure.[159] What concerned the Cubans was how to safeguard the arms they had stored for the MIR, how to take their own arms with them without them being discovered, and how they could protect Max Marambio, a Mirista and former leader of the GAP with close links to the Cubans who was at the embassy on the day of the coup and whom the military refused to let leave.

Eventually, Havana entrusted Sweden's ambassador, Harald Edelstam, with Cuban interests. When this left-wing Swedish aristocrat, with experience of covert operations during World War II, arrived at the embassy, Estrada led him down to the cellar where the Cubans had stored the arms they wanted to distribute to the MIR. And although Edelstam was reportedly shocked at their quantity, Estrada remembers that his attitude was "magnificent." He immediately agreed to protect Marambio, safeguard the arms, and help distribute them as soon as possible. For the time being, though, he covered the cellar's trap door with a sofa and vowed to sleep on it.[160] Meanwhile, on 12 September, the Cubans collected documents and money from Cuba's commercial office, rescued those that had not been able to get to the embassy from their safe houses, and packed their empty diplomatic crates with Cuban arms.[161]

Cubans later recalled it was pure luck that a Soviet plane was at Puda-huel airport to fly them out of Chile.[162] It was also only because Soviet personnel were neither vulnerable nor being asked to leave that they agreed to donate their plane when asked by the Cubans to do so. The only other country the junta immediately broke relations with was North Korea, on the grounds that it, like Cuba, had "actively intervened in internal national politics."[163] However, despite the discovery of North Korean arms at Tomás Moro, which served as the pretext, Pyongyang's leaders knew nothing about the weapons (the Cubans had brought North Korean weapons into the country because the USSR and Eastern Europeans had put restrictions on Cubans transferring their weapons to Chile).[164]

Cuba's three-year mission in Chile thus came to a disastrous end far more abruptly than the Cubans themselves had anticipated. Their improvised escape and the extensive embassy preparations for withstanding a prolonged struggle reveal that the Cubans had never expected to abandon the country like this. Although Marambio and Edelstam, together with Argentine Montoneros clandestinely in Chile, delivered approximately three hundred arms to the MIR in the weeks after the coup, these did not offer any significant relief for the desperate situation Chile's left wing faced.[165] As the CIA noted, the junta planned "severe repression" to "stamp out all vestiges of communism in Chile for good."[166]

Of course, the junta's fear that the Cubans could lead mass resistance, nurtured over the course of three years of psychological campaigns to play up Cuban involvement in Chile, was exaggerated. Even with prior knowledge and unity, it is far from certain whether a few hundred (or even a few thousand) partially trained Chilean militants could have resisted Chile's armed forces. The Chilean Left was hopelessly divided and was unprepared to face the military onslaught that followed, having been severely weakened by the arms raids in the weeks leading up to the coup. There also does not appear to have been a joint Cuban-Chilean plan to defend the government. Rather, there was a general expectation that the Cubans would assist if the time came.[167] And although their embassy remained a central point of reference to the various sectors of the Chilean Left, in the context of fragmented left-wing planning the Cubans had become dislocated and unable to direct any decisive countermeasures for a coup. Ultimately, Havana's role depended on Allende to take decisive action to unite these forces and request the Cubans' help. But this request never came. "The only option was to try to arm the popular forces," Castro later told Honecker; "Naturally it would have been dangerous, but it was more dangerous to do nothing. . . . For the enemy was mobilized, the fascists were mobilized, and the masses were nowhere to be seen because the government had not mobilized them."[168]

New Friendships

One week after the Chilean coup, Cuba's representative at the United Nations, Ricardo Alarcón, labeled Nixon the "intellectual author" of the military's intervention.[169] From Berlin to Tanzania, Paris to Rome, and Montreal to Honduras, other fingers also pointed at the United States as the architect of Allende's downfall.[170] Chile's new regime certainly looked like Nixon's most-favored ally in Latin America, Brazil's dictatorship. But as one external observer noted two years later, "the level of oppression" was a "major difference": "Chile's military junta has not only utilized the experience of Brazil but leapfrogged the early experimental stages of the Brazilian process."[171] Washington played a role in encouraging the new Chilean dictatorship to speedily learn the lessons from Brazil. Indeed, U.S. contingency planners had been examining ways of persuading a hypothetical military regime to seek close relations with Brasilia even before the Chilean coup took place. And now that it had, policy makers in Washington—among them the previously reticent Davis and members of the State Department—paid considerable attention to ensuring that a potential military regime succeeded.

The day after the coup, the State Department instructed Davis to discreetly convey Washington's "desire to cooperate" and to "assist" the junta.[172] As Kissinger privately argued, "however unpleasant," the new government was "better for us than Allende."[173] Over a month before the coup took place, intelligence analysts had also unsurprisingly predicted that Allende's "demise" would be a "psychological setback to the cause of doctrinaire socialism in the hemisphere" and that his successors would "be favorably disposed toward the U.S." and to foreign investment.[174]

Pinochet also quite clearly wanted to "strengthen . . . friendly ties" and contacted the U.S. Embassy in Santiago on 12 September as a means of doing so.[175] Although he had apparently not communicated his plans to Washington before, he now notably played up Allende's alleged pressure on the army to purchase Soviet equipment as a lever to extract adequate assistance.[176] Indeed, looking back on the days before the coup when he was minister of defense, Letelier recalled that he had asked Pinochet to look into the prospect of purchasing arms from the USSR and that the latter had expressed opposition to the idea of Soviet arms and training programs in Chile.[177] This attitude appears to have impressed U.S. officials in the immediate aftermath of the coup. On 14 September, intelligence sources noted somewhat belatedly that he was "decisive" and "prudent . . . the priority concerns are to restore order and economic normalcy. Political reform apparently will wait."[178] The DIA also later described him as "very businesslike. Very honest, hard working, dedicated." And Davis went as far as to call him "gracious and eloquent."[179]

The embrace U.S. officials gave Pinochet was nevertheless predetermined even before Washington became acquainted with him personally. Predicting a violent confrontation between coup leaders and UP supporters, the United States had wanted to ensure that any military leaders who seized power succeeded in defeating their opponents. On 1 August, CIA analysts had therefore noted, "repressive measures would be necessary" to quell "strikes, demonstrations, and other forms of protest." A "favorable" scenario they listed was one in which, "after some, perhaps considerable, bloodletting, Chile could eventually achieve a greater measure of political and social stability."[180] On 8 September, the U.S. Ad Hoc Interagency Working Group on Chile had subsequently concluded that "a united military could control violent resistance" but warned that this would not be assured if thousands of armed workers seized factories and marched downtown. It had therefore suggested that the United States be willing (even if at this late stage it was still not completely ready) to step in by providing riot control equipment, supplying Chile by means of military airlifts from Panama, and providing food and other "minimum essential" assistance. This working group had also urged that items already requested by the Chilean military under Foreign Military Sales credits be delivered rapidly. To lessen charges of supporting coup leaders, varied and complex scenarios had also simultaneously been explored to see how the United States could respond positively to expected requests for foodstuffs and financial assistance. Overall, the working group had calculated that the new government could not "possibly succeed without very substantial external help" and recommended that Washington be "prepared . . . through special congressional action if necessary, to provide substantial additional resources."[181]

As predicted, after 11 September, Chile's new regime asked for help. Davis concluded that the Chilean military ascribed to a National Security Doctrine that prioritized economic stability and a "healthy social structure" as essential pillars of defense. The ambassador observed that "under the broader interpretation, most recently enunciated by former army CINC general Carlos Prats, officers [had] looked on in anger as they saw the Allende government plunge Chile into economic disaster and increased foreign dependency, and watched the UP parties and extreme left elements actively seek to undermine traditional military precepts of discipline and chain of command."[182] After Allende's overthrow, military leaders were explicit about what they needed to create this "healthy" society: at the top of their list was equipment—one thousand flares, a thousand steel helmets, portable housing—to put down resistance to the coup, equip draftees, and deal with the large numbers of prisoners they detained. The Chilean air force also asked the United States to send medical supplies and, in sharp contrast to his worries about precipitating a coup before it took place, Davis now advised Washington to accommodate requests, albeit as "discreetly as possible."[183] Meanwhile, Orlando Saenz, a Chilean businessman who had led strikes against Allende and had considerable influence in the new regime, approached a U.S. official in Nairobi. He spelled out that Chile needed $500 million before the end of 1973 ($200 million for imports, $300 million for debt payments) and indicated that the new government was also seeking credits from U.S. banks and, through "very" confidential talks, from U.S. copper companies.[184]

Henceforth, Washington delivered as much assistance as it deemed possible without attracting undue attention and condemnation. On 21 September, Foreign Minister Admiral Ismael Huerta expressed his "deep appreciation" when Washington agreed to send an airlift of supplies worth $100,000.[185] Kissinger then privately conveyed his support for the junta and expressed his "best wishes . . . for the success of the Chilean government" to Huerta when the latter visited the UN in October 1973. In separate meetings, U.S. policy makers also underlined their intention to be as "helpful as possible" in arranging meetings with New York banks.[186] Indeed, when Kubisch met Huerta on 12 October, he promised the Chilean government the "widest collaboration."[187] Huerta also recorded Kissinger as stating "emphatically that U.S. policy would not be modified by mistaken information in the press," which condemned the military regime's brutality.[188] And when Pinochet approached Davis in Santiago on the same day, emphasizing that Chile was "broke" and needed "help getting on its feet," the ambassador "reiterated assurances."[189]

By the end of October 1973, Washington had given Pinochet a loan of $24 million for wheat purchases (eight times the total commodity credit offered to Allende's government). In 1974 Chile—which accounted for 3 percent of Latin America's population—also received 48 percent of U.S. "Food for Peace" (PL480) grants to the region.[190] In the three years that followed, Chile assumed a preferential status in Latin America, as the recipient of 88 percent of U.S. AID's housing guarantees and $237.8 million from the Inter-American Development Bank. Pinochet's government also became the fifth-largest purchaser of U.S. military equipment until U.S. congressional leaders put a stop to this in subsequent years on account of Chilean human rights abuses.[191]

Simultaneously, the CIA established close ties with the military regime's new security and intelligence services. In early 1974 General Walters, by then deputy director of the CIA, invited Manuel Contreras, the head of Chile's new secret policy agency (the DINA) to Washington, where Contreras, in his own words, learned about "how to do national intelligence."[192] As the former *Washington Post* correspondent John Dinges concludes in his book, *The Condor Years*, the United States also had "amazingly complete and intimate details" about the regional counterrevolutionary network that Pinochet formally established in late 1975 under the name "Operation Condor."[193] After all, immediately after the coup, U.S. policy makers had reemphasized their preference for encouraging coordination between the new Chilean government and its regional neighbors, noting that "for financial and technical as well as political reasons," the United States should lead "part of a larger effort of various international and other sources of assistance."[194]

Surveying other Latin American countries that might be "disposed" to help, analysts predictably noted that Brazil would be "particularly important because of its likely ideological identification with the new GOC and its substantial and growing economic strength." It is therefore unsurprising that when Davis conveyed Washington's desires to assist the new Chilean regime with countering "urban terrorism," he also insisted "Chile's Latin American friends" had "considerable experience . . . in this area" that the junta could draw on.[195] Similarly, Huerta recorded Kissinger as insinuating to him that Chileans should acquire military equipment in Brazil if it was needed "urgently."[196] Fortunately for the Nixon administration, the United States' efforts to organize such a multilateral support effort appear to have been well received. As Davis observed in late October, "in regard to third country channeling of aid," Pinochet was "showing considerable understadint [*sic*]."[197]

The Brazilians were also obviously inclined to help. Not only had they been given prior information about coup plotting, but Pinochet later recalled that the Brazilian ambassador in Santiago personally extended recognition to the junta early on 11 September. "We won!" he reportedly exclaimed.[198] Brasilia then offered the Chilean junta immediate help with suppression, working as advisers to the new regime, as well as directly interrogating and torturing prisoners in Chile's National Stadium.[199] As Contreras would recall three decades later, Chilean intelligence services quickly established exchange and training programs with Brasilia.[200] Meanwhile, the Brazilian regime conducted an immediate review of how to extend lines of credit, reportedly offering the junta "significant economic assistance in the near future . . . $50 million or more" days after the coup.[201]

Other right-wing regimes in the Southern Cone also supported the Chilean junta on account of the implications that it had for their own internal Cold War battles against the Left. On the one hand, Bolivian newspapers cheerfully reported the expulsion of 315 Bolivian "leftists" from Chile.[202] And on the other hand, U.S. diplomats reported that with more than 300 Uruguayans in Chile, a group of hard-line military leaders in Montevideo were hoping the Chileans would "take care" of the Tupamaros.[203] Indeed, without any apparent U.S. coordination, planes from Argentina, Brazil, Bolivia, Uruguay, and Ecuador had arrived with provisions for the new regime days after the coup.[204]

Chile's neighbors, alongside Washington, did their best to bolster the incoming regime's international standing. When Huerta appeared at the United Nations in October 1973, Brazil's permanent representative at the organization helped draft his speech.[205] Acknowledging the role of public relations, the State Department had also sent instructions to Santiago days after the coup, emphasizing that Chile would need to defend itself eloquently in international forums.[206] Subsequently, a Chilean Foreign Ministry spokesman told Davis that the new regime was "deeply appreciative" for advice on this matter, and in the months that followed, the United States helped launch a propaganda offensive justifying the junta's actions.[207] According to Davis, Pinochet also showed "sensitivity to the need for both U.S. and GOC caution in development of overly close public identifications." The dictator informed the U.S. ambassador that he would send Chilean civilian leaders to the United States to alleviate "Chile's public image problem."[208] As Chile's new ambassador in Washington surmised, the American public's hostility toward the new regime was not just about the junta but rather the result of ongoing battles between Congress and the Executive in the context of Watergate and Vietnam.[209]

Nixon and Kissinger were equally frustrated by the reaction to the coup in the United States. The president dismissed press speculation that the United States was involved as "crap," and Kissinger commented on the "filthy hypocrisy" of those that condemned the new military regime: "In Eisenhower's day it would have been celebrated!"[210] It was an "absurd situation where we have to apologize for the overthrow of . . . a government hostile to us," he privately complained.[211] Even so, Kissinger acknowledged he had to be cautious about what he said. "To get in to this [Chile], even in executive session," his assistant, William Jorden, counseled, "will open a

Pandora's box . . . once a precedent of discussing CIA activities before the Foreign Relations Committee is established, no programs in other countries will be immune."[212] What followed in 1974 and 1975—the publication of two congressional reports, *Covert Operation in Chile, 1963–73* and *Alleged Assassination Plots Involving Foreign Leaders*—confirmed his fears. Indeed, one scholar has since argued that U.S. foreign policy subsequently suffered from a "'Chile syndrome'—supplementing the Vietnam syndrome of national reticence to U.S. military intervention in distant lands" when it came to covert operations abroad.[213]

The coup also dramatically altered Chile's place in the world as well as Cuban and U.S. positions in Latin America. In the Southern Cone, Allende's hopes of redesigning the inter-American system had backfired even before he was overthrown. And now that he had been, growing ranks of counterrevolutionary forces emerged from the ruins of the left-wing tide of the 1960s and the early 1970s to create a new antirevolutionary order. Without a doubt, this shifting regional balance of power was directly related—though by no means exclusively—to Allende's election, presidency, and demise. And it was also helped by U.S. policymakers, who got what they had wanted from the start of Allende's presidency, even if they had not masterminded precisely how this occurred. Certainly, the mortal struggle to determine Chile's future had been won, and Latin America was back within the United States' sphere of influence. As Davis noted a month after the coup had taken place, "*grosso modo* Chile has been shunted out of the column of left-leaning Third World admirers of the Soviet Union.[214]

Conclusion

The international history of Allende's overthrow is a far more complex story than a simple case of "who did it?" To appreciate its significance, we need to ask why foreigners got involved in the battle for Chile between 1970 and 1973 and with what consequences for that country, the hemisphere, and beyond. A confluence of different local and international actors driven apart in a battle between socialism and capitalism determined what happened on 11 September 1973. And although neither the victors nor the vanquished in Chile were manipulated from abroad, the decisions they made were in part the result of their belief that an international battle was taking place within their country and region. Indeed, both the Left and the Right conceptualized themselves as nationalists who were fighting against foreign enemies. Thus, while Allende pictured himself as freeing Chile from

U.S. capitalist exploitation, Pinochet justified outlawing left-wing parties by blaming the "foreign doctrine of Marxism" for having driven Chile to chaos.[215] In this context, the opposition media's skillful manipulation of Cuba's role in Chile, helped by funds and intelligence feeds from the CIA (both true and false), was highly effective in drumming up fear among an already highly charged and divided population. There is another international dimension to the coup that also needs underlining and which has received little attention to date: instead of being *the* decisive turning point in the defeat of revolution in the Southern Cone, which it is often depicted as being, the Chilean coup of 1973 was one pivotal moment in a much larger counterrevolutionary wave that had begun in the mid-1960s and had gathered pace in the three years following Allende's election, isolating Chile in the process.

So what of the United States and its responsibility for toppling Allende's Chile? As it turned out, U.S. intervention in the final months of Allende's presidency was a messy reaction to events on the ground rather than a simplistic tale of the White House masterminding the Chilean coup. In a conversation at the end of 1973, Kissinger remarked to President Houari Boumedienne of Algeria that the world had given the United States "too much credit" for the coup that overthrew Allende.[216] And contrary to the accusations that circulated after the coup, and much of the literature available since 11 September 1973, this assessment now seems to be reasonably accurate. The Nixon administration had certainly willed a coup to take place and had been frustrated by the slow progress of coordinating military action. However, question marks as to where the United States would fit into the equation of any successful military intervention had overshadowed policy formulation right up until the last minute. It is therefore not surprising that historians and commentators have agonized over the United States' direct responsibility for the coup, considering the fragmented direction of U.S. policy at this crucial moment in Chilean politics.

However, as it turns out, what we know now about the United States' involvement in Chile is even less palatable than a story of Nixon and Kissinger working alone to overthrow Allende. As we have seen, once a military coup or the fall of Allende's government seemed a decided possibility, the whole Nixon administration took calculated decisions to help a future repressive military dictatorship survive and consolidate its hold over its citizens. Washington's leaders also enthusiastically propounded a hemispheric support system between similar dictatorships, something that was eagerly taken up and encouraged by like-minded strongmen in the Southern Cone. And more than any smoking gun that proves U.S. responsibility for the coup itself, contingency planning before it took place and the actions that followed tell a far more uncomfortable story of willing complicity throughout Washington's foreign policy-making establishment in securing the junta's subsequent dictatorship and encouraging the formation of a regional right-wing network.

The story of Cuba's growing frustration, despair, and impotency in Chile before the coup took place is also complicated. As the Cubans who participated in the events suggested years later, had Havana been in charge in 1973 (or even earlier for that matter), it would have made different—implicitly, better—strategic decisions. In what Castro perceived to be a zero-sum game between revolution and reaction, Havana advocated a life-and-death struggle that, however costly, would have eventually led Chile and Latin America closer to socialism. While Allende preferred to symbolically sacrifice himself at La Moneda instead of mobilizing his supporters to regroup and then launch a resistance that would almost certainly have led to a bloody civil war, the Cubans were thus willing to risk the consequences of fighting back. It is impossible to tell what would have happened had Cubans been able to change the course of Chilean events. More effective resistance to the coup may well have delayed the counterrevolutionary onslaught as Havana hoped, and Allende alive may well have been more important to the resistance than dead, but the result of civil war would also have been scores of casualties and destruction—probably even more than the junta subsequently unleashed. As Merino's message made clear on 9 September, those who prepared to crush Chile's democracy believed the coup they launched would be a matter of life and death, and they were not prepared to take any chances.

Indeed, rather than dissuading the coup leaders from acting, the growing possibility of a left-wing combative force, the specter of Cuban involvement in preparing it, and the prospect of an impending showdown radicalized Chilean society and propelled the armed forces to act. To be sure, there were only 120 Cubans in Santiago on 11 September, not the thousands that the right-wing media had warned of. But the military's targeting of the Cuban Embassy and all foreigners, factories, and poor neighborhoods, together with the ruthlessness with which it did so, clearly illustrates the power of wildly exaggerated fears regarding what the Cubans and left-wing revolutionaries from the Southern Cone could achieve.

CONCLUSION

A concerned scholar once asked me whether my researching the details of Cuba's role in Chile meant that I thought the United States was justified in destabilizing Chilean democracy. Having spent decades uncovering the many wrongs of U.S. interventionism in the Third World, he wanted to know whether by writing about Cuban arms transfers and military training of the Left I was condoning U.S. covert operations, those who celebrated the bombing of La Moneda, and the violent repression in the years that followed. This question, together with fears expressed by some who shared their memories with me for the purpose of this book, has troubled me over the past few years. My immediate answer was (and is) a resounding no. However, beyond this, I answered him by saying that history should never be regarded as a zero-sum game—that understanding the role that one side played in the complex inter-American Cold War should not preclude investigation of another. Or to put it another way, to catalog one lot of wrongdoing should not automatically lead to us into the trap of thinking that the other side was passive and blameless or vice versa. Not only is this not what history is about—the past is mostly far more nuanced than a simple battle between good and evil—but to omit the role of the Cubans and the Chileans they worked with is actually to do an injustice to what they believed in and what both groups fought for. Just as many argue that the story of U.S. intervention in Chile should be "exposed," therefore, the Cubans' and the Chileans' story—their "agency," as academics like to call it—deserves rescuing, inconvenient as some of the details of Havana's role in particular might be for those on the Left who would prefer now to pretend it had never taken place. Not making an effort to tell *all* sides of the story and how they related to each other makes it difficult to fully understand what happened. And inexcusable as the crimes committed by those who seized power on 11 September 1973 might be, examining all possible dimensions of the past is part and parcel of what history is all about.

As it turns out, there is enough responsibility for what happened in

Chile to be spread around—about which more in a moment. First and foremost, however, my interest in writing the international history of Allende's Chile was not to add one more voice to the historiography of blame. Since the end of the Cold War and the collapse of the Soviet Union, the New Cold War History has thankfully moved away from traditional narratives that focused on cyclical debates about whose *fault* the conflict was and has moved on to examining questions of why and how it took place.[1] While scholarship on the Cold War in Latin America has so far tended to lag behind historiography of the ideological struggles that dominated other parts of the world in the latter part of the twentieth century, it has also begun to move beyond the blame game to explore other dimensions of the struggle.[2] This has a lot to do with growing generational distance from the events that took place, which means that historians approaching this topic now do not feel compelled to refight battles of the past. But it is also thanks to new sources that are available for scholars to consult, which allow for a multidimensional and comprehensive examination of the past.

For my part, I wanted to use these new sources to get to the heart of what shaped the intense struggles that consumed Chile, the Southern Cone, and the inter-American system in the early 1970s. Primarily, I was interested in understanding who the main protagonists of that conflict were, what they believed in and fought over, how the ideological struggles they engaged in evolved, and with what consequences. Yet, equally, I was keen to explore them with a view to examining broader questions, such as what détente meant to parts of the global South, how Third World revolutionary states dealt with the outside world during the Cold War years, and the extent to which this coincided with North-South divides in international politics.

Like so many other views from the Third World, the international history of Allende's Chile that emerged is a rather depressing story. The Cold War in Latin America, as the historian Gilbert Joseph has argued, "was rarely cold."[3] And Chile's story ended up being no exception, despite what many Chileans—Allende among them—believed before 11 September 1973. Yet the internationalization of Chilean politics during the early 1970s provides a fascinating snapshot of the inter-American Cold War, those who shaped it, and the way in which allies and antagonists within it interacted with each other. As well as shedding light on diplomatic negotiations and covert arms deliveries, on the disputes *between* revolutionaries as much as the battles they fought with their adversaries, it also shows how actors in the South experienced Cold War ideological struggles at regional and global levels. In this respect, as I suggested in the introduction, focusing on the intersection between bilateral relations and the multilateral arenas in which they were played out helps us to get to the bottom of the dynamic historical processes that unfolded.

In exploring these dimensions, this book examined two main issues: the impact that international actors had on Chile, and that country's significance for what occurred beyond its borders. Beginning with the latter of these two issues, it is quite clear that the rise and fall of La Vía Chilena had a profound impact both in Latin America and much further afield as well. Alone, the sizable interest that Allende's presidency and his overthrow sparked worldwide, not to mention the dynamic nature of Chile's foreign relations during this period, makes it an interesting story to tell. But the apparent disconnect between it and the history of the relaxation of superpower tensions, the United States' opening to China, and European détente during the same period make it all the more intriguing. When Chileans talk of the early 1970s, they speak of their county's most "ideological years." Yet this was precisely when ideological conflict was supposed to have been abandoned—or at least recalibrated and postponed—in favor of pragmatism and realpolitik.

So how do we make sense of this apparent contradiction? By the 1970s, there were different ideas around the globe about what the Cold War was and how it should be fought. As a result of the varied experiences of living—and for a whole new generation, growing up—with the Cold War for over two decades, the ideological conflict at its core between different varieties of communism and capitalism was far more diffuse, fragmented, and global. For one, developments had splintered the Cold War parameters of earlier decades, adding new ingredients along the way. These included—but were not confined to—decolonization and the emerging North-South divide, the Cuban revolution, the Sino-Soviet split, and divisions over Vietnam. Beyond these issues, the Cold conflict was also being fought by a far greater array of ideologically driven warriors than it had been in the immediate aftermath of World War II. When General Médici traveled to Washington in 1971, it was the Brazilian president more than Nixon who drove the conversation about the anticommunist agenda in the Southern Cone. And when Castro went to Poland shortly after Nixon's visit in June 1972, he denounced détente and the very concept of peaceful coexistence with U.S. imperialism in no uncertain terms. So much so, in fact, that his hosts privately derided him as being "aggressive," "demagogic," and "primitive." Castro simply did not understand the "significance" of East-West negotiations or grasp what was at stake, they lamented—he believed "that everything is good and important if it directly contributes to the revolutionary struggle" and therefore failed to take "consequences and other perspectives" into account.[4]

In a sense, Castro and his hosts were both right. For the Soviet bloc, there was a lot to be gained from détente in the shape of arms negotiations, security, trade, and a sense of legitimacy. And Castro's commitment to revolutionary upheaval, his rejection of armistices, and his insistence on a fight to the death with imperialism *was* extreme. But Castro was also right to be worried about his island's position within the game of détente and what this meant for his efforts to survive as a revolutionary leader only ninety miles away from the opposing camp's superpower that his principal backers halfway across the globe now seemed so eager to placate.[5] Would the Cuban revolution's future be negotiated over his head as it had been during the Cuban Missile Crisis? Would the Soviet bloc withdraw its support from its allies? What did this mean for the cause of revolutionary struggle in the Third World to which Castro's regime was so inextricably tied? As Castro's bewildered East European allies observed, "Cuba's full strength is its attachment to principles: that it will not compromise . . . sometimes irritates even friends and allies." If Cuba gave up this position it would have to give up what to its leaders and its population was most important, its role in Latin America and its global ambitions going beyond its size or the opportunities normally available to a small island. Havana could therefore not bargain for concessions from the United States in the same way that the Soviets and the PRC believed they could. As the U.S. representative to the OAS simply put it, "Cuba is not China."[6]

Neither was Chile. Allende's hope of benefiting from détente by engaging in the policies and language of ideological pluralism fell on deaf ears in Washington. When Allende's Chile then ended up trying to play the Cold War at a superpower level, the Soviets were not interested either. Indeed, Allende's Chile seemed to be excluded at every turn—"East-West rapprochement had restricted peace to the prosperous countries of the world," noted a commentator from India, another southern nation that was seemingly neglected within the context of détente.[7]

Meanwhile, Chile was consumed by the bitter regional—inter-American—manifestation of the global Cold War that abided by its own internal logic, chronology, dimensions, and cast of characters. Indeed, the United States' reasons for opposing Allende become clearer if we look at them in the context of the Nixon administration's broader approach to Latin America. The separate concerted efforts it made to boost right-wing forces and curtail left-wing advances in the region during the early 1970s were part of a bigger strategy that was renewed as a result of Allende's election, but which governed Washington's policy toward Latin America throughout the Cold War era—and détente. At the core of this strategy was a belief that the United States had a "vital interest" in regaining political influence in its traditional sphere, recovering lost prestige among potential anticommunist allies, and ensuring that the "battle of ideas" between different modes of social and economic development was won by those essentially rooted in capitalism. By virtue of the instincts instilled by the Monroe Doctrine, which sought to exclude other world powers from the region, officials in Washington feared Latin American countries' voluntary separation from the United States as threatening its own political, economic, and security interests by undermining its position as a superpower. As George Kennan had written in 1950, "If the countries of Latin America should come to be generally dominated by an outlook which views our country as the root of all evil and sees salvation only in the destruction of our national power, I doubt very much whether our general political program in other parts of the non-communist world could be successful."[8] For a superpower with global aspirations, Latin America's position was therefore pivotal. And in spite of superpower détente, U.S. policy makers' frames of reference vis-à-vis Latin America consequently remained wedded to the concept of a "mortal struggle" against communism and regional examples set by the likes of Castro and Allende.

Nixon in particular seems to have seen history running along two parallel tracks for structuring society, economics, and politics. On one side lay capitalism, which could appear in the guise of liberal democracy or authoritarian dictatorship. On the other side lay communism of whatever stripe, be it a dictatorship of the proletariat or, as in the case of Allende, a pluralistic liberal democracy. As far as Nixon was concerned, there was little possibility of altering the pattern of logical progression along either track, which would ultimately lead Latin America (once "mature" enough) either toward the United States or toward Cuba and then the Soviet Union. Vernon Walters, whom Nixon admired, trusted, and listened to, later explained that "authoritarian rightist regimes always disappear eventually. They have never been able to perpetrate themselves. Communist regimes, once they seize power, never let it go."[9] While the Nixon administration resigned itself to the fact that it could not turn back the clock when it came to the USSR and the PRC on the global stage and thus engaged in negotiations with both powers, it was determined to try to help roll it back in Latin America, where it had more influence and could prevent the consolidation or the spread of communist control—"save Chile!" as Nixon put it.

Of course, the mistake the Nixon administration made in Chile was to disregard Allende's unbending commitment to constitutional government and the anomaly of La Vía Chilena. However, it would be an error to suggest, as others have done, that the Nixon administration's obsessive anticommunism led it to misinterpret Allende's Chile completely. Unlike other right-wing coups in Latin America before 1973, the Chilean coup actually overturned a socialist revolutionary process in train rather than a reformist government. Chilean foreign policy *was* explicitly anti-imperialist (in the sense of being anti-American) to the extent that a Chilean Foreign Ministry report in April 1973 concluded that "the very existence and actions of the Chilean government are damaging to U.S. national interests in Chile, and . . . its example can have great influence on power relations in Latin America and on the Third World in general. . . . Chile succeeds Vietnam . . . in reinforcing and extending anti-imperialist action around the world."[10] Moreover, those who led Chile in the years between 1970 and 1973 were part of a radicalized generation of Third World leaders who believed in not only the struggle for full political and economic independence but also the overhaul of world capitalism and world revolution. Allende was not hoodwinked by Castro or subverted by Cuban revolutionary and far left forces operating in Chile. Although he was a committed democrat stubbornly wedded to Chile's proud constitutional history, he was deeply impressed by Che Guevara, invited Tupamaros and Cuban revolutionaries to his weekend home, and carried the rifle Fidel gave him to La Moneda on the day of the coup. The relations between Castro and Allende were a logical expression of both leaders' ideals and the manifestation of more than a decade of intimate ties. Both shared a commitment to socialism and were also bound by the belief that the United States had exploited the region's resources, thereby undermining development and independence.

Indeed, the real challenge to the United States' regional—and, by extension, its global—influence came from the likes of Allende and Castro in the early 1970s, not the USSR. With the exception of Soviet-Cuban relations, the ideological component of Moscow's lukewarm support for Chile during the Allende years stood in stark contrast to the USSR's burgeoning economic ties with right-wing dictatorships and non-Marxist nationalists in the Americas. (By the late 1970s, for example, Argentina and Brazil were the first and second recipients of all Council of Mutual Economic Assistance aid to the Third World.)[11] More than a struggle against the Soviet Union—temporarily on hold in the age of superpower détente—the Nixon administration's intervention in Chile was a result of an inter-American struggle against Latin Americans who themselves challenged that agenda. Like other revolutionary leaders, Allende went to Havana far more frequently and enthusiastically than he did to Moscow to seek support, recognition, and inspiration, joining a collection of democrats and dictators, civilians and military leaders, nationalists, revolutionaries, Soviet-style communists, and extremist guerrillas. Although the lessons these leaders took away from Cuba were as diverse as the nature of their goals to begin with, they all went to marvel at the only Latin American country to have wrestled with the United States and survived.

Meanwhile, three years after Allende's election had awoken left-wing leaders to the hope of a different type of revolution—a benign version of the Soviet Union or indeed the Cuban reality, itself romanticized for its radical aspirations—Chile became an emblematic example of the failure of that possibility. As it did, its experience was bitterly debated and fought over. "Distant and small though it is," one of Kissinger's advisers told him in 1974, "Chile has long been viewed universally as a demonstration area for economic and social experimentation. Now it is in a sense in the front line of world ideological conflict."[12]

Given Chile's size and the short period Allende was in office, the widespread impact that La Vía Chilena's failure had around the world is surprising. I would argue that any explanation of why should include reference to the ambitious scope of Chilean foreign policy in the 1970s. Chile's international relations during the Allende years were not merely imposed from outside but rather reflected Chilean government officials' own worldviews, their own efforts to reorient Santiago's international standing, and the country's extensive diplomatic outreach over the course of only three years in power. To a lesser extent, the same could also be said of the Chilean opposition's simultaneous search for support in the United States and the Southern Cone and the way in which this galvanized those who were already predisposed to fear Allende and help overthrow him.

Quite simply, the three years of Allende's presidency increased Chile's visibility around the globe. While his government embraced the concept of "ideological pluralism," it enthusiastically invited outsiders to look at Chile both as an example of socialism being attained by peaceful democratic means and as a model for what the global South could achieve by way of shaking off the shackles of dependency. Consequently, the UP put

Santiago forward to host UNCTAD III, Chile's embassy in Washington ran press campaigns to raise awareness of the UP's aims, and Allende called for Latin Americans to speak with "one voice" as a means of spurring others on to challenge the logic of regional political and economic relations. Later, the Chilean government asked for concrete assistance from Latin America, the Third World, and the Soviet bloc so as to survive what Chilean spokesmen conceptualized as a frontline battle in a worldwide struggle for social justice, equality, and liberty in the global South. In these instances, Chilean foreign policy was profoundly linked to La Vía Chilena's progress at home, but rather than being a purely defensive strategy, it also contained essential offensive characteristics that drew attention to what was happening in Chile during the UP years. Indeed, like Castro before him, albeit through international forums rather than guerrilla struggles, Allende sought to safeguard his own revolution by changing the world as opposed to sacrificing his cause.

Although Allende was wildly optimistic about what he could achieve, his failure resonated loudly in the global South, where his government had previously attracted interest and sympathy. Indeed, one African editorial—itself testimony to Chilean foreign policy's reach by 1973—described Allende's overthrow as "a slap in the face of the third world."[13] True, the Third World as a whole faced a large collection of different challenges—a few months earlier, in June 1973, for example, Chilean Foreign Ministry analysts had cataloged serious divisions over the Provisional Government of South Vietnam's entry into the Non-Aligned Movement and a growing "crisis" within the G77 as a result of its heterogeneity and its members' inability to overcome their own interests as just two difficult issues undermining harmonious relations between Third World countries.[14] However, Allende's overthrow only a few days after the Non-Aligned Movement's conference in Algeria appeared to spell out these wider Third World problems with clarity. Not only had the Chilean coup demonstrated the ongoing nature of the Cold War conflict in the global South, but Allende's struggle to assert Chile's economic independence through nationalization of Chile's raw materials and the failure of the UP's broader international agenda also underscored the obstacles involved in promoting systemic change at a national and international level.

With the majority of the former colonial areas of the world nominally independent by the 1970s and with Cold War tensions apparently diminishing, the Third World—to which Allende very much saw himself as belonging—had focused increasingly on guaranteeing economic security and independence for its member states as a means to definitive political power. Within this context, Chile had contributed to the radicalization of the Non-Aligned Movement and the divisions within the G77 during the UP years. It had also played a key role in laying the groundwork for what would, after the Algiers conference in 1973, be the global South's demand for a New International Economic Order (NIEO) in 1974. And yet, by the 1980s, the NIEO had collapsed amid divisions in the Third World, the intransigence of developed industrial nations, and a staggering debt crisis—echoing many of the difficulties that Chile had faced a decade before. Indeed, Allende's own efforts to assert independence and bring about revolutionary change—in Chile and abroad—reflected some of the Third World's essential dilemmas. Aside from the resistance to serious renegotiation of the basic principles and structure of international economic and political relations in the global North, it had to cope with differences within the global South itself.

Moreover, Santiago's perspective during the 1970s exemplifies a central contradiction that underlay much of the Third Worldist project with which Allende identified, namely the simultaneous demand for independence and the request for developmental assistance. In *The Wretched of the Earth*, Frantz Fanon heralded the moment when colonial states asserted independence and demanded that past exploitation be compensated: "Colonialism and imperialism have not paid their score when they withdrew their flags and their police forces from our territories," he wrote; "when we hear the head of a European state declare with his hand on his heart that he must come to the help of the poor underdeveloped peoples, we do not tremble with gratitude. Quite the contrary; we say to ourselves: 'It's a just reparation which will be paid to us.' . . . The Third World does not mean to organize a great crusade of hunger against the whole of Europe. What it expects from those who for centuries have kept it in slavery is that they will help it to rehabilitate mankind, and make man victorious everywhere, once and for all."[15] A decade after Fanon wrote from the vantage point of Algeria's struggle for independence, Allende demanded that Chile be accorded the right to claim back excessive profits, but in the absence of ready alternatives, he needed Washington to secure an easy passage toward revolution by granting credits and approval. As he put it, his rebellion was reasonable and just, and Chile was owed compensation for past exploitation, but he continually appealed for understanding that was simply not there. Moreover, his last-minute trip to Moscow and stalemated bilateral negotiations with Washington in the last year of his presidency demonstrated that, despite efforts to rejuggle Chile's international relations, Santiago was ultimately still dependent on the vertical North-South relationships that the UP had hoped to set to one side in favor of South-South ties and ideological pluralism. Even if Washington had extended détente to the global South (rather than merely attempting to limit the USSR's involvement in the Third World) and even if the Soviet Union had not backed away from risking its relations with the United States to help sustain a revolutionary process it increasingly believed would fail, this essential dilemma would not have been solved.

Certainly, since the early twentieth century, Latin Americans have always had to work within the confines of the U.S. economic, geostrategic, and cultural sphere. Directly challenging the logic of this system and trying to negotiate an amicable separation or, in extreme cases, a favorable divorce has consistently proved to be unfeasible. To a large degree this has stemmed from traditional patterns of trade and industrial development that, once established, have been difficult to undo. But it was also because Latin American countries' geographic position, coupled with their relative poverty and the limited resources other great powers could provide, made negotiating an end to the region's dependence acutely difficult. As Letelier warned the UP during the Allende years, diversifying trade and aid in Europe and the Soviet bloc could simply not compensate for the loss of U.S. credits, spare parts, and trade. Only Castro, by tying himself firmly to the Soviet bloc and embarking on a new (but, in his estimation, still unsatisfactory) dependence was able to survive dislocation from the United States and escape what many Cubans regarded to be their geographic and historical fate, and even this proved to be monumentally difficult.

In this context, the United States rarely countenanced the idea of renegotiating its prescriptions for economic development or its principles for involvement in regional affairs. Even during a brief interlude when it proclaimed a "mature partnership" with the region, the Nixon administration continued to use the threat of estrangement or promise of cooperation as a means of maintaining influence over Latin America. "We have the only system that works," George H. W. Bush and Secretary Rogers respectively told Allende in 1972 and 1973. Although the ideological makeup of those that rebelled against this system determined how the United States would oppose them, any country that chose a different path was essentially deemed as being wrong by successive administrations in Washington who felt they knew better than the unruly Latin Americans that they were forced to deal with (Nixon's admiration for General Médici aside). Thus, although Kennan had argued that Latin America's loyalty was essential to the United States' great power status, he had also advised Secretary of State Acheson that it was up to the Latin Americans to conform as opposed to the other way round. As he put it, U.S. officials had to remember "that we are a great power; that we are by and large much less in need of them than they are in need of us."[16]

Following the Chilean coup of 1973 and the counterrevolutionary advances made in the Southern Cone during the two years preceding it, the United States could relax in the knowledge that Kennan's observation was still true. To be sure, when he assumed the position of secretary of state in late September 1973, Kissinger "confessed he really didn't know much about Latin America" and set up study groups to engage more with the problems of the region. He told Mexico's foreign minister that he wanted a "more active" Latin American policy and announced the latest of what have been a stream of initiatives to begin a so-called New Dialogue with Latin America since Franklin Roosevelt's rather more successful Good Neighbor Diplomacy back in the 1930s. (This time, he acknowledged that the United States could no longer "overpower" its "foreign policy problems" as it had in the past and that it could do "very little" without "understanding.") Beyond surface platitudes, however, Kissinger resisted Latin American demands to transform U.S. regional policy, compromise on issues of economic assistance, practice nonintervention, or give preferential access to U.S. markets.[17]

After the long decade of the 1960s that lasted from the Cuban revolution until Allende's overthrow or, as I have argued, just before this point, the United States had regained the initiative in the inter-American Cold War that it had previously lost with the help of local allies and the failings of those it opposed. Certainly, compared to 1970, when Allende's election had pushed the White House to pay more attention to Latin America, Washington's position was much more secure thanks to the new level of understanding it could count on from dictatorships in the Southern Cone and the new relations it had fostered with non-Marxist nationalists as a means of neutralizing the threat of more Allendes and Castros. This is not to say that Washington could henceforth stage-manage events on the ground. To the contrary, as recent international histories of U.S.–Latin American relations have convincingly shown — and as the Chilean chapter of the inter-American Cold War demonstrates — the United States' power to *control* events south of the Rio Grande was more limited than is commonly suggested, despite the interest it had in doing so. Instead, it is to acknowledge that from the early 1970s onward Washington could once more rely on mutual interests and a similar worldview with Cold Warriors in South America who were happy to accept U.S. funds, arms, or training to fight their own cause and share—or in some cases assume—the burden of fighting so-called communism in all its various forms.

For Cuba, this renewed inter-American Cold War offensive in the early 1970s was disastrous. When more than a hundred Cubans descended the steps of an especially commissioned Aeroflot plane at Havana's international airport on 13 September 1973, Raúl Castro had been there to embrace them while hundreds of onlookers applauded their arrival.[18] Less than twenty-four hours earlier, it had been touch-and-go whether these Cubans would escape Chile alive. Now that they were back in Havana, they had to accept that their hasty departure from Santiago had marked a devastating end to three years of intimate involvement in Chile. And once back in Havana after his tour of Asia, Fidel Castro moderated even his previously new so-called mature stance toward Latin America that had evolved since 1968, backing away from the steadfast principles he had held up until that point. In essence, this is because he had very little choice after September 1973. Reflecting on "recent setbacks" in early 1974, Manuel Piñeiro also warned that "even harder times" awaited revolutionaries in the region.[19]

Ultimately, Cuba's leaders concluded that the objective conditions for successful revolution no longer existed in South America. When far Left revolutionary movements in the Southern Cone—including the MIR—moved from Chile to Argentina to instigate a regional insurgency in November 1973, Castro was therefore reluctant to help, reportedly calling their collective Junta Coodinadora Revolucionaria "a waste of time."[20] As he told East Germany's Erich Honecker a few months later, "The situation is difficult, the persecution is great, the struggle is hard." Explaining that the Cubans were not "interfering" any more, he also sharply criticized the MIR, noting that "They had conflicts with Allende, and Allende was right. . . . They had really extremist positions."[21] It is partly as a result of such observations—and their implications for the way in which Cuba conceptualized the opportunities for supporting a revolutionary campaign in Latin America—that the CIA in 1975 was able to report that Cuban support to insurgent groups was at its "lowest levels since 1959."[22] Certainly, when speaking privately to Allende's doctor after the coup, Piñeiro dismissed hopes of reversing Chile's coup for at least a decade.[23]

Without the "objective" conditions to support revolutionary upheaval, Castro reluctantly acknowledged that he had to work with the regional dynamics he confronted if his revolution was to survive. In view of its options, and referring to ongoing nationalization disputes between South American states and the United States, or Panama's efforts to regain control of the Canal Zone, Piñeiro explained to DGLN employees in mid-1974 that Cuba was now "employing flexible tactics." As he put it, it would be "childish" not to take advantage of the fact that sectors of the national bourgeoisie in the region were "adopting attitudes that clash objectively with U.S. policy" because of their "secondary economic contradictions with imperialism." In Piñeiro's words, forming relationships with these actors favored revolutionary progress by promoting "organization, strengthening and preparation for the final battle to seize political power," be it in one, two, or three decades ahead.[24]

In terms of its relations with a variety of different sectors of the national bourgeoisie, Allende's reestablishment of relations with Cuba in 1970 had been pivotal in breaking Castro's isolation in the hemisphere. Before and during Cuban involvement in Chile's revolutionary process, Havana had also been simultaneously developing a new multifaceted regional policy that responded to the failure of previous guerrilla struggles and allowed it to keep up its support for a range of different revolutionary processes. Now that Chile's revolutionary process lay in tatters, this more flexible policy became ever more elastic and important to Cuba's hopes of playing a role within the inter-American system. The fact that Castro had resigned himself to new circumstances and downgraded his appraisal of revolutionary conditions in the Americas also led Havana to engage in exploratory talks with Kissinger in 1974–75, who for his part pragmatically realized that the United States no longer needed to block the normalization of Cuba's relations with a growing variety of Latin American states.[25] Indeed, by 1975, revolutionary Cuba had diplomatic relations with Peru, Argentina, Panama, Venezuela, and Colombia at least in part thanks to the precedent of Allende's reestablishment of diplomatic relations with Cuba and his support for an end to the island's formal isolation within the hemisphere. Finally, after more than a decade of collective sanctions, the majority of the OAS also voted in 1975 to allow sanctions to be dropped without a two-thirds majority to overturn it. Henceforth, states were to be able to deal independently with Cuba without opposition from the United States (albeit with no help from Havana's bitter new ideological foe in Latin America, General Pinochet).

Even so, Cuba's new pragmatism in the Americas did not mean that it rejected principles of revolutionary internationalism or that it was willing to sacrifice its global revolutionary ambitions for the sake of its own détente with the inter-American system. With a firm U.S. commitment to containing Cuba's role in its own backyard and slim prospects for revolution in Latin America, Castro turned to Africa, urging the Soviet Union to join him in his support for national liberation and socialism. Indeed, after fewer than 150 Cubans left Chile in 1973, Havana sent 36,000 Cuban soldiers to fight alongside the People's Movement for the Liberation of Angola (the Movimento Popular de Libertação de Angola, or MPLA) in Angola's civil war between 1975 and 1976, followed by 16,000 to aid Ethiopia in 1978. Africa had certainly not been the Cuban leaders' priority when they seized power in 1959. However, partly as a result of the United States' dominance closer to home in Latin America and decisive setbacks there—including Chile in 1973—Africa is where they were able to make the most decisive impact on the struggle against imperialism.[26]

As a battle between Cuba and the United States developed first in southern Africa and then with renewed vigor in Central America during the 1980s, the international struggle for Chile—a sliver of land far away from either superpower—came to prominence as a lesson in a new phase of this global confrontation, even if the lessons people drew from Allende's Chile depended on who they were and what they wanted to learn. Faced with the fall of détente and renewed superpower hostility in the late 1970s and early 1980s, the Soviets rhetorically pointed the finger at U.S. intervention in Chile as having caused Allende's overthrow when they invaded Afghanistan. As Brezhnev explained in 1980, "to have acted otherwise would have meant leaving Afghanistan prey to imperialism, allowing the forces of aggression to repeat in that country what they had succeeded in doing for example in Chile, where the people's freedom was drowned in blood."[27]

Interestingly, in the immediate aftermath of the coup seven years earlier, Moscow's leaders had been far been more cautious and circumspect about holding the United States accountable for Chilean events. In the months that followed 11 September 1973, Anatoly Dobrynin, the Soviet ambassador in Washington, approached Nixon administration officials privately to exert leverage on the junta on only one issue, the release of the Chilean Communist Party's secretary-general, Luis Corvalán.[28] True, the Soviet Union broke off relations with the Chilean junta a week after the coup, but as others have suggested, this seems to have been related more to Moscow's desire to assume a leading role in mourning Allende's death in the socialist bloc as well as the West, together with the relative insignificance of Soviet-Chilean economic relations, than to its ideological distaste for Santiago's new regime.[29]

Meanwhile, the Chilean coup sparked introspective, self-reflective discussions within the international communist movement centering on the lessons to be drawn from Allende's overthrow and what this meant for strategies of winning power and building socialism. As communist leaders began analyzing what had happened in Chile, what is striking is that more often than not they tended to focus on internal factors, and primarily those associated with the UP's record as opposed to its enemies. In China, Zhou Enlai essentially agreed when Kissinger denied U.S. involvement in bringing down Allende during Sino-American talks in 1973, criticizing Allende's "rashness" and telling his U.S. counterpart that the UP had been "much too complicated."[30] In Western Europe, where the UP's victory had initially been enthusiastically welcomed as a potential model for reaching socialism by peaceful democratic means, Allende's failure also provoked divisions regarding the lessons communist parties should draw.[31] In Italy, the secretary-general of Italy's Communist Party, Enrico Berlinguer, laid out a new strategy for "Historic Compromise." His ideas—that the Left would have to make concessions to the center, work within institutional structures, and embrace pluralism as an end in itself—were heavily shaped by the UP's experience and failings in these areas.[32] Elsewhere, the Portuguese Communist Party concentrated on its relations with the country's armed forces as a means of resisting another Chile after the unexpected fall of Portugal's dictatorship in 1974.[33] And, together with the PCCh, the Soviets now concluded that a revolution needed the means to defend itself and that the UP had not been sufficiently prepared, which led it to focus on armed struggle within Chile during the 1970s and 1980s.[34] Overall, it seemed, Soviet analysts primarily ascribed the coup to the Chilean Left's mistakes (and particularly those of the far Left).[35]

For all Fidel Castro's public condemnation of U.S. imperialism's responsibility for Allende's overthrow and "murder," this is also partly what the Cubans concluded. In private, Piñeiro certainly touched on other lessons that the Cubans should learn from the past beyond what the United States' role had been (something which the Cubans knew lots about anyway and did not need to be persuaded of). Progress could not be "erased by torture or other crimes," he promised his officers in the DGLN, but equally it was now clearer than ever that socialism would not triumph with "reformist formulas, such as 'bloodless revolutions.'" To the contrary, quoting Castro, he argued that "revolution and social change require[d] a revolutionary dictatorship." Indeed, as seen from Cuba, Allende's overthrow proved that the rules of revolution involved discipline, intolerance of opposition, and military fortitude. In April 1974, therefore, Piñeiro instructed that more than ever there was a need to "channel any doubts . . . through the party; and declare an open war on liberalism, using the Marxist-Leninist principle of criticism and self-criticism to cleanse our ranks."[36]

Although Allende would have strenuously disagreed with these conclusions—at least when applied to Chile—they pointed to the underlying reasons why he failed to bring about the peaceful democratic revolution in Chile. Allende had a fundamental belief in the expansion of democracy, the promises of socialist revolution "at no social cost," and the birth of a new, fairer, equal, world order. But his vision was compromised by fundamental weaknesses within Chile itself that lessened his ability to confront the challenges of resisting a domestic opposition and a formidable economic crisis.

The first of these was that he did not lead a united government. The various elements of the left wing in Chile were fractious and increasingly divided to such an extent that it is unlikely that Salvador Allende, even if he had taken a more decisive path to the Left or Right, could not have married its disparate constituencies together. He had tried to neutralize the MIR during his presidential campaign by bribing its leaders to stop its urban guerrilla campaign, but this had not been enough for it to give up its increasingly radical criticism of the UP's commitment to "bourgeois constitutionalism." Meanwhile, within the UP, the PCCh complained to foreign representatives from the socialist bloc about its "extremist" coalition partners, and the Socialists—Allende's own party—increasingly attacked the shape and pace of La Vía Chilena. Allende therefore ended up as a president without a party, and an increasingly isolated one at that. Many inside and outside of his country agreed that he was the only possible figure who could lead the diffuse Left in Chile. Yet uniting his supporters behind him proved impossible. Tied to these divisions, and Allende's ability to overcome them, was also the fact that he lacked a definitive end goal and a precise means of how to get there. At home and abroad, he trod a middle, and increasingly improvised, ground that shrank progressively over three years in government. And if coalition members were unable to convince each other of the right path ahead, the UP's chances of persuading its enemies of the merits of the government's cause were nonexistent.

These political weaknesses were pivotal when considering the obstacles that La Vía Chilena was up against. With a small mandate and a power-ful—externally funded—and increasingly united opposition, Allende's government was even more vulnerable divided than it might otherwise have been united. To be sure, his government held up exceptionally well given the circumstances as evidenced by the separate UP parties actually increasing their percentage of the national vote in municipal and con-gressional elections. And in this respect, as U.S. commentators wistfully observed, the economic crisis that befell Chile during the early 1970s—in part manipulated from abroad in the shape of restricted credits, a refusal to sell spare parts to Chile's industrial sector, and a sizable fall in the price of copper—was not nearly as decisive as the opposition had hoped it would be. But the fact that the government fragmented when faced by this eco-nomic crisis combined with a spiraling opposition movement, multiple strikes, and military plotting meant that its ability to survive its full term was significantly compromised.

Within this context, the failure to arrive at a comprehensive and coor-dinated plan for the defense of the government in the event of a coup was devastating. Not only did Allende and the PCCh stand mistakenly by their belief that Chile's armed forces—or enough of them at least—were pro-fessional bystanders of the political system and loyal to the government, but those who began planning for what might happen if the military was not severely overestimated their own strength within a hugely unequal national balance of power. Moreover, the far Left's loud pronouncements about its military might raised fears of subversion and internal maneuvers within the armed forces to such an extent that the leaders who launched the coup of 11 September 1973 were terrified, despite the size of their own forces. Believing the right wing's propaganda about the Left and multiply-ing the evidence of armaments they found before September when they imagined what they might confront, the coup plotters preempted a sup-posed resistance that never materialized by launching a violent war on the Left in all its various forms.

As much as those who ascribe all wrongdoing in Latin America to pup-pet masters in Washington would like to place the blame for this repres-sion on the United States, the United States cannot be held entirely responsible. Yes, the Nixon administration initially condoned the junta's brutality and had been poised to help any military successor regime to Allende's government that so many—in the United States, Cuba, and Chile—expected to be on the horizon. The Nixon administration also did its best to stop Allende from assuming office, albeit in an initially desperate, disorganized, and chaotic way. Then, having pulled itself together, the administration worked systematically, overtly and covertly, not only to ensure that La Vía Chilena failed but also to contain Allende's influence in Latin America and roll back left-wing advances wherever possible elsewhere in the region. On the one hand, U.S. funding for opposition groups and their media outlets in Chile bolstered the challenge they were able to pose to Allende's presidency. The CIA's propaganda and black operations campaigns fueled doubts concerning the UP's democratic credentials and the far Left's relationship with Allende. And the Nixon administration's credit freezes, together with private companies' lawsuits against Santiago, forced the Allende government into a defensive scramble for economic support abroad. On the other hand, Washington's approach to diplomacy was calculating, remarkably flexible, and effective in lessening the benefits that Allende might have accrued from facing an all-out confrontation with the United States. Nor was this confined to Richard Nixon and Henry Kissinger, although the president's role, in particular, was pivotal in framing the administration's overall approach to Latin America from late 1970 onward. After Allende's election, even the more moderate Bureau of Inter-American Affairs reverted to anticommunist stereotypes for Allende. True, the year before Allende was elected, Assistant Secretary for Latin American Affairs Charles Meyer had stated that in Latin America "dissent among friends is not a disaster." But Allende's key problem was that he was never considered a friend by *anyone* in the administration, and it was by no means only Kissinger, Nixon, and the CIA that wanted Allende overthrown or increasingly believed the "solution" to his democratic government lay in the military. Furthermore, the United States did not manipulate or force its Chilean contacts to do anything that they did not want to. As the U.S. ambassador in Santiago wrote back to Washington a month after Allende's overthrow, "the military men who now rule Chile are nationalistic as is evidenced in their extreme pride that they managed their own coup without the assistance of the USG or other nations."[37] In short, the coup did not take place merely because "Nixon ordered [it] to happen," as I recently heard one of Allende's aides explain to an unquestioning and sympathetic audience in London.[38]

Instead, the picture is more complicated when it comes to the balance between domestic and international factors. There is no doubt, for example, that right-wing Chileans internationalized their own political disputes, reacted to international factors, and sought help from outsiders in a number of specific instances where they felt that they needed it. However, more than the United States' influence, it was the coup plotters' immediate external environment and the role of other Latin American actors on the Chilean national stage that seems to have shaped the way in which they conceived of the threats and opportunities in front of them. The Chilean navy's effort to gain assurance that there would be no Peruvian intervention in Chile in the event of a coup—a key concern for a navy schooled on the lessons of Chile's nineteenth-century War of the Pacific with its northern neighbor and fearful of Lima's recent arms deal with the USSR— is a case in point. The fact that the coup leaders went to the Brazilian intelligence services—and not the CIA—to get this assurance is also telling of the independent and autonomous links between both countries, irrespective of U.S. matchmaking (the Brazilians also seem to have informed U.S. officials about their contacts with the Chileans rather than being asked to establish them). What is more, the military regime in Brasilia offered a useful model of what those in the Chilean armed forces who were plotting to overthrow Allende's democratically elected government aspired to (the junta certainly did not pattern its future government on the United States' liberal democracy). And yet, just as many on the left in Chile neglected to look seriously at Brazil's significance as a direct sponsor and supporter of coup plotters—the MIR and Cuban intelligence agents included—historians have previously, and mistakenly, tended to assign Brasilia the role of a passive, ineffectual appendage to the United States.

When it came to those they opposed, Chile's military plotters were also deeply worried about the arrival of revolutionaries from the Southern Cone, Cuba's influence in Chile, and how these foreigners interacted with Chilean developments. They did not take orders from Washington to attack the Cuban Embassy on the day of the coup (the declassified record available shows that the U.S. ambassador in Santiago heard of it only after the event via his Israeli and Mexican counterparts). Rather, Cuba's revolutionary credentials, the belief of others in those credentials, and Allende's association with Havana ironically undermined La Vía Chilena's chances by fueling right-wing fears of Cuban guerrilla tactics and subversion within Chile—fears that the coup plotters had at the front of their minds when they seized power.

On the Left, the relationship between domestic and international actors appears fluid and interactive as well. There is, of course, no doubt that Castro believed that the UP's political program would have to be accompanied by determined force to defend the revolutionary process and push it forward, especially after he saw Allende running into difficulty during his visit to Chile in 1971. And yet, when Castro argued that Allende's road to socialism was unlikely to succeed if the president did not learn the right lessons from history—and in particular, Cuba's history—Allende refused Castro's advice to expand preparations (covertly or overtly) for a forthcoming armed struggle. Indeed, when it came to Chile, Castro and Allende stood poles apart on the methodology of revolution: on questions of winning power, retaining it, and converting it into progressive systems of government. Crucially, however, Castro refused to go behind Allende's back despite the Cubans' different views on what was needed. All of which suggests once again that we need to look at bilateral relationships such as the Chilean-Cuban one as two-sided affairs. As the Cuban Ulises Estrada explained to me, "revolutionaries fight to live. We are not afraid of death and this is why we do not die."[39] But in Chile, on 11 September, it was Allende who determined he did not want the Cubans to make the ultimate sacrifice in defending the so-called *Chilean* road to socialism.

The ones who paid the price were more than three thousand Chileans who were murdered and tens of thousands more who were tortured or forced into exile during the Pinochet years. And it was, in the end, other Chileans who let this happen. Right-wing Chileans themselves had worked hard to undermine General Prats as the key obstacle to military intervention after he led loyal units against plotters during the Tanquetazo; they then supported his successor, General Augusto Pinochet, as he acted decisively to overthrow Allende and destroy all remnants of the UP years in Chile; the Chilean navy's high command had vehemently condemned left-wing Chileans who had tried to infiltrate its ranks (with the Cubans' and Soviet bloc's disapproval); Chilean military officers freely exchanged information with their Brazilian counterparts and invited them into the National Stadium to help when it came to practicing torture after the coup; Chilean truckers and miners had staged strikes in the hope of bringing their country to a standstill, with funding from outside but with a will of their own nevertheless; Chile's ex-president, Eduardo Frei, sought help from the U.S. ambassador in Santiago, and his Christian Democrat Party directly requested CIA dollars to help with its political campaigns; Chile's civilian opposition movement increasingly chose to block UP government programs in Congress and ultimately sided with the armed forces in the mistaken belief that the military would soon return Chile to democracy, in which it could play a major role; and the central Chilean in this story, Salvador Allende, worked hard to achieve his own lifelong goal of bringing peaceful democratic revolution to his country before he ultimately failed alongside the members of his Chilean left-wing coalition.

In the last few days of his life, it was also Allende who resigned himself to this failure and decided to take his own life when a coup struck. Turning to those who accompanied him as the aerial bombardment of La Moneda started on the day of the coup, Allende had proclaimed this was "how the first page of history is written. My people and Latin America will write the rest."[40] His belief in history's predetermined path spurred him on to believe that the failure of a peaceful democratic road to socialism in Chile would be only a temporary setback on the inevitable road to revolution. "Sooner rather than later," he promised, "the great avenues through which free men walk to build a better society will open."[41] In the end, however, the future was quite plainly not for Allende to decide.

A Note on Sources

[W]e want to be sure the paper record doesn't look bad. No matter what we do [in Chile]
it will probably end up dismal. So our paper work should be done carefully.
                    —William Rogers to Kissinger, 14 September 1970.[1]

As one scholar warned not long ago in *Diplomatic History*, "mono-national research tends to produce mono-national explanations and to ignore the role of players from countries other than those whose words are examined."[2] This book is an explicit effort to avoid such a pitfall. Although uncovering other angles and perspectives has not been straightforward, it has not been impossible either, and in presenting one chapter of the inter-American Cold War, I am consciously suggesting there are many more multinational narratives to write. Indeed, thanks to the New Cold War History, we now have a better idea of how the world was viewed from the East, but the view from the South, and Latin America in particular, is comparatively less clear. In the future, instead of numerous studies on U.S. policy toward individual Latin American countries—invaluable as they are—it is thus hoped that scholars will pay attention to the multisided dynamics of relationships within and between inter-American states. As Thomas Blanton recently argued, "the opportunities for Cold War scholarship based on newly recovered archives in Latin America and the United States are immense."[3] I would go further: the opportunity is not only in the documents available but in asking different questions when we look at them.

   Writing an international history of Allende's Chile that brings Chile, Cuba, inter-American affairs, and global developments to the forefront of its analysis was possible in this case thanks to the exciting range of newly available historical sources in Latin America, the United States, and Europe. Of utmost importance was the declassification of documents at Chile's Foreign Ministry archives and, in particular, the availability of miscellaneous memorandum files as well as records of secret, confidential, and ordinary correspondence between Santiago and Chile's embassies abroad.[4] A further collection of the Chilean Embassy in Havana's files from this period that was not transferred back to Santiago after the coup can also be found at Casa Memorial Salvador Allende in Havana. In addition, Orlando Letelier's papers—recently opened to researchers at the National Archives in Santiago—are rich in information pertaining to the internal decision-making processes within the UP. Over the past decade, General Augusto Pinochet's arrest in London and the thirtieth anniversary of Allende's presidency and the Chilean coup also reawakened interest in the period. Subsequently, Chilean, Cuban, and other Latin American protagonists added important new testimonies to an already rich collection of memoirs pertaining to the subject. And, as well as these sources, this book makes use of recent collections of Chilean left-wing sources and Soviet archival documents published by the Centro de Estudios Publicos in Santiago.[5]

Outside Chile, Brazil's Foreign Ministry Archive has also partially released files related to the period (though confidential and secret files remain classified at the time of writing). In an effort to find more information on the Cuban and Chilean sides of the story, and with the invaluable help of Anita Prazmowska and Laura Wiesen, I was able to incorporate key insights from Polish and East German Foreign Ministry Archives in Berlin and Warsaw. However, beyond these, it is clear that the documents of the former Soviet bloc remain a veritable treasure trove waiting to be opened by Latin Americanists who seek to understand how their left-wing subjects interacted with the East and presented their policies to their allies.

By far the most extensive (albeit scattered) collection of archival material this book has drawn on is in the United States. In addition to the thousands of documents relating to U.S. covert intervention and human rights abuses in Chile released in the late 1990s as part of the online "Chile Declassification Project," the Nixon administration's National Security Council files, presidential materials, and State Department records are also now open at the U.S. National Archives II in College Park, Maryland, online at the National Archives and Records Administration Archival Database, and partially published in *Foreign Relations of the United States* document collections.[6]

Last but by no means least, this book benefits from the author's extensive interviews with key protagonists of the story. In Chile, Allende's personal physician; his representatives in New York and Cuba; his nephew, Andrés Pascal Allende; and his ambassador in Buenos Aires were among those who shared their recollections with me. In the United States, State Department official John H. Crimmins and Kissinger's assistant on Latin American affairs, Viron Pete Vaky, also shared their views. In Mexico City, former Mexican ambassador to Chile Gonzalo Martínez Corbalá agreed to an interview. And in Havana, Cubans such as Ulises Estrada, a senior intelligence official in charge of Cuba's embassy in Santiago on the day of the coup, and Luis Fernández Oña,

Allende's Cuban son-in-law, engaged in hours of exclusive conversations. And during a final research trip to Chile in March and April 2010, I was also lucky enough to have many more hours of informal conversations with Oña, during which he shared yet more information in a patient, collaborative, sincere, and open way.

Unfortunately, however, there are many sources that are still not available to researchers. On the Chilean side, not only do historians not have access to Allende's presidential papers and the UP parties' confidential files, but there is widespread agreement that most of these papers were destroyed either immediately before and/or during the Chilean coup by the Left itself or by the military when it seized power.[7] Despite my numerous requests for at least partial access to Cuban documents, Havana's archives also remain firmly closed. In 2008 there was a small glimmer of hope in regard to the Cuban side of the story when, on the centenary of Allende's birth, Fidel Castro published theretofore unseen letters that he sent to the Chilean president between 1970 and 1973 (excerpts of which are included in this book). But as Castro tantalizingly said at the time, "Much remains to be said about what [the Cubans] were willing to do for Allende."[8] Sadly, one of the key players in the story of Cuba's Latin American policy, Manuel Piñeiro, died in 1998 just before he was due to offer his testimony on the subject.[9] Questions also remain regarding the relationship between Cuba and the Soviet Union and their policies toward Chile's revolutionary process, but until Havana and Moscow declassify their documents, the relationship cannot be fully clarified.[10]

The main problem with not having more access to Chilean and Cuban sources is that scholars are forced to rely on interviews, memoirs, and the documentary record pertaining to others' intelligence sources at the time (and intelligence, as we know, is not always the same as fact). Indeed, while Piero Gleijeses was struck by how close the CIA and the State Department's Bureau of Intelligence and Research were in understanding the motives behind Cuban activities in Africa, there is surprisingly little information on Cuban activities in Chile in U.S. records. There are two explanations for this: one is that the documents remain classified and/or destroyed, and the other is that the United States simply did not have good information. As with most of these things, the truth probably lies somewhere in between. Certainly the information that exists on the Cuban personnel operating in Chile or Cuban training of Chilean parties offers only partial and inconclusive analysis of what was happening. There is no mention of Estrada in any of the U.S. or British documents I have seen, for example. Furthermore, as Kristian Gustafson has observed as a result of his interviews with U.S. covert operatives in Chile, Washington's task of collecting intelligence in Chile after Allende came to power became considerably more difficult (one CIA operative's recollection of the number of Cubans in Chile being over a thousand is a case in point).[11] It appears that this got easier, and that the United States had many more informants within left-wing parties as well as the military by the time of the coup. But the intelligence Washington had—or that we know it had—is far too little to base a detailed historical study of Allende's relationship with the Cubans or the Chilean Left on.

Obviously, these circumstances have implications for methodology. It means that scholars have to cast the net wide and be assiduous in cross-referencing the pieces of the jigsaw puzzle that they have. It also means that the balance of sources is not what it might be. And it means having to write a first draft of history in the knowledge that it may well be improved upon with the benefit of new materials in future years. Oral history sources that I have drawn on for the purposes of writing this book are by no means 100 percent accurate or the last word on Cuban involvement in Chile, but in an effort to ensure information gained through them was as accurate as possible, I conducted numerous separate interviews with the individuals involved and utilized documents found elsewhere to jog memories and clarify ambiguities. Whatever their limitations, these sources are also the first significant contribution to understanding the rise and fall of Allende's Chile from Cuban perspectives.

On the other side of the Cold War divide, where scholars have access to a comparative mountain of material, there are also substantial gaps in the U.S. documentary record. While I was fortunate to be given some information about Vernon Walters's personal diaries, for example, their full contents are blocked by the Pentagon for the time being. Many other documents—or redacted parts of documents—relating to Washington's covert operations and the Pentagon's links to military leaders in Latin America are also unavailable, and details of covert operations, ample as they are, still do not tell the full extent of the story. One frustrating aspect of information on U.S. covert operations to contain Chile's influence in Latin America is that we do not have more information about the disinformation and propaganda campaign that was launched through the press. When shifting through Chilean and Brazilian press sources, therefore, we do not know for sure where opinions or information are coming from. While alarmist newspaper reports quoting a Brazilian official as warning that Allende's election would be followed by Russian flotillas arriving at Valparaiso, for example, must be treated with caution in these circumstances, they can equally not be disregarded as Washington's viewpoint alone until we have more information.[12] Indeed, to fall into the trap of ascribing every negative piece of reporting on Allende to the CIA is to misunderstand the hostility that *both* Brazilian and American officials felt toward Chilean events, something that I have found is evident in private Brazilian records, in recently declassified U.S. transcripts of conversations with Brazilian officials, and in Chilean diplomatic correspondence between Santiago and Brasilia during these years (and after).

Overall, then, there is still much to learn from U.S. and Latin American archives. When they are fully opened, it is hoped this book will act as a springboard for further research in two key areas. First, beyond "the Chile chapter," Castro's policies toward Latin America, and Cuba's interaction with hemispheric developments, clearly need further examination and explanation. Second, historians need more information about the other extremity of the inter-American Cold War, namely the Latin American right-wing military leaders who took up arms against the Left and the relationships between them. (Both the Cubans and the Americans that led foreign policy toward Latin America during this period witnessed a clear solidarity between military leaders in the hemisphere founded on a mutual distrust for civilian politicians and a shared analysis of the region's threats.)[13]

For now, though, the challenge is to work with what we have—always, of course, being wary that what Americans might write down and what Cubans might recall years later is not necessarily the whole truth and nothing but the truth. Indeed, one interesting feature of the international history of Allende's Chile is the extent to which actors across political divides of this story put a premium on how their story would be told in future generations, and then how the effort to conceal that history has come back to haunt key participants involved. This effort notwithstanding, the view is now at least far clearer than it was.

Notes

Abbreviations

AMRE	Archivo General Histórico, Ministerio de Relaciones Exteriores, Santiago, Chile
AMRE-Brasilia	Arquivo Histórico, Ministério das Relações Exteriores, Brasilia, Brazil
AMSZ	Archiwum Ministerstwa Spraw Zagranicznych, Warsaw, Poland
CDP-CIA	Chile Declassification Project, Freedom Of Information Act Reading Room, Department of State, CIA Documents
CDP-DOD	Chile Declassification Project, Freedom Of Information Act Reading Room, Department of State, Department of Defense Documents
CDP-NARA	Chile Declassification Project, Freedom Of Information Act Reading Room, Department of State, NARA Documents
CDP-NSC	Chile Declassification Project, Freedom Of Information Act Reading Room, Department of State, NSC Documents
CMSA	Casa Memorial Salvador Allende, Havana, Cuba
COS	Chief of Station
CREST/NARA	Central Intelligence Agency Records Search Tool, NARA
CSD	Castro Speech Database
DCI	Director of Central Intelligence
DOS	Department of State
DOS/CFP	Department of State, Central Foreign Policy Files, NARA
E.	Enviados (Sent)
EEUU	Estados Unidos (United States)
FBIS	Foreign Broadcast Information Service
FCO	Foreign and Commonwealth Office (United Kingdom)
FD	Frontline Diplomacy
FHSC	Fondo Hernán Santa Cruz, AMRE
FJTM	Fondo José Toribio Merino, Centro de Investigación y Documentación en Historia de Chile Contemporáneo, Universidad Finis Terrae, Santiago, Chile
FOL	Fondo Orlando Letelier, National Archive, Chile
FRUS	Foreign Relations of the United States
HAK	Henry A. Kissinger

HQ	Headquarters
MfAA	Ministerium für Auswärtige Angelegenheiten, Berlin, Germany
MRE/MINREL	Ministerio de Relaciones Exteriores (Chilean Foreign Ministry)
NARA	National Archives and Record Administration
NIE	National Intelligence Estimate
NPMP	Nixon Presidential Materials Project
NSA	National Security Archive
NSCF	National Security Council Files
NSCIF	National Security Council Institutional Files
OE-SA	V. Pey et al., eds. *Salvador Allende, 1908–1973: Obras Escogidas.* Santiago: Centro de Estudios Políticos Latino Americanos Simon Bolivar, 1992.
R.	Recibidos (Received)
RG	Record Group
SAPMO	Stiftung Archiv der Parteien und Massenorganisationen der DDR im Bundesarchiv, Berlin, Germany
TNA	The National Archives, Kew, London
WHD	Western Hemisphere Division (CIA)
WHT	White House Tapes

Introduction

1. Jara, *Victor*, 155; "Fiesta Popular," *El Mercurio*, 3 November 1970; and "Dijo Allende en el Estadio Nacional: Chile Forja su Propio Destino," *El Mercurio*, 6 November 1970.

2. Memorandum of Conversation (USSR), Kissinger and Dobrynin, 13 April 1972, in Geyer and Selvage, *Soviet-American Relations*, 661–62.

3. Memorandum, General Vernon Walters to Henry Kissinger, 3 November 1970, enclosure, Memorandum, Kissinger to Nixon, 5 November 1970, box H029/NSCIF/ NPMP. When it comes to Chile's exclusion from the benefits of détente, and Latin America's position within the bipolar détente process, it is telling to note that neither Chile, Allende, nor Latin America came up once in secret U.S.-Soviet negotiations between 1969 and 1972. See Geyer and Selvage, *Soviet-American Relations*.

4. Memorandum of Conversation, the President et al., the Cabinet Room, 9:40 A.M., 6 November 1970, in Kornbluh, *Pinochet File*, 116–20.

5. Dinges, *Condor Years*, 41.

6. Charles Meyer as cited in Memorandum, Armando Uribe, "Estada en Chile del Jefe de la Delegacion Especial de EEUU a la Transmisión de Mando, Secretario Charles Meyer," 6 November 1970, MINREL 1961–1979/Memorandos Políticos/ AMRE.

7. Brands, *Latin America's Cold War*, 7.

8. Bethell and Roxborough, "The Impact of the Cold War on Latin America," 431.

9. On the issue of a crisis-driven approach, see Grandin, "Off the Beach."

10. McAllister, "Rural Markets, Revolutionary Souls, and Rebellious Women," 350.

11. For the most recent publications on U.S. intervention in Chile, see Gustafson, *Hostile Intent*; Haslam, *Assisted Suicide*; and Kornbluh, *Pinochet File*. Before the

recent declassification of documents on the subject, some of the most comprehensive accounts of the Allende years were Davis, *Last Two Years*; Kaufman, *Crisis in Allende's Chile*; and Sigmund, *Overthrow of Allende*. On Kissinger's "criminality" in subverting democracy, see Hitchens, *Trial of Henry Kissinger*. On consensus, see Maxwell and Rogers, "Fleeing the Chilean Coup," and Fermandois, "Pawn or Player?"

12. Kornbluh, *Pinochet File*, and Maxwell and Rogers, "Fleeing the Chilean Coup."

13. Haslam, *Assisted Suicide*, 230.

14. To date, access to Walters's diaries is restricted, and they remain in control of the Defense Intelligence Agency. Pending the outcome of my Freedom of Information Act request, I am very grateful to an employee of the National Defense Intelligence College who was kind enough to share this information with me. According to Walters's diaries, he was in Palm Beach and Miami on 11 September 1973 and made no trips to South America that year.

15. Hanhimäki, "'Dr. Kissinger' or 'Mr. Henry'?" 676.

16. For example, see Hanhimäki, *Flawed Architect*, 105; LaFeber, *Inevitable Revolutions*, 197; Lawrence, "History from Below"; Smith, *Last Years of the Monroe Doctrine*, 6, 130–37; Grandin, *Empire's Workshop*, 1; Ferguson, "Trends in Inter-American Relations: 1972–Mid-1974," 1; Stephansky, "'New Dialogue' on Latin America: The Cost of Policy Neglect," 154; and Kaplan, "U.S. Arms Transfers to Latin America." While there have been recent efforts to step outside Chile-focused parameters when it comes to Nixon's Latin American policy, these have not connected what happened in Chile to other areas of interest. See for example, Brands, "Richard Nixon and Economic Nationalism," and Spektor, *Kissinger e o Brasil*.

17. For similar conclusions, see *Covert Action in Chile*, 50–52; Gustafson, *Hostile Intent*; Michael, "Nixon, Chile and the Shadows of the Cold War," 1; and Kaufman, *Crisis in Allende's Chile*, 4–5.

18. Briefing Memorandum, Nachmanoff to Kissinger, 17 June 1971, enclosure, Memorandum, Nachmanoff to Kissinger, 11 August 1971, box H059/NSCIF/NPMP.

19. Kissinger, 27 June 1970, as quoted in Davis, *Last Two Years*, 6.

20. On the U.S.-Cuban Cold War in Africa, see Gleijeses, *Conflicting Missions*.

21. Spenser, "Final Reflections: Standing Conventional Cold War History on Its Head," 392. The only works on Cuban foreign policy based on archival documents are Gleijeses, *Conflicting Missions*, and Kirk and McKenna, *Canada-Cuba Relations*. Other useful studies on Cuban foreign policy include Domínguez, *To Make a World Safe*; Mesa-Lago, *Cuba in the 1970s*; Erisman, *Cuba's International Relations*; and D'Esteséfano Pisani, *Política Exterior de la Revolución Cubana*. On the problems associated with studying the history of revolutionary Cuba for Cuban historians and those outside, see Miller, "The Absolution of History."

22. Kissinger, *White House Years*, 681–83, 686, and Nixon, *Memoirs of Richard Nixon*, 490.

23. Quiroga, *Compañeros*, 136, 173, 251–52.

24. Haslam, *Assisted Suicide*, 75, 126, 153.

25. See Memorandum, "Covert Action Program for Chile," 17 November 1970, CDP-NSC, and *Covert Action in Chile*, 38.

26. On Allende's supposed lack of control, see Haslam, *Assisted Suicide*, 155.

27. Rojas Pizarro interview, 1 November 2004. On different sides to Allende—in public, but mostly in terms of his private life—see Labarca, *Biografía Sentimental*.

28. Fermandois, *Mundo y Fin de Mundo*, 338–41.

29. To date, the Chilean historian Joaquin Fermandois has written the most comprehensive survey of the period, drawing on interviews, Chilean archival documents, and published material. See Fermandois, *Mundo y Fin de Mundo*. On Soviet-Chilean relations, see Miller, *Soviet Relations with Latin America*, and Ulianova, "La Unidad Popular y el Golpe Militar." Another invaluable examination of the UP's foreign policy conducted by ex-Chilean diplomats and scholars with documents is Vera Castillo, *Política Exterior Chilena*.

30. For varying views, see Sigmund, *Multinationals*, 168; Haslam, *Assisted Suicide*, 30, 64; Andrews and Mitrokhin, *The Mitrokhin Archive II*, 69–88; Fortin, "Principled Pragmatism in the Face of External Pressure," 12.

31. Fortin, "Principled Pragmatism in the Face of Pressure," 221–42.

32. Colburn, *Vogue of Revolution*, 13.

33. Red Cross estimates at Derechos Chile and Rettig Commission (1991) at Strategic Choices in the Design of Truth Commissions.

Chapter 1

1. Huerta interview, 23 March 2010.

2. Muñoz, "The International Policy of the Socialist Party," 153.

3. Marambio, *Armas de Ayer*, 41.

4. Estrada, *Tania*, 12–13, 15.

5. Frei Montalva, "The Alliance That Lost Its Way."

6. Gray, *Latin America and the United States*, vii.

7. Agenda Annex, "The Setting for Policy Choice," enclosure, Memorandum, NSC Staff Secretary, Jeanne Davis, to the Vice President et al., 13 October 1969, box H040/NSCIF/NPMP.

8. See Kruijt, *Revolution by Decree*, 101–2; Lehman, *Bolivia and the United States*, 159; Winn, *Americas*, 478–81; and Berríos, "The USSR and the Andean Countries."

9. Allende, Speech to UN General Assembly, 4 December 1972, published as "Address to the United Nations General Assembly," in Cockcroft, *Allende Reader*, 205–12. See also Allende, Speech from the Federation of Students Building, 5 September 1970, published as "Victory Speech to the People of Santiago," in Cockcroft, *Allende Reader*, 50, 48.

10. Hart Dávalos, *Homenaje a Miguel Enríquez*, 8.

11. Fidel Castro, "Second Declaration of Havana," 4 February 1962.

12. Fidel Castro, "History Will Absolve Me" (1953), Fidel Castro History Archive, and Fidel Castro to Celia Sánchez, 5 June 1958, as quoted in Gleijeses, *Conflicting Missions*, 13.

13. Record of Conversations, Raúl Roa and Polish minister of foreign affairs Stefan Jedrychowski, 24–26 June 1971, Urgent Note, "Notes on the Conversations with Roa," 30 June 1971, wiazka 3/40/75/AMSZ.

14. Gleijeses, *Conflicting Missions*, 377.

15. Manuel Piñeiro, Speech to the DGLN, 8 June 1973, in Suárez, *Manuel Piñeiro*, 102.

16. Miller, *Soviet Relations with Latin America*, 2, 217–18; Armony, "Transnationalizing the Dirty War," 138; and Blight and Brenner, *Sad and Luminous Days*.

17. Venezuelan Communist Party statement, 1967, as quoted in Skierka, *Fidel Castro*, 187.

18. Castro as quoted in Blight and Brenner, *Sad and Luminous Days*, 122.

19. Che Guevara, Message to the *Tricontinental*, April 1967, Che Guevara Internet Archive.

20. Gleijeses, *Conflicting Missions*, 23.

21. Marambio, *Armas de Ayer*, 48–50, and Huerta interview, 20 April 2010.

22. Gleijeses, *Conflicting Missions*, 377–78. Gleijeses claims that fewer than forty Cubans fought in Latin America during the 1960s compared to more than one thousand Cubans who went to Algeria, Zaire and the Congo, and Guinea-Bissau. While the figure for those who went to Latin America is probably far higher, there is no doubt that a significantly higher number went to Africa. On a different view of Cuban involvement in Latin America—albeit with an exaggerated emphasis on the Soviet Union's role in this venture—see Brands, *Latin America's Cold War*, 40–44.

23. Debray, *Guerrilla del Che*, 83, and Castañeda, *Compañero*, 331–33.

24. On disagreements between Che and Fidel, see Castañeda, *Compañero*. On Che's impatience, see Suárez, *Manuel Piñeiro*, 19.

25. Blight and Brenner, *Sad and Luminous Days*, 128–29.

26. Debray, *Guerrilla del Che*, 82–83.

27. Suárez interview, 10 December 2004, and Berríos, "The USSR and the Andean Countries," 349.

28. Suárez interview, 10 December 2004.

29. Edwards, *Persona Non Grata*, 55–56. On Cuban interest and praise for Velasco Alvarado's government, see also Record of Conversations, Raúl Roa and Polish minister of foreign affairs Stefan Jedrychowski, 24–26 June 1971, Urgent Note, "Notes on the Conversations with Roa," 30 June 1971, wiazka 3/40/75/AMSZ.

30. Plank, "We Should Start Talking to Castro," 244. Regarding Latin American opinion, see Intelligence Note, INR, "Latin America: Chile's Renewed Relations with Cuba—A Potential Problem for the OAS," 30 November 1970, box 2199/RG59/NARA.

31. Estrada interview, 13 December 2004.

32. Huerta interview, 20 April 2010, and conversations with Oña, March–April 2010. On the second Bolivian guerrilla struggle, see Bodes Gómez, *En la Senda del Che*, and Rodríguez Ostria, *Teoponte*.

33. Directorate of Intelligence: Central Intelligence Bulletin, 28 August 1971, CREST/NARA.

34. Labrousse, *Tupamaros*, 84, and Record of Conversations, Raúl Roa and Polish minister of foreign affairs Stefan Jedrychowski, 24–26 June 1971.

35. Oña interview, 3 September 2005, and Castillo Estay, "Mucha Gente Me Culpó Cuando Se Suicidó la Tati."

36. Domínguez, *To Make a World Safe*, 4.

37. Castro, Speech at Havana's Plaza de la Revolución, 26 July 1970, CSD.

38. Castro, Speech to Plenum of Basic Industrial Workers, 9 December 1970, CSD.

39. Blight and Brenner, *Sad and Luminous Days*, 124–31.

40. "Account of the delegation of the PZPR [Polska Zjednoczona Partia Robotnicza; Polish United Workers' Party] in the Republic of Cuba," 24 June 1971, wiazka 5/40/75/AMSZ. Emphasis in original.

41. Estrada interview, and Gleijeses, *Conflicting Missions*, 373–74.

42. Memorandum, Ambassador Marian Renke, Polish Embassy, Havana, to the Ministry of Foreign Affairs, "Certain Aspects of Cuba's Situation and Politics on the American Continent," 15 October 1971, wiazka 5/40/75/AMSZ.

43. Castro as quoted in Blight and Brenner, *Sad and Luminous Days*, 142, 122–25.

44. Memorandum of Conversation, Mario Campora (Argentine Embassy, Washington) and Robert L. Funseth (Coordinator of Cuban Affairs, State Department) et al., 9 April 1970; and Memorandum of Conversation, Counselor Igor D. Bubnov, First Secretary Vladimir A. Romanchencko, and First Secretary Lev C. Ilyin (Soviet Embassy, Washington) and Madison M. Adams Jr. (Economic Officer, Office of the Coordinator of Cuban Affairs, State Department), 11 May 1970, box 223/RG59/NARA.

45. "Cuba in Latin America," enclosure, Briefing Memorandum prepared for Fidel Castro's visit to Poland, no date, c. June 1972, wiazka 3/12/78/AMSZ.

46. On KGB activities in Peru, see Andrews and Mitrokhin, *Mitrokhin Archive II*, 60–64.

47. "Report on a Discussion between Comrade Markowski (Head of the Latin America Sector, Foreign Relations Department, Central Committee, Socialist Unity Party of Germany) and Comrade Montes (member of the political commission of the PCCh)," 15 July 1970, DY/30/IV A2/20/712/SAPMO.

48. Fidel Castro, "Salvador Allende: His Example Lives On."

49. Martínez Pírez interview, 15 December 2004. Pírez recalls first meeting Ulises Estrada in Chile prior to 1964 when he was serving as a political counselor at the Cuban Embassy in Chile.

50. Chain interview, 8 December 2004.

51. Ibid., and Vierra interview, 28 April 2006.

52. Piñeiro recalls that Argentina, Bolivia, and Peru were the key countries considered. Suárez, *Manuel Piñeiro*, 12, and Oña interview, 2 May 2006.

53. Carlos Rafael Rodríguez as quoted in "Summary of Press Conference," 24 November 1970, FCO7/1991/TNA.

54. Marambio, *Armas de Ayer*, 46.

55. Ibid., 57; Intelligence Note, INR, "Times Article Exaggerates Appeal of Revolutionary Group," 14 January 1970, box 2196/RG59/NARA; and Haslam, *Assisted Suicide*, 53.

56. Marambio, *Armas de Ayer*, 61–65.

57. Rojas Pizarro interview.

58. Haslam, *Assisted Suicide*, 27–29.

59. Marambio, *Armas de Ayer*, 69.

60. Pascal Allende interview, 6 April 2010. Pascal Allende believes that this money

came from a variety of sources, including Allende's own funds and businesses, his campaign funds, and "help" that he received from the Cubans.

61. On the MIR's decision, see Quiroga, *Compañeros*, 50. Cubans dismiss the importance of their role in making this decision for the MIR. See Oña interview, 9 December 2004, and Estrada interview.

62. Allende, Speech at Chile's National Stadium, 5 November 1970, published as "Inaugural Address in the National Stadium," in Cockcroft, *Allende Reader*, 53.

63. Muñoz, "The International Policy of the Socialist Party," 152.

64. See Colburn, *Vogue of Revolution*, and Frank, *Latin America: Underdevelopment or Revolution*.

65. Allende, Speech to Chilean Senate, 4 July 1956, published as "El Socialismo Chileno," *OE-SA*, 186.

66. Allende cited the United Kingdom, France, and Germany as alternative markets for Chile, being capable of receiving 400,000 tons of copper. Allende, July 1964, published as "Cómo vamos a nacionalizar el cobre," *OE-SA*, 234.

67. Colburn, *Vogue of Revolution*, 5–6, 8–9. By Colburn's definition of revolutionary transformation, he does not include Chile in his list of Third World states that underwent successful revolutions, but his analysis of the intellectual *mentalité* that revolutionary elites around the world adopted is particularly useful for understanding the ideas that Chilean revolutionaries drew from.

68. Malley, *Call from Algeria*, 173–74, and Fermandois, *Mundo y Fin de Mundo*, 354.

69. Allende, "Victory Speech," in Cockcroft, *Allende Reader*, 51. See also Veneros, *Ensayo Psicobiográfico*, 298; Allende, interview with Augusto Olivares, November 1971, published as "Interview with Salvador Allende and Fidel Castro," in Cockcroft, *Allende Reader*, 134.

70. Almeyda, Speech to OAS General Assembly, San José, Costa Rica, 15 April 1971, in Vera Castillo, *Política Exterior Chilena*, 432.

71. Juan Osses and Ernesto Guitierrez as quoted in Quiroga, *Compañeros*, 17–18, 61, and Jaramillo Edwards, "Testimonios: Vuelo de Noche," 88. See also Fermandois, *Mundo y Fin de Mundo*, 383.

72. Alejandro Cid as quoted in Quiroga, *Compañeros*, 63.

73. Debray, "Allende Habla con Debray," 33, 35; Almeyda, *Reencuentro con mi Vida*, 165; Jorquera, *El Chicho Allende*, 266, 261; Veneros, *Allende*, 252; and Otero, *Razón y Fuerza de Chile*, 69.

74. Allende, *Conferencia Ofrecida por el Dr. Salvador Allende*.

75. Allende, Speech at Plaza Bulnes, Santiago, 1 May 1971, published as "Address to International Workers Day Rally," in Cockcroft, *Allende Reader*, 81.

76. For a detailed examination of Chile's copper industry and successive efforts to gain control of it, see Sigmund, *Multinationals*, 131–78.

77. Collier and Sater, *History of Chile*, 318.

78. Popular Unity Programme, in Cockcroft, *Allende Reader*, 259–61; Allende, *Conferencia Ofrecida por el Dr. Salvador Allende*; and Collier and Sater, *History of Chile*, 334.

79. Allende, Speech, 25 October 1938, published as "Homenaje al Frente Popular," *OE-SA*, 66–67. On his early reference to the pursuit of a "second indepen-

dence," see Allende, Speech at Chamber of Deputies, 7 June 1939, published as "La géstion del Gobierno del Frente Popular," *OE-SA*, 61–62.

80. Allende, 1944, as quoted by Joan Garcés in *OE-SA*, 22.

81. Allende, Speech to the Chilean Senate, 4 July 1956, published as "Homenaje al Gobierno de Arbenz en Guatemala," *OE-SA*, 181–82.

82. Allende, *El Siglo*, 15 March 1954, and *Pravda*, 13 August 1954, as quoted in Hove, "The Arbenz Factor," 634, 643, 659–60.

83. Allende, Speech at the University of Montevideo, 1967, published as "Critica a la Alianza para el Progreso," *OE-SA*, 265.

84. Allende as quoted in Debray, "Allende habla con Debray," 32.

85. Allende, *Conferencia Ofrecida por el Dr. Salvador Allende*; Jorquera, *El Chicho Allende*, 269; Estrada interview; and Marambio, *Armas de Ayer*, 70–71. Details of Allende's support for armed struggle in Latin America are almost nonexistent, although Estrada stated that he helped (particularly in Venezuela) with both money and moral support. See also Haslam, *Assisted Suicide*, 34; Pascal Allende interview and Huerta interviews, 23 March and 20 April 2010.

86. Allende, Speech to Chilean Senate, no date, as quoted in Veneros, *Allende*, 251.

87. *O Globo*, 10 November 1970, as quoted in Oficio, Embachile Rio to Señor Ministro, 13 November 1970, Oficios Conf., E./R./Brasil/1970/AMRE.

88. Allende as quoted in Labarca, *Biografía Sentimental*, 172.

89. Oña interviews, 9 December 2004 and 3 September 2005.

90. Oña interview, 3 September 2005; Pascal Allende interview; and conversations with Oña, March–April 2010. Allende appears to have known about the broad outlines of the Chilean ELN's activities and supported it, but he never knew details or became involved directly.

91. Oña interview, 9 December 2004. See also Suárez, *Manuel Piñeiro*, 26, and Quiroga, *Compañeros*, 26–27.

92. *Covert Action in Chile*, 15, 20, 22.

93. Oña interview, 3 September 2005.

94. On Cuba's refusal to give the PDC "electioneering material," see Record of Conversation with Olga Chamorro, 17 September 1970, Briefing, East German Embassy, Havana, to Berlin, "Information on Questions of Cuba's Position on the Election Results in Chile," 25 September 1970, DY/30/IV A2/20/286/SAPMO. On Cuba's commercial relations with Chile during the last year of Frei's presidency, see Gleijeses, *Conflicting Missions*, 221.

95. Oña interview, 9 December 2004.

96. Allende, interview with Peter Gzowski, 4 September 1970, published as "Election Day Interview with Canada's CBC Radio," in Cockcroft, *Allende Reader*, 44.

97. Memorandum of Conversation, Rogers, Kubisch, and Allende, 25 May 1973, Chilean Embassy, Buenos Aires, Telegram, SecState to Amembassy Santiago, 29 May 1973, box 953/NSCF/NPMP.

98. Vaky interview, 27 April 2005. On senior government priorities and a lack of attention to Latin America, and Chile in particular, see also Memorandum, "Why did the U.S. Government Not Take More Vigorous Political Action Measures to Prevent the Election of the Marxist candidate, Salvador Allende, as President of Chile?"

4 March 1971, The Nixon Presidential Library and Museum, "December 9, 2010 Materials Release." Specifically, this postmortem memorandum notes that in 1970 "much of the time and attention of policy-making level officials was taken up by the situation in Southeast Asia (the Cambodia operation) and the Middle East—40 Committee meetings on Chile were cancelled or postponed."

99. Kissinger, *White House Years*, 666, and Kubisch interview, FD.

100. The original source of this oft-quoted remark is Hersh, *Price of Power*, 263. Its accuracy was nevertheless confirmed to the author by Ramon Huidobro, who was present at the meeting with Valdés and who personally heard it. See Huidobro interview, 28 October 2004.

101. Rabe, *Eisenhower and Latin America*, 100.

102. Nixon, *Six Crises*, 213–14.

103. Rabe, *Eisenhower and Latin America*, 107–12.

104. Nixon's handwritten notes (1967) as quoted in Michael, "Nixon, Chile and Shadows of the Cold War," 95–104. Emphasis in original.

105. Ibid., 102–4.

106. Nixon, *Six Crises*, 191, 208–9; Nixon, *Memoirs*, 490; Nixon as quoted in Rabe, *Eisenhower and Latin America*, 104; and Nixon, as quoted in Schoultz, *Beneath the United States*, 352.

107. Louis Halle as quoted in McPherson, *Intimate Ties*, 21.

108. George Kennan to Dean Acheson, 29 March 1950, published as "A Realist Views Latin America," in Holden and Zolov, *Latin America and the United States*, 196–97.

109. Thomas Jefferson, 1813, as quoted in Westad, *Global Cold War*, 10–11. On U.S. views of Latin Americans as being inferior, see also Schoultz, *Beneath the United States*.

110. Nelson Rockefeller, "The Official Report of a United States Presidential Mission for the Western Hemisphere," 30 August 1969, in Holden and Zolov, *Latin America and the United States*, 265.

111. White House Tape, Nixon to Daniel P. Moynihan, 7 October 1971, Conversation: 116-10/WHT/NPMP.

112. Telcon, Kissinger and Dean Rusk, 3 October 1973, box 22/HAK Telcons/NSC/NPMP.

113. Consensus of Viña del Mar as quoted in Fermandois, *Mundo y Fin de Mundo*, 322–24.

114. Guerra Vilaboy, *Breve Historia de América Latina*, 273.

115. Uribe, *Black Book of Intervention*, 30, and Huidobro interview, 28 October 2004.

116. NSSM 15 as quoted in Agenda Annex, "The Setting for Policy Choice," box H040/NSCIF/NPMP.

117. Agenda Annex, "The Setting for Policy Choice."

118. Rockefeller, "The Official Report," 265.

119. Kissinger, "Central Issues of American Foreign Policy" (1968), in Kissinger, *American Foreign Policy*, 80.

120. Memorandum, Crimmins to Meyer, "Comments on Rockefeller Report

Recommendation," 3 October 1969, Bureau of Inter-American Affairs, Office of the Deputy Assistant Secretary, 1969–ca. 1975, RG59/NARA.

121. Richard Nixon, Speech to the Inter-American Press Association, 31 October 1969, published as "Action for Progress for the Americas," in Gray, *Latin America and the United States*, 264; and Crimmins interview, 3 May 2005.

122. Meyer, Speech to Subcommittee on Inter-American Affairs of the House Committee on Foreign Affairs, 8 May 1969, published as "Future U.S Relations with Latin America," in Gray, *Latin America and the United States*, 261.

123. Records of the Staff Secretary, NSDM Working Files, National Decision Memorandum 28, 20 October 1969, and Memorandum, Kissinger for Chairman, NSC Under Secretaries Committee, 20 October 1969, box H285/NSCIF/NPMP. See also Brands, "Richard Nixon and Economic Nationalism," 219. Sanctions against Bolivia and Peru were not as extensive as those subsequently launched against Chile, and little is known about them. On what is known about Bolivia, see Lehman, *Limited Partnership*, 160.

124. See Memorandum, William Merriam (Vice-President, ITT, Washington) to John McCone, 9 October 1970, and Memorandum, H. Hendrix (ITT) to E. J. Gerrity (ITT), 30 October 1970, in *Subversion in Chile*, 52, 90–91.

125. Kissinger, "Central Issues," 52.

126. Huerta interview, 23 March 2010.

127. Memorandum, "Why did the U.S. Government Not Take More Vigorous Political Action Measures to Prevent the Election of the Marxist candidate, Salvador Allende, as President of Chile?" 4 March 1971, The Nixon Presidential Library and Museum, "December 9, 2010 Materials Release."

128. Ibid., and *Covert Action in Chile*, 1, 9, 13, 22.

Chapter 2

1. *Granma*, 5 September 1970; Debray, "Allende habla con Debray," 33; Suárez interview, 12 September 2005; Oña interview 3 September 2005; and conversations with Oña, March–April 2010. See also Fidel Castro to Beatriz Allende as quoted in Record of Conversation, Ambassador Alexseev and Volodia Teitelboim, 14 October 1970, published as "Conversación del Embajador Alexseev con Volodia Teitelboim," in Ulianova and Fediakova, "Chile en los Archivos de la URSS (1959–1973)," 412.

2. Memorandum, Kissinger to Nixon, 18 October 1970, and Memorandum, Kissinger to Nixon, 5 November 1970, box H029/NSCIF/NPMP.

3. Kissinger, *White House Years*, 670.

4. Agenda Annex, "The Setting for Policy Choice," enclosure, Memorandum, NSC Staff Secretary, Jeanne Davis, to the Vice President et al., 13 October 1969, box H040/NSCIF/NPMP.

5. Memorandum, General Vernon Walters to Henry Kissinger, 3 November 1970, enclosure, Memorandum, Kissinger to Nixon, 5 November 1970, box H029/NSCIF/NPMP.

6. Telcon, Kissinger and Roger, 14 September 1970, in Kornbluh, "New Kissinger 'Telcons' Reveal Chile Plotting."

7. Memorandum, Kissinger to Nixon, 5 November 1970.

8. See *Covert Action in Chile*, 23–26, and Kornbluh, *Pinochet File*, 11–35.

9. Fidel Castro, Speech at Teatro Municipal, Santiago, 25 November 1971, published as "Teatro Municipal Santiago," *Cuba-Chile*, 380.

10. Fidel Castro as quoted in Information Report, FBIS, "Trends in Communist Propaganda," 19 September 1970, CDP-CIA.

11. Chain interview; Estrada interview; and conversations with Oña, March–April 2010.

12. Castillo Estay, "Mucha Gente Me Culpó Cuando Se Suicidó la Tati."

13. Veneros, *Allende*, 267.

14. Estrada interview; Oña interviews, 9 and 16 December 2004, 3 September 2005; and Pérez, "Salvador Allende, Apuntes Sobre su Dispositivo de Seguridad," 49.

15. Pérez, "Salvador Allende, Apuntes Sobre su Dispositivo de Seguridad," 39–46.

16. Quiroga, *Compañeros*, 51, 54.

17. Oña interview, 3 September 2005, and Quiroga, *Compañeros*, 47–48.

18. Estrada, *Tania*, 17–21, 34–42.

19. Amat interview, 24 April 2006.

20. Oña interviews, 16 December 2004, 2 May 2006, and 15 April 2006.

21. Oña interview, 16 December 2004; conversations with Oña, March–April 2010; and Suárez, *Manuel Piñeiro*, 97, n. 1.

22. Estrada interview; Oña interviews, 2004–10; Otero interview, 17 December 2004; and Vázquez and Cubillas interview, 11 September 2005. Before Chile, Estrada was assigned to accompany Guevara out of Africa. Estrada, Testimony, 2003, CMSA. See also, Estrada, *Tania*, 17–21.

23. Castillo Estay, "Mucha Gente Me Culpó Cuando Se Suicidó la Tati," and Oña interviews, 15 April and 2 May 2006.

24. Oña interviews, 3 September 2005 and 2 May 2006.

25. Oña interview, 2 May 2006. Unfortunately, the author has not seen or heard this interview. Oña believes it to be the most detailed interview in existence with the president-elect about his aims after being elected.

26. Oña interview, 9 December 2004, and conversations with Oña, March–April 2010.

27. Quiroga, *Compañeros*, 51, 54, 49, and Pérez, "Salvador Allende, Apuntes Sobre su Dispositivo de Seguridad," 45–46.

28. Marambio, *Armas de Ayer*, 69–70, 81.

29. Oña interviews, 2004–6; Estrada interview; and Quiroga, *Compañeros*, 58. There is some debate as to whether Cubans actually joined the GAP. Together with the Cubans' own accounts, Marambio rejects the idea that Cubans were ever integrated, albeit recalling that a few Cubans did help to train members of the escort. Marambio, *Armas de Ayer*, 90. On the importance of Cuban support with training, see Pascal Allende interview.

30. Estrada interview; Oña interviews, 2004–6; Vázquez and Cubillas interview, 11 September 2005; Suárez interview, 10 December 2004; Jaramillo Edwards interviews, 24 November 2004 and 21 September 2005; and Soto interview, 7 July 2005.

31. Oña interview, 9 December 2004.

32. Oña interview, 3 September 2005.

33. Records of the Staff Secretary, NSDM Working Files, Minutes, SRG Meeting on Chile, 14 October 1970, box H289/NSCIF/NPMP.

34. Kissinger, "Domestic Structure and Foreign Policy" (1966), in Kissinger, *American Foreign Policy*, 14.

35. Talking Points, Kissinger, SRG Meeting on Chile, 18 August 1970, box H047/NSCIF/NPMP.

36. Nixon, *Memoirs*, 490.

37. Telcon, Kissinger and Nixon, 12 September 1970, in Kornbluh, "New Kissinger 'Telcons' Reveal Chile Plotting."

38. NSSM 97 as quoted in Kornbluh, *Pinochet File*, 8, and Memorandum, "Why did the U.S. Government Not Take More Vigorous Political Action Measures to Prevent the Election of the Marxist candidate, Salvador Allende, as President of Chile?" 4 March 1971, The Nixon Presidential Library and Museum, "December 9, 2010 Materials Release."

39. Crimmins interview.

40. Telcon, Kissinger and Rogers, 24 October 1970, box 7/HAK Telcons/NSC/NPMP, and Memorandum, "Why did the U.S. Government Not Take More Vigorous Political Action Measures?" 4 March 1971.

41. White House Tape, Nixon, Kissinger, and Haldeman, 11 June 1971, doc. 139, FRUS/1969–1976/E-10.

42. Telcons, Kissinger and Nixon, and Kissinger and Helms, 12 September 1970, in Kornbluh, "New Kissinger 'Telcons' Reveal Chile Plotting."

43. This group was formed by Eisenhower and was known as the 303 Committee under President Lyndon Johnson. Hitchens, *Trial of Henry Kissinger*, 16–18.

44. Telcon, Kissinger and Rogers, 14 September 1970, in Kornbluh, "New Kissinger 'Telcons' Reveal Chile Plotting"; and Memorandum for the Record, Frank Chaplin, "Minutes of the Meeting of the Forty Committee, September 8 1970," September 9, CDP-NSC. For Korry's telegrams, see Telegram, Korry to SecState, 5 September 1970, NSA. Kissinger refers to Nixon as underlining passages of the cable. Kissinger, *White House Years*, 654.

45. Memorandum, Vaky to Kissinger, 14 September 1970, CDP-NSC; Memorandum, William McAfee (INR) to Johnson (Under Secretary of State), 8 September 1970, CDP-NARA; Telegram, Johnson to Korry, 25 September 1970, CDP-CIA.

46. Intelligence Memorandum, Directorate of Intelligence, "Situation Following the Chilean Presidential Election," 7 September 1970, CDP-NSC; and "Minutes of the Meeting of the Forty Committee, September 8 1970." For State Department views, see Intelligence Note, INR, 1 October 1970, box H048/NSCIF/NPMP; and Telegram, Robert Hurwitch to the Secretary, 3 November 1970, box 2201/RG59/NARA. For Defense Department views, see Telcon, Kissinger and Laird, 10 October 1970, box 7/HAK Telcons/NSCF/NPMP.

47. "Minutes of the Meeting of the Forty Committee, September 8 1970"; Memorandum, McAfee to Johnson, 8 September 1970; and Memorandum, Vaky to Kissinger, 14 September 1970.

48. "Minutes of the Meeting of the Forty Committee, September 8 1970."

49. "HAK Talking Points—Chile" enclosure, Memorandum, Vaky to Kissinger, 7 September, CDP-NSC. Newly released documents from the Nixon Presidential Library and Museum have revealed that the first of these measures was initially proposed by the U.S. ambassador in Santiago back in June 1970 but that this was shelved and ignored by decision makers until late August, when the Senior Review Group of the National Security Council again proposed that an Action Plan be drawn up to prevent an Allende victory in a congressional run-off. Amid evidence suggesting that Allende would lose, however, there is no indication that an Action Plan was in fact produced before the 40 Committee met on 8 September. Memorandum, "Why did the U.S. Government Not Take More Vigorous Political Action Measures?" 4 March 1971.

50. Memorandum, Vaky to Kissinger, 14 September 1970.

51. Telcon, Kissinger and Rogers, 14 September 1970.

52. Telcon, Kissinger and Nixon, 12 September 1970. Telephone call logs and Nixon's daily schedule list Don Kendall calling Nixon on 12 September followed by a meeting on 15 September with Edwards and Kissinger at the White House. Log, 12 September 1970, box 106/Presidential Telephone Calls June 1970–December 1970/President's Office Files/NPMP; box 102/President's Daily Schedule July 1970 to May 1971/President's Office Files/NPMP; and Kissinger, *White House Years*, 673. On Edwards's "escape" from Chile, see Arancibia Claval, *Conversando con Roberto Kelly*, 123–24.

53. CIA Report, "Review of Political and Military Options in Chilean Electoral Situation," 14 September 1970, CDP-NSC.

54. Memorandum, Vaky to Kissinger, 14 September 1970, and Memorandum, Vaky to Kissinger, 16 September 1970, CDP-NSC.

55. Intelligence Telegram, David Philips (CIA Chile Task Force) to CIA Station, Santiago, 27 September 1970, CDP-CIA (filed as 28 September).

56. Memorandum for the Record, "Minutes of the 40 Committee, 6 October 1970," 7 October 1970, CDP-NSC.

57. Quotations from Handwritten Notes, Helms, 15 September 1970, in Kornbluh, *Pinochet File*, 36.

58. Memorandum, Kissinger to Nixon, 17 September 1970, enclosure, Memorandum, Vaky to Kissinger, 17 September 1970, CDP-NSC.

59. Intelligence Telegram, Philips to CIA Station, Santiago, "Need Station New Possibilities," 27 September 1970, CDP-CIA.

60. Kissinger, *White House Years*, 673.

61. Nixon, *Memoirs*, 490.

62. "Minutes of the 40 Committee Meeting, 6 October 1970."

63. Telegram, SecState to All American Republic Diplomatic Posts, 10 September 1970, box 18/RG84/NARA. On allusions to this lobbying, see Walters, *Silent Missions*, 566, and Kissinger, *White House Years*, 675.

64. Memorandum of Conversation, Nixon and Saragat, Rome, 27 September 1970, box 467/NSCF/NPMP.

65. Memorandum of Conversation, Nixon and Pope Paul VI, 28 September 1970, box 467/NSCF/NPMP; Memorandum, Haig to Kissinger, 28 September 1970, box

467/NSCF/NPMP; and Record of a Meeting between the Prime Minister and President Nixon, 3 October 1970, Prime Minister's Files, 15/714/TNA. Nixon also urged British prime minister Edward Heath to defer two relatively unimportant loans to Chile, which the latter did.

66. Memorandum for the Record, "Minutes of the 40 Committee, 14 October 1970," 16 October 1970, CDP-NSC.

67. Intelligence Telegram, CIA Headquarters to CIA Station, 16 October 1970, CDP-CIA.

68. Paul Wimert, interview with CNN, 21 February 1999, NSA.

69. Kissinger, *White House Years*, 667.

70. Telcon, Kissinger and Nixon, 23 October 1970, box 7/HAK Telcons/NSCF/NPMP.

71. "Minutes of the 40 Committee, 14 October 1970."

72. Memorandum, Kissinger to Nixon, 18 October 1970, enclosure Memorandum, Vaky to Kissinger, 18 October 1970, CDP-NSC.

73. Memorandum, Vaky to Kissinger, 16 October 1970, box H048/NSCIF/NPMP. On the SRG, see National Security Decision Memorandum 85, box H219/NSCIF/NPMP.

74. Records of the Staff Secretary, NSDM Working Files, Minutes, SRG Meeting on Chile, 14 October 1970. On the lack of an "effective analysis of interests," see also Memorandum, "Why did the U.S. Government Not Take More Vigorous Political Action Measures?" 4 March 1971.

75. Kissinger, *White House Years*, 665.

76. Records of the Staff Secretary, NSDM Working Files, Minutes, SRG Meeting on Chile, 29 October 1970, box H289/NSCIF/NPMP.

77. Quotation from Memorandum, Dwight Chaplin for H. R. Haldeman, 4 November 1970, box H029/NSCIF/NPMP.

78. Memorandum, Kissinger to Nixon, 5 November 1970.

79. Note, Kissinger to Nixon, enclosure, ibid.

80. See, for example, Memorandum, Vernon Walters to Kissinger, "Brazil," c. December 1968, doc. 116/FRUS/1969–1976/E-10.

81. Author's correspondence with an employee at the U.S. National Defense Intelligence College regarding Walters's personal diaries, 3 January 2008.

82. Memorandum, Walters to Kissinger, 3 November 1970.

83. Handwritten note, Nixon to Kissinger, 5 November 1970, on Note, Kissinger to Nixon, 5 November 1970. Emphasis in original.

84. Memorandum, Kissinger to Nixon, 5 November 1970.

85. Letter, Osvaldo Dorticós, President of Cuba to Allende, 1 November 1970, Cuba/1970/AMRE. See also Vázquez and Cubillas interviews.

86. Rodríguez as quoted in "Summary of Press Conference," 24 November 1970, FCO7/1991/TNA.

87. Timossi interview, 14 September 2005.

88. Quotation from Record of Conversation, Ambassador Alexseev and Volodia Teitelboim, 14 October 1970, 411. Allende also recounted Castro's counsel to Galo Plaza. Memorandum of Conversation, Galo Plaza and Allende, 2 November 1970,

Tomás Moro, enclosure, Memorandum, Rogers to Nixon, 29 December 1970, box 2196/RG59/NARA.

89. Quotation from Memorandum of Conversation, Plaza and Allende, 2 November 1970. See also Castro as quoted in Record of Conversation, Ambassador Alexseev and Volodia Teitelboim, 14 October 1970. On Castro similarly advising the Peruvians to wait, see Oficio, Jorge Edwards (chargé d'affaires), Embachile Havana to Señor Ministro, 10 December 1970, Cuba/1970/AMRE.

90. Oña interview, 16 December 2004.

91. Estrada interview. On Carretero's role in Bolivia, see Castañeda, *Compañero*, 239, 346.

92. Oña interviews, 2004–6; Otero interview; Vázquez and Cubillas interview, 11 September 2005; and Soto interviews, 29 April and 7 July 2005.

93. Telcon, Kissinger and Rogers, 30 October 1970, box 7/HAK Telcons/NSCF/NPMP.

94. Memorandum, Armando Uribe, "Estada en Chile del Jefe de la Delegacion Especial de EEUU a la Transmisión de Mando, Secretario Charles Meyer," 6 November 1970. See also, Memorandum, Ramon Huidobro, c. 4 November 1970, Memos Politicos/MINREL, 1961–1979/AMRE.

95. Memorandum for the Record, "Minutes of the Meeting of the 40 Committee, 13 November 1970," 17 November 1970, CDP-NSC.

96. "HAK Talking Points on Chile, NSC Meeting—Thursday, November 6," box H029/NSCIF/NPMP. Emphasis in original.

97. Memorandum, Kissinger to Nixon, 5 November 1970.

98. Quotations from Intelligence Note, INR, "Latin America: Top Officials Assess the Implications of the Allende Victory," 2 November 1970, box 2196/RG59/NARA.

99. Telegram, Hurwitch to the Secretary, 3 November 1970.

100. Memorandum of Conversation, the President et al., the Cabinet Room, 9:40 A.M., 6 November 1970, in Kornbluh, *Pinochet File*, 116–20.

101. Telcon, Kissinger and Rogers, 6 November 1970, box 7/HAK Telcons/NSCF/NPMP.

102. Memorandum, Kissinger to Nixon, 5 November 1970.

103. "HAK Talking Points," NSC Meeting, 6 November 1970. See also David Packard's comments in Minutes, SRG Meeting on Chile, 14 October 1970, and Kissinger, *White House Years*, 665.

104. Memorandum, Walters to Kissinger, 3 November 1970, and Note, Nixon to Kissinger, 5 November 1970.

105. Memorandum of Conversation, the President et al., 6 November 1970.

106. National Security Decision Memorandum 93, "Policy towards Chile," 9 November 1970, CDP-NSC.

107. Memorandum of Conversation, the President et al., 6 November 1970.

108. Ibid.

109. Memorandum, "Covert Action Program for Chile," 17 November 1970.

110. National Security Decision Memorandum 93.

111. Allende interview with Radio Habana Cuba as quoted in *Granma*, 5 September 1970.

112. Volodia Teitelboim, 3 January 1971, as quoted in Special Report, FBIS, 25 March 1971, CDP-CIA.

113. Record of Conversations, Raúl Roa and Polish minister of foreign affairs Stefan Jedrychowski, 24–26 June 1971, Urgent Note, "Notes on the Conversations with Roa," 30 June 1971, wiazka 3/40/75/AMSZ.

114. Ibid.

115. Castro as quoted in "Interview with Salvador Allende and Fidel Castro," in Cockcroft, *Allende Reader*, 134.

Chapter 3

1. Allende, "Victory Speech," in Cockcroft, *Allende Reader*, 50, 48.

2. Oficio, Embachile Rio to Señor Ministro, 26 October 1970, Oficios Conf. E./R./Brasil/1970/AMRE.

3. Speech, General Canaverro Pereira on the occasion of Argentine General Alcides Lópes Aufranc's visit to Brazil, October 1970, as quoted in Embachile Rio to Señor Ministro, 26 October 1970, Oficios Conf., E./R./Brasil/1970/AMRE.

4. This possibility and the decision not to break relations were later conveyed to Secretary of the Treasury John Connally during conversations with President Médici on 8 June 1972 in Brasilia. For an account of this conversation, see Telegram, Amembassy Wellington to SecState, 23 June 1972, Executive Secretariat, Briefing Books, 1958–1976, lot 720373, box 135/RG59/NARA.

5. Allende, "Inaugural Address in the National Stadium," in Cockcroft, *Allende Reader*, 54, 60; and Popular Unity Programme, 1969, in Cockcroft, *Allende Reader*, 276–78.

6. Allende, "Victory Speech," in Cockcroft, *Allende Reader*, 48, 51.

7. Almeyda, "La Política Exterior del Gobierno de la Unidad Popular," in Almeyda, *Obras Escogidas*, 97, 131.

8. Letter, Hernán Santa Cruz to Señor Don Salvador Allende, 12 September 1970, vol. 2/FHSC/AMRE.

9. Memorandum Secreto, Ministro de Relaciones Exteriores al Señor Embajador de Chile en Washington, no. 14, 24 June 1971, 2/16/2/FOL.

10. Allende, "Address to the United Nations General Assembly," 4 December 1972, in Cockcroft, *Allende Reader*, 205.

11. Popular Unity Programme, in Cockcroft, *Allende Reader*, 270–71.

12. Debray, "Allende habla con Debray," 40.

13. Oficio, Domingo Santa Maria (Chilean Ambassador), Embachile Washington to Señor Ministro, 17 November 1970, Oficios Conf./EEUU/1970/AMRE. On scrutinizing the press, see Jaramillo Edwards interview, 21 September 2005. Certain reports on the U.S. press from Chile's embassy in Washington were passed directly to Allende. See Telex, Letelier to MRE, 7 April 1971, Telex: 1–400/EEUU/1971/AMRE.

14. Kissinger, *White House Years*, 654. Although the Nixon administration expressed worries about increasing Soviet activity in Cuba in August 1970, the Cienfuegos crisis did not erupt until late September. See Memorandum of Conversation, Kissinger and Minister Counselor Vorontsov, 7 August 1970, and Memorandums of

Conversations, Kissinger and Dobrynin, 25 September and 9 October 1970, in Geyer and Selvage, *Soviet-American Relations*, 186–88, 199–200, 202, and 207–8.

15. Letter, Santa Cruz to Allende, 12 September 1970.

16. Memorandum of Conversation, Galo Plaza and Allende, 2 November 1970, Tomás Moro, enclosure, Memorandum, Rogers to Nixon, 29 December 1970, box 2196/RG59/NARA.

17. Letter, Orlando Letelier to Aniceto Rodríguez, 12 October 1970, 12/2/11/FOL. See also, Almeyda, "Foreign Policy of the Unidad Popular," 84.

18. Letter, Letelier to Rodríguez, 12 October 1970.

19. Almeyda, "Exposición del Ministro de Relaciones Exteriores, Señor Clodomiro Almeyda, ante la Comisión de Relaciones Exteriores del Senado," 22 December 1970, enclosure, Circular, MRE, 25 January 1971, Discursos: S. Allende Gossens/1971/AMRE.

20. Huidobro interview, 18 October 2004, and Urrutia interview, 27 October 2004.

21. Urrutia interview, 27 October 2004. Urrutia recalled that he was one of those who suggested Letelier to Allende as an alternative. On speculation that Herrera might be offered the post, see "Allende May Offer Chilean Post to Inter-American Bank Head," *New York Times*, 8 October 1970.

22. Fermandois, *Mundo y Fin de Mundo*, 361–62.

23. Ibid., 360; Huidobro interviews, 18 and 28 October 2004; and Humberto Diaz Casanueva, "Política Multilateral del Presidente Salvador Allende," 168.

24. Huidobro interview, 28 October 2004. Although Castro advised Allende to keep Valdés on, Huidobro insisted this was Allende's decision. E-mail correspondence with the author, 16 February 2005. On Castro's advice, see Memorandum of Conversation, Plaza and Allende, 2 November 1970, and Record of Conversation, Ambassador Alexseev and Volodia Teitelboim, 14 October 1970, published as "Conversación del Embajador Alexseev con Volodia Teitelboim," in Ulianova and Fediakova, "Chile en los Archivos de la URSS (1959–1973)."

25. Huidobro interview, 28 October 2004. Huidobro, a career diplomat and Allende's close confidant, also stayed at the ministry with Almeyda for two months until he went to Buenos Aires as Chile's ambassador.

26. Almeyda, "Foreign Policy of the Unidad Popular," 80–81, 84. See also Urgent Note, "Summary of Visit of the Chilean Delegation," 2 June 1971, wiazka 3/40/75/AMSZ.

27. Memorandum Secreto, Ministro de Relaciones Exteriores al Señor Embajador de Chile en Washington et al., no. 14, 24 June 1971, 2/16/2/FOL.

28. Ulianova, "La Unidad Popular y el Golpe Militar," 89.

29. Almeyda, "Foreign Policy of the Unidad Popular," 83.

30. Oficio, Jorge Edwards to Señor Ministro, 10 December 1970, Cuba/1970/AMRE.

31. For a detailed examination of the UP's policies toward East and West Germany, see Fermandois, "Del Malestar al Entusiasmo."

32. Almeyda as quoted in Urgent Note, "Summary of Visit of the Chilean Delegation," 2 June 1971.

33. Memorandum of Conversation, Plaza and Allende, 2 November 1970.

34. Ibid; Almeyda as quoted in Urgent Note, "Summary of Visit of the Chilean Delegation," 2 June 1971.

35. Memorandum of Conversation, Plaza and Allende, 2 November 1970; Almeyda as quoted in Urgent Note, "Summary of Visit of the Chilean Delegation," 2 June 1971.

36. Allende, Speech in Punta Arenas, 27 February 1971, published as "Estados Unidos de Norteamérica," *OE-SA*, 565. See also Almeyda, Speech to OAS, San José, Costa Rica, 15 April 1971, in Vera Castillo, *Política Exterior Chilena*, 432–33.

37. Paper, "Enfoque y Conceptos sobre la coperacion cientifico-tecnica internacional," enclosure, Memorandum, Embachile Havana, no date, "Negociaciones para el establecimiento de cooperacion cientifico-tecnica chileno-cubana," CMSA.

38. Memorandum, Santa Cruz, "Posibilidades de la Realizacion en Chile de la Tercera UNCTAD," 17 February 1971, vol. 2/FHSC/AMRE.

39. Oficio, Santa Maria to Señor Ministro, 27 November 1970, Oficios Conf./EEUU/1970/AMRE; and Officio, Manuel Sánchez (chargé d'affaires), Embachile Washington, to Señor Ministro, 22 January 1971, Oficios Conf., R./EEUU/1971/AMRE.

40. Davis, *Last Two Years*, 27–28; *Covert Action in Chile*, 35; and Telex, MRE to Embachile Washington, 2 March 1971, Telex E: 1–367/EEUU/1971/AMRE. On indications of U.S. hostility, see also Diaz Casanueva, "Política Multilateral del Presidente Salvador Allende," 170. Although the Easter Island incident was probably unrelated to Nixon's policy to undermine Allende, the White House was directly responsible for canceling the *Enterprise* visit. Kissinger noted that he did not want Allende to be able to "use it to say they have great relations with us." See Telcons, Kissinger and Admiral Elmo Zumwalt, 24 February 1971, Kissinger and Rogers, 25 February 1971, and Kissinger and Melvyn Laird, 25 February 1971, box 9/HAK Telcons/NSC/NPMP. On Chilean complaints to Washington regarding both incidents as evidence of hostility, see Telex, MRE to Embachile Washington, 14 October 1972, Telex E./EEUU/1972/AMRE.

41. Nixon as quoted in Oficio, Sánchez to Señor Ministro, 8 January 1971 Oficios Conf., R/EEUU/1971/AMRE.

42. Telex, Embachile Washington to MRE, 26 February 1971, Telex R: 1–400/EEUU/1971/AMRE.

43. Allende, "Estados Unidos de Norteamérica," *OE-SA*, 567.

44. Memorandum Secreto, MRE al Señor Embajador, no. 14, 24 June 1971. The working group consisted of Allende, the president of the state's Council of Defense, Letelier, and functionaries from the Foreign Ministry, the National Copper Corporation of Chile (Corporación Nacional del Cobre de Chile or CODELCO), and the Production Development Corporation (Corporación de Fomento de la Producción de Chile or CORFO). On working group meetings, see also Huidobro interview, 28 October 2004. Huidobro recalls that he attended one early meeting of the working group at which six or seven people were present, including Letelier, Almeyda, and Allende's minister in charge of mines, Orlando Cantuarias.

45. Allende, "Inaugural Address," in Cockcroft, *Allende Reader*, 58.

46. Telegrams, Rogers to Amembassy Santiago and Korry to SecState, 1 February 1971, box 18/RG84/NARA. See also Record of Conversation, Almeyda and Korry, 1

February 1971, Memorandum, 2 February 1971, Memorandos/Dirección Economica, 1967–1974/AMRE.

47. Telegram, Korry to SecState, 4 February 1971, box 18/RG84/NARA.

48. Record of Conversations, Korry and José Toha (Chilean Minister of the Interior), 8 February 1971, Telegram, Korry to SecState, 9 February 1971, box 18/RG84/NARA.

49. Telegram, Korry to SecState, 9 February 1971.

50. Telex, Embachile Washington to MRE, 26 February 1971.

51. Annex III: Memorandum Armando Uribe, enclosure, Oficio, MRE to Embachile Washington, 14 April 1971, Oficios Conf., E./EEUU/1971/AMRE.

52. Oficio, Letelier to Señor Ministro, 23 April 1971, Oficios Conf., R./EEUU/1971/AMRE.

53. Memorandum, William R. Joyce to Mr. Navarro, 30 March 1971, Oficios Conf., R./EEUU/1971/AMRE.

54. Telex, Letelier to MRE, 6 July 1971, Telex R: 1–400/EEUU/1971/AMRE.

55. Oficio, Sánchez to Señor Ministro, 3 February 1971, Oficios Conf., R./EEUU/1971/AMRE.

56. Record of Conversation, Letelier and Crimmins, 17 March 1971, Telex, Letelier to MRE, 17 March 1971, Telex R: 1–400/EEUU/1971/AMRE.

57. "The President's Reply to the Remarks of the Newly Appointed Ambassador of Chile Orlando Letelier del Solar upon the Occasion of the Presentation of His Letter of Credence," 2 March 1971, 2/16/10/FOL.

58. Record of Conversation, Letelier and Kissinger, 23 March 1971, Telex, Letelier to Almeyda, 23 March 1971, Telex R: 1–400/EEUU/1971/AMRE.

59. Oficio, Letelier to Señor Ministro, "La prensa norteamericana y Chile. Elecciones municipales," 9 April 1971, Oficios Conf., R./EEUU/1971/AMRE.

60. On lobbying and Nixon's views, see *Subversion in Chile*, 22–103, 96, 46, 53.

61. "HAK Talking Points—Chile SRG Meeting," 17 February 1971, box H052/NSCIF/NPMP.

62. Ibid., and Memorandum, Nachmanoff to Kissinger, 16 February 1971, box H052/NSCIF/NPMP.

63. Memorandum, Kissinger to the Under Secretary of State et al., 25 February 1971, box H052/NSCIF/NPMP.

64. Record of Conversation, Letelier and Kissinger, 23 March 1971, Telex, Letelier to Almeyda, 23 March 1971.

65. Memorandum, Crimmins (Acting Chairman, Ad Hoc Working Group on Chile) to Irwin, 19 December 1970, box 2201/RG59/NARA.

66. See Memorandums, Kissinger to the Under Secretary of State et al., 27 November 1970 and 30 December 1970, box H050/NSCIF/NPMP; Paper "Status Report on Discussions with Export-Import Bank on Discontinuation of New Credits and Guarantees," enclosure, Memorandum, Crimmins to Kissinger, 4 December 1970; and Paper, "Feasible Reductions, Delays or Terminations of AID Commitments to Chile," enclosure, Memorandum, Crimmins to Kissinger, 19 December 1970, box H172/NSCIF/NPMP. Kissinger also personally discouraged Ford's chairman from visiting Chile. See Telcons, Kissinger and Edward Molina (Ford Motors),

19 December 1970; Kissinger and Irwin, 15 December 1970; and Kissinger and Molina, 10 December 1971, box 8/HAK Telcons/NSCF/NPMP.

67. Kornbluh, *Pinochet File*, 84. See also *Covert Action in Chile*, 34.

68. *Covert Action in Chile*, 57.

69. Memorandum for the 40 Committee, 28 January 1971, enclosure, Memorandum, Nachmanoff to Kissinger, 28 January 1971; Memorandum, Richard Helms for the 40 Committee, 15 March 1971, enclosure, Memorandum, Chaplin to Kissinger, 17 March 1971; and Memorandum, CIA for the 40 Committee, 21 April 1971, CDP-NSC. See also, *Covert Action in Chile*, 59.

70. Memorandum, CIA for the 40 Committee, 21 April 1971, enclosure, Memorandum, Nachmanoff to Kissinger, 11 May 1971, CDP-NSC.

71. "Covert Action Program for Chile," 17 November 1970, CDP-NSC.

72. *Covert Action in Chile*, 38, and U.S. Congressional Findings (1971) as quoted in Schoultz, *Beneath the United States*, 359.

73. Paper, Department of Defense, "Paper on M-41 Tanks," enclosure, Memorandum, Crimmins to Kissinger, 16 February 1971, box H220/NSCIF/NPMP.

74. Telcon, Kissinger and Rogers, 25 February 1971, box 9/HAK Telcons/NSCF/NPMP.

75. Memorandum Secreto, MRE al Señor Abajador, no. 14, 24 June 1971.

76. Ibid.

77. Crimmins interview.

78. Memorandum Secreto, MRE al Señor Abajador, no. 14, 24 June 1971.

79. *Washington Post*, 13 November 1970, as quoted in Telegram, Brazilian Embassy, Washington, to Secretaria de Estado das Relações Exteriores, 13/14 November 1970, Rolo 423, Telegramas recebidos da Embaixada em Washington/AMRE-Brasilia.

80. Intelligence Note, INR, "Latin America: Chile's Renewed Relations with Cuba—A Potential Problem for the OAS," 30 November 1970, box 2199/RG59/NARA.

81. Circular Telegram, DOS to All American Republic Diplomatic Posts, 15 November 1970, box H220/NSCIF/NPMP, and Memorandum, Nachmanoff and R. T. Kennedy to Kissinger, 5 December 1970, box H050/NSCIF/NPMP. On Kissinger's views that the United States' Cuba policy should not change, see Memorandum, Johnson to Rogers and Irwin, 8 December 1970, box 2201/RG59/NARA. On Nixon's refusal to contemplate altering Washington's Cuba policy, see Memorandum of Conversation, the President et al., the Cabinet Room, 9:40 A.M., 6 November 1970, in Kornbluh, *Pinochet File*, 116–20.

82. "More Latin Lands Seem Willing to End Ban on Cuba," *New York Times*, 14 August 1971, as quoted in Telegram, Brazilian Embassy, Washington, to Secretario de Estado das Relações Exteriores, 14 August 1971, Rolo 423/Telegramas recebidos da Embaixada em Washington/AMRE-Brasilia. On U.S.-Brazilian cooperation on this issue, see Record of Conversation, William Rountree (U.S. Ambassador in Brasilia), and Gibson Barbosa, 22 December 1970, Telegram, Rountree to SecState, 23 December 1970, box 2199/RG59/NARA. See also Mesa-Lago, *Cuba in the 1970s*, 123.

83. Telegram, DOS to All American Republic Diplomatic Posts, 22 January 1971, box 2199/RG59/NARA.

84. Telegram, DOS to All American Republic Diplomatic Posts, 15 November 1970, and Memorandum, Kissinger to the Under Secretary of State et al., 10 December 1970, box H050/NSCIF/NPMP.

85. Memorandum, DOS to SRG, "Status Report on Implementation of NSDM 93 and SRG Directives," 9 April 1971, box 2201/RG59/NARA; and Draft Telegram, DOS to All ARA Chiefs of Mission in Paper "Status Report of U.S Actions to Discourage Further Resumptions of Relations with Cuba," enclosure, Memorandum, Crimmins to Kissinger, 4 December 1970, box H172/NSCIF/NPMP. The exact content of the information passed on by the CIA is still unknown. However, various stories about Cuban agents in Chile appeared in the U.S. press alone. See "Cuban Agents in Chile Hide Debray," *Washington Star*, 10 January 1971, Oficio, Sánchez to Señor Ministro, 22 January 1971, Oficios Conf., R./EEUU/1971/AMRE; and Telex, Sánchez to MRE, 11 January 1971, Telex R: 1–400/EEUU/1971/AMRE.

86. Vaky and Crimmins interviews.

87. Oficio, Antonio Castro da Câmara Canto (Brazilian Ambassador in Chile) to Secretario de Estado das Relações Exteriores, 23 February 1971, Oficios/Embaixada do Brasil, Santiago 1971 (01)/AMRE-Brasilia.

88. Nixon as quoted in Oficio, Letelier to Señor Ministro, 1 March 1971, Oficios Conf., R./EEUU/1971/AMRE; Telex, Magnet (Chilean Representative, OAS) to MRE, 21 December 1970, Aerogram y Telex/OEA/1970/AMRE; and Record of Conversation, Valdés and Antonio Sánchez de Lozoda (Bolivian Ambassador, Washington), 8 February 1971, Oficio, Valdés to Señor Ministro, 9 February 1971, Oficios Conf., R./EEUU/1971/AMRE.

89. Telex, Valdés to MRE, 26 February 1971, Telex R: 1–400/EEUU/1971/AMRE.

90. See Oficio, MRE to Letelier, 24 March 1971, Oficios Conf., E./EEUU/1971/AMRE; and Oficio, Letelier to Señor Ministro, 9 April 1971, Oficios Conf., R./EEUU/1971/AMRE.

91. Telex, Valdés to MRE, 26 February 1971.

92. Oficios, Luis Jerez Ramirez (Chilean Ambassador), Embachile Lima to Señor Ministro, 25 March and 13 April 1971, Oficios Conf., E./EEUU/1971/AMRE; and Oficios, Jerez Ramirez to Señor Ministro, 2 February and 6 April 1971, Oficios Res., E./R./Perú/1971/AMRE. On U.S-Peruvian relations, see Airgram, Belcher (U.S. Ambassador), Amembassy Lima to DOS, box 2196/RG59/NARA. Belcher acknowledged that U.S.-Peruvian relations had improved but stated this was for "reasons other than Peruvian reaction to the Allende election."

93. Telex, Pedro Vuskovic Bravo (Acting Minister) and Daniel Vergara Bustos (Under Secretary of the Interior) to Letelier, 13 March 1971, Telex E: 1–367/EEUU/1971/AMRE.

94. Oficio, MRE to Letelier, 24 March 1971, and Oficio, Letelier to Señor Ministro, 9 April 1971, Oficios Conf., R./EEUU/1971/AMRE.

95. Oficio, Embachile Rio to Señor Ministro, 13 November 1970, Oficios Conf., E./R./Brasil/1970/AMRE; and "Paises Latinoamericanos no han contestado consulta de

EE.UU para bloqear a Chile; Departamento de Estado inició contactos en noviembre. Norteamérica y Brasil observan Gobierno de Allende," *El Diario* and *La Prensa*, 13 March 1971, enclosures, Telex, Vuskovic and Vergara to Letelier, 13 March 1971.

96. Oficio, Rettig to Señor Ministro, 2 March 1971, Oficios Conf., E./R./ Brasil/1971/AMRE.

97. Oficio, Rettig to Señor Ministro, 14 May 1971, Oficios Conf., E./R./Brasil/1971/ AMRE.

98. Quotations from Oficio, Embachile Rio to Señor Ministro, 17 September 1970, Oficios Conf., E./R./Brasil/1970/AMRE.

99. *O Estado de São Paulo*, 10 November 1970, as quoted in Oficio, Embachile Rio to Señor Ministro, 23 November 1970, and Oficio, Embachile Rio to Señor Ministro, 13 November 1970, Oficios Conf., E./R./Brasil/1970/AMRE.

100. Oficio, Rettig to Señor Ministro, 23 March 1971, Oficios Conf., E./R./Brasil/1971/AMRE. On evidence of communication between Brazilian naval officials and anti-Allende sectors of the Chilean navy, see Record of Conversation, Rountree and Admiral Figueiredo, c. 14 January, São Paulo, Telegram, Rountree to SecState, 14 January 1971, box 1697/RG59/NARA.

101. Oficio, Rettig to Señor Ministro, 30 March 1971, Oficios Conf., E./R./Brasil/1971/AMRE.

102. "Paises Latinoamericanos no han contestado consulta de EE.UU para bloqear a Chile; Departamento de Estado inició contactos en noviembre. Norteamérica y Brasil observan Gobierno de Allende," *El Diario* and *La Prensa*, 13 March 1971, enclosures, Telex, Vuskovic and Vergara to Letelier, 13 March 1971.

103. Oficio, Embachile Rio to Señor Ministro, 29 April 1970, Oficios Conf., E./R./ Brasil/1970/AMRE.

104. Almeyda as quoted in Urgent Note, "Summary of Visit of the Chilean Delegation," 2 June 1971, wiazka 3/40/75/AMSZ.

105. On reactions to Brazil's diplomatic offensive, see Oficios Conf., Rettig to Señor Ministro, 2 June 1971, and MRE to Señor Embajador de Chile en Brasil-Brasilia, 11 June 1971, Oficios Conf., E./R./Brasil/1971/AMRE. On Brazil's outreach to Peru, see Oficio Conf., Rettig to Señor Ministro, 27 March 1971, enclosure, Oficio, MRE to Embachile Washington, 15 April 1971, Oficios Conf., E./EEUU/1971/AMRE.

106. Oficio, Ramon Huidobro (Chilean Ambassador), Embachile Buenos Aires to Señor Ministro, 16 July 1971, Oficios Conf., E./EEUU/1971/AMRE.

107. Oficio, Rettig to Señor Ministro, 26 March 1971, enclosure, Oficio, MRE to Embachile Washington, 15 April 1971, Oficios Conf., E./EEUU/1971/AMRE.

108. Almeyda, "Foreign Policy of the Unidad Popular," 88, and Almeyda as quoted in Urgent Note, "Summary of Visit of the Chilean Delegation," 2 June 1971. On levels of trade, see Diplomatic Report no. 338/72, FCO, 19 April 1972, FCO7/2174/TNA.

109. Record of Conversation, Hugo Vigorena Ramirez (Chilean Ambassador), Embachile Mexico, and Emilio Rabasa (Mexican Foreign Minister), no date, Oficio, Vigorena Ramirez to Señor Ministro, Oficios Conf., E./R./México/1971/AMRE.

110. "Conferencia de Prensa del Presidente de la Republica, Compañero Salvador Allende," 5 May 1971, Discursos/AMRE.

111. Almeyda, Speech to OAS, San José, Costa Rica, 15 April 1971, in Vera Castillo,

Política Exterior Chilena, 427–37; and Telex, Herrera to MRE, 1 April 1971, Aerograma y Telex/OEA/1971/AMRE.

112. Special Report, FBIS, "Cuban and Other Communist Views of Chile: Elements of Competition with the Cuban Model," 15 March 1971, CDP-CIA.

113. Telegram, Hildyard (British Ambassador in Santiago) to FCO, 14 June 1971, FCO7/2091/TNA.

114. Letter, Hildyard to J. M. Hunter (Latin America Department), FCO, 30 June 1971, FCO7/2091/TNA.

115. Record of Conversation, Letelier and Crimmins, 17 March 1971. See also Telegram, SecState to Amembassy Santiago, 18 March 1971, box 18/RG84/NARA.

116. Record of Conversation, Letelier and Kissinger, 23 March 1971.

117. Oficio, Letelier to Señor Ministro, 9 April 1971.

118. Crimmins interview.

119. Memorandum of Conversation, H. E. Argentina's Ambassador Pedro Real et al., Washington, 22 December 1970, Bureau of Inter-American Affairs, Deputy Assistant Secretary, Subject and Country Files, box 1/RG59/NARA.

120. Paper, "A Study of Options for U.S. Strategy Concerning Chile's Future Participation in the Organization of American States," enclosure, Memorandum, Crimmins to Kissinger, 4 December 1970.

121. Spektor, "Equivocal Engagement," 43–80.

122. "Brazil Program Analysis (NSSM 67)," enclosure, Memorandum, Wayne Smith to Kissinger, 3 December 1970, box H049/NSCIF/NPMP.

123. Letter, Edward M. Kennedy to Rogers, 25 March 1971, box 2134/RG59/NARA.

124. Memorandum, Irwin to the Secretary, "Policy toward Brazil," c. 1 December 1970, box 2134/RG59/NARA; and Memorandum, Wayne Smith to Kissinger, 27 November 1970, box H049/NSCIF/NPMP.

125. Memorandum, Nachmanoff to Kissinger, 25 November 1970, box H049/NSCIF/NPMP.

126. Memorandum, Nachmanoff to Kissinger, 1 December 1970, box H049/NSCIF/NPMP. Although he was invited in early 1971, Médici finally visited in December. Handwritten note, Kissinger, on Memorandum, Nachmanoff and Kennedy to Kissinger, 5 December 1970, box H050/NSCIF/NPMP.

127. Country Analysis and Strategy Paper (CASP), 30 November 1970, enclosure, Airgram, Rountree to DOS, 19 January 1971, box 2136/RG59/NARA.

128. White House Tape, Nixon, Kissinger and Haldeman, 11 June 1971, doc. 139/FRUS/1969–1976/E-10.

129. Memorandum, Irwin to the Secretary, "Policy toward Brazil," c. 1 December 1970.

130. Memorandum, Crimmins to Irwin, 19 December 1970.

131. Memorandum, Laird to Nixon, 30 November 1970, box H220/NSCIF/NPMP.

132. Telcon, Kissinger and Laird, 26 December 1970, box 8/HAK Telcons/NSCF/NPMP.

133. Memorandum, Kissinger to the Undersecretary of State et al., 8 December 1970, box H049/NSCIF/NPMP.

134. Study, "U.S Military Presence in Latin America," enclosure, Memorandum,

Meyer (Chairman, Interdepartmental Group for Inter-American Affairs) to Kissinger, 12 January 1971, box H178/NSCIF/NPMP.

135. Telcon, Kissinger and Laird, 22 April 1971, box 9/HAK Telcons/NSCF/NPMP.

136. Oficio, da Câmara Canto to Secretario de Estado das Relações Exteriores, 25 March 1971, Oficios/Embaixada do Brasil, Santiago 1971 (01)/AMRE-Brasilia.

137. Record of Conversation, Rountree and Admiral Figueiredo, c. 14 January 1971.

138. Record of Conversation, Rountree and Mario Gibson Barbosa, 12 November 1970, Telegram, Amembassy Brasilia to SecState, 12 November 1970, doc. 129/FRUS/1969–1976/E-10.

139. Memorandum of Conversation, Rogers, Meyer, Robert W. Dean (Brazil Country Director), Gibson Barbosa, and Celso Diniz (chargé d'affaires, Brazilian Embassy), 1 February 1971, box 2134/RG59/NARA.

140. Oficio, Embachile Rio to Señor Ministro, 26 October 1970, Oficios Conf., E./R./Brasil/1970/AMRE.

141. Oficio, Huidobro to Señor Ministro, 16 July 1971, Airgram, Rountree to DOS, 28 May 1971, box 2132/RG59/NARA; and Oficio, Rettig to Señor Ministro, 2 July 1971, Oficios Conf., E./R./Brasil/1971/AMRE.

142. Bautista Yofre, *Misión Argentina*, 63–64, 78–79. Memorandum, Huidobro, 18 December 1970, MINREL: Memorandos Políticos/AMRE; and Almeyda, Speech to OAS, San José, Costa Rica, 15 April 1971, in Vera Castillo, *Política Exterior Chilena*, 431. On Argentina's concerns regarding Chile, see also Telegram, Lodge to SecState, 27 April 1971, box 1697/RG59/NARA.

143. Letter, Letelier to Rodriguez, 12 October 1970.

144. Cable, Ambassador Noworyt, Polish Embassy, Santiago, to Ministry of Foreign Affairs, 22 May 1971, wiazka 3/40/75/AMSZ.

145. Almeyda, "Política Exterior de la Unidad Popular," in Almeyda, *Obras Escogidas*, 122–23, and Huidobro interview, 18 October 2004.

146. Almeyda as quoted in Urgent Note, "Summary of Visit of the Chilean Delegation," 2 June 1971.

147. Ibid.

148. Memorandum of Conversation, H. E. Argentina's Ambassador Pedro Real et al., Washington, 22 December 1970.

149. Pablo Pardo as quoted in Telegram, Lodge to SecState, 2 July 1971, box 2193/RG59/NARA. See also Bautista Yofre, *Misión Argentina*, 63–64, 78–79.

150. "Declaración de Salta," 24 Argentina 1971, in Vera Castillo, *Política Exterior Chilena*, 465–68.

151. *Washington Post*, 25 July 1971, as quoted in Telegram, Brazilian Embassy, Washington to Secretario de Estado das Relçoes Exteriores, 26 July 1971, Rolo 424/Telegramas recebidos da Embaixada em Washington/AMRE-Brasilia.

152. Oficio, Letelier and Valdés to Señor Ministro, 4 June 1971, Oficios Conf., R./EEUU/1971/AMRE.

153. Fidel Castro, 26 July 1971, as quoted in Oficio, Vega to Señor Ministro, 13 August 1971, Oficios Conf./Cuba/1971/AMRE.

154. Record of Conversation, Salum (Chilean Ambassador), Embachile Argel, and

President Boumedienne, 23 July 1971, Oficio, Salum to Señor Ministro, 27 July 1971, Argelia/1971/AMRE.

155. Oficio, Jerez Ramirez to Señor Ministro, "Asamblea Gobernadores BID: Discurso Presidente Velasco Alvarado," 11 May 1971, Oficios Res., E./R./Perú/1971/AMRE.

156. Directorate of Intelligence: Central Intelligence Bulletin, 28 August 1971, CREST/NARA.

157. Letter, Castro to Allende, 21 May 1971, in Castro, "Salvador Allende: His Example Lives On."

158. Record of Conversations, Raúl Roa and Polish minister of foreign affairs Stefan Jedrychowski, 24–26 June 1971, Urgent Note, "Notes on the Conversations with Roa," 30 June 1971, wiazka 3/40/75/AMSZ.

159. Memorandum Secreto, MRE al Señor Ambajador, no. 14, 24 June 1971.

160. Telegram, DOS to Amembassy Brasilia, 15 July 1971, box 2134/RG59/NARA.

Chapter 4

1. Castro, Speech at Regional Stadium, Concepción, 17 November 1971, published as "Estadio Regional de Concepción," *Cuba-Chile*, 242.

2. Cable, Ambassador Noworyt, Polish Embassy, Santiago, to Ministry of Foreign Affairs, 11 June 1971, wiazka 3/40/75/AMSZ, and Telegram, Korry to SecState, 9 June 1971, box 2193/RG59/NARA.

3. Logevall and Preston, *Nixon in the World*, 4.

4. Castro, interview for Chilean Television, 12 November 1971, in *Fidel in Chile: "A Symbolic Meeting Between Two Historical Processes,"* 67. See also documentary, Alvarez, *De América Soy Hijo*.

5. Letter, Allende to Nixon, 4 September 1971 [English translation], 2/15/23/FOL. See also draft letter, Almeyda to Rogers, in Telex, Letelier to Almeyda (in Lima), 1 September 1971, Telex R: 401–839/EEUU/1971/AMRE; and Jaramillo Edwards interview, 21 September 2005.

6. Allende, 15 July 1971, published as "Palabras del Presidente de la Republica, Compañero Salvador Allende, en la ceremonia de firma del decreto que promulga la reforma constitucional que permite la nacionalizacion del Cobre," in Vera Castillo, *Política Exterior Chilena*, 408–9.

7. Memorandum of Conversation, Almeyda and Rogers, no date, c. 7 October 1971, 2/13/32/FOL.

8. Estrada interview.

9. Record of Conversation, Valdés and Nachmanoff, 13 May 1971; Telex, Valdés to MRE, 13 May 1971; and Record of Conversation, Letelier and Meyer, 28 June 1971, Telex, Letelier to MRE, 29 June 1971, Telex R: 1–400/EEUU/1971/AMRE.

10. Telex, Letelier to Almeyda, 9 July 1971, Telex R: 1–400/EEUU/1971/AMRE.

11. Record of Conversation, Letelier and Kearns, 11 August 1971; Telex, Letelier to Almeyda, 11 August 1971; and Telex, Letelier to Almeyda, 5 August 1971.

12. Record of Conversation, Letelier and Kissinger, 5 August 1971; Telex, Letelier to Almeyda, 5 August 1971, Telex R: 401–839/EEUU/1971/AMRE.

13. Oficio, Letelier to Señor Ministro, 10 August 1971, Oficios Conf., R./EEUU/ 1971/AMRE; and Telexes, Letelier to Almeyda, 11 August 1971, and Letelier to MRE, 12 October 1971, Telex R: 401–839/EEUU/1971/AMRE.

14. Record of Conversation, Ambassador Noworyt and Allende, 29 July 1971, Urgent Cable, Polish Embassy, Santiago, to the Ministry of Foreign Affairs, 31 July 1971, wiazka 3/40/75/AMSZ.

15. Telex, Letelier to Almeyda, 5 August 1971, Telex R: 401–839/EEUU/1971/AMRE.

16. Telex, Letelier to Almeyda, 8 September 1971, Telex R: 401–839/EEUU/1971/ AMRE.

17. Telexes, Letelier to Almeyda, 11 August 1971, 13 and 21 August 1971, Telex R: 401–839/EEUU/1971/AMRE; and Telex, Letelier to Almeyda, 8 September 1971, 2/13/ 33/FOL. See also Record of Luncheon offered by the Chilean embassy, attended by Marilyn Berger (*Washington Post*), Benjamin Welles (*New York Times*), George Gedda (AP), Ricardo Utrilla (France Press), Juan Walte (UPI), and Jones Rozenthal (Latin), Oficio, Letelier to Señor Ministro, 24 August 1971, Oficios Conf., R./EEUU/1971/ AMRE. Another key embassy contact included Senator Edward Kennedy. See Record of Conversation, Letelier and Kennedy, 5 December 1971, Telexes (2), Letelier to MRE, 7 December 1971, and Record of Conversation, Letelier, Almeyda, and Kennedy, 6 October 1971, Telex, Letelier to MRE, 6 October 1971, Telex R: 401–839/ EEUU/1971/AMRE.

18. Vázquez and Cubillas interview, 11 September 2005. Vázquez and Cubillas recall that the Cubans advised Chile throughout the nationalization process and encouraged Allende to negotiate with the companies. On PS pressure, see Special National Intelligence Estimate, "The Outlook for Chile under Allende," 4 August 1971, CDP-CIA; and Cable, Polish Embassy, Santiago, to Ministry of Foreign Affairs, 7 June 1971, wiazka 3/40/75/AMSZ.

19. "Decreto No. 92, firmado por el Presidente de la Republic de Chile, Salvador Allende Gossens, Relativo a las Rentabilidades excesivas de las empresas de la gran mineria del cobre afectadas por la nacionalizacion," 28 September 1971, in Vera Castillo, *Política Exterior Chilena*, 409–10.

20. Allende, "Address to the United Nations," in Cockcroft, *Allende Reader*, 203–4. Allende stated that Anaconda and Kennecott mines reaped $774 million in "excess profits." This was then deducted from the compensation figure of $333 million determined by Chile's controller general.

21. "Contraloría General de la República: Fijación de la Indemnización a las Empresas Cupreras Nacionalizadas, Resolution No. 529," 11 October 1971, in Vera Castillo, *Política Exterior Chilena*, 414–17.

22. Allende, Speeches in Quito, 25 August 1971, and Guayaquil, 27 August 1971, in Allende, *Voz de Un Pueblo Continente*, 53, 86. See also Telegram, Amembassy Quito, to SecState, 26 August 1971, box 2193/RG59/NARA.

23. Almeyda, *Reencuentro con mi Vida*, 194–95.

24. "Declaración Conjunta suscrita entre los Presidentes de la República del Ecuador, José María Velasco y de la Republica de Chile, Salvador Allende Gossens" Quito, 26 August 1971; "Declaración Conjunta suscrita entre los Presidentes de la Republica de Colombia, Misael Pastrana Borrero y de la República de Chile, Salva-

dor Allende Gossens," Bogotá, 31 August 1971; "Declaración Conjunta suscrita entre los Presidentes de la Repúblic del Perú, Juan Velasco Alvadardo y de la República de Chile, Salvador Allende Gossens," Lima, 3 September 1971, in Vera Castillo, *Política Exterior Chilena*, 469–80; and Almeyda, Speech to UN General Assembly, 1 October 1971, in Vera Castillo, *Política Exterior Chilena*, 371.

25. Letter, Castro to Allende, 11 September 1971, in Castro, "Salvador Allende: His Example Lives On."

26. Allende, Press Conference in Quito, 26 August 1971, in Allende, *Voz de Un Pueblo Continente*, 66.

27. Allende, Speech to Presidential Banquet, Bogotá, 29 August 1971, in Allende, *Voz de Un Pueblo Continente*, 109–10.

28. Telegram, Allen (U.S. Ambassador), Embachile Bogotá to SecState, 1 September 1971, box 2193/RG59/NARA.

29. Allende, interview with Augusto Olivares, November 1971, published as "Interview with Salvador Allende and Fidel Castro," in Cockcroft, *Allende Reader*, 134. See also Allende, San Augustin, Ecuador, 24 August 1971, in Allende, *Voz de Un Pueblo Continente*, 45.

30. Almeyda, Speech to UN General Assembly, in Vera Castillo, *Política Exterior Chilena*, 368–71.

31. "Declaracion del Ministerio de Relaciones Exteriores de Chile," Santiago Chile, 13 October 1971, in Vera Castillo, *Política Exterior Chilena*, 418–19; and Almeyda, Speech to G77, Lima, Peru, 29 October 1971, in Vera Castillo, *Política Exterior Chilena*, 401–3.

32. Almeyda, Speech to G77, Lima, Peru, 29 October 1971, in Vera Castillo, *Política Exterior Chilena*, 400.

33. "Resolucion 1803 (XVII). Soberania Permanente Sobre los Recursos Naturales (11941. Sesion Plenaria, 14 December 1962)," in Vera Castillo, *Política Exterior Chilena*, 419–22.

34. Almeyda, Speeches to UN General Assembly, 1 October 1971, and G77, Lima, Peru, 29 October 1971, in Vera Castillo, *Política Exterior Chilena*, 370, 399. On the Third Word's lack of progress, see Mortimer, *Third World Coalition*, 35.

35. Almeyda, Speech to G77 Meeting, Lima, Peru, 29 October 1971, in Vera Castillo, *Política Exterior Chilena*, 400.

36. Memorandum, Hernán Santa Cruz, "Consideraciones políticas adicionales sobre la Reunión de las 77 y respecto a las perspectives para la Tercera Conferencia de Comercio y Dessarrollo," no date, c. October 1971, vol. 2/FHSC/AMRE.

37. Almeyda, Speech to G77 Meeting, Lima, Peru, 29 October 1971, in Vera Castillo, *Política Exterior Chilena*, 406.

38. Diplomatic Report, no. 532/71, 18 November 1971, and Telegram, Morgan to FCO, 10 October 1971, FCO61/836/TNA.

39. Memorandum, Baker-Bates, UN (E & S) to MacInnes, 22 November 1971, FCO61/836/TNA.

40. Vera Castillo, *Política Exterior Chilena*, 547.

41. Urgent Note, "Summary of Visit of the Chilean Delegation," 2 June 1971, wiazka 3/40/75/AMSZ.

42. Report by Ambassador Noworyt, "Basic Elements of Chile's Internal Political Situation After the Municipal Elections, 4 April 1971," no date, c. May 1971, wiazka 3/40/75/AMSZ.

43. Cables, Ambassador Noworyt to the Ministry of Foreign Affairs, 11 October and 11, 12, and 16 November 1971, wiazka 3/40/75/AMSZ.

44. Special NIE, 4 August 1971, and Fermandois, *Mundo y Fin de Mundo*, 384.

45. East German Ministry of Foreign Trade Report, "Information on the Development of Economic Relations between the GDR and Chile," 20 April 1971, DY/30/IV A2/20/728/SAPMO.

46. Miller, *Soviet Relations with Latin America*, 138.

47. Prats, *Memorias*, 214–19. Details of the Allende government's interest in purchasing arms from the Soviet bloc are hazy. However, the available evidence suggests that the UP remained interested in acquiring arms from the USSR after this trip and that Allende raised the issue directly with Brezhnev. In a later testimony given to the Centro de Estudios Publicos in Chile, Leonov, then head of the Analytical Department in the KGB, recalled that the USSR provided Chile with a $100 million credit to buy Soviet arms (primarily tanks) in 1973 and that these were on their way to Chile in August of that year when Moscow called the ships that were carrying them back on account of the fear that a military coup was on the horizon. See Ulianova, "La Unidad Popular y el Golpe Militar," 108–10.

48. Memorandum, Javier Urrutia to Ministro de Relaciones Exteriores et al., "Algunos Aspectos de Las relaciones Financieras de Chile con la Banca de EE.UU," 22 October 1971, 2/13/44/FOL. The reasons Urrutia offered for the European banking sector's inability to counteract U.S. obstacles were that Chile's relations with them had been modest in the past, that European financial credits were mostly linked to purchases, and that the European banking sector was "less agile and more complex" than its U.S. counterpart.

49. Oficio, Letelier to Señor Ministro, 10 August 1971, Oficios Conf., R./EEUU/1971/AMRE.

50. Ibid., and Oficio, Valdés to Señor Ministro, 12 November 1971, Oficios Conf., R./EEUU/1971/AMRE.

51. Memorandum, Orlando Letelier, "Algunos Aspectos del Estado Actual de las Relaciones de Chile con Estados Unidos," 3 November 1971, 2/16/6/FOL.

52. Record of Conversation, Allende and Hollis Moore, President of Bowling Green State University, Letter, Hollis to Nixon, 12 November 1971, box 2193/RG59/NARA.

53. Letter, Almeyda to His Excellency William P. Rogers, 4 September 1971 (delivered by hand by Letelier on 7 September 1971), 2/15/18/FOL.

54. In September and October, ITT representatives contacted U.S. officials to urge Nixon to abandon what it perceived was a "soft-line" against the UP. After a meeting between Rogers and business leaders with investments in Chile, ITT submitted a White Paper on 1 October 1971 detailing eighteen points of economic warfare, among them efforts to disrupt UNCTAD III and sabotage trade, to ensure Allende did not survive a further six months. Davis, *Last Two Years*, 69. On Treasury joining SRG discussions, see Memorandum, Keith Guthrie to General Haig, 1 June 1971, box H056/NSCIF/NPMP.

55. Memorandum, Connally to Nixon, 11 June 1971, doc. 154/FRUS/1969–1976/IV.

56. Ibid. See also Memorandum, Connally to Nixon, 9 June 1971, box H056/NSCIF/NPMP.

57. Handwritten notes, Nixon to Kissinger on Memorandum, Kissinger to Nixon, 9 June 1971, and Kissinger to Nachmanoff on Memorandum, Nachmanoff to Kissinger, 14 June, box H056/NSCIF/NPMP. On the review itself, see Memorandum, Kissinger to the Secretary et al., 23 June 1971, doc. 155/FRUS/1969–1976/IV; and Memorandum, Keith Guthrie to General Haig, 1 June 1971.

58. Memorandum, Crimmins to Irwin, 4 August 1971, doc. 159/FRUS/1969–1976/IV.

59. "HAK Talking Points for SRG Meeting on Chile," 3 June 1971, and Memorandum, Kissinger to Nixon, 9 June 1971, box H056/NSCIF/NPMP.

60. Telegram, Korry to SecState, 1 June 1971, Special NIE, 4 August 1971, CDP-CIA; and Intelligence Note, INR, "Chile: Copper and Domestic Politics," 14 October 1971, box 2193/RG59/NARA.

61. Paper, Ad Hoc Interagency Working Group, "Chile: Strategy Review," enclosure, Memorandum for the Under Secretary of State et al., 8 September 1971, box H220/NSCIF/NPMP.

62. National Security Decision Memorandum 136, 8 October 1971, doc. 169/FRUS/1969–1976/IV, and Speeches, Connally, World Bank, 30 September 1971, Undersecretary of State Walker, U.S. Congressional Subcommittee on International Finance, 6 July 1971 and 26 October 1971, as cited in Oficio, Letelier to Señor Ministro, 26 January 1973, Oficios Conf., E./R./EEUU/1973/AMRE.

63. See retrospective account of this offer in Aide Memoire, Letelier, "Situación Relaciones Chile con Estados Unidos," 11 August 1972, 2/16/5/FOL.

64. Memorandum of Conversation, Kissinger, Almeyda, and Letelier, c. 7 October 1971, 2/13/49/FOL.

65. Record of Conversation, Letelier and Kissinger, Joseph Alsop's House, 5 December 1971, Telex, Letelier to MRE, 7 December 1971, Telex R: 401–839/EEUU/1971/AMRE.

66. Aide Memoire, Letelier, "Situación Relaciones Chile con Estados Unidos," 11 August 1972, 2/16/5/FOL; and Memorandum, Letelier, "Medidas que podríamos adoptar para establecer algún 'modus vivendi' con Estados Unidos," 5 September 1972, enclosure, Letter, Orlando [Letelier] to Clodomiro [Almeyda], 6 September 1972, 2/17/12/FOL.

67. Telegram, Davis to SecState, 7 December 1971, CDP-NARA.

68. Paper, Ad Hoc Interagency Working Group, "Chile: Strategy Review," enclosure, Memorandum, Jeanne W. Davis to the Under Secretary of State et al., 8 September 1971, box H220/NSCIF/NPMP.

69. Telegram, DOS to Amembassy, Lima, "Soviet-Chilean Economic Relations," c. June 1971, box 2193/RG59/NARA. See Telegrams, Korry to SecState, 28 May 1971, and Korry to SecState, 1 June 1971, box 2193/RG59/NARA; and Telegram, Shlaudeman to SecState, 24 June 1971, box 478/RG59/NARA.

70. Special NIE, 4 August 1971.

71. Telegram, Korry to SecState, 7 June 1971, box 2193/RG59/NARA.

72. Transcript of Conversation, Nixon and Daniel P. Moynihan, 7 October 1971, in Doyle, "The Nixon Tapes."

73. Memorandum, Nachmanoff to Kissinger, 9 June 1971, box H056/NSCIF/ NPMP. Javier Urrutia, a financial adviser to the Chilean Embassy in Washington, was involved in the Boeing negotiations and recalled Santiago was interested in more profitable U.S. and European routes for the Boeings. Javier Urrutia, e-mail correspondence with author, 3 December 2005.

74. Telexes, Letelier to Almeyda, 5 August and 11 August 1971.

75. Telegram, DOS to Lima, "Soviet-Chilean Economic Relations." In the end, although the vice president of LAN-Chile visited Moscow after Eximbank's deferral on the Boeing loans, the UP ended up paying $5.5 million in cash the following year to purchase a Boeing airplane from the United States. Miller, *Soviet Relations with Latin America*, 140–41.

76. Transcripts of Conversations, Nixon and Rockefeller, 29 October 1971, and Nixon and Kissinger, 20 September 1971, in Doyle, "The Nixon Tapes."

77. Joseph Jova interview (1991), FD. See also, Transcript of conversation, Nixon and Connally, Oval Office, 2 June 1971, in Doyle, "The Nixon Tapes."

78. Briefing Memorandum, Nachmanoff to Kissinger, 17 June 1971, enclosure, Memorandum, Nachmanoff to Kissinger, 11 August 1971, box H059/NSCIF/NPMP.

79. Memorandum, Nachmanoff to Kissinger, 11 August 1971.

80. Custom Country Report for Latin America and the Caribbean, The Green Book of U.S. Overseas Loans and Grants.

81. Memorandum, Kissinger to the Under Secretary of State et al., 18 August 1971, box H178/NSCIF/NPMP.

82. Telephone Conversation, Nixon and Rogers, 7 December 1971, Conversation 16:36/WHT/NPMP; and Memorandum of Conversation for the President's File from Henry Kissinger, 20 December 1971, in Osorio, "Nixon: 'Brazil Helped Rig the Uruguayan Elections' 1971."

83. Memorandum, Nachmanoff to Kissinger, 17 June 1971, box H055/NSCIF/ NPMP.

84. Lehman, *Limited Partnership*, 161.

85. Siekmeier, "A Sacrificial Llama?"

86. Briefing Memorandum, Nachmanoff to Kissinger, 17 June 1971.

87. Handwritten note, Kissinger on Briefing Memorandum, Nachmanoff to Kissinger, 17 June 1971.

88. "U.S. Denies Bolivia Rule," *New York Times*, 30 August 1971.

89. Handwritten note, Kissinger on Memorandum, Hewitt to Kissinger, 4 March 1972, box 232/NSCIF/NPMP. Banzer was a graduate of the School of the Americas and a former military attaché in Washington. On CIA involvement in coup plotting, see McSherry, *Predatory States*, 55.

90. On this "multinational coup," see McSherry, *Predatory States*, 55. On Brazil's involvement, see Gaspari, *Ditadura Derrotada*, 346–47.

91. Raúl Roa as quoted in FBIS, "Trends in Communist Propaganda," 25 August 1971, CDP-CIA.

92. Record of Conversations, Raúl Roa and Polish minister of foreign affairs

Stefan Jedrychowski, 24–26 June 1971, Urgent Note, "Notes on the Conversations with Roa," 30 June 1971, wiazka 3/40/75/AMSZ.

93. Memorandum, Ambassador Marian Renke, Polish Embassy, Havana, to the Ministry of Foreign Affairs, "Certain Aspects of Cuba's Situation and Politics on the American Continent," 15 October 1971, wiazka 5/40/75/AMSZ.

94. Airgram, Ortiz (U.S. Embassy, Montevideo) to DOS, 25 August 1971, in Osorio, "Nixon: 'Brazil Helped Rig the Uruguayan Elections' 1971."

95. McSherry, *Predatory States*, 56.

96. Telcon, Nixon and Rogers, 7 December 1971, and Memorandum of Conversation for the President's File from Henry Kissinger, 20 December 1971, in Osorio, "Nixon: 'Brazil Helped Rig the Uruguayan Elections' 1971."

97. Memorandum of Conversation, Médici, Nixon, and Walters, 10:00 A.M., the President's Office, 9 December 1971, doc. 143/FRUS/1969–1976/E-10.

98. Memorandum of Conversation, Médici, Nixon, and Walters, 11:30 A.M., the President's Office, 7 December 1971, doc. 141/FRUS/1969–1976/E-10.

99. Memorandum of Conversations, Médici, Nixon and Walters, 7 and 9 December 1971.

100. Memorandum, Acting Director of Central Intelligence (Cushman) to Kissinger, 29 December 1971, doc. 145/FRUS/1969–1976/E-10.

101. Memorandum of Conversation, Médici, Nixon, and Walters, 9 December 1971.

102. Memorandum of Meeting, Médici, Gibson Barbosa, Ambassador Araujo Castro, Kissinger, Walters, and Nachmanoff, Blair House, 5:15 P.M., 8 December 1971, doc. 142/FRUS/1969–1976/E-10.

103. Memorandum of Conversation, Médici, Nixon, and Walters, 9 December 1971.

104. White House Tapes, Nixon, Kissinger, and Haldeman, 11 June 1971, doc. 139/FRUS/1969–1976/E-10.

105. Memorandum of Conversation, Médici, Nixon, and Walters, 9 December 1971.

106. Memorandum of Meeting, Médici, Gibson Barbosa, Ambassador Araujo Castro, Kissinger, Walters, and Nachmanoff, Blair House, 5:15 P.M., 8 December 1971.

107. Telcon, Kissinger and Nixon, 8 December 1971, box 12/HAK Telcons/NSCF/NPMP.

108. Crimmins interview.

109. Telephone Conversation, Nixon and William Rogers, 7 December 1971, and Telephone Conversation, Nixon and John Connally, 8 December 1971, Conversation 16:44/WHT/NPMP.

110. "Brazil Leader to Meet Nixon," *Washington Post*, 6 December 1971, as cited in Telegram, Brazilian Embassy, Washington, to Secretario de Estado das Relações Exteriores, 6 December 1971, Rolo 42/Telegramas recebidos da Embaixada em Washington/AMRE-Brasilia.

111. "Médici Visit: Important but Why?" *Washington Post*, 13 December 1971; Telegram, Brazilian Embassy, Washington, to Secretario de Estado das Relações Exteriores, 6 December 1971, Rolo 424/Telegramas recebidos da Embaixada em Washington/AMRE-Brasilia.

112. Castro, Press Conference, Santiago, 3 December 1971, published as "Conferencia de Prensa," *Cuba-Chile*, 493–94.

113. Intelligence Telegram, CIA Station, Santiago to DCI, 19 August 1971, CDP-CIA.

114. Record of Conversation, Korry and Frei, 9 October 1971, Telegram, Korry to SecState, 11 October 1971, box 2197/RG59/NARA.

115. Memorandum of Conversation, Frei and Meyer, Waldorf Towers, New York, 23 October 1971, 26 October 1971, box 2193/RG59/NARA.

116. Memorandum, Irwin to Kissinger, 22 December 1971, box 289/NSIF/NPMP.

117. *Covert Action in Chile*, 37.

118. Dispatch, COS, Santiago, to Chief, WHD, 3 November 1971, CDP-CIA; and Intelligence Information Special Report, 9 November 1971, CDP-CIA. On monitoring and speculation about key players, see Intelligence Telegram, CIA Station, Santiago, to Director, 31 August 1971, CDP-CIA. Of those mentioned, General Pinochet is noted as favoring a coup but happier to "close eyes to events." Dispatch, COS, Santiago, to Chief, WHD, 12 November 1971, CDP-CIA.

119. Dispatch, Chief, WHD, to COS, Santiago, 1 December 1971, CDP-CIA.

120. Memorandum, Irwin to Kissinger, 22 December 1971.

121. Lopez interview, 28 October 2004.

122. Fidel Castro, Press Conference, Havana, 10 November 1971, published as "Entrevista," *Cuba-Chile*, 14.

123. Allende, Speech at National Stadium, Santiago, 2 December 1971, published as "Farewell Address to Fidel Castro," in Cockcroft, *Allende Reader*, 137 (the *Allende Reader* mistakenly cites this as 4 December 1971); and "Interview with Allende and Castro," in Cockcroft, *Allende Reader*, 135–36.

124. Allende, Speech at National Stadium, 4 November 1971, published as "First Anniversary of the Popular Government," in Cockcroft, *Allende Reader*, 122.

125. Fidel Castro, Universidad de Punta Arenas, 22 November 1971, *Cuba-Chile*, 326.

126. Oficio, Manuel Sánchez Navarro to Señor Ministro, 23 April 1971, Oficios Ordinarios, Cuba/1971/AMRE.

127. Castro as quoted in FBIS, "Trends in Communist Propaganda," 14 April 1971, CDP-CIA.

128. Memorandum, "Cooperación tecnica y cientifica entre la Republica de Chile y la republica de Cuba," November 1972, CMSA. Agreements signed included collaborative programs in publishing (Quimantú and Instituto Cubano del Libro, 2 December 1971), health (10 December 1971), and education, culture, and sport (2 December 1971). On the Cuban-Chilean cinema agreement between Chile Films and ICAIC, see Ortega, *La Habana-Arica-Magallanes*.

129. Informe del Intercambio Comercial Chileno-Cubano, no date, c. December 1972, CMSA.

130. Record of Conversation, Miret and Juan Enrique Vega, Chilean Ambassador in Havana, Oficio, Vega, to Señor Ministro, 21 June 1971; and Oficio, Vega to Señor Ministro, 9 July 1971, Oficios/Cuba/1971/AMRE.

131. Informe del Intercambio Comercial Chileno-Cubano, c. December 1972.

132. Almeyda, Speech to UN General Assembly, in Vera Castillo, *Política Exterior Chilena*, 376.

133. Vázquez and Cubillas interview, 11 September 2005, and Suárez interview, 12 September 2005. On the improving links with Latin American revolutionary movements, see Oña interview, 3 September 2005.

134. Quiroga, *Compañeros*, 71–74.

135. Figures of arms transfers are difficult to verify, although some members of the GAP later testified that they had received one .30 machine gun, eight Uzis, forty MP-40 submachine guns, twelve P-38 automatic pistols, and twelve Colt pistols from the island at the beginning of 1971. Ibid., 251.

136. Pascal Allende interview.

137. Estrada interview; Oña interviews, 2004–6; and Jaramillo Edwards interview, 21 September 2005.

138. Soto interview, 7 September 2005.

139. Dispatch, COS, Santiago, to Chief, WHD, 3 November 1971, CDP-CIA. Specifically, the CIA Station listed the GAP's new arsenal as containing "Cuban-provided .45 caliber Colt automatic pistols, 9mm Browning automatic pistols and Czech P-38 automatic pistols." The Chilean historian Cristian Pérez claims that the biggest Cuban donation of arms to Chile occurred during Castro's visit. Pérez, "Salvador Allende, Apuntes Sobre su Dispositivo de Seguridad," 52.

140. CIA Information Report, 1 October 1971, CDP-CIA. Quiroga cites the number as twenty and twenty rather than thirty and thirty. Quiroga, *Compañeros*, 76, and Intelligence Information Special Report, 9 November 1971, CDP-CIA.

141. *Covert Action in Chile*, 38.

142. Telegram, Korry to SecState, 17 August 1971, box 2194/RG59/NARA.

143. Quiroga, *Compañeros*, 57. On the reason for the split, see Oña interview, 2 May 2006. On the split, see Dispatch, COS, Santiago, to Chief, WHD, 3 November 1971, CDP-CIA.

144. Pascal Allende interview. Luis Fernández Oña, who was present at this interview, confirmed the story.

145. Dispatch, COS, Santiago, to Chief, WHD, 3 November 1971.

146. Memorandum of Conversation, "Meeting with [redacted]," 17 August 1971, CDP-CIA.

147. Allende, "First Anniversary of the Popular Government," in Cockcroft, *Allende Reader*, 123–24.

148. Castro as cited in Airgram, Shlaudeman to SecState, 17 August 1971, box 2194/RG59/NARA.

149. Oña interview, 9 December 2004. On armed forces reaction, see Quiroga, *Compañeros*, 119–20.

150. Minute, FCO Research Department, 3 August 1971, FCO7/1991/TNA.

151. "Santiago Plagado de Cubanos Armados," *La Tribuna*, 8 November 1971, and "Con el Despliegue Armado Caracteristico de los Tiranos: Y . . . ¡Nos Puso La Pata Encima!," *La Tribuna*, 11 November 1971. On the Right's press campaigns against the GAP, see Quiroga, *Compañeros*, 110–11.

152. Coltman, *The Real Fidel Castro*, 233, and Castro, as quoted in Record of Con-

versation, Ambassador Alexseev and Volodia Teitelboim, 14 October 1970, 411. On Fidel's desire not to cause problems, see also Fidel Castro, "Conferencia de Prensa," 3 December 1971, *Cuba-Chile*, 506–7.

153. Teitelboim interview, 5 November 2004.

154. Castro, "Entrevista," 10 November 1971, *Cuba-Chile*, 16; Palma interview, 23 October 2004; and Huidobro interviews, 18 and 28 October 2004.

155. Letter, Castro to Allende, 11 September 1971, in Castro, "Salvador Allende: His Example Lives On."

156. Vázquez and Cubillas interview, 11 September 2005. See also Debray as quoted in Haslam, *Assisted Suicide*, 32.

157. Record of Conversation, Director General, MRE, and Hildyard, Letter, British Chancery, Santiago to Latin America Department, FCO, 15 November 1971, FCO7/1991/TNA. On Castro's attention to Chile, see also Suárez interview, 10 December 2004; Estrada interview; and Oña interviews, 2004–6.

158. Goméz interview, 24 October 2004, and Soto interview 29 April 2005. See also Alvarez, *De América Soy Hijo*.

159. Timossi interview.

160. Castro, Speech at National Stadium, Santiago, 2 December 1971, published as "Acto de Despedida," *Cuba-Chile*, 474–76.

161. Castro, "Conferencia de Prensa," 3 December 1971, *Cuba-Chile*, 494, 520; and "Interview with Allende and Castro," in Cockcroft, *Allende Reader*, 130.

162. "El Comandante Fidel Estuvo 'Aminado' con 'El Teniente,'" *La Tribuna*, 25 November 1971.

163. "Interview with Allende and Castro," in Cockcroft, *Allende Reader*, 130.

164. Ibid., 129–30, and Castro, "Acto de Despedida," 477. On reports of Castro's comments to Czechoslovakia's ambassador in Havana about his trip to Chile, see Memorandum, Renke, Polish Embassy, Havana, to the Ministry of Foreign Affairs, 15 March 1972, wiazka 3/12/78/AMSZ.

165. Interviews with Armando Hart and Pascal Allende, in Ortega, *La Habana-Arica-Magallanes*.

166. Pascal Allende interview.

167. Castro as quoted in Intelligence Information Cable, 2 December 1971, CDP-CIA.

168. Castro, Speech to Rancagua Stadium, 24 November 1971, published as "Estado Rancagua," *Cuba-Chile*, 360; and Castro, Speech in Santa Cruz, 25 November 1971, published as "Santa Cruz, Colchagua," *Cuba-Chile*, 375.

169. Castro, "Acto de Despedida," *Cuba-Chile*, 480.

170. Castro, Dialogue with Students, 29 November 1971, published as "Universidad Técnica del Estado," *Cuba-Chile*, 439, 444; Castro, "Conferencia de Prensa," 3 December 1971, *Cuba-Chile*, 497–98, 517; and Castro, "Santa Cruz," *Cuba-Chile*, 377. See also Suárez interview, 10 December 2004.

171. Castro, Speech to Teatro Municipal, Santiago, 25 November 1971, published as "Teatro Municipal," *Cuba-Chile*, 380.

172. "Interview with Allende and Castro," in Cockcroft, *Allende Reader*, 133.

173. Castro, "Santa Cruz," *Cuba-Chile*, 275.

174. Otero, *Llover Sobre Mojado*, 190; Estrada interview; and Vázquez and Cubillas interview, 11 September 2005.

175. Vázquez and Cubillas, Otero, and Estrada interviews.

176. Castro, "Conferencia de Prensa," *Cuba-Chile*, 493.

177. CIA Intelligence Information Special Report, enclosure, Memorandum, Thomas Karamessines, Deputy Director of Plans to DCI Helms, "Cuban Disappointment with the Chilean Experiment," 31 May 1972, CREST/NARA.

178. Oña interview, 3 September 2005.

179. Castro to Czechoslovakia's ambassador in Havana as cited in Memorandum, Renke to the Ministry of Foreign Affairs, 15 March 1972, wiazka 3/12/78/AMSZ.

180. Letter, Castro to Allende, 4 February 1972, in Castro, "Salvador Allende: His Example Lives On."

181. Allende, "Farewell Address," in Cockcroft, *Allende Reader*, 140, 138; Castro, "Acto de Despedida," *Cuba-Chile*, 477; and "Interview with Salvador Allende and Fidel Castro," in Cockcroft, *Allende Reader*, 132.

182. Allende, "Farewell Address," in Cockcroft, *Allende Reader*, 141–42.

183. Telegram, Davis to SecState, 3 December 1971, box 2197/RG59/NARA; and Allende, "Farewell Address," in Cockcroft, *Allende Reader*, 138.

184. Allende, "Farewell Address," in Cockcroft, *Allende Reader*, 135–45.

185. Quiroga, *Compañeros*, 76.

186. Cables, Noworyt to the Ministry of Foreign Affairs, 8 and 20 August 1971, wiazka 3/40/75/AMSZ. See also references to the MIR's and the PS's "left wing extremism" in "Report on the First Year of the Government of the UP," East German Embassy, Santiago, to Berlin, 12 December 1971, V-33/MfAA.

187. Allende, 20 December 1971, and "Declaration of December" as quoted in Telegram, Shlaudeman to SecState, 21 December 1971, box 2194/RG59/NARA.

188. Record of Conversation, Almeyda and Davis, 1 December 1970, Telex, MRE to Embachile Washington, 1 December 1971, Telex E: 1–367/EEUU/1971/AMRE.

189. Renán Fuentealba, 16 December 1971, as quoted in Telegram, Shlaudeman to SecState, 17 December 1971, box 2194/RG59/NARA. On Fuentealba's election at the PDC National Junta on 27–28 November 1971, see Telegram, Davis to SecState, 29 November 1971, box 2194/RG59/NARA.

190. Airgram, Davis to DOS, 24 December 1971, box 2197/RG59/NARA.

191. "Report on the First Year of the Government of the UP," East German Embassy, Santiago, 12 December 1971.

192. Allende, "First Anniversary of the Popular Government," in Cockcroft, *Allende Reader*, 121–22.

193. Collier and Sater, *History of Chile*, 336–45.

194. Special NIE, 4 August 1971, and Allende, "First Anniversary of the Popular Government," in Cockcroft, *Allende Reader*, 123.

195. Corvalán as quoted in "Report on the First Year of the Government of the UP," East German Embassy, Santiago, 12 December 1971.

196. Telegram Amembassy Santiago to SecState, 14 December 1971, box 2198/RG59/NARA, and "Report on the First Year of the Government of the UP," East German Embassy, Santiago, 12 December 1971.

197. Telex, Letelier to MRE, 30 November 1971, Telex R: 401–839/EEUU/1971/ AMRE.

198. Memorandum, Letelier, "Algunos Aspectos del Estado Actual de las Relaciones de Chile con Estados Unidos," 3 November 1971, 2/16/6/FOL.

199. Allende, "Farewell Address," in Cockcroft, *Allende Reader*, 141.

200. Frei as quoted in Telegram, Korry to SecState, 11 October 1971, box 2197/ RG59/NARA.

201. NIE 93-72, "The New Course in Brazil," doc. 146/FRUS/1969–1976/E-10.

202. Telex, Luis Herrera, Chilean Delegate, OAS, to MRE, 14 and 15 December 1971, Aerogramas, Telexes, OEA/1971/AMRE. OAS members voted 7 in favor, 13 against, and 3 abstained.

203. Intelligence Note, INR, "Cuba: New Orleans plus Kosygin Equals What?" 8 November 1971, box 2223/RG59/NARA; and Memorandum, Renke to the Ministry of Foreign Affairs, "Certain Aspects of Cuba's Situation and Politics on the American Continent," 15 October 1971, wiazka 3/12/78/AMSZ.

Chapter 5

1. Allende, Speech at National Stadium, 4 November 1971, published as "First Anniversary of the Popular Government," in Cockcroft, *Allende Reader*, 22. See also Almeyda, Speech to the G77, Lima, Peru, 29 October 1971, in Vera Castillo, *Política Exterior Chilena*, 403.

2. Memorandum of Conversation, Médici, Nixon, and Walters, 10:00 A.M., the President's Office, 9 December 1971, doc. 143/FRUS/1969–1976/E-10.

3. See, for example, Summary of Minutes of Connally's meeting with President Pastrana, 7 June 1972, Telegram, Amembassy Bogotá to SecState, 17 June 1972; Memorandum of Conversation, Connally, Médici, et al., 8 June 1972, Telegram, Amembassy Brasilia to SecState, 17 June 1972; and Record of Conversation, Connally and President Lannusse, 12 June 1972, Telegram, Amembassy Buenos Aires to SecState, 17 June 1972, Executive Secretariat, Briefing Books, 1958–1976, lot 720373, box 135/RG59/NARA.

4. Jova as quoted in Memorandum, Ambassador Marian Renke, Polish Embassy in Havana to the Ministry of Foreign Affairs, "Certain Aspects of Cuba's Situation and Politics on the American Continent," 15 October 1971, wiazka 5/40/75/AMSZ. On private reassurances to Latin Americans that détente did not apply to Cuba, see Telegram, Amembassy Montevideo to SecState, 3 March 1972, and Memorandum of Conversation, Celso Diniz (Brazilian Embassy, Washington) and Marvin J. Hoffenberg (Economic Officer, Office of the Coordinator for Cuban Affairs, ARA), 2 December 1972, 5 December 1972, box 2223/RG59/NARA. On State Department answers to criticism, see Robert Hurwitch as cited in Telegram, DOS to All American Republics, 20 September 1972, box 2223/RG59/NARA; Rogers as cited in Telex, DelChile OEA, "Subsecretario dice" to Almeyda, 12 April 1972, Aerog y Telex/ OEA/1972/AMRE; and Telex, Valdés to MRE, 15 March 1972, Telex R./EEUU/1972/ AMRE.

5. Oficio, Armando Uribe, Chilean Ambassador, Beijing, to Señor Ministro, 10

February 1972, enclosure, MRE to Letelier, 6 March 1972, Oficios Conf., E./R./ EEUU/1972/AMRE.

6. Oficio, Letelier to Señor Ministro, 23 June 1972, Oficios Conf., E./R./ EEUU/1972/AMRE.

7. Allende, Speech at the opening session of UNCTAD III, Santiago, published as "Discurso ante la Tercera UNCTAD," *OE-SA*, 608.

8. Notes, Comrade Markowski (Head of the Latin America Sector, Foreign Relations Department, Central Committee, Socialist Unity Party of Germany [CC SED]) to Hermann Axen (Leader of Foreign Relations Department, CC SED), 11 February 1972, DY/30/IV A2/20/286/SAPMO.

9. "Cuba in Latin America," enclosure, Briefing Memorandum prepared for Fidel Castro's visit to Poland, no date, c. June 1972, wiazka 3/12/78/AMSZ.

10. Frei as quoted in Telegram, Davis to SecState, 26 January 1972, box 2194/ RG59/NARA.

11. "Serio Quebranto de la Economía Nacional," *El Mercurio*, 15 March 1972; "Temas Económicas," *El Mercurio*, 29 April 1972; and "La Semana Política," *El Mercurio*, 21 May 1972, in Gonzalez Pino and Fontaine Talavera, *Mil Días (I)*, 312–31, 369–73, 389–92.

12. Record of Conversation, Letelier and Irwin, 24 March 1972, Telex, Letelier to MRE, 24 March 1972, Telex R./EEUU/1972/AMRE; Informe, Central Committee, PCCh, as quoted in "Balance de Éxitos; Batida Contra las Fallas.," *El Siglo*, 16 March 1972; Gonzalez Pino and Fontaine Talavera, *Mil Días (I)*, 319; and Petras and LaPorte, "Can We Do Business with Radical Nationalists?"

13. Internal Document, Political Commission, PCCh, as quoted in Airgram, Davis to DOS, 11 February 1972, box 2194/RG59/NARA; and "La Declaración de el Arrayan," 9 February 1972, in Pérez, "La Izquierda," 412–19.

14. Internal Document, Political Commission, PCCh, as quoted in Airgram, Davis to DOS, 11 February 1972.

15. "Partido Socialista: Informe del Comité Central al Pleno de Algarrobo," February 1972, in Pérez, "La Izquierda," 420.

16. Allende, "Informe al Pleno Nacional del Partido Socialista en Algarrobo," February 1972, in Pérez, "La Izquierda," 421.

17. Telegram, Davis to SecState, 20 March 1972, box 2198/RG59/NARA; and Airgram, Davis to DOS, 27 April 1972, box 2194/RG59/NARA.

18. "Report, Latin American Institute, Soviet Academy of Sciences," c. July 1972, in Ulianova and Fediakova, "Chile en los Archivos de la URSS (1959–1973)," 429; "Corvalán cantó claro en conferencia de prensa," *Clarín*, 26 May 1972, in Gonzalez Pino and Fontaine Talavera, *Mil Días (I)*, 394–95; and Airgram, Davis to DOS, 27 April 1972.

19. "La Semana Política," *El Mercurio*, 21 May 1972; Gonzalez Pino and Fontaine Talavera, *Mil Días (I)*, 390.

20. Memorandum of Conversation, Felipe Amunategui (Third Vice President, PDC), Richard Schwartz (USAID), and Arnold Isaacs (U.S. Embassy), 4 May 1972, enclosure, Airgram, Davis to DOS, 17 May 1972, box 2194/RG59/NARA.

21. Castro as quoted by Alain Peyrefitte, French Union of Democrats for the

Republic Party, public statement, 24 September 1972, Santiago, Telegram, Davis to SecState, 26 September 1972, box 2196/RG59/NARA.

22. Telegram, Davis to SecState, 2 May 1972, box 2197/RG59/NARA; and Memorandum, Jorden to Kissinger, 10 April 1972, box H064/NSCIF/NPMP.

23. Telegram, Davis to SecState, 26 June 1972, box 2197/RG59/NARA; "Constituida Comision Para Investigar la Internacion Illegal por Aviones Cubanos," *El Mercurio*, 4 April 1972; and Gonzalez Pino and Fontaine Talavera, *Mil Días (I)*, 333. Whether these crates contained weapons has not yet been convincingly proved or disproved. Pinochet's dictatorship published apparent proof that they contained weapons, but Lisandro Otero, Havana's cultural attaché, insists that these boxes *did* contain works of art for an exhibition he was organizing, as the Cuban embassy asserted at the time. Otero interview. Arms were brought into Chile by the Cubans, but in other ways. Conversations with Oña, March–April 2010.

24. Quiroga, *Compañeros*, 107.

25. Estrada interview. Allende's decision can be narrowed down to 26–30 May 1972 on account of Estrada's recollection of being in Romania with Fidel Castro when he found out.

26. Estrada interview and author's interview with a former member of the MIR, who would prefer to remain anonymous. Besides the MIR, Quiroga asserts that two groups from the GAP traveled to Cuba in 1972, one at the beginning and one at the end of the year for one week and fifteen days respectively. Quiroga, *Compañeros*, 90.

27. Memorandum, Letelier, "Algunos Aspectos del Estado Actual de las Relaciones de Chile con Estados Unidos," 3 November 1971, 2/16/6/FOL.

28. Oficio, Letelier to Señor Ministro, 10 August 1971, Oficios Conf., R./ EEUU/1971/AMRE; and Telex, Letelier to MRE, 27 May 1972, Telex R./EEUU/1972/ AMRE. For details of the lawsuits and embargoes against Chile in early 1972, see Telexes, Letelier to MRE, 9 and 22 February 1972, Telex R./EEUU/1972/AMRE.

29. Urrutia interviews, and Telex, Letelier to MRE, 21 January 1972, Telex R./ EEUU/1972/AMRE.

30. Memorandum, Letelier, "Algunos Aspectos del Estado Actual de las Relaciones de Chile con Estados Unidos," 3 November 1971; and Aide Memoire, Letelier, "Situación Relaciones Chile con Estados Unidos," 11 August 1972, 2/16/5/FOL.

31. Record of Conversation, Letelier and John Fisher, 6 January 1972, Telex, Letelier to MRE, 6 January 1972, Telex R./EEUU/1972/AMRE.

32. Telexes, Hugo Cubillos to Embachile Washington, 27 January 1972, and MRE to Embachile Washington (Por instrucciónes del Presidente de la República), 24 February 1972, Telex E./EEUU/1972/AMRE; Telegram, Davis to SecState, 28 February 1972, box 2193/RG59/NARA. See also Record of Conversation, Letelier, Sidney Weintraub, Economic Department, et al., 6 January 1971, Telexes, Letelier to MRE, 6 January 1972, Telex R./EEUU/1972/AMRE.

33. Vázquez and Cubillas interview, 11 September 2005. Despite threatening to take the painting back, she never went to collect it. Conversations with Oña, March–April 2010.

34. Allende, "First Anniversary of the Popular Government," in Cockcroft, *Allende Reader*, 123, and Davis, *Last Two Years*, 72. For an in-depth examination of Chile's

debt problems and Washington's leverage over Santiago, see Michael, "Nixon, Chile and Shadows of the Cold War," 319–47.

35. Circular Telex, Hugo Cubillos to Embachile Washington, 8 January 1972, Telex E./EEUU/1972/AMRE. See also Directorate of Intelligence, Weekly Review, 3 December 1971, CDP-CIA. In February 1972, Chile also rescheduled payments to private U.S. banks. Davis, *Last Two Years*, 72.

36. Oficio, Letelier to Señor Ministro, 2 June 1972, Oficios Conf., E./R./EEUU/1972/AMRE.

37. "Temas Económicas," *El Mercurio*, 29 April 1972, in Gonzalez Pino and Fontaine Talavera, *Mil Días (I)*, 369–73; and Memorandum, Jorden to Kissinger, 10 April 1972.

38. Telegram, Davis to SecState, 26 January 1972, box 2194/RG59/NARA.

39. Telegram, Davis to SecState, 7 December 1971, CDP-NARA, and Telegram, Crimmins to Amembassy Rome, 14 December 1971, box 2193/RG59/NARA.

40. Diplomatic Report, no. 562/71, FCO, 15 December 1971, FCO7/1991/TNA.

41. Record of Conversation, I. B. Puchkov (Soviet Embassy, Santiago) and Hugo Cubillios, 25 January 1972, published as "Conversación del Ministro Consejero de la Embajada Soviética con el director del departamento económico del Ministerio de Relaciones Exteriores de Chile," in Ulianova and Fediakova, "Chile en los Archivos de la URSS (1959–1973)," 421–22.

42. "Report, Latin American Institute, Soviet Academy of Sciences," c. July 1972, in Ulianova and Fediakova, "Chile en los Archivos de la URSS (1959–1973), 438–40, and Miller, *Soviet Relations with Latin America*, 139. The figure of $5 million is based on the Soviet official exchange rate of .64 rubles to the dollar up to the 1980s.

43. Record of Conversation, Hildyard and Altamirano, 27 February 1972, Letter, Hildyard to Hankey (FCO), 8 March 1972, FCO7/2212/TNA.

44. Circular Telegram, FCO, 5 May 1972, FCO59/795/TNA; and Telex, Herrera to MRE (Gabinete Ministro), 13 April 1972, Aerogram y Telex/OEA/1972/AMRE.

45. Chilean Foreign Ministry statement as quoted in Oficio, da Câmara Canto to Gibson Barbosa, 11 March 1971, Oficios/Embaixada do Brasil, Santiago 1971 (01)/AMRE-Brasilia.

46. "Report on the first year of the Government of the UP," East German Embassy, Santiago, 12 December 1971, V-33/MfAA.

47. Almeyda, Speech to G77, 29 October 1971, Lima, Peru, in Vera Castillo, *Política Exterior Chilena*, 405–6.

48. Memorandum of Conversation, Parsons (FCO), Lam (Department of Trade and Industry), Williams (Overseas Development Administration), Kemmis (Department of Trade and Industry), Kater-Bates (FCO), and Hernán Santa Cruz, 28 January 1972, FCO59/794/TNA; and Telegram, Amembassy Dar-es-Salaam to SecState, 22 February 1972, box 2913/RG59/NARA.

49. Memorandum, Santa Cruz to Almeyda, "Consideraciones políticas adicionales sobre la Reunión de los 77 y respecto a las perspectivas para la Tercera Conferencia de Comercio y Desarrollo," no date, vol. 2/FHSC/AMRE.

50. For ITT documents, see *Subversion in Chile*.

51. Telex, Letelier to MRE, 27 March 1972, Telex R./EEUU/1972/AMRE.

52. Allende, "Discurso ante la Tercera UNCTAD," *OE-SA*, 613–14.

53. Telegram, Davis to SecState, 17 May 1972, box 2198/RG59/NARA.

54. Letter, Letelier to Clodomiro (in Paris), 31 March 1972, 2/17/11/FOL.

55. Options Paper, DOS, "Next Steps Options on Chile," 4 April 1972, enclosure, Memorandum, Jorden to Kissinger, 10 April 1972, box H064/NSCIF/NPMP.

56. Memorandum, Jorden to Kissinger, 10 April 1972.

57. Options Paper, DOS, "Next Steps Options on Chile," 4 April 1972.

58. Telegram, Davis to SecState, 28 February 1972, box 2193/RG59/NARA. See also Davis, *Last Two Years*, 77.

59. Telegram, Davis to SecState, 1 April 1972, box H064/NSCIF/NPMP.

60. See NSSM 158, NSC Interdepartmental Group (Latin America), "Review of US policy toward Peru," 26 September 1972, box H193/NSCIF/NPMP.

61. Davis, *Last Two Years*, 74.

62. Memorandum, Jorden to Kissinger, 10 April 1972. Emphasis in original.

63. Options Paper, DOS, "Next Steps Options on Chile," 4 April 1972.

64. Telegram, Davis to SecState, 28 March 1972, box H064/NSCIF/NPMP; Options Paper, DOS, "Next Steps Options on Chile," 4 April 1972; and Analytic Summary, NSC, enclosure, Memorandum, Jorden to Kissinger, 10 April 1972.

65. Memorandum, Jorden to Kissinger, 10 April 1972.

66. "Memorandum of agreement regarding the consolidation of Chilean Debt," 19 April 1972, accessed online at http://untreaty.un.orgunts/1_60000/27/3/00052134.pdf.

67. Zammit as quoted in Jones, *North-South Dialogue*, 30; and Telegram, Amembassy Caracas to SecState, 11 June 1972, Executive Secretariat, Briefing Books, 1958–1976, lot 720373, box 135/RG59/NARA.

68. Bouteflika (1972) as quoted in Mortimer, *Third World Coalition*, 37. On similar Chilean conclusions, see Prats, *Memorias*, 263.

69. UNCTAD III's Resolution no. 46 condemned U.S. pressure against Chile. Telex, MRE to Embachile Washington, 14 October 1972, Telex E./EEUU/1972/AMRE; and Letter, Hildyard to Hunter, 20 April 1972, FCO7/2212/TNA.

70. Oficio, Letelier to Señor Ministro, 11 August 1972, Oficios Conf., E./R./ EEUU/1972/AMRE.

71. Diplomatic Report no. 338/72, FCO, 19 April 1972, FCO7/2174/TNA.

72. Letter, W. R. McQuillan, British Embassy, Santiago, to Latin America Department, FCO, 12 June 1972, FCO7/2174/TNA; and Almeyda, "Foreign Policy of the Unidad Popular," 88.

73. Letter, Antony Walter, British Embassy, Lima, to Robson, FCO, 3 July 1972, FCO7/2174/TNA.

74. Kissinger, 5 January 1972, as quoted in Spektor, "Equivocal Engagement," 108.

75. Airgram, DOS to All ARA Diplomatic Posts, 8 June 1972, box 404/RG59/NARA.

76. Memorandum of Conversation, Connally, Médici, et al., 8 June 1972, Telegram, Amembassy Brasilia to SecState, 17 June 1972, Executive Secretariat, Briefing Books, 1958–1976, lot 720373, box 135/RG59/NARA.

77. Ibid.

78. Letter, Médici to Nixon, 27 April 1972, as quoted in Spektor, "Equivocal Engagement," 101.

79. Telegram, Amembassy Brasilia to SecState, 7 March 1972, doc. 147/ FRUS/1969–1976/E-10.

80. Memorandum of Conversation, Connally, Médici, et al., 8 June 1972, Telegram, Amembassy Brasilia to SecState, 17 June 1972.

81. Memorandum of Conversation, Connally, Banzer, et al., 13 June 1972, Telegram, Amembassy La Paz to SecState, 23 June 1972, Executive Secretariat, Briefing Books, 1958–1976, lot 720373, box 135/RG59/NARA.

82. Handwritten note, Kissinger on Memorandum, Hewitt to Kissinger, 4 March 1972, box 232/NSCIF/NPMP. The IMF finally insisted on the devaluation of Bolivia's peso, and La Paz froze wages at half the level of rising living costs. Lehman, *Limited Partnership*, 165–66.

83. Memorandum, Hewitt to Kissinger, 4 March 1972.

84. Telex, Letelier to MRE, 8 June 1972, Telex R./EEUU/1972/AMRE.

85. Gaspari, *Ditadura Derrotada*, 348, and Options Paper, DOS, "Next Steps Options on Chile," 4 April 1972. See also conversations with Oña, March–April 2010. On the Right, the author has found no evidence that the United States used this route to channel arms to Chile. Instead, sources cited suggest weapons for the right wing came from Brazil and Argentina.

86. Memorandum of Conversation, Diniz and Hoffenberg, 7 September 1972, box 2223/RG59/NARA.

87. Telex, Letelier to MRE, 6 June 1972, Telex R./EEUU/1972/AMRE.

88. Oficios, Enrique Bernstein to Letelier, 11 July 1972, and Letelier to Señor Ministro, 23 June 1972, Oficios Conf., E./R./EEUU/1972/AMRE.

89. Martínez Corbalá interview, 30 December 2009.

90. Bussi interview, 9 April 2010.

91. Retrospective Record of Conversation, McBride, U.S. Ambassador, Mexico City, and Mexican Foreign Minister, Emilio Rabasa, Telegram, McBride to SecState, 26 September 1973, DOS/CFP.

92. Almeyda as quoted in Urgent Note, "Summary of Visit of the Chilean Delegation," 2 June 1971, wiazka 3/40/75/AMSZ. On Cuban suspicions regarding Mexico's position and an analysis of its "pre-revolutionary" character, see also Record of Conversations, Raúl Roa and Polish minister of foreign affairs Stefan Jedrychowski, 24–26 June 1971, Urgent Note, "Notes on the Conversations with Roa," 30 June 1971, wiazka 3/40/75/AMSZ.

93. Transcript, Nixon and Echeverría, Oval Office, 15 June 1972, in Doyle, "The Nixon Tapes."

94. Record of Conversations, Raúl Roa and Polish minister of foreign affairs Stefan Jedrychowski, 24–26 June 1971.

95. Julien-Landelius, "Resumidas Cuentas," 48.

96. Suárez interview, 10 December 2004.

97. Oficios, Vega to Señor Ministro, 13 September 1972 and 24 July 1972, Oficios Conf./Cuba/1972/AMRE.

98. Amat and Vierra interviews. Between 1964 and 1972 there were only "a couple" of Latin American specialists at MINREX.

99. Suárez interview, 10 December 2004; and Raúl Roa as cited in Oficio, Vega to Señor Ministro, 10 July 1972, Oficios Conf./Cuba/1972/AMRE.

100. Manuel Piñeiro to DGLN, 5 August 1972, in Suárez, *Manuel Piñeiro*, 98–99.

101. Vierra interview.

102. Foreign Ministry Report, "Political Evaluation of Fidel Castro's Visit and Program for Action," 23 June 1972, and Minutes of Central Committee Meeting, "Discussion on Evaluating Fidel Castro's Visit," 14 June 1972, wiazka 3/12/78/AMSZ.

103. Mesa-Lago, *Cuba in the 1970s*, 20–21.

104. Castro, 26 July 1972, as quoted in Erisman, *Cuba's International Relations*, 53–54.

105. Memorandum of Conversation, Connally, Médici, et al., 8 June 1972.

106. Memorandum of Conversation, Rogers and Gibson Barbosa, 29 September 1972, Waldorf Hotel, Telegram, USMission, UN to SecState, 6 October 1972, box 2130/RG59/NARA; and Gaspari, *Ditadura Derrotada*, 349–51. On Brazilian government and military concerns regarding the Tupamaro threat and the security situation in Uruguay, see Telegram, Amembassy Brasilia to SecState, 7 March 1972, doc. 147/FRUS/1969–1976/Vol. E-10.

107. Memorandum of Conversation, Connally and de la Flor, 14 June 1972, Telegram, Amembassy Lima to SecState, 23 June 1972, Executive Secretariat, Briefing Books, 1958–1976, lot 720373, box 135/RG59/NARA.

108. NSSM 158. The United States' policy of "non-overt pressure" on Peru included a freeze on U.S. government bilateral assistance, including Eximbank lending, lobbying of U.S. banks to put financial pressures on Peru, and a discreet position against Lima at the IBRD and the IMF.

109. Annex to NSSM 158, enclosure, Memorandum, A. Arenales (INR/RAA/OD) to Bloomfield (ARA/NSC-IG), 6 September 1972, box H193/NSCIF/NPMP.

110. NSSM 158. On the differentiation in the minds of policy makers between Peru and Chile, see Vaky interview. For a previous study of the differentiation, see also Cottam, *Images and Intervention*.

111. NSSM 158.

112. Memorandum, Peter M. Flanigan and Kissinger to Nixon, 28 December 1972, box H237/NSCIF/NPMP; Memorandum, Thomas R. Pickering, Executive Secretary DOS, to Brent Scowcroft, 13 September 1973, box 2196/RG59/NARA; and Country Report, Peru, The Green Book.

113. Oficio, Letelier to Señor Ministro, 13 October 1973, Oficios Conf., E./R./EEUU/1972/AMRE.

114. Memorandum, Urrutia to Ministro de Relaciones Exteriores et al., "Algunos Aspectos de Las relaciones Financieras de Chile con la Banca de EE.UU," 22 October 1971, 2/13/44/FOL.

115. Aide Memoire, Letelier, "Situación Relaciones Chile con Estados Unidos," 11 August 1972, 2/16/5/FOL; and Memorandum, Letelier, "Medidas que podríamos adoptar para establecer algún 'modus vivendi' con Estados Unidos," 5 September 1972, enclosure, Letter (personal and confidential), Orlando to Clodomiro, 6 September 1972, 2/17/12/FOL.

116. Letter (personal and confidential), Orlando to Clodomiro, 6 September 1972.

117. Aide Memoire, Letelier, "Situación Relaciones Chile con Estados Unidos," 11 August 1972; and Memorandum, Letelier, "Medidas que podríamos adoptar para establecer algún 'modus vivendi' con Estados Unidos," 5 September 1972.

118. For negative PS reaction to PCCh analysis of the situation, see Arnoldo Camú, "Respuesta al Partido Comunista," *Punto Final*, 18 July 1972, in Pérez, "La Izquierda," 460–65.

119. Allende, 7 August 1972, as quoted in Telegram, Davis to DOS, 9 August 1972, box 478/RG59/NARA.

120. Report, Latin American Institute, Soviet Academy of Sciences, c. July 1972, in Ulianova and Fediakova, "Chile en los Archivos de la URSS (1959–1973)," 425–26, 436, and Ulianova, "La Unidad Popular y el Golpe Militar," 96–101.

121. Letter, Ambassador Fries, East German Ambassador, Santiago, to Comrade Georg Stibi, Minister of Foreign Affairs, Berlin, 25 June 1972, V-33/MfAA.

122. *Pravda*, 23 November 1972, as quoted in Miller, *Soviet Relations with Latin America*, 132.

123. Memorandum, Letelier, "Medidas que podríamos adoptar para establecer algún 'modus vivendi' con Estados Unidos," 5 September 1972.

124. Miller, *Soviet Relations with Latin America*, 139–40.

125. Edmundo Eluchans as quoted in Memorandum of Conversation, Jorge Ross (Businessman), Joaquin Figueroa (ex–General Manager Mina Andina), Orlando Saenz (President SOFOFA), Javier Vial (President FENSA), Edmundo Eluchans (Lawyer), Davis, Joel W. Biller (Acting DCM, U.S. Embassy), and Calvin C. Berlin (U.S. Commercial Attaché), 26 July 1972, enclosure, Airgram, Davis to DOS, 2 August 1972, box 2197/RG59/NARA.

126. Aide Memoire, Letelier, "Situación Relaciones Chile con Estados Unidos," 11 August 1972, and Memorandum, Letelier, "Medidas que podríamos adoptar para establecer algún 'modus vivendi' con Estados Unidos," 5 September 1972.

127. Urrutia interviews, and Huidobro interview, 18 October 2004.

128. Telex, Letelier to Almeyda (exclusivo), 15 May 1972, Telex R./EEUU/1972/AMRE; and Oficios, Letelier to Señor Ministro, 23 May 1972, and Letelier to Señor Ministro, 20 June 1972, Oficios Conf., E./R./EEUU/1972/AMRE. See also Davis, *Last Two Years*, 94.

129. Telex, Carlos Negri, Direccion Economica, MRE, to Embachile Washington, 7 August 1972, Telex E./EEUU/1972/AMRE.

130. Aide Memoire, Letelier, "Situación Relaciones Chile con Estados Unidos," 11 August 1972, and Memorandum, Letelier, "Medidas que podríamos adoptar para establecer algún 'modus vivendi' con Estados Unidos," 5 September 1972.

131. Memorandum, Letelier, "Medidas que podríamos adoptar para establecer algún 'modus vivendi' con Estados Unidos," 5 September 1972.

132. Letter (personal and confidential), Orlando to Clodomiro, 6 September 1972.

133. Handwritten letter, Cloro to Orlando, 30 September 1972, 2/17/13/FOL.

134. Telexes, Almeyda to Embachile Washington, 5 September 1972, and Letelier to Almeyda (exclusivo), 29 September 1972, Telex R./EEUU/1972/AMRE; and Record of Conversation, Subsecretary Luis Orlandini, MRE, and Davis, 18 October 1972, Telex, Orlandini to Almeyda (in Washington), 18 October 1972, Telex E./EEUU/1972/AMRE.

135. Draft Note, MRE to U.S. Embassy, Santiago, Telex, MRE to Embachile Washington, 14 October 1972, Telex E./EEUU/1972/AMRE.

136. Record of Conversation, Orlandini and Davis, 18 October 1972, and Davis, *Last Two Years*, 102–3.

137. Record of Conversation, Letelier and Hennessy, 29 September 1972, Telex, Letelier to Almeyda, 29 September 1972, Telex R./EEUU/1972/AMRE.

138. CIA Information Report, Directorate of Plans, 31 October 1972, CDP-CIA; and Background Study, Shlaudeman "Toward a Working Hypothesis of the Gremialista Movement, Its Origin, Structure and Implications," enclosure, Airgram, Davis to DOS, 15 December 1972, box 2194/RG59/NARA. See also Memorandum, Jorden to Kissinger, 29 August 1973, CDP-NSC. Jorden describes the possibility of supporting Gremialistas as "new territory."

139. Memorandum for 40 Committee, 21 January 1972, and Memorandum for the 40 Committee, 10 October 1972, CDP-NSC.

140. Memorandum for the 40 Committee, 6 April 1972, and Memorandum for the 40 Committee, 15 August 1972, CDP-NSC.

141. Memorandum, Rob Roy Ratliff (CIA) to Kissinger, 16 June 1972, CDP-NSC.

142. Memorandum of Conversation, Gustavo Alessandri Valdes, Second Vice-President (PN) and Arzac, 28 July 1972, enclosure, Airgram, Davis to DOS, 23 August 1972, box 2194/RG59/NARA.

143. *Covert Action in Chile*, 37–39.

144. Conversation, Ambassador A. V. Basov with Corvalán and Teitelboim, 13 September 1972, published as "Conversación del embajador A. V. Basov con Luis Corvalán y Volodia Teitelboim," in Ulianova and Fediakova, "Chile en los Archivos de la URSS (1959–1973)," 441. See also "Discussion between First Secretary Erich Honecker with the General Secretary of the Central Committee of the PCCh, Luis Corvalán, November 24, 1972, Berlin," DY/30 2432/SAPMO.

145. Telegram, Davis to SecState, 22 August 1972, box 2198/RG59/NARA; Telegram, Davis to SecState, 15 September 1972, CDP-NARA; and Record of Conversation, Davis and Frei, 16 August 1972, Telegram, Davis to SecState, 19 August 1972, box 2193/RG59/NARA.

146. Allende as quoted in "'Si Hubiera Guerra Civil la Ganariamos,' djo S.E.," *La Tercera de la Hora*, 31 August 1972, Gonzalez Pino and Fontaine Talavera, *Mil Días (I)*, 441.

147. Quiroga, *Compañeros*, 84.

148. Letter, Castro to Allende, 6 September 1972, in Castro, "Salvador Allende: His Example Lives On."

149. "Discussion between First Secretary Erich Honecker with the General Secretary of the Central Committee of the PCCh, Luis Corvolan, November 24, 1972, Berlin."

150. Nolff, *Salvador Allende*, 87.

151. Quiroga, *Compañeros*, 121.

152. Ibid., 82, 116–17.

153. Huerta interview, 18 October 2004; Pascal Allende interview; conversations with Oña, March–April 2010; and Cabieses interview, 25 March 2010.

154. Bautista Yofre, *Misión Argentina*, 261–69, and "Avión con Guerrilleros Argentinos Llegó a Chile," *La Tercera de la Hora*, 16 August 1972, Gonzalez Pino and Fontaine Talavera, *Mil Días (I)*, 528–30.

155. Huidobro interview, 28 October 2004. See also Bautista Yofre, *Misión Argentina*, 267–69.

156. Dinges, *Condor Years*, 50–51.

157. Gaspari, *Ditadura Derrotada*, 357; McSherry, *Predatory States*, 57; and Telegram, Davis to SecState, 28 September 1973, DOS/CFP.

158. Dinges, *Condor Years*, 50–51.

159. Jaramillo Edwards interview, 21 September 2004, and Oña interview, 2 May 2006.

160. Record of Conversation, Davis and Frei, 15 March 1972, Telegram, Davis to SecState, 16 March 1972, and Record of Conversation, Davis and Frei, 16 August 1972, Telegram, Davis to SecState, 19 August 1972, box 2193/RG59/NARA.

161. Vuskovic as quoted in Memorandum for the 40 Committee, 15 August 1972, CDP-NSC.

162. Oficio, Letelier to Señor Ministro, 13 October 1972, Oficios Conf., E./R./EEUU/1972/AMRE.

163. Transcript, Nixon and Haldeman, 15 June 1972, in Doyle, "The Nixon Tapes."

164. Memorandum, Connally, Médici, et al., 8 June 1972.

165. Transcript, Nixon and Echeverría, Oval Office, 15 June 1972.

166. Summary of Minutes, Connally and Pastrana, 7 June 1972, Telegram, Amembassy Bogotá to SecState, 17 June 1972.

167. Aerogram, Herrera to MRE, 9 September 1972, Aerogram y Telex/OEA/1972/AMRE; and Leacock, *Requiem for Revolution*, 228–29.

168. Gamani Corea as quoted in Nossiter, *Global Struggle for More*, 40.

169. Memorandum, Letelier, 23 November 1972, 2/16/7/FOL.

Chapter 6

1. Allende, "Address to the United Nations General Assembly," in Cockcroft, *Allende Reader*, 202, 212.

2. Record of Conversation, Díaz Casanueva and Bush, 15 November 1972, Telegram, Bush to SecState, 15 November 1972, box 2193/RG59/NARA.

3. Intelligence Note, INR, "Chile: Quest for the unreachable," 30 November 1972, box 2193/RG59/NARA.

4. Neruda, *Incitación al Nixonicidio*, and Allende, Speech at Kremlin Banquet, 6 December 1972, published as "Palabras del Presidente de la República de Chile, Salvador Allende Gossens, pronunciadas en la Cena Ofrecida en su Honor en el Kremlin, Moscú," in Pérez, "La Izquierda," 491.

5. Letter, Orlando to Clodomiro, 11 November 1972, 2/17/8/FOL.

6. Telexes, Letelier to Almeyda, 8 and 10 November 1972, Telex R./EEUU/1972/AMRE; and Letter, Orlando to Clodomiro, 11 November 1972.

7. Memorandum of Conversation, Letelier and Davis, Santiago, no date, Telegram, Davis to SecState, 23 November 1972, box 2193/RG59/NARA.

8. Memorandum, Crimmins to the Secretary, 11 November 1972, box 2193/RG59/NARA.

9. Intelligence Note, INR, "Chile: Quest for the unreachable," 30 November 1972, and Intelligence Note, INR, "Chile: Cabinet Changes Should End Confrontation" 6 November 1972, box 2197/RG59/NARA.

10. For en masse cancellation of TV channels' interest in interviewing Allende hours after networks fought over access to the president, see Oficio, Letelier to Señor Ministro, 19 January 1973, Conf., E./R./EEUU/1973/AMRE.

11. Ibid.

12. Allende as quoted in Telegram, McBride to SecState, 7 December 1972, box 2193/RG59/NARA.

13. Allende, "Address to the United Nations General Assembly," in Cockcroft, *Allende Reader*, 205–12.

14. Ibid., 202–3, 214–18.

15. Record of Conversation, Bush and Allende, Waldorf Towers, 4 December, Telegram, DOS to Amembassy Santiago, 4 December 1972, box 2197/RG59/NARA.

16. Almeyda, *Reencuentro con mi Vida*, 182–83.

17. Estrada interview.

18. "Discussion between First Secretary Erich Honecker with the General Secretary of the Central Committee of the PCCh, Luis Corvalán, November 24, 1972, Berlin," DY/30 2432/SAPMO. For other accounts of Corvalán's trip, see Haslam, *Assisted Suicide*, 151–52, and Telegram, Beam, Amembassy Moscow, to SecState, 24 November 1972, box 2193/RG59/NARA.

19. Ulianova, "La Unidad Popular y el Golpe Militar," 102.

20. Allende, "Palabras del Presidente de la República de Chile, Salvador Allende Gossens, pronunciadas en la Cena Ofrecida en su Honor en el Kremlin, Moscú," in Pérez, "Izquierda," 491.

21. Soto interviews. See also Soto, *El Ultimo Día*, 24.

22. Haslam, *Assisted Suicide*, 152–53.

23. Intelligence Note, INR, "USSR-Chile: Allende Visit Produces Limited Results," 12 December 1972, box 2193/RG59/NARA; and Haslam, *Assisted Suicide*, 153.

24. Huidobro interviews.

25. "Gigantesco Recibimiento Popular al Presidente Allende," *Granma*, 10 December 1972.

26. Letter, Castro to Allende, 4 February 1972, in Castro, "Salvador Allende: His Example Lives On."

27. Oficio, Rojas Pizarro to Señor Ministro, 20 December 1972, Oficios Conf./Cuba/1972/AMRE.

28. Castro, Speech at the Plaza de la Revolución, Havana, 13 December 1972, published as "Castro Allende Exchange Speeches," CSD.

29. Ibid.

30. Soto interviews.

31. Allende, Speech at the Plaza de la Revolución, Havana, 13 December 1972, published as "Castro Allende Exchange Speeches," CSD.

32. Oficio, Rojas to Señor Ministro, 20 December 1972, Oficios Conf./Cuba/1972/AMRE.

33. Airgram, Rojas to MRE, 14 November 1972, Aerograms Conf./Cuba/1972/AMRE.

34. Informe del Intercambio Comercial Chileno-Cubano, no date, c. 1972, CMSA; and Carta Personal, Vega to Almeyda, 6 July 1972, CMSA.

35. Interview with Vega, *Bohemia*, as quoted in Oficio, Gonzalo Rojas to Señor Ministro, 31 October 1972, Oficios Conf./Cuba/1972/AMRE.

36. Telegrams, Davis to SecState, 13 and 18 December 1972, box 2193/RG59/NARA.

37. "Minuta," [U.S.-Chilean Talks, 20–23 December 1972, Washington], 26 December 1972, MINREL 1961–1971/Memorandos Políticos/AMRE.

38. "Minutas de Conversaciones Sostenidas Entre Delegaciones de Chile y Los Estados Unidas: 20, 21 y 22 de diciembre de 1972, Departamento de Estado Washington DC," c. 23 December 1972, Oficios Conf./E./R./EEUU/1972/AMRE.

39. Prizel, *Latin America through Soviet Eyes*, 164.

40. Briefing on Chile Elections, CIA, 1 March 1973, CDP-CIA; and Memorandum for Deputy Director for Plans, 18 November 1972, CDP-CIA.

41. Memorandum, Rogers to Nixon, 15 November 1972, box 2193/RG59/NARA.

42. "Minutas de Conversaciones Sostenidas Entre Delegaciones de Chile y Los Estados Unidas," c. 23 December 1972.

43. Ibid., and "Minuta," 26 December 1972.

44. Memorandum, MRE, 3 January 1973, Memorandos/Dirección de Asuntos Juridicos 1971–1980/AMRE. On the importance of keeping Paris Club creditors on Chile's side, see Circular Telex, MRE to Embachile Paris Club countries, 16 January 1973, Telex E./EEUU/1973/AMRE.

45. Telex, Letelier to MRE, 30 January 1973, Telex R: 1–400/EEUU/1973/AMRE.

46. Telex, Letelier to Almeyda, 17 January 1973, Telex R: 1–400, EEUU/1973/AMRE; and Telex, MRE to Embachile Washington, 5 February 1973 Telex E./EEUU/1973/AMRE.

47. Telegram, Davis to SecState, 21 February 1973, box 2196/RG59/NARA.

48. Airgram, Davis to DOS, 24 January 1973, box 2196/RG59/NARA.

49. Telegram, Davis to SecState, 21 February 1973.

50. Allende as quoted by Phillipe Mengin (architect) in Memorandum of Conversation, Mengin and Judd L. Kessler (Regional Legal Advisor), 23 January 1973, enclosure, Airgram, Davis to DOS, 30 January 1973, box 2197/RG59/NARA.

51. Soviet Foreign Ministry Report, O. Grek, 21 February 1973, in Ulianova, "La Unidad Popular y el Golpe Militar," 104–5.

52. Telegram, Davis to SecState, 1 March 1973, box 2196/RG59/NARA.

53. Airgram, Chief, WHD, to COS, Santiago, 12 January 1973, and Cable, COS, Santiago, to Chief, WHD, 13 February 1973, CDP-CIA.

54. Cable, CIA Station, Santiago, to CIA HQ, 8 February 1973, CDP-CIA; Memorandum, James Gardner (INR) to William McAfee (INR), 27 February 1973, CDP-NSC; Memorandum, Chief, WHD, to DCI, 29 March 1973, CDP-CIA; Information Report, CIA, 28 February 1973, CDP-CIA; Cable, Chief, WHD, to COS, 14 March 1973, CDP-CIA; and Cable, CIA HQ to CIA Station, Santiago, 6 February 1973, CDP-CIA.

55. Record of Conversation, HQ Officers and Davis, 10 January 1973, Cable, CIA HQ to CIA Station, Santiago, 10 January 1973, CDP-CIA.

56. Airgram, COS, Santiago, to Chief, WHD, 21 February 1973, CDP-CIA.

57. Central Intelligence Bulletin, Directorate of Intelligence, 22 February 1973, and Intelligence Report, CIA, 28 February 1973, CDP-CIA.

58. Cable, Chief, WHD, to COS, Santiago, 14 March 1973, CDP-CIA.

59. Telegram, Davis to SecState, 6 March 1973, box 2196/RG59/NARA. Martínez Corbalá, *Instantes de Decisión*, 78, and Bautista Yofre, *Misión Argentina*, 325.

60. Telegram, Davis to SecState, 23 March 1973, box 2194/RG59/NARA; and Memorandum Chief, WHD, to DCI, 29 March 1973, CDP-CIA.

61. Record of Conversation, Davis and Frei, 15 March 1973, Telegram, Davis to SecState, 16 March 1973, box 2196/RG59/NARA.

62. Telegram, Davis to SecState, 23 March 1973.

63. "Ahora mas que nunca avanzar sin transar," *Las Noticias de Ultima Hora*, 9 March 1973, Gonzalez Pino and Fontaine Talavera, *Mil Días (I)*, 600.

64. Report, Soviet Foreign Ministry, 16 March 1973, as quoted in Ulianova, "La Unidad Popular y el Golpe Militar," 104.

65. Memorandum of Conversation, Claudio Huepe (PDC Deputy) and Arnold Isaacs (U.S. Embassy), 14 March 1973, enclosure, Airgram, Davis to DOS, 30 March 1973, box 2194/RG59/NARA.

66. Cable, CIA Station to DCI, 26 April 1973, CDP-CIA.

67. CIA Memorandum, 30 June 1973, CDP-CIA.

68. Cable, COS, Santiago, to DCI, 14 March 1973, CDP-CIA.

69. Telegram, Davis to Rogers, 23 March 1973.

70. Cable, COS to DCI, 14 March 1973.

71. Memorandum for Chief, WHD, 17 April 1973, CDP-CIA.

72. Memorandum, CIA, 31 March 1973, CDP-CIA.

73. Memorandum for Chief, WHD, 17 April 1973.

74. *Covert Action in Chile*, 38.

75. Quiroga, *Compañeros*, 88.

76. Corvalán, *Gobierno de Salvador Allende*, 215.

77. Allende as quoted in "No ocultamos las horas dificiles que tengamos que vivir," *Las Ultimas Noticias*, 28 March 1973, in; Gonzalez Pino and Fontaine Talavera, *Mil Días (I)*, 610–11.

78. Report, Soviet Foreign Ministry, 16 March 1973, as quoted in Ulianova, "La Unidad Popular y el Golpe Militar," 105.

79. *Pravda* as quoted in Telegram, Dubs, Amembassy Moscow to SecState, 26 March 1973, DOS/CFP.

80. Hart, *Homenaje a Miguel Enríquez*, 2–3.

81. Rodríguez as quoted in "Discurso en el acto de celebración de los 40 años del Partido Socialista," *Chile Hoy*, 27 April 1973, in Pérez, "La Izquierda," 549–50.

82. Chain interview, and Castro to Honecker, 21 February 1974, as quoted in Skierka, *Castro*, 204.

83. Suárez interviews.

84. DIA Intelligence Summary, 28 April 1973, CDP-DOD.

85. Quiroga, *Compañeros*, 91–92.

86. Haslam, *Assisted Suicide*, 165, and Prats, *Memorias*, 378–79.

87. Prats, *Memorias*, 378–79, and "PDC Rechaza la Escuela Nacional Unificada," *El Mecurio*, 6 April 1973, Gonzalez Pino and Fontaine Talavera, *Mil Días (I)*, 378–79.

88. Airgram, Davis to DOS, 9 February 1973, box 2193/RG59/NARA.

89. Telegram, Davis to SecState, 16 May 1973, DOS/CFP; and NIE, "Chile," 14 June 1973, CDP-CIA.

90. DIA Intelligence Summary, 16 March 1973, CDP-DOD; and Prats, *Memorias*, 369.

91. Oscar Garretón (MAPU) as quoted in Telegram, Davis to SecState, 11 January 1973, and MAPU document as cited in Telegram, Davis to SecState, 1 March 1973, box 2196/RG59/NARA.

92. Record of Conversation, Davis and Letelier, 31 March 1973, Telegram, Davis to SecState, 31 March 1973, DOS/CFP.

93. "Minutas de Conversaciones Sostenidas Entre Delegaciones de Chile y Los Estados Unidas," 20–23 December 1972; "Minutas de Conversaciones Sostenidas Entre Delegaciones de Chile y Los Estados Unidos, 22 y 23 de Marzo de 1973, Departamento de Estado, Washington DC," c. 24 March 1973, Oficios Conf., E./R./EEUU/1973/AMRE; and Telegram, Rogers to Amembassies, Paris Club Countries, 4 April 1973, DOS/CFP.

94. "Minutas de Conversaciones Sostenidas Entre Delegaciones de Chile y Los Estados Unidos," c. 24 March 1973.

95. On Chilean views of the Senate hearings, see Oficio, Enrique Bernstein, MRE to Chilean missions abroad, 16 May 1973, Oficios Conf., E/R, EEUU/1973/AMRE.

96. "Minutas de Conversaciones Sostenidas Entre Delegaciones de Chile y Los Estados Unidos," c. 24 March 1973.

97. Record of Conversation, Davis and Letelier, 31 March 1973.

98. Telegram, Rogers to White House, 1 April 1973, DOS/CFP.

99. Memorandum, "Conversaciones Sostenidas Entre Delegaciones de Chile y Estados Unidos," 24 March 1973, DIGEN de Pol. Exterior 1961–1979/Memorandos Politicos/AMRE.

100. Record of Conversation, Davis and Letelier, 31 March 1973.

101. Telegrams, Rogers to White House, White House to Rogers and Rush, and DOS to Davis, 1 April 1973, DOS/CFP.

102. Telegram, Rogers to Amembassy Santiago, 13 April 1973, DOS/CFP; and "Memorandum Sobre Conversaciones Sostenidas Entre representantes de Chile y Los Estados Unidos (1)," 27 June 1973, DIGEN de Pol. Exterior 1961–1979/Memorandos Políticos/AMRE.

103. Allende, *Chile Hoy*, 19 April 1973, as quoted in Telegram, Davis to SecState, 19 April 1973, DOS/CFP.

104. Telegram, Davis to SecState, 25 July 1973, DOS/CFP.

105. "Minutas de Conversaciones Sostenidas Entre Delegaciones de Chile y Los Estados Unidas," c. 24 March 1973.

106. Oficio, MRE to Embachile Washington, 4 June 1973, Oficios Conf., E./R./EEUU/1973/AMRE.

107. Almeyda as cited in Telegram, SecState to All American Republic Diplomatic Posts, 7 April 1973, DOS/CFP.

108. Almeyda, April 1973, as quoted in Sater, *Chile and the United States*, 168.

109. Telegram, SecState to All American Republic Diplomatic Posts, 14 April 1973, DOS/CFP.

110. Rogers, "Interim Report on Latin American Trip," as paraphrased in Memorandum, Brent Scowcroft to Nixon, 22 May 1973, box 953/NSCF/NPMP.

111. Handwritten note, Nixon to Rogers, 23 May 1973, box 953/NSCF/NPMP.

112. Rogers, "Interim Report on Latin American Trip," as paraphrased in Memorandum, Brent Scowcroft to Nixon, 22 May 1973.

113. Rogers as quoted in Memorandum, Kissinger to Nixon, 28 May 1973, box 953/NSCF/NPMP.

114. Memorandum of Conversation, Rogers, Kubisch, and Allende, Chilean embassy, Buenos Aires, 25 May 1973, Telegram, SecState to Amembassy Santiago, 29 May 1973, box 953/NSCF/NPMP.

115. Ibid.

116. Memorandum, "La gira del Secretario de Estado, William Rogers por America Latina," enclosure, Oficio, MRE to Embachile, Washington, 19 June 1973, and Oficio, Letelier to Señor Ministro, 24 April 1973, Oficios Conf., E./R./EEUU/1973/AMRE.

117. Telex, Letelier to Embachile, Washington, 28 May 1973, Telex E./EEUU/1973/AMRE; Huidobro interviews; and Uribe, *Black Book*, 150.

118. Memorandum of Conversation, Rogers, Kubisch, and Allende, Chilean embassy, Buenos Aires, 25 May 1973.

119. Oficio, MRE to Embachile, Washington, 4 June 1973, Oficios Conf., E./R./EEUU/1973/AMRE.

120. Luis Herrera as quoted in Telegram, Belcher, Amembassy Lima, to SecState, 12 July 1973, DOS/CFP; and Records of Conversation, Davis and Letelier, 10 July 1973, Telegram, Davis to SecState, 10 July 1973, and Memorandum Confidencial, enclosure, Oficio, MRE to Embachile, 10 July 1973, Oficios Conf., E./R./EEUU/1973/AMRE.

121. Telegram, Belcher to SecState, 12 July 1973, DOS/CFP.

122. Telegram, Belcher to SecState, "OAS Special Committee: Wrap-up of Subcommittee Three (Structure)," 15 July 1973, DOS/CFP.

123. Telegram, Belcher to SecState, "OAS Special Committee: Preliminary Observations about Just Concluded Lima Meeting," 15 July 1973, DOS/CFP.

124. Telegram, Brewin, Amembassy La Paz, to SecState, 10 August 1973, DOS/CFP.

125. Telegram, SecState to Amembassy Brasilia, 9 August 1973, DOS/CFP. On U.S.-Brazilian cooperation in an inter-American setting and President Médici's communication with Washington about standing "firm" against the possibility of lifting sanctions against Cuba, see Memorandum for Kissinger from Scowcroft, 9 March 1973, The Nixon Presidential Library and Museum, "December 9, 2010, Materials Release."

126. Record of Conversation, Rogers and Velasco Alvarado, 16 May 1973, Telegram, Amconsul Rio de Janeiro to SecState, 19 May 1973, DOS/CFP.

127. Allende as quoted by Huidobro. Huidobro interview, 18 October 2004.

128. Sigmund, *Multinationals*, 167.

129. NIE, "Chile," 14 June 1973.

130. Airgram, Davis to DOS, 13 June 1973, box 2193/RG59/NARA. Emphasis added.

131. Ismael Huerta Díaz, c. July 1973, as quoted in Fermandois, *Mundo y Fin de Mundo*, 357.

132. Merino as quoted by Roberto Kelly, in Arancibia Claval, *Conversando con Roberto Kelly*, 138.

Chapter 7

1. Arancibia Claval, *Conversando con Roberto Kelly*, 144–47.

2. Telcon, Kissinger and Nixon, 16 September 1973, box 22/HAK Telcons/NSCF/NPMP.

3. Allende, Radio Magallanes, 11 September 1973, published as "Last Words," in Cockcroft, *Allende Reader*, 240.

4. For detailed examinations of the coup itself as opposed to these international dimensions, see Davis, *Last Two Years*; Soto, *El Ultimo Día*; and Verdugo, *Interferencia Secreta*.

5. Telegram, Col. Gerald H. Sills to M. G. Aaron, 11 April 1974, CREST/NARA. For reference to an alleged Chilean purchase of Soviet arms in 1973 using a $100 million credit offered by Moscow, see also Ulianova, "La Unidad Popular y el Golpe Militar," 108–10.

6. The number 15,000 surfaced repeatedly before the coup among military plotters. CIA Information Report, 9 July 1973, CDP-CIA.

7. On the figure of 120, most of whom were members of Cuba's Tropas Especiales, see conversations with Oña, March–April 2010. The number also reflects the figure of 142 given by *Bohemia* for the Cubans, Prensa Latina staff, and selected Chilean colleagues including Beatriz Allende and her daughter, Maya, who landed in Havana on 13 September 1973. *Bohemia*, 21 September 1973, 46–49.

8. Edict no. 1, 11 September 1973, as quoted in Fermandois, *Mundo y Fin de Mundo*, 405; and Airgram, Davis to DOS, "The Military Junta at One Month," 12 October 1973, box 2198/RG59/NARA.

9. Fermandois, *Mundo y Fin de Mundo*, 393.

10. Telexes, Embachile Argel (Salum) to Gabinete del Ministro, 31 August and 7 September 1973; and Allende to Boumedienne, in Telex, MRE to Ministro Almeyda, 7 September 1973, Oficios et al./Argelia/1973/AMRE.

11. Herrera, as quoted in Telegram, Belcher to SecState, 12 July 1973, DOS/CFP.

12. Airgram, Davis to SecState, 16 May 1973, box 2194/RG59/NARA.

13. Information Report, CIA, 2 May 1973, CDP-CIA.

14. Cable, DCI to CIA Station, Santiago, 1 May 1973, CDP-CIA.

15. Cables, DCI to CIA Station, Santiago, 2 and 9 May 1973; Cables, CIA Station, Santiago, to DCI, 2 and 7 May 1973; Cable, CIA Station, Santiago, to DCI, 26 May 1973; and Cable, CIA Station, Santiago, to DCI, 25 June 1973, CDP-CIA.

16. Record of Meeting, ARA-CIA, 11 June 1973, Memorandum James Gardener (ARA) to William McAffee (INR), 11 June 1973, CDP-NARA.

17. On the Tanquetazo, see Gustafson, "Double-Blind: Predicting the Pinochet Coup," 80, and Davis, *Last Two Years*, 171–75.

18. Quiroga, *Compañeros*, 95–96.

19. Pérez, "Salvador Allende, Apuntes Sobre su Dispositivo de Seguridad," 61–63.

20. Quiroga, *Compañeros*, 97.

21. Memorandum for Chief, WHD, "Chile—What Now?" 30 June 1973, CDP-CIA.

22. DIA Intelligence Summary, 5 July 1973, CDP-DOD.

23. Intelligence Telegram, 23 July 1973, CDP-CIA.

24. Quotation from Memorandum, David Atlee Philips to Deputy Director of Operations, "Recent Visit of [redacted] to Santiago," 13 August 1973, CDP-CIA.

25. *Covert Action in Chile*, 39. See also Intelligence Memorandum, "Consequences of a Military Coup in Chile," 1 August 1973, CDP-CIA.

26. Record of Conversation, Kubisch and Valdés, 24 July 1973, Telegram, SecState to Amembassy Santiago, 26 July 1973, DOS/CFP.

27. Record of Conversation, Davis and Letelier, 4 July 1973, Telegram, Davis to SecState, 4 July 1973, DOS/CFP.

28. Record of Conversation, Davis and Tomic, 24 August 1973, Airgram, Davis to DOS, 29 August 1973, box 2193/RG59/NARA.

29. Telegram, SecState to Amembassy Wellington and Canberra, 6 August 1973, DOS/CFP.

30. Telegram, Wood, Amembassy Wellington, to SecState, 13 August 1973, DOS/CFP.

31. Telegram, Annenberg, Amembassy London, to SecState, 6 July 1973, DOS/CFP. See also Telegram, SecState to Amembassy Wellington and Canberra, 6 August 1973. On United Kingdom views of Chile's "dismal" economic performance to this point, see Letter, G. J. MacGillivray, Bank of England, to Hunter, FCO, 26 July 1973, FCO7/2426/TNA.

32. Sweden doubled its aid to Chile to $9.5 million in 1973. Telegram, Olsen, Amembassy Stockholm, to SecState, 5 September 1973, DOS/CFP.

33. DIA Intelligence Summary, 2 August 1973, CDP-DOD.

34. Memorandum, Philips to Deputy Director of Operations, "Recent Visit of [redacted] to Santiago," 13 August 1973.

35. See Otero, *Razón y Fuerza de Chile*, 16–24, and Davis, *Last Two Years*, 196–98.

36. DIA Intelligence Summary, 24 August 1973, CDP-DOD.

37. Memorandum for the 40 Committee, enclosure, Rob Roy Ratcliff to Kissinger, 10 August 1973, CDP-NSC.

38. *Ultima Hora* published a list of embassy staff supposedly working for the CIA on 15 August. See Telegram, Davis to SecState, 15 August 1973, DOS/CFP; Davis, *Last Two Years*, 190–91; Telegram, Davis to SecState, 10 August 1973, DOS/CFP.

39. Kissinger as quoted in Memorandum, Richard T. Kennedy to Kissinger, 15 August 1973, CDP-NSC, and Kubisch interview, FD.

40. See Cable, Philips to CIA Station, 21 August 1973, CDP-CIA; Memorandum, William Colby to Kissinger and Kubisch, 28 August 1973, CDP-NSC; and *Covert Action in Chile*, 30.

41. Davis, *Last Two Years*, 152–54. On possible private Argentine sources of funding for Chilean paramilitary organization Fuerzas Nacionalistas de Ataque (FNA), see CIA Information Report, 28 August 1973, CDP-CIA.

42. This was denied by Banzer. Telegram, Brewin, Amembassy La Paz, to Sec-State, 24 August 1973, DOS/CFP.

43. Gaspari, *Ditadura Derrotada*, 348, and Davis, *Last Two Years*, 154.

44. Prats, *Memorias*, 394–96, and Intelligence Telegram, 23 July 1973, CDP-CIA.

45. Martínez Corbalá interview.

46. Davis, *Last Two Years*, 331–32.

47. "Chile Contingency Paper: Possible Military Action," Ad Hoc Interagency Working Group on Chile, enclosure, Memorandum, Pickering to Scowcroft, 8 September 1973, box 2196/RG59/NARA. On the DOS's desire to be in a position to "influence the situation," see Kornbluh, *Pinochet File*, 112.

48. Leacock, *Requiem for Revolution*.

49. Frei as recalled by Lincoln Gorden. Gordon interview, 2 May 2005.

50. Davis, *Last Two Years*, 214, 221, 356–58.

51. Memorandum to Pinochet, "Memorandum sobre la Situación Nacional," 27 August 1973, as quoted in Quiroga, *Compañeros*, 124–25.

52. Letter to Comandante en Jefe de la Armada Almirante José Toribio Merino Castro, Valparaiso, 5 September 1973, FJTM.

53. Memorandum, Jorden to Kissinger, 29 August 1973, CDP-NSC.

54. Marambio, *Armas de Ayer*, 76.

55. Report, Soviet Foreign Ministry, 16 July 1973, as quoted in Ulianova, "La Unidad Popular y el Golpe Militar," 105.

56. Ambassador Basov as quoted in Letter, East German embassy, Santiago (Friedel Trappen), to Berlin, 5 August 1973, V-33/MfAA. See also Haslam, *Assisted Suicide*, 210.

57. Almeyda, *Reencuentro con mi Vida*, 184–85. On similar advice voiced in public, see "Chou-en-lai: En la entrevista al periódico mexicano," *Excelsior*, 6 September 1972, in Pérez, "La Izquierda," 385–86.

58. Corvalán to Pajetta (Italian Communist Party) as quoted in Haslam, *Assisted Suicide*, 175.

59. Letter, Castro to Allende, 30 June 1973, in Castro, "Salvador Allende: His Example Lives On."

60. Otero interview; Oña interview, 16 December 2004; and Vázquez and Cubillas interview, 11 September 2005.

61. Oña interview, 16 December 2004.

62. Letter, Castro to Allende, 29 July 1973, in Timossi, *Grandes Alamedas*, 187–88.

63. Quiroga, *Compañeros*, 83.

64. Oña interview, 9 December 2004.

65. Ibid., and Estrada interview.

66. Conversations with Oña, March–April 2010.

67. Castro as quoted in Telegram, Schneider, Amembassy New Delhi, to SecState, 15 September 1973, DOS/CFP.

68. Estrada interview. On Allende's aversion to civil war, see Laura Allende as quoted in Davis, *Last Two Years*, 244.

69. Estrada Testimony, CMSA.

70. Pérez, "Salvador Allende, Apuntes Sobre su Dispositivo de Seguridad," 34, n. 8.

71. Estrada interview.

72. Telegram, Davis to SecState, 30 July 1973, DOS/CFP.

73. Estrada, "Allende's Death in Combat," 10, and Oña interview, 9 December 2004. See also, Timossi, *Grandes Alamedas*, 95.

74. Vázquez and Cubillas interview, 11 September 2005.

75. Otero, *Razón y Fuerza de Chile*, 58; Estrada interview; and Timossi, *Grandes Alamedas*, 96.

76. Otero interview, and Oña interview, 9 December 2004. Oña later recalled that around 80 percent of those stationed at Cuba's embassy in Santiago in the final month of Allende's government were members of the Tropas Especiales. Conversations with Oña, March–April 2010.

77. Oña interview, 16 December 2004, and Estrada interview. Carretero was due to leave Chile on 13 September.

78. Quiroga, *Compañeros*, 251–52. According to these testimonies, they also had fifty Walther P-50 submachine guns that did not come from the Cubans.

79. Estrada interview. Estrada says Havana trained and armed ten MAPU members before the coup.

80. Castro to Honecker, 21 and 26 February 1974, as quoted in Gleijeses, *Conflicting Missions*, 222.

81. Estrada interview.

82. "Dictadura Popular: Unico Remedio Contra Los Golpes de Estado," *Punto Final*, Extra Supplement, c. 3 July 1973, enclosure, Airgram, Davis to DOS, 13 July 1973, box 2197/RG59/NARA.

83. Dinges, *Condor Years*, 51.

84. Estrada Testimony, CMSA.

85. Letter, East German Embassy, Santiago (Friedel Trappen), to Berlin, 5 August 1973. See also Haslam, *Assisted Suicide*, 210–11.

86. CIA Information Report, 25 June 1973, CDP-CIA.

87. CIA Information Report, 3 August 1973, CDP-CIA. On general party directives to burn documents before the coup, see Silva interview, 31 March 2005.

88. Quiroga, *Compañeros*, 147.

89. Ibid., 101, 138.

90. Davis, *Last Two Years*, 204.

91. Oña interview, 16 December 2004.

92. DIA Intelligence Summary, 14 August 1973, CDP-DOD; Telegram, Davis to SecState, 14 August 1973, DOS/CFP; and Altamirano, 9 September 1973, as quoted in Davis, *Last Two Years*, 220.

93. Quiroga, *Compañeros*, 103, 136.

94. Ibid, 52.

95. Garcés, *Allende y la Experiencia Chilena*, 363.

96. Quiroga, *Compañeros*, 130–31.

97. Telegram, Davis to SecState, 17 August 1973, DOS/CFP.

98. Letter, Allende to Houari Boumedienne, 10 August 1973, in Vera Castillo, *Política Exterior Chilena*, 501–2.

99. Letter, Allende to Houari Boumedienne, 29 August 1973, in Vera Castillo, *Política Exterior Chilena*, 506–7.

100. Memorandum of Conversation, Letelier and Chile's Naval Council, 1 September 1973, FJTM.

101. Otero interview.

102. Isabel Allende interview, *South Bank Show* (ITV-UK), broadcast 22 April 2007.

103. Huerta interview, 23 March 2010.

104. Quiroga, *Compañeros*, 141.

105. Oña interview, 16 December 2004.

106. Soto, *El Ultimo Día*, 49.

107. Timossi, *Grandes Alamedas*, 16.

108. CIA Information Report, 8 September 1973, CDP-CIA.

109. Quotation from Verdugo, *Interferencia Secreta*, 23–24.

110. Telegram, Davis to SecState, 10 September 1973, DOS/CFP.

111. Garcés, *Allende y la Experiencia Chilena*, 360–61.

112. Ulianova, "La Unidad Popular y el Golpe Militar," 106–7. The East Germans also appear to have been persuaded that, although a coup was likely, it was not yet immediately imminent. As late as 9 September, the East German embassy—informed as always by its close relationship with the PCCh—reported that the armed forces were loyal to the constitution, the Carabineros could be "entirely trusted" to reinstate order in Chile, and the UP still had available reserves to combat reactionary forces. See "Report on Main Political Developments in Chile from the Embassy in Santiago," 9 September 1973, C/3320/BD/3/MfAA.

113. Oña interview, 16 December 2004.

114. Kornbluh, *Pinochet File*, 112.

115. Allende as quoted in Garcés, *Allende y la Experiencia Chilena*, 368–74.

116. DIA Intelligence Summary, "01.10 EDT," 11 September 1973, CDP-DOD (emphasis added).

117. Sigmund, *Overthrow of Allende*, 288–89.

118. Estrada, Vázquez, and Cubillas interviews.

119. Estrada interview; Estrada Testimony, CMSA; and Estrada, "Allende's Death in Combat." On the reasons for the Cuban embassy's stockpiling of weapons, see chapter 5.

120. Mario García Incháustegui Testimony, in Timossi, *Grandes Alamedas*, 98.

121. Otero interview; Estrada interview; Oña interview, 3 September 2005; and Vázquez and Cubillas interview, 11 September 2005.

122. Estrada interview, and Estrada Testimony, CMSA.

123. Perez, "Salvador Allende, Apuntes Sobre su Dispositivo de Seguridad," 36–37, n. 16, and Timossi, *Grandes Alamedas*, 76.

124. Allende, 8:45 A.M., 11 September, published as "La Moneda, 11 de Septiembre de 1973," *OE-SA*, 668.

125. Soto, *El Ultimo Día*, 69–70, 73, and Timossi, *Grandes Alamedas*, 52.

126. Espejo interview, 31 March 2010.

127. Soto, *El Ultimo Día*, 69–70, 73, and Beatriz Allende, Speech at the Plaza de la Revolución, Havana, 28 September 1973, in Timossi, *Grandes Alamedas*, 55.

128. Estrada Testimony, CMSA, and Estrada interview.

129. Soto, *El Ultimo Día*, 68, and Verdugo, *Interferencia Secreta*, 54.

130. "Andrés Pascal [Allende] recuerda la participación del MIR en el gobierno de Salvador Allende," La Fogata Digital, and Beatriz Allende, 28 September 1973, in Timossi, *Grandes Alamedas*, 53.

131. Davis, *Last Two Years*, 253; Soto, *El Ultimo Día*, 82, 90; and Verdugo, *Interferencia Secreta*, 59.

132. Beatriz Allende, 28 September 1973, in Timossi, *Grandes Alamedas*, 53.

133. Allende, "Last Words," in Cockcroft, *Allende Reader*, 239.

134. Timossi, *Grandes Alamedas*, 36–38, and Davis, *Last Two Years*, 252–63.

135. Estrada interview, and Jaramillo Edwards interviews. See also Jaramillo Edwards, "Vuelo de Noche," 90, and Mario García Incháustegui Testimony, in Timossi, *Grandes Alamedas*, 96.

136. Estrada interview, and Oña interview, 3 September 2005.

137. Timossi, *Grandes Alamedas*, 96. The number 200 is also cited in Telegram, Davis to SecState, "Cubans Go Home," 12 September 1973, DOS/CFP. The first U.S. reference the author has found of military attacks against the embassy is a CIA Information Report on 11 September that details a planned attack due to take place at 6:30 P.M. Davis reports that he learned of events via the Israeli ambassador who had heard about them from Mexico's ambassador. See also Oña interview, 16 December 2004.

138. Estrada interview.

139. Oña interview, 9 December 2004.

140. Quotation from Davis, *Last Two Years*, 242, and Telegram, SecState to U.S. Mission, UN, "Noon Wrapup," 15 September 1973, DOS/CFP.

141. Quotation from Davis, *Last Two Years*, 263.

142. Soto, *El Ultimo Día*, 87, and Davis, *Last Two Years*, 263.

143. Soto, *El Ultimo Día*, 87–88.

144. Verdugo, *Interferencia Secreta*, 38; Davis, *Last Two Years*, 232; and Silva interview.

145. Quiroga, *Compañeros*, 150–52, and Pérez, "Años de Disparos y Tortura," 359–60.

146. Davis, *Last Two Years*, 247.

147. Estrada interview, and Oña interviews, 15 April and 2 May 2006.

148. Estrada interview.

149. Cable, Davis to SecState, "Cubans Go Home," 12 September 1973, and Central Intelligence Bulletin, 13 September 1973, CDP-CIA.

150. Testimony, Mario García Incháustegui, in Timossi, *Grandes Alamedas*, 99–91.

151. Timossi interview.

152. Estrada claims there were close to 100 casualties. See Estrada interview. Oña recalled that ambulances arrived to collect wounded or dead but thinks it was far fewer than 100. Oña interview, 16 December 2004, and conversations with Oña, March–April 2010. On Cuban wounded, see *Bohemia*, 21 September 1973, 46–49.

153. Fidel Castro, Speech at the Plaza de la Revolución, Havana, 28 September 1973, in Timossi, *Grandes Alamedas*, 191.

154. *Testimonios Chile*, 32, 34, 36.

155. Ulianova, "La Unidad Popular y el Golpe Militar," 112.

156. Quotations from Verdugo, *Interferencia Secreta*, 89–90.

157. Pinochet as quoted in Soto, *El Ultimo Día*, 112.

158. Estrada, "Allende's Death in Combat," 11.

159. Telegram, Bennett, U.S. Mission UN, to SecState, 14 September 1973, and Telegram, Olson, Amembassy Freetown, to SecState, 17 September 1973, DOS/CFP.

160. Estrada, "Allende's Death in Combat," 10–11; Estrada Testimony, CMSA; and Estrada interview.

161. Vázquez and Cubillas interview, 11 September 2005, and Oña interviews, 2004–10.

162. Ibid., and conversations with Oña, March–April 2010.

163. "Ruptura de Relaciones Diplomaticas," 14 September 1973, *Memoria del Ministerio*, AMRE, 41.

164. Estrada interview.

165. Marambio, *Armas de Ayer*, 121–76.

166. CIA Information Report, 21 September 1973, CDP-CIA.

167. Quiroga, *Compañeros*, 136.

168. Castro to Honecker, 21 February 1974, as quoted in Skierka, *Castro*, 204.

169. Alarcón, 17 September 1973, as quoted in Telegram, Scali, U.S. Mission UN, to SecState, 18 September 1973, DOS/CFP.

170. Telegrams, Amembassy Dar-Es-Salaam to SecState, 14 September 1973, U.S. Mission Berlin to SecState, 15 September 1973, and Volpe, Amembassy Rome, to SecState, 18 September 1973, DOS/CFP; and Situation Report no. 12, DOS Operations Center, "Situation in Chile as of 0700 hours (EDT) Sept. 14, 1973," 14 September 1973, box 2196/RG59/NARA.

171. MacEoin, *Struggle for Dignity*, 194–99.

172. Telegram, SecState to Amembassy, Santiago, "USG Attitude toward Junta," 12 September 1973, DOS/CFP.

173. Kissinger, 1 October 1973, as quoted in Kornbluh, *Pinochet File*, 203.

174. Intelligence Memorandum, "Consequences of a Military Coup in Chile," 1 August 1973, CDP-CIA

175. Telegrams, Davis to SecState, "Gen Pinochet's Request for Meeting with MILGP [Military Group] Officer," 12 September 1973, and Davis to SecState "Relations with New Chilean Government," 13 September 1973, DOS/CFP.

176. Telegram, Davis to SecState, "Gen Pinochet's Request for Meeting with MILGP Officer," 12 September 1973.

177. Garcés and Landau, *Orlando Letelier*, 44–46.

178. DCI Briefing, Washinton Special Actions Group Meeting, 14 September 1973, CDP-NSC.

179. Kornbluh, *Pinochet File*, 155, and Record of Conversation, Davis and Pinochet, 12 October 1973, Telegram, Davis to SecState, 12 October 1973, DOS/CFP.

180. Intelligence Memorandum, "Consequences of a Military Coup in Chile," 1 August 1973.

181. "Chile Contingency Paper," 8 September 1973.

182. Airgram, Davis to DOS, 12 October 1973, box 2198/RG59/NARA.

183. Telegram, Davis to SecState, "FMS Sales to FACH," 15 September 1973, DOS/ CFP; and Kornbluh, *Pinochet File*, 203.

184. Record of Conversation, Hennessy, Weintraub, and Saenz, no date, Telegram, SecState to U.S. Mission, UN, 25 September 1973, DOS/CFP.

185. Telegram, Davis to SecState, 21 September 1973.

186. Record of Conversation, Hennessy, Weintraub, and Saenz, no date, Telegram, SecState to U.S. Mission, UN, 25 September 1973.

187. Record of Conversation, Huerta and Kubisch, 11 October 1973, Telex, Eberhard, Embachile Washington to MRE, 11 October 1973; and Record of Conversation, Huerta and Kissinger, 12 October 1973, Telex, Eberhard to MRE, 12 October 1973, Telex R: 491-/EEUU/1973/AMRE. See also Record of Conversation, Huerta and Kubisch, 11 October 1973, Telegram, SecState to Amembassy Santiago, 12 October 1973, DOS/CFP.

188. Record of Conversation, Huerta and Kissinger, 12 October 1973.

189. Record of Conversation, Davis and Pinochet, 12 October 1973.

190. PL480 allocations dropped to 40 percent in 1975 and 28 percent in 1976. Schoultz, *Beneath the United States*, 360–61.

191. Kornbluh, *Pinochet File*, 204–6.

192. Ibid., 212–17, and Dinges, *Condor Years*, 68–71, 101–5.

193. Dinges, *Condor Years*, 5.

194. Briefing Paper "Economic Assistance Needs of the New Government of Chile and Possible Responses," enclosure, Memorandum Pickering to Scowcroft, 14 September 1973.

195. Ibid., and Record of Conversation, Davis and Heitman, Ambassador Designate, 27 September 1973, Telegram, Davis to SecState, 28 September 1973, DOS/CFP.

196. Record of Conversation, Huerta and Kissinger, 12 October 1973.

197. Record of Conversation, Davis and Pinochet, 18 October 1973, Telegram, Davis to SecState, 18 October 1973, DOS/CFP.

198. Quotation from Gaspari, *Ditadura Derrotada*, 355.

199. McSherry, *Predatory States*, 57, and Dinges, *Condor Years*, 264. See also Record of Conversation, Davis and Heitman, 27 September 1973, and Gaspari, *Ditadura Derrotada*, 357–58.

200. Robin, *Escuadrones de la Muerte: La Escuela Francesa*.

201. Oficio, Brazilian Embassy, Santiago, to Itamaraty, "Compra de ascensores ATLAS. Dificuldades de crédito," 17 September 1973, Oficios/Chile 1973 (9)/AMRE-Brasila; and Telegram, Davis to Amembassy Brasilia, 21 September 1973, DOS/CFP.

202. Telegram, Davis to SecState, 18 September 1973, DOS/CFP.

203. Telegram, Ernest Siracusa, Amembassy Montevideo, to SecState, 18 September 1973, DOS/CFP.

204. DIA Intelligence Summary, 15 September 1973, CDP-DOD; and Telegram, Siracusa to SecState, 18 September 1973.

205. Telegram, Scali to SecState, 10 October 1973, DOS/CFP.

206. Telegram, SecState to Amembassy Santiago, "Security Council Meeting," 14 September 1973, DOS/CFP.

207. Record of Conversation, Davis and Enrique Bernstein, MRE, 15 September 1973, Telegram, Davis to SecState, 15 September 1973, DOS/CFP; and Kornbluh, *Pinochet File*, 206–8.

208. Record of Conversation, Davis and Pinochet, 18 October 1973.

209. See, for example, Oficio Sec., Embachile Washington to Señor Ministro, 6 December 1974, Oficios Sec., Res., Conf., E./R./EEUU/1974/AMRE.

210. Telcon, Kissinger and Nixon, 16 September 1973, box 22/Telcons/NSCF/NPMP.

211. Telcon, Kissinger and Rush, 13 September 1973, box 22/Telcons/NSCF/NPMP; and Kissinger, *Years of Upheaval*, 411.

212. Memorandum, Jorden to Kissinger, 16 September 1973, CDP-NSC.

213. Kornbluh, *Pinochet File*, 222–23.

214. Airgram, Davis to DOS, 12 October 1973, box 2198/RG59/NARA.

215. Pinochet as paraphrased in ibid.

216. Memorandum of Conversation, President Houari Boumedienne, Foreign Minister Bouteflika, Secretary of State Henry Kissinger, Assistant Secretary Joseph Sisco, and Peter Rodman (NSC Staff), the Presidency, Algiers, 13 December 1973, box 1027/NSCF/NPMP.

Conclusion

1. See for example, Lundestad, "How (Not) to Study the Origins of the Cold War," 69–75.

2. See, for example, Joseph and Spenser, *In from the Cold*.

3. Joseph, "What We Now Know," in Joseph and Spenser, *In from the Cold*, 3. See also Brands, *Latin America's Cold War*.

4. Foreign Ministry Report "Initial Assessment of Comrade Fidel Castro's Visit to Poland," 13 June 1972, wiazka 3/13/78/AMSZ.

5. On Soviet efforts to reassure the United States that the USSR meant no harm to U.S. interests or the Nixon administration's domestic position when it came to the "sensitive" issue of Cuba, see Dobrynin's apologies for any inconvenience caused to the United States as a result of a Soviet naval flotilla's visit to Cuba and his promises that Kosygin's October 1971 visit to Havana would be "short" and "low profile." Memorandum of Conversation (U.S.), Kissinger and Dobrynin, 15 October 1971, in Geyer and Selvage, *Soviet-American Relations*, 491–92.

6. Jova as quoted in Memorandum, Ambassador Marian Renke, Polish Embassy, Havana, to the Ministry of Foreign Affairs, "Certain Aspects of Cuba's Situation and Politics on the American Continent," 15 October 1971, wiazka 5/40/75/AMSZ.

7. Jaipal, *Non-Alignment*, 100.

8. Kennan to Acheson, 29 March 1950, in Holden and Zolov, *Latin America and the United Sates*, 195–98.

9. Walters, *Silent Missions*, 389. This was also the thesis that underscored Ronald Reagan's Latin American policies in the 1980s and was outlined explicitly in Kirkpatrick, "Dictatorships and Double Standards."

10. MRE Study, 13 April 1973, in Uribe, *Black Book*, 138.

11. Prizel, *Latin America through Soviet Eyes*, 153. See also Miller, *Soviet Relations with Latin America*, 148–84, 218.

12. Quotation from Kornbluh, *Pinochet File*, xiv.

13. Quotation from Intelligence Note, INR, "Coup in Chile Reveals African Mistrust of US," 10 October 1973, box 2198/RG59/NARA; and Telegram, Schneider to SecState, 16 September, DOS/CFP.

14. Foreign Ministry Memorandum, Asesor Político to Señor Ministro, "Preparación de Conferencia de Países No Alineados," 5 June 1973, Cumbre de Paises No Alineados: Zambia-1970/AMRE.

15. Fanon, *Wretched of the Earth*, 79–84.

16. Kennan to Acheson, 29 March 1950, in Holden and Zolov, *Latin America and the United Sates*, 195–98.

17. Kubisch interview, FD; Telcon, Kissinger and Emilo Rabasa, 18 September 1973, box 22/Telcons/NSCF/NPMP; Kissinger, Address to Luncheon for Latin American Foreign Ministers, Other Heads of Delegations to General Assembly, and UN Permanent Representatives, 5 October 1973, Telegram, SecState to All American Republic Diplomatic Posts, 7 October 1973, DOS/CFP; and *Memoria del Ministerio*, 71.

18. *Bohemia*, 21 September 1973, 46–49.

19. Piñeiro, Speeches to DGLN, 2 March and 28 April 1974, in Suárez, *Manuel Piñeiro*, 109.

20. Dinges, *Condor Years*, 56.

21. Castro to Honecker, 21 February 1975, as quoted in Skierka, *Fidel Castro*, 206.

22. Intelligence Memorandum, Office of Current Intelligence and Directorate of Operations, "The Status of Cuban Subversion in Latin America," 2 May 1975, CREST/NARA.

23. Soto interview, 7 July 2005.

24. Piñeiro, Speech to DGLN, 25 July 1974, in Suárez, *Manuel Piñeiro*, 120.

25. Kornbluh and Blight, "Our Hidden Dialogue with Castro."

26. Gleijeses, *Conflicting Missions*, 228, 390–99

27. Brezhnev, 13 January 1980, as quoted in Garthoff, *Détente and Confrontation*, 928–29.

28. Telegram, SecState to Chargé Thompson, 5 December 1973, box 2194/RG59/NARA.

29. Ulianova, "La Unidad Popular y el Golpe," 112–13.

30. Memorandum of Conversation, Zhou Enlai, Kissinger, et al., 13 November 1973, and Memorandum from the President's Assistant for National Security Affairs to President Nixon, 19 November 1973, docs. 59 and 62/FRUS/1969–1976/XVIII.

31. Schmitter, "Lessons of the Chilean Coup," 343.

32. Santoni, "La Via Cilena al Socialismo nella Riflessione del Partito Comunista Italiano"; Urban, *Moscow and the Italian Communist Party*, 268–69; and Schmitter, "Lessons of the Chilean Coup in Europe," 347.

33. Schmitter, "Lessons of the Chilean Coup in Europe," 347–55.

34. Furci, *Chilean Communist Party*, 121–24.

35. Ulianova, "La Unidad Popular y el Golpe," 127, and Prizel, *Latin America through Soviet Eyes*, 167.

36. Piñeiro, Speech to DGLN, 28 April 1974, in Suárez, *Manuel Piñeiro*, 12, 107, 114.

37. Airgram, Davis to SecState, "The Military Junta at One Month," 12 October 1973, box 2198/RG59/NARA.

38. Joan Garcés at "The Pinochet Case and Its Consequences 10 Years On" conference, London, 11 November 2008.

39. Estrada interview.

40. Allende as quoted by Fidel Castro, 28 September 1973, in Timossi, *Grandes Alamedas*, 179.

41. Allende, "Last Words," in Cockcroft, *Allende Reader*, 241.

A Note on Sources

1. Telcon, Kissinger and Rogers, 14 September 1970, in Kornbluh, "New Kissinger 'Telcons' Reveal Chile Plotting at Highest Levels of U.S. Government."

2. Friedman, "Retiring the Puppets, Bringing Latin America Back In," 625.

3. Blanton, "Recovering the Memory of the Cold War," 67

4. Documents from this period have not yet been indexed. At present they are filed by document type (Oficios, Telex, Aerogram), classification (Confidenciales/Ordinarios), direction of correspondence, (Enviados/Recibidos or E./R.), country, and year.

5. For example, see Quiroga, *Compañeros*; Soto, *El Ultimo Día*; Estrada, "Allende's Death In Combat"; Bautista Yofre, *Misión Argentina*; Martínez Corbalá, *Instantes de Decisión*; Marambio, *Armas de Ayer*; interviews with Paul Wimert and Nathaniel Davis (1999); Pérez, "La Izquierda"; Ulianova and Fediakova, "Chile en los Archivos de la URSS (1959-1973)"; and Gonzalez Pino and Fontaine Talavera, *Mil Días (I and II)*.

6. All online documents were accessed over the period 2003–10. Documents belonging to the Chile Declassification Project can be located by date after selecting declassification tranches and using the "List All" function.

7. On the burning of Allende's papers, see Oña interview, 16 December 2004, and Soto, *El Ultimo Día*, 69–70, 73.

8. Castro, "Salvador Allende: His Example Lives On."

9. Suárez, *Manuel Piñeiro*, 4.

10. On underlying questions, see Miller, *Soviet Relations with Latin America*, 127–29.

11. Gustafson, *Hostile Intent*, 172–73.

12. UPI Press report, 11 September 1970, as quoted in Oficio Conf., Embachile Rio to Señor Ministro, 17 September 1970, Oficios Conf., E./R./Brasil/1970/AMRE.

13. Mario García Incháustegui, Press Conference, 15 September 1973, in *Bohemia*, 29 September 1973, 49; and Crimmins interview.

Bibliography

Primary Sources

Archival Documents

Brazil
Arquivo Histórico, Ministério das Relações Exteriores, Brasilia
    Oficios Recebidos da Embaixada do Brasil, Santiago, 1970–73
    Oficios Recebidos da Embaixada do Brasil, Washington, D.C., 1970–73
    Telegramas Recebidos da Embaixada do Brasil, Washington, D.C., 1970–73

Chile
Archivo General Histórico, Ministerio de Relaciones Exteriores, Santiago
    Discursos del Presidente S. Allende Gossens, 1971
        Fondo, Hernán Santa Cruz
        Memorandos
            Dirección Economica, 1967–74
            Gabinete del Ministro, 1963–87
            Jurídicos
            Políticos
        Memoria del Ministerio de Relaciones Exteriores, 1970–73
    Oficios, Telexes y Aerograms (Enviados y Recibidos)
        Argelia
        Brasil
        Cuba
        Estados Unidos
        México
        Naciones Unidas
        OEA
        Perú
        URSS
Archivo Nacional, Santiago
    Fondo Orlando Letelier de Solar
Centro de Investigación y Documentación en Historia de Chile Contemporáneo,
        Universidad Finis Terrae, Santiago
    Fondo José Toribio Merino

Cuba
Casa Memorial Salvador Allende, Havana
  Press Archive, 1971
  Private Collection (Miscellaneous Chilean Embassy Files)
  Testimonies (Ulises Estrada and Jorge Timossi)

German Democratic Republic
Bundesarchiv, Berlin, Germany
  Stiftung Archiv der Parteien und Massenorganisationen der DDR im
    Bundesarchiv
Ministerium für Auswärtige Angelegenheiten Berlin, Germany

Poland
Archiwum Ministerstwa Spraw Zagranicznych, Warsaw
  Zespoly 40/75, 41/75, 12/78, and 13/78

United Kingdom
The National Archives, Kew, London
  Prime Minister's Files
  Records of the Foreign and Commonwealth Office
    FCO7: American and Latin American Departments, 1967–76
    FCO59: Economic Relations Department and Foreign and Commonwealth
      Office, Financial Policy and Aid Department and Financial Policy
      Department, 1967–75
    FCO61: United Nations (Economic and Social) Department, 1967–76

United States
National Archives and Records Administration, College Park, Maryland
  Central Intelligence Agency Records Search Tool
    Record Group 59: General Records of the Department of State, Subject and
      Numeric Files, 1970–73
    Record Group 84: American Embassy Files, Santiago
Nixon Presidential Materials Project, National Archives, College Park, Maryland
  National Security Council Files
    Institutional Files
    Henry A. Kissinger Telephone Conversation Transcripts
    Subject Files
  Nixon White House Tapes
  President's Office Files
  President's Personal Files

Interviews by the Author

Carlos Alzugaray, Cuban diplomat, 10 September 2005, Havana, Cuba.
Carlos Amat, Cuban diplomat, 24 April 2006, Havana, Cuba.

Ana Maria Bussi, Allende's niece, 9 April 2010, Santiago, Chile.

Manuel Cabieses, Mirista and managing editor, *Punto Final*, 25 March 2010, Santiago, Chile.

Carlos Chain, Cuban intelligence officer (early 1960s) and vice minister for foreign affairs (1967–72), 8 December 2004, Havana, Cuba.

John H. Crimmins, deputy assistant secretary for Latin American Affairs (1969–73) and U.S. ambassador in Brasilia (1973–78), 3 May 2005, Maryland.

Patricia Espejo, private secretary to Allende, 31 March 2010, Santiago, Chile.

Ulises Estrada Lescaille, head of Chilean operations at the DGLN (1970–73) and chargé d'affaires for political work and defense of the Cuban embassy in Chile (August–September 1973), 13 December 2004, Havana, Cuba.

Carlos Goméz, PS militant and member of the Chilean ELN, 23 October 2004, Los Andes, Chile.

Lincoln Gordon, U.S. ambassador to Brazil (1961–66), 2 May 2005, Washington, D.C.

Felix Huerta, PS militant and member of the Chilean ELN, 23 March and 20 April 2010, Santiago, Chile.

Ramon Huidobro, Chilean diplomat and ambassador to Argentina (1971–73), 18 and 28 October 2004, Santiago, Chile.

Isabel Jaramillo Edwards, private secretary to Allende, 24 November 2004 and 21 September 2005, Havana, Cuba.

Hilda Lopez, Quimantú employee and PCCh militant, 28 October 2004, Santiago, Chile.

Gonzalo Martínez Corbalá, Mexican ambassador in Santiago (1972–73), 30 December 2009, Mexico City, Mexico.

Pedro Martínez Pírez, first secretary of Cuban embassy in Chile, (1962–64), 15 December 2004, Havana, Cuba.

Luis Fernández Oña, DGLN officer and political counselor at the Cuban embassy in Chile (1970–73), 9 and 16 December 2004, 3 September 2005, 15 April and 2 May 2006, Havana, Cuba, and conversations, March–April 2010, Santiago, Chile.

Lisandro Otero, Cuban cultural attaché in Chile (1970–73), 17 December 2004, Havana, Cuba.

Anibal Palma, PR member and Chilean deputy foreign minister (1972), 23 October 2004, Santiago, Chile.

Andrés Pascal Allende, Mirista and Allende's nephew, 6 April 2010, Santiago, Chile.

Gonzalo Rojas Pizarro, chargé d'affaires at Chilean embassy in Cuba (1972–73), 1 November 2004, Chillán, Chile.

Luis Suárez Salazar, DGLN analyst, 10 December 2004 and 12 September 2005, Havana, Cuba.

Luis Silva, PS militant, 31 March 2005, London.

Oscar Soto Guzman, Allende's private cardiologist, 29 April 2005, Washington, D.C., and 7 July 2005, Madrid, Spain.

Volodia Teitelboim, PCCh senator, 5 November 2004, Santiago, Chile.

Jorge Timossi, Prensa Latina journalist in Santiago (1970–73), 14 September 2005, Havana, Cuba.

Javier Urrutia, representative of CORFO in the United States and financial advisor to the Chilean embassy in Washington, D.C., 27 October and 3 November 2004, Santiago, Chile.

Viron "Pete" Vaky, assistant to Kissinger for Latin American affairs (April 1969–November 1970), 27 April 2005, Washington, D.C.

Michel Vázquez Montes de Oca and Nelly A. Cubillas Pino, commercial attaché in Chile (1970–73) and his wife, 11 September 2005 and 23 April 2006, Havana, Cuba.

José Vierra, Cuban diplomat, 28 April 2006, Havana, Cuba.

Online Documents

Castro, F. "Salvador Allende: His Example Lives On." *Escambray*, 30 June 2008. http://www.escambray.cu/Eng/Special/Comradefidel/Callende080630857. htm.

———. "The Second Declaration of Havana." 4 February 1962. http://www.walterlippmann.com/fc-02-04-1962.pdf.

Central Foreign Policy Files, Access to Archival Databases (AAD), NARA. http://.aad.archives.gov/add/.

Che Guevara Internet Archive. http://www.marxists.org/archive/guevara/index.htm.

Chile Declassification Project. Freedom of Information Act Reading Room, Department of State.

   CIA Documents. http://foia.state.gov/SearchColls/CIA.asp.

   Defense Department Documents. http://foia.state.gov/SearchColls/DOD.asp.

   NARA Documents. http://foia.state.gov/SearchColls/Nara.asp.

   National Security Council Documents. http://foia.state.gov/SearchColls/ NSC.asp.

CNN Cold War Series (Interviews), Episode 18: Backyard, National Security Archive. http://www.gwu.edu/~nsarchiv/coldwar/interviews/.

Derechos Chile. http://www.chipsites.com/derechos/1973_eng.html.

Fidel Castro History Archive. http://www.marxists.org/history/cuba/archive/castro/.

Fidel Castro Speech Database, LANIC. http://lanic.utexas.edu/la/cb/cuba/ castro.html.

Foreign Relations of the United States, 1969–1976. Vol. 4: *Foreign Assistance, International Development, Trade Policies, 1969–1972.* http://www.state.gov/r/pa/ho/ frus/nixon/iv/index.htm.

Foreign Relations of the United States, 1969–1976. Vol. 12: *China, 1969–1972.* http://history.state.gov/historicaldocuments/frus1969-76v17.

Foreign Relations of the United States, 1969–1976. Vol. 13: *China, 1973–1976.* http://history.state.gov/historicaldocuments/frus1969-76v18.

Foreign Relations of the United States, 1969–1976. Vol. E-10: *Documents on American Republics, 1969–1972.* http://history.state.gov/historicaldocuments/ frus1969-76ve10.

Frontline Diplomacy: The Foreign Affairs Oral History Collection of the Association for Diplomatic Studies and Training, Library of Congress. http://memory.loc.gov/ammem/collections/diplomacy/index.html.

The Green Book of U.S. Overseas Loans and Grants. http://www.usaid.gov/policy/greenbook.html.

The National Security Archive, George Washington University, Washington, D.C. http://www.gwu.edu/~nsarchiv/.

Doyle, K., ed. "The Nixon Tapes: Secret Recording from the Nixon White House on Luis Echeverria and Much Much More." August 2003. http://www.gwu.edu/~nsarchiv/NSAEBB/NSAEBB95/index2.htm.

Kornbluh, P., ed. "Brazil Conspired with U.S. to Overthrow Allende." August 2009. http://www.gwu.edu/~nsarchiv/NSAEBB/NSAEBB282/index.htm.

———, ed. "Chile Documentation Project." http://www.gwu.edu/~nsarchiv/latin_america/chile.htm.

———, ed. "New Kissinger 'Telcons' Reveal Chile Plotting at Highest Levels of U.S. Government." September 2008. http://www.gwu.edu/~nsarchiv/NSAEBB/NSAEBB255/index.htm.

Osorio, C., ed. "Argentine Military Believed U.S. Gave Go-Ahead for Dirty War." August 2002. http://www.gwu.edu/~nsarchiv/NSAEBB/NSAEBB73/index3.htm.

———, ed. "Nixon: 'Brazil Helped Rig the Uruguayan Elections' 1971." June 2002. http://www.gwu.edu/~nsarchiv/NSAEBB/NSAEBB71/.

The Nixon Presidential Library and Museum, "December 9, 2010 Materials Release." http://nixonlibrary.gov/virtuallibrary/documents/dec10.php#selection.

Pascal Allende, A. "Andrés Pascal ecuerda la Participación del MIR en el Gobierno de Salvador Allende." La Fogata Digital. http://www.lafogata.org/chile/sep_pascal.htm.

Strategic Choices in the Design of Truth Commissions. www.truthcommission.org.

Memoirs, Interviews, Speeches, and Collated Documents

Allende, S. *America Latina: Voz de Un Pueblo Continente; Discursos del Presidente Allende en sus Giras por Argentina, Ecuador, Colombia y Perú.* Santiago: Consejería de Difusión de la Presidencia de la Republica, 1971.

———. *Conferencia Ofrecida por el Dr. Salvador Allende en la Sala Teatro de los Trabajadores de Ministro de Hacienda el dia 7 de Febrero de 1962.* Havana: Ministerio de Hacienda, Sección Sindical, 1962.

Almeyda Medina, C. "The Foreign Policy of the Unidad Popular Government." In *Chile at the Turning Point: Lessons of the Socialist Years, 1970–1973,* edited by F. G. Gill, R. E. Lagos, and H. A. Landsberger. Philadelphia: ISHI, 1979.

———. *Obras Escogidas, 1947–1992.* Santiago: Centro de Estudios Políticos Latino Americanos Simon Bolivar, 1992.

———. *La Política Internacional del Gobierno de la Unidad Popular.* Mexico City: UNAM, Facultad de Ciencas Políticas y Sociales, Mexico City, 1977.

———. *Reencuentro con mi Vida.* Guadalajara: Universidad de Guadalajara, 1988.

Arancibia Claval, P., ed. *Conversando con Roberto Kelly V.: Recuerdos de una Vida.* Santiago: Editorial Biblioteca Americana, 2005.

Arrate, J. "Cuando Perdimos a un Gran Dirigente." *Rocinante: Arte, Cultura, Sociedad* 72, no. 7 (October 2004).

Castillo Estay, N. "Mucha Gente Me Culpó Cuando Se Suicidó la Tati." *La Tercera: Reportajes,* 14 October 2007.

Cockcroft, J. D., ed. *Chile's Voice of Democracy: Salvador Allende Reader.* Melbourne: Ocean Press, 2000.

Colby, W., and P. Forbath. *Honourable Men: My Life in the CIA.* London: Hutchison, 1978.

Cooper, M. *Pinochet and Me: An Anti-Memoir.* London: Verso, 2002.

Corvalán, L. *El Gobierno de Salvador Allende.* Santiago: LOM, 2003.

Covert Action in Chile, 1963–1973: Staff Report of the Select Committee to Study Governmental Operations with Respect to Intelligence Activities. 1975. Honolulu, Hawaii: University Press of the Pacific, 2005.

Cuba-Chile. Havana, 1972.

Davis, N. *The Last Two Years of Salvador Allende.* London: I. B. Tauris, 1985.

Debray, R. "Allende habla con Debray." *Punto Final,* special issue, 126, no. 16 (March 1971).

Diaz Casanueva, H. "Política Multilateral del Presidente Salvador Allende en sus Aspectos Políticos y de Derechos Humanos, a la Luz de las Experiencias de un Embajador." In *La Política Exterior Chilena Durante el Gobierno del Presidente Salvador Allende 1970–1973,* edited by J. Vera Castillo. Santiago: Ediciones IERIC, 1987.

Edwards, J. *Persona Non Grata.* 4th ed., Santiago: Tiempo de Memoria, 2000.

Estrada Lescaille, U. "Allende's Death in Combat." *Tricontinental,* year 37, no. 157 (2003).

———. *Tania: Undercover with Che Guevara in Bolivia.* Melbourne: Ocean Press, 2006.

Fidel in Chile: "A Symbolic Meeting between Two Historical Processes." Selected Speeches of Major Fidel Castro during His Visit to Chile, November 1971. New York: International Publishers, 1972.

Frei Montalva, E. "The Alliance That Lost Its Way." *Foreign Affairs* 45, no. 3 (1967): 437–48.

Garcés, J. E. *Allende y La Experiencia Chilena; Las Armas de la Política.* 3rd ed. Santiago: Ediciones BAT, 1990.

Garcés, J. E., and S. Landau, eds. *Orlando Letelier: Testimonio y Vindicación.* Madrid: Siglo Vientiuno de España Editores, S.A., 1998.

Geyer, D. C., and D. E. Selvage, eds. *Soviet-American Relations: The Détente Years, 1969–1972.* Washington, D.C.: U. S. Government Printing Office, 2007.

Gonzalez Pino, M., and A. Fontaine Talavera, eds. *Los Mil Días de Allende.* Tomo I y II. Santiago: Centro de Estudios Publicos, 1997.

Gray, R. B., ed. *Latin America and the United States in the 1970s.* Itasca, Ill.: F. E. Peacock Publishers, 1971.

Haldeman, H. R. *The Haldeman Diaries: Inside the Nixon White House*. New York: G. P. Putnam's, 1994.

Hart Dávalos, A. *Homenaje a Miguel Enríquez*. Havana: Ediciones De La Cultural, 1990.

Holden, R., and E. Zolov, eds. *Latin America and the United States: A Documentary History*. New York: Oxford University Press, 2000.

Interview with Isabel Allende. *South Bank Show* (ITV-UK). Broadcast 22 April 2007.

Jara, J. *Victor: An Unfinished Song*. London: Jonathan Cape, 1983.

Jaramillo Edwards, I. "Testimonios: Vuelo de Noche." *Casa de Las Americas*, no. 3 (January–March 1996).

Jorquera, C. *El Chicho Allende*. Santiago: Ediciones BA, 1990.

Julien-Landelius, N. "Resumidas Cuentas." Unpublished manuscript, 2004.

Kissinger, H. A. *American Foreign Policy: Three Essays*. New York: Weidenfeld & Nicolson, 1969.

———. *The White House Years*. London: Weidenfeld and Nicolson, 1979.

———. *Years of Renewal*. New York: Simon & Schuster, 1999.

———. *Years of Upheaval*. London: Weidenfeld and Nicolson, 1982.

Korry, E. "Los Estados Unidos en Chile y Chile en los Estados Unidos: Una Retrospectiva Política y Económica (1963–1975)." *Estudios Publicos*, no. 72 (1998): 1–48.

Marambio, M. *Las Armas de Ayer*. 3rd ed. Santiago: La Tercera-Debate, 2008.

Martínez Corbalá, G. *Instantes de Decisión: Chile 1972–1973*. Mexico City: Grijalbo, 1998.

Martner, G. *El Gobierno del Presidente Salvador Allende, 1970–1973: Una Evaluación*. Concepción: Ediciones Literatura Americana Reunida, 1988.

Muñoz, H. "The International Policy of the Socialist Party and Foreign Relations of Chile." In *Latin American Nations in World Politics*, edited by H. Muñoz and J. S. Tulchin. Boulder, Colo.: Westview, 1984.

Neruda, P. *Incitación al Nixonicidio y Alabanza de la Revolución Chilena*. Santiago: Quimantú, 1973.

Nixon, R. *The Memoirs of Richard Nixon*. London: Arrow, 1979.

———. *Six Crises*. London: Allen, 1962.

Otero, L. *Llover Sobre Mojado: Una Reflexión Sobre La Historia*. Havana: Editorial Letras Cubanas, 1997.

———. *Razón y Fuerza de Chile*. Mexico City: Katún, 1984.

Pérez, C., ed. "La Izquierda Chilena Vista por la Izquierda." *Estudios Publicos*, no. 81 (2001): 337–579.

Pey, V., et al., eds. *Salvador Allende, 1908–1973: Obras Escogidas*. Santiago: Centro de Estudios Políticos Latino Americanos Simon Bolivar, 1992.

Pinochet Ugarte, A. *Augusto Pinochet: Diálogos con su Historia. Conversasiones Inéditas con María Eugenia Oyarzún*. Santiago: Editorial Sudamericana, 1999.

Plank, J. "We Should Start Talking to Castro." In *Latin America and the United States in the 1970s*, edited by R. B. Gray. Itasca, Ill.: F. E. Peacock Publishers, 1971.

Prats Gonzalez, C. *Memorias: Testimonio de un Soldado*. Santiago: Pehuén, 1985.

Soto Guzmán, O. *El Ultimo Día de Salvador Allende*. Santiago: Aguila Chilena de Ediciones, 1999.

Suárez Salazar, L., ed. *Manuel Piñeiro: Che Guervara and the Latin American Revolutionary Movements*. Melbourne: Ocean Press, 2001.

Subversion in Chile: A Case Study in U.S. Corporate Intrigue in the Third World. Nottingham: Spokesman Books, 1972.

Testimonios Chile: Septiembre 1973. Argentina: Ediciones de Crisis, 1974.

Timossi, J., ed. *Fascismos Parallelos: A 30 Años del Golpe de Estado en Chile*. Havana: Ciencias Sociales, 2003.

Ulianova, O., and E. Fediakova, eds. "Chile en los Archivos de la URSS (1959–1973): Comité Central del PCUS y del Ministerio de Relaciones Exteriores de la URSS." *Estudios Publicos* 72 (1998): 391–476.

Uribe, A. *The Black Book of Intervention in Chile*. Boston: Beacon Press, 1975.

Vera Castillo, J., ed. *La Política Exterior Chilena Durante el Gobierno del Presidente Salvador Allende 1970–1973*. Santiago: Ediciones IERIC, 1987.

Walters, V. A. *Silent Missions*. New York: Doubleday, 1978.

Witiker Velázquez, A. *Historia Documental del PSCH, 1933–1993*. Concepción: IELCO-Chile, 1993.

Zaradov, K., ed. *One Thousand Days of Revolution: Communist Party Leaders on Lessons of the Events in Chile*. Prague: Peace and Socialism International Publishers, 1978.

Zumwalt, E. *On Watch: A Memoir*. New York: Quadrangle/New York Times Book Co., 1976.

Newspapers and Periodicals

Bohemia, Havana, Cuba
Granma, Havana, Cuba
El Mercurio, Santiago, Chile.
La Tribuna, Santiago, Chile

Documentary Films

Alvarez, S. *De América Soy Hijo y a Ella Le Debo*. ICAIC, Sweden, April 1975.

Guzmán, P. *La Batalla de Chile*. In cooperation with ICAIC. Part 1, Cannes International Film Festival, 1975; Part 2, Cannes International Film Festival, 1976; Part 3, Cannes International Film Festival, 1979.

———. *Salvador Allende*. Mediapro, CV Filmproduktions, Les Films de la Passerelle, 2004.

Ortega, A. *La Habana-Arica-Magallanes*. ICAIC y La Casa Memorial Salvador Allende en Cuba, September 2008.

Robin, M. *Escuadrones de la Muerte: La Escuela Francesa*. France, 2003.

Secondary Sources

Published

Alba, V. *Alliance without Allies: The Mythology of Progress in Latin America*. New York: Frederick A. Praeger, 1965.

Ambrose, S. E. *Nixon*.Vol. 2: *The Triumph of a Politician, 1962–1972*. London: Simon & Schuster, 1989.

Andrews, C., and V. Mitrokhin. *The Mitrokhin Archive II: The KGB and the World*. London: Allen Lane, 2005.

Armony, A. C. "Transnationalizing the Dirty War: Argentina in Central America." In *In from the Cold: Latin America's New Encounter with the Cold War*, edited by G. Joseph and D. Spenser. Durham: Duke University Press, 2008.

Arora, K. C. *Imperialism and the Non-aligned Movement*. New Delhi: Sanchar Publishing House, 1998.

Atkins, G. P. *Latin America in the International Political System*. 2nd ed. Boulder, Colo.: Westview Press, 1989.

Bautista Yofre, J. *Misión Argentina en Chile (1970–1973): Los Registros Secretos de Una Difícil Gestión Diplomatica*. Santiago: Editorial Sudamericana Chilena, 2000.

Bell, C. "Kissinger in Retrospect: The Diplomacy of Power Concert." *International Affairs* 53, no. 2 (1977): 202–16.

Benítez, H. *Las Muertes de Salvador Allende: Insospechados Detalles, Incógnitas y Enimgmas de las Ultimas Horas del Presidente*. Santiago: Ril Editores, 2006.

Berríos, R. "The USSR and the Andean Countries: Economic and Political Dimensions." In *The USSR and Latin America: A Developing Relationship*, edited by E. Mujal-León. London: Unwin Hyman, 1989.

Bethell, L., and I. Roxborough. "The Impact of the Cold War on Latin America." In *Origins of the Cold War: An International History*, edited by M. P. Leffler and D. S. Painter. 2nd ed. New York: Routledge, 2005.

Blanton, T. "Recovering the Memory of the Cold War: Forensic History and Latin America." In *In from the Cold: Latin America's New Encounter with the Cold War*, edited by G. Joseph and D. Spenser. Durham: Duke University Press, 2008.

Blazier, C. *The Hovering Giant: US Responses to Revolutionary Change in Latin America 1910–1985*. Rev. ed. Pittsburgh, Pa.: University of Pittsburgh Press, 1985.

Blight, J. G., and P. Brenner. *Sad and Luminous Days: Cuba's Struggle with the Superpowers after the Missile Crisis*. Lanham, Md.: Rowman and Littlefield, 2002.

Bodes Gómez, J. *En la Senda del Che: Biografía de Elmo Catalán*. Havana: Prensa Latina, 2009.

Boorstein, E. *Allende's Chile: An Insiders View*. New York: International Publishers, 1977.

Brands, H. *Latin America's Cold War*. Cambridge, Mass.: Harvard University Press, 2010.

———. "Richard Nixon and Economic Nationalism in Latin America: The Problem of Expropriations, 1969–1974." *Diplomacy and Statecraft* 18, no. 1 (2007): 215–35.

Braveboy-Wagner, J. A., ed. *The Foreign Policies of the Global South: Rethinking Conceptual Frameworks*. Boulder, Colo.: Lynne Rienner Publishers, 2003.

Bundy, W. *A Tangled Web: The Making of Foreign Policy in the Nixon Presidency*. New York: Hill and Wang, 1998.

Castañeda, J. *Compañero: The Life and Death of Che Guevara*. London: Bloomsbury, 1997.

Colburn, F. D. *The Vogue of Revolution in Poor Countries*. Princeton, N.J.: Princeton University Press, 1994.

Collier, S. "Allende's Chile: Contemporary History and the Counterfactual." *Journal of Latin American Studies* 12, no. 2 (1980): 445–52.

Collier, S., and W. F. Sater. *A History of Chile, 1808–2022*. 2nd ed. Cambridge: Cambridge University Press, 2004.

Coltman, L. *The Real Fidel Castro*. New Haven: Yale University Press, 2003.

Connelly, M. *A Diplomatic Revolution: Algeria's Fight for Independence*. Oxford: Oxford University Press, 2002.

———. "Taking Off the Cold War Lens: Visions of North-South Conflict during the Algerian War for Independence." *American Historical Review* 105, no. 3 (2000): 739–69.

Cottam, M. L. *Images and Intervention: US Policies in Latin America*. Pittsburgh, Pa.: University of Pittsburgh Press, 1994.

Debray, R. *La Guerrilla del Che*. Siglo Veinteuno: Ediciones SA, 1973.

D'Esteséfano Pisani, M. A. *Política Exterior de la Revolución Cubana*. Havana: Editorial de Ciencias Sociales, 2002.

Dinges, J. *The Condor Years: How Pinochet and His Allies Brought Terrorism to Three Continents*. New York: New Press, 2004.

Domínguez, J. I. "Insurgency in Latin America and the Common Defense." *Political Science Quarterly* 101, no. 5 (1986): 807–23.

———, ed. *Latin America's International Relations and Their Domestic Consequences: War and Peace, Dependency and Autonomy, Integration and Disintegration*. New York: Garland Publishing, 1994.

———. *To Make a World Safe for Revolution: Cuba's Foreign Policy*. Cambridge, Mass.: Harvard University Press, 1989.

Duke, L. "A Plot Thickens." *Washington Post*, 27 February 2005.

Ellner, S. "The Latin American Left since Allende: Perspectives and New Directions." *Latin American Research Review* 24, no. 2 (1989): 143–67.

Erisman, H. M. *Cuba's International Relations: The Anatomy of a Nationalistic Foreign Policy*. Boulder, Colo.: Westview Press, 1985.

Fagen, R. R. "The United States and Chile: Roots and Branches." *Foreign Affairs* 53, no. 2 (1975): 297–313.

Fanon, F. *The Wretched of the Earth*. London: Penguin Books, 1963.

Ferguson, Y. "Trends in Inter-American Relations: 1972–Mid-1974." In *Latin America: The Search for a New International Role*, edited by R. G. Hellman and H. J. Rosenbaum. New York: Sage Publications, 1975.

Fermandois, J. *Chile y el Mundo 1970–1973: La Política Exterior del Gobierno de la*

Unidad Popular y el Sistema Internacional. Santiago: Ediciones Universidad Católica de Chile, 1985.

———. "Del Malestar al Entusiasmo: La Reacción de Bonn ante el Gobierno de la Unidad Popular 1970–1973." *Boletín de la Academia Chilena de la Historia*, no. 117 (2008).

———. *Mundo y Fin de Mundo: Chile en la Política Mundial 1900–2004*. Santiago: Ediciones Universidad Catolica de Chile, 2005.

———. "Pawn or Player? Chile in the Cold War (1962–1973)." *Estudios Publicos* 72 (1998).

Fortin, C. "Principled Pragmatism in the Face of External Pressure: The Foreign Policy of the Allende Government." In *Latin America: The Search for a New International Role*, edited by R. G. Hellman and H. J. Rosenbaum. New York: Sage Publications, 1975

Fousek, J. *To Lead the Free World: American Nationalism and the Cultural Roots of the Cold War*. Chapel Hill: University of North Carolina Press, 2000.

Frank, A. G. *Latin America: Underdevelopment or Revolution; Essays on the Development of Underdevelopment and the Immediate Enemy*. New York: Monthly Review Press, 1970.

Fraser, Cary. "The 'New Frontier' of Empire in the Caribbean: The Transfer of Power in British Guiana, 1961–1964." *International History Review* 22, no. 3 (2000): 583–610.

Friedman, M. P. "Retiring the Puppets, Bringing Latin America Back In: Recent Scholarship on United States–Latin American Relations." *Diplomatic History* 27, no. 5 (2003): 621–36.

Furci, C. *The Chilean Communist Party and the Road to Socialism*. London: Zed Books, 1984.

Gaddis, J. L. *Strategies of Containment: A Critical Appraisal of Postwar American National Security Policy*. New York: Oxford University Press, 1982.

Garthoff, R. *Détente and Confrontation: American-Soviet Relations from Nixon and Reagan*. Rev. ed. Washington, D.C.: Brookings Institution, 1994.

Gaspari, E. *A Ditadura Derrotada*. São Paulo: Companhia das Letras, 2003.

Gilderhus, M. T. "An Emerging Synthesis? U.S.–Latin American Relations since the Second World War." In *America in the World: The Historiography of American Foreign Relations since 1941*, edited by M. J. Hogan. New York: Cambridge University Press, 1995.

Gleijeses, P. "A Bone in the Throat." In *London Review of Books* 26, no. 16 (19 August 2004): 24–25.

———. *Conflicting Missions: Havana, Washington, and Africa, 1959–1976*. Chapel Hill: University of North Carolina Press, 2003.

———. *Shattered Hope: The Guatemalan Revolution and the United States, 1944–1954*. Princeton, N.J.: Princeton University Press, 1991.

Gott, R. *Cuba: A New History*. New Haven: Yale University Press, 2004.

Gould-Davies, N. "Rethinking the Role of Ideology in International Politics during the Cold War." *Journal of Cold War Studies* 1, no. 1 (1999): 90–109.

Grandin, G. *Empire's Workshop: Latin America, the United States, and the Rise of the New Imperialism*. New York: Metropolitan Books, 2006.

———. "Off the Beach: The United States, Latin America, and the Cold War." In *A Companion to Post-1945 America*, edited by J. Agnew and R. Rosenzweig. Malden, Mass.: Blackwell Publishers, 2002.

Greenberg, D. *Nixon's Shadow: The History of an Image*. New York: W. W. Norton, 2003.

Guerra Vilaboy, S. *Breve Historia de América Latina*. Havana: Ciencias Sociales, 2006.

Gustafson, K. "Double-Blind: Predicting the Pinochet Coup." *RUSI Journal* 150, no. 6 (2005): 78–83.

———. *Hostile Intent: U.S. Covert Operations in Chile, 1964–1974*. Washington, D.C.: Potomac Books, 2007.

Hanhimäki, J. "'Dr. Kissinger' or 'Mr. Henry'? Kissingerology, Thirty Years and Counting." *Diplomatic History* 27, no. 5 (November 2003): 637–76.

———. *Flawed Architect: Henry Kissinger and American Foreign Policy*. Oxford: Oxford University Press, 2004.

Haslam, J. "Collecting and Assembling Pieces of the Jigsaw; Coping with Cold War Archives." *Cold War History* 4, no. 3 (April 2004): 140–52.

———. *The Nixon Administration and the Death of Allende's Chile: A Case of Assisted Suicide*. London: Verso, 2005.

Hellman, R. G., and H. J. Rosenbaum, eds. *Latin America: The Search for a New International Role*. New York: Sage Publications, 1975.

Hennessy, A., and G. Lambie, eds. *The Fractured Blockade: West European–Cuban Relations during the Revolution*. London: Macmillan, 1993.

Hersh, S. M. *The Price of Power: Kissinger in the Nixon White House*. London: Faber, 1983.

Hershberg, J. G. "The United States, Brazil and the Cuban Missile Crisis, 1962 (Part 1)." *Journal of Cold War Studies* 6, no. 2 (2004): 3–20.

———. "The United States, Brazil and the Cuban Missile Crisis, 1962 (Part 2)." *Journal of Cold War Studies* 6, no. 3 (2004): 5–48.

Hilton, I. "The General." *Granta* 31 (1990).

Hitchens, C. *The Trial of Henry Kissinger*. London: Verso, 2001.

Hite, K. *When the Romance Ended: Leaders of the Chilean Left, 1968–1998*. New York: Columbia University Press, 2000.

Hoff, J. *Nixon Reconsidered*. New York: Basic Books, 1994.

Hogan, M. J., and T. G. Paterson, eds. *Explaining the History of American Foreign Relations*. 2nd ed. Cambridge: Cambridge University Press, 2004.

Horne, A. *Small Earthquake in Chile*. 2nd ed. London: Papermac, 1990.

Hove, M. T. "The Arbenz Factor: Salvador Allende, U.S.-Chilean Relations, and the 1954 U.S. Intervention in Guatemala." *Diplomatic History* 31, no. 4 (2006): 623–63.

Hunt, M. *Ideology and U.S. Foreign Policy*. New Haven: Yale University Press, 1987.

Husain, A. "Covert Action and US Cold War Strategy in Cuba, 1961–62." *Cold War History* 5, no. 1 (2005): 23–53.

Jaipal, R. *Non-alignment: Origins, Growth and Potential for World Peace.* Ahmedabad: Allied Publishers, 1987.

Jones, C. A. *The North-South Dialogue: A Brief History.* London: Frances Pinter, 1983.

Joseph, G., and D. Spenser, eds. *In from the Cold: Latin America's New Encounter with the Cold War.* Durham: Duke University Press, 2008.

Kaplan, S. S. "U.S. Arms Transfers to Latin America, 1945–1974: Rational Strategy, Bureaucratic Politics, and Executive Parameters." *International Studies Quarterly* 19, no. 4 (1975): 399–431.

Karabell, Z. *Architects of Intervention: The United States, the Third World and the Cold War, 1946–1962.* Baton Rouge: Louisiana State University Press, 1999.

Kaufman, E. *Crisis in Allende's Chile: New Perspectives.* New York: Praeger, 1988.

Kay, C. *Latin American Theories of Development and Underdevelopment.* London: Routledge, 1989.

Kerr, M. *The Arab Cold War, 1958–1964: A Study of Ideology in Politics.* London: Oxford University Press, 1965.

Kimball, J. *Nixon's Vietnam War.* Lawrence: University Press of Kansas, 1998.

Kirk, J. M. *Cuba: Twenty-five Years of Revolution, 1959–1984.* New York: Praeger, 1985.

Kirk, J. M., and P. McKenna. *Canada-Cuba Relations: The Other Good Neighbor Policy.* Gainesville: University Press of Florida, 1997.

Kirkpatrick, J. "Dictatorships and Double Standards." *Commentary*, November 1979, 34–45.

Kornbluh, P. *The Pinochet File: A Declassified Dossier on Atrocity and Accountability.* New York: New Press, 2003.

Kornbluh, P., and J. G. Blight. "Our Hidden Dialogue with Castro—A Secret History." *New York Review of Books*, 6 October 1994.

Kruijt, D. *Revolution by Decree: Peru 1968–1975.* Amsterdam: Thela Publishers, 1994.

Labarca, E. *Salvador Allende: Biografía Sentimental.* Santiago: Catalonia, 2007.

Labrousse, A. *The Tupamaros: Urban Guerrillas in Uruguay.* London: Penguin, 1973.

LaFeber, W. *Inevitable Revolutions: The United States in Central America.* New York: W. W. Norton, 1993.

Langley, L. D. "The United States and Latin American Revolution in the 1960s." *Diplomatic History* 28, no. 2 (2004): 277–80.

Lawrence, M. A. "History from Below: The United States and Latin America in the Nixon Years." In *Nixon in the World: American Foreign Relations, 1969–1977*, edited by F. Logevall and A. Preston. Oxford: Oxford University Press, 2008.

Leacock, R. *Requiem for Revolution: The United States and Brazil, 1961–1969.* Kent, Ohio: Kent State University Press, 1990.

Lehman, K. D. *Bolivia and the United States: A Limited Partnership.* Athens: University of Georgia Press, 1999.

———. "Revolutions and Attributions: Making Sense of Eisenhower Administration Policies in Bolivia and Guatemala." *Diplomatic History* 21, no. 2 (1997): 185–213.

Logevall, F., and A. Preston, eds. *Nixon in the World: American Foreign Relations, 1969–1977.* Oxford: Oxford University Press, 2008.

Loveman, B. *Chile: The Legacy of Hispanic Capitalism*. New York: Oxford University Press, 2001.

Lundestad, G. "How (Not) to Study the Origins of the Cold War." In *Reviewing the Cold War: Approaches, Interpretations, Theory*, edited by O. A. Westad. London: Frank Cass Publishers, 2000.

MacEoin, G. *Chile, the Struggle for Dignity*. London: Conventure, 1975.

Malley, R. *The Call from Algeria: Third Worldism, Revolution, and the Turn to Islam*. Berkeley: University of California Press, 1996.

Martner, G. *El Gobierno del Presidente Salvador Allende, 1970–1973: Una Evaluación*. Concepción: Ediciones Literatura Americana Reunida, 1988.

Maxwell, K., and W. D. Rogers. "Fleeing the Chilean Coup: The Debate over U.S. Complicity." *Foreign Affairs* 83, no. 1 (2004): 160–65.

McAllister, C. "Rural Markets, Revolutionary Souls, and Rebellious Women in Cold War Guatemala." In *In from the Cold: Latin America's New Encounter with the Cold War*, edited by G. Joseph and D. Spenser. Durham: Duke University Press, 2008.

McPherson, A. *Intimate Ties, Bitter Struggles: The United States and Latin America since 1945*. Washington, D.C.: Potomac Books, 2006.

———. *Yankee No! Anti-Americanism in U.S–Latin American Relations*. Cambridge, Mass.: Harvard University Press, 2003.

McSherry, J. P. *Predatory States: Operation Condor and Covert War in Latin America*. Oxford: Rowman and Littlefield, 2005.

Mesa-Lago, C. *Cuba in the 1970s: Pragmatism and Institutionalization*. Albuquerque: University of New Mexico Press, 1974.

Miller, N. "The Absolution of History: Uses of the Past in Castro's Cuba." *Journal of Contemporary History* 38, no. 1 (2003): 147–62.

———. *Soviet Relations with Latin America, 1959–1987*. Cambridge: Cambridge University Press, 1989.

Mortimer, R. A. *The Third World Coalition in International Politics*. 2nd ed. Boulder, Colo.: Westview Press, 1984.

Moss, R. *Chile's Marxist Experiment*. Newton Abbot, Devon: David and Charles, 1973.

Moulian, T. *Conversacion Interrumpida con Allende*. Santiago: LOM, 1998.

Mujal-León, E., ed. *The USSR and Latin America: A Developing Relationship*. London: Unwin Hyman, 1989.

Muñoz, H., and J. S. Tulchin, eds. *Latin American Nations in World Politics*. Boulder, Colo.: Westview Press, 1984.

Murphy, C. N. "What the Third World Wants: An Interpretation of the Development and Meaning of the New International Economic Order Ideology." *International Studies Quarterly* 27, no. 1 (1983): 54–76.

Nelson, K. L. *The Making of Détente: Soviet-American Relations in the Shadow of Vietnam*. Baltimore: John Hopkins University Press, 1995.

Neustadt, R. E., and E. May. *Thinking in Time: The Uses of History for Decision-Makers*. New York: Free Press, 1986.

Nolff, Max. *Salvador Allende: El Político, El Estadista*. Santiago: Ediciones Documenatas, 1993.

Nossiter, B. D. *The Global Struggle for More: Third World Conflicts and Rich Nations.* New York: Harper and Row, 1987.

Oppenheim, L. H. "The Chilean Road to Socialism Revisited." *Latin America Research Review* 24, no. 1 (1989): 155–83.

Palast, G. "A Marxist Threat to Coca Cola Sales?" *Observer*, 8 November 1998.

Parkinson, F. *Latin America, the Cold War and the World Powers, 1945–1973: A Study in Diplomatic History.* London: Sage Publications, 1974.

Petras, J. F., and R. LaPorte. "Can We Do Business with Radical Nationalists? Chile: No." *Foreign Policy*, no. 7 (1972): 132–58.

Petras, J. F., and M. M. Morley. *How Allende Fell: A Study in U.S.-Chilean Relations.* Nottingham: Spokesman Books for the Bertrand Russell Foundation, 1974.

Pérez, C. "Años de Disparos y Tortura (1973–1975): Los Ultimos Días de Miguel Enríquez." *Estudios Publicos* 96 (2004): 355–82.

———. "Che Guevara's Army and Its Chilean Followers." *Estudios Publicos* 89 (2003).

———. "Rural Guerrilla in Chile: The Battle at the Farm of San Miguel (1968)." *Estudios Publicos* 78 (2000): 181–208.

———. "Salvador Allende, Apuntes Sobre su Dispositivo de Seguridad: El Grupo de Amigos Personales (GAP)." *Estudios Publicos* 79 (2000): 31–81.

Pérez, L. A. *Cuba and the United States: Ties of Singular Intimacy.* 3rd ed. Athens: University of Georgia Press, 2003.

Power, M. "The Engendering of Anticommunism and Fear in Chile's 1964 Presidential Elections." *Diplomatic History* 32, no. 5 (2008): 931–53.

Prizel, I. *Latin America through Soviet Eyes, the Evolution of Soviet Perceptions during the Brezhnev Era, 1964–1982.* Cambridge: Cambridge University Press, 1990.

Quiroga, P. Z. *Compañeros: El GAP, La Escolta de Allende.* Santiago: Aguilar, 2001.

Rabe, S. G. *Eisenhower and Latin America: The Foreign Policy of Anticommunism.* Chapel Hill: University of North Carolina Press, 1988.

———. *The Most Dangerous Area in the World: John F. Kennedy Confronts Communist Revolution in Latin America.* Chapel Hill: University of North Carolina Press, 2000.

———. *U.S. Intervention in British Guiana: A Cold War Story.* Chapel Hill: University of North Carolina Press, 2005.

Riquelme Segovia, A. *Rojo Atardecer. El Comunismo Chileno Entre Dictadura y Democracia.* Santiago, Chile: Dibam, 2009.

Rodman, P. W. *More Precious than Peace: The Cold War and the Struggle for the Third World.* New York: C. Scribner's Sons, 1994.

Rodríguez Ostria, G. *Teoponte: La Otra Guerrilla Guevarista en Bolivia.* Cochabamba, Bolivia: Grupo Editorial Kipus, 2006.

Ronning, C. N., and A. P. Vannucci, eds. *Ambassadors in Foreign Policy: The Influence of Individuals on U.S.-Latin American Policy.* New York: Praeger, 1987.

Roxborough, I., P. O'Brien, and J. Roddick. *Chile: The State and Revolution.* London: Macmillan, 1977.

Sater, W. F. *Chile and the United States: Empires in Conflict.* Athens: University of Georgia Press, 1990.

Schlesinger, C., and S. Knizer. *Bitter Fruit: The Untold Story of the American Coup in Guatemala*. Garden City, N.Y.: Doubleday, 1982.

Schmitter, P. "Lessons of the Chilean Coup in Europe: The Case of Portugal." In *Chile at the Turning Point: Lessons of the Socialist Years, 1970–1973*, edited by F. G. Gill, R. E. Lagos, and H. A. Landsberger. Philadelphia: ISHI, 1979.

Schoultz, L. *Beneath the United States*. Cambridge, Mass.: Harvard University Press, 1998.

Siekmeier, J. F. "A Sacrificial Llama? The Expulsion of the Peace Corps from Bolivia in 1971." *Pacific Historical Review* 69, no. 1 (2000): 65–87.

———. "Trailblazer Diplomat: Bolivian Ambassador Victor Andrade Uzquicino's Efforts to Influence U.S Policy, 1944–1962." *Diplomatic History* 28, no. 3 (2004): 385–406.

Sigmund, P. E. *Multinationals in Latin America*, Madison: University of Wisconsin Press, 1980.

———. *The Overthrow of Allende and the Politics of Chile, 1964–1976*. Pittsburgh: University of Pittsburgh Press, 1977.

Skidmore, T. E., and P. H. Smith. *Modern Latin America*. 5th ed. New York: Oxford University Press, 2001.

Skierka, V. *Fidel Castro*. Cambridge: Polity Press, 2004.

Smirnow, G. *The Revolution Disarmed: Chile 1970–1973*. New York: Monthly Review Press, 1979.

Smith, G. *The Last Years of the Monroe Doctrine*. New York: Hill and Wang, 1994.

Smith, J. *History of Brazil, 1500–2000: Politics, Economics, Society, Diplomacy*. New York: Longman, 2002.

Smith, P. *Talons of the Eagles: Dynamics of US–Latin American Relations*. 2nd ed. New York: Oxford University Press, 2000.

Smith, T. "'The Spirit of the Sierra Maestra': Five Observations on Writing about Cuban Foreign Policy." *World Politics* 41, no. 1 (1988): 98–119.

Spektor, M. *Kissinger e o Brasil*. Rio de Janeiro: Zahar, 2009.

Spenser, D. "Final Reflections: Standing Conventional Cold War History on Its Head." In *In from the Cold: Latin America's New Encounter with the Cold War*, edited by G. Joseph and D. Spenser. Durham: Duke University Press, 2008.

Spooner, M. H. *Soldiers in a Narrow Land: The Pinochet Regime in Chile*. Berkeley: University of California Press, 1999.

Stephansky, B. S. "'New Dialogue' on Latin America: The Cost of Policy Neglect." In *Latin America: The Search for a New International Role*, edited by R. G. Hellman and H. J. Rosenbaum. New York: Sage Publications, 1975.

Stephanson, A. "Fourteen Notes on the Very Concept of the Cold War." *H-Diplo: Essays*, http://www.h-net.org/~diplo/essays/PDF/stephanson-14notes.pdf.

Suárez Salazar, L. "The Cuban Revolution and the New Latin American Leadership: A View from Its Utopias." *Latin American Perspectives* 36, no. 114 (2009): 114–27.

———. *Madre America: Un Siglo de Violencia y Dolor (1898–1998)*. Havana: Ciencias Sociales, 2004.

———. "La Política de la Revolución Cubana Hacía América Latina y el Caribe:

Notas Para Una Periodización." *Cuadernos de Nuestra América* 3, no. 6 (July–December 1986).

Sulzberger, C. L. *The World and Richard Nixon*. New York: Prentice Hall, 1987.

Suri, J. *Power and Protest: Global Revolution and the Rise of Détente*. Cambridge, Mass.: Harvard University Press, 2003.

Sweig, J. *Inside the Cuban Revolution: Fidel Castro and the Urban Underground*. Cambridge, Mass.: Harvard University Press, 2002.

Szulc, T. *Fidel: A Critical Portrait*. London: Hutchinson, 1986.

Timossi, J. *Grandes Alamedas: El Combate del Presidente Allende*. Havana: Ciencias Sociales, 1974.

Ulianova, O. "La Unidad Popular y el Golpe Militar en Chile: Percepciones y Análisis Soviéticos." *Estudios Publicos* 79 (Winter 2000): 83–171.

Urban, J. B. *Moscow and the Italian Communist Party*. London: I. B. Tauris, 1986.

Veneros, D. *Allende: Un Ensayo Psicobiográfico*. Santiago: Editorial Suamericana, Señales, 2003.

Verdugo, P. *Interferencia Secreta: 11 de Septiembre de 1973*. Santiago: Editorial Sudamericana Chilena, 1998.

Wesson, R. *The United States and Brazil: Limits of Influence*. New York: Praeger, 1981.

Westad, O. A. *The Global Cold War: Third World Interventions and the Making of Our Times*. Cambridge: Cambridge University Press, 2005.

———, ed. *Reviewing the Cold War: Approaches, Interpretations, Theory*. London: Frank Cass Publishers, 2000.

Winn, P. *Americas: The Changing Face of Latin America and the Caribbean*. 3rd ed. Berkley: University of California Press, 2006.

Unpublished

Michael, D. "Nixon, Chile and Shadows of the Cold War: U.S.-Chilean Relations during the Government of Salvador Allende, 1970–1973." Ph.D. diss., George Washington University, 2005.

Santoni, A. "La Via Cilena al Socialismo nella Riflessione del Partito Comunista Italiano. Un Mito per una Strategia Politica, 1960–1973." Ph.D. diss., University of Bologna, 2006.

Spektor, M. "Equivocal Engagement: Kissinger, Silveira and the Politics of U.S.-Brazil Relations (1969–1983)." Ph.D. diss., Oxford University, 2006.

Index

with Chilean Road, 11, 234, 246, 269–70, 273–74; historiography on, 10–11, 13, 281; on Latin American balance of forces, 43, 60, 103, 130, 171, 266–67; and Latin American revolution, 21, 22, 23, 25, 28, 29, 30, 36, 72, 103, 130, 258; letters to Allende, 104–5, 113, 141–42, 184, 199, 231, 279; moderation of stance by, 29, 48, 92, 266; on need for Chilean Left unity, 136, 139–40; opposition attacks on, 136, 143; on options during Pinochet coup, 246; provides Allende security assistance, 4, 52, 53, 55; respect for Allende authority by, 11–12, 136, 144, 274; self-criticism of 1970 by, 28, 149; and Soviet Union, 28, 29, 30, 150, 158, 172–73, 196, 264; urges caution to Allende, 65, 78, 136; on Velasco Alvarado, 26; warns of impending confrontation, 133, 139, 140–42, 184, 199–200, 209, 221, 231, 232, 233, 254, 274. *See also* Cuba

Castro, Raúl, 266

Central Intelligence Agency (CIA), 7–8, 21, 37, 53, 56, 78, 119, 127, 135–36, 183, 227, 235, 252; and Bolivia coup, 125; and Chile coup plotting, 130–31, 207, 223–25, 226, 227, 238, 248, 273, 314 (n. 118); definition of tasks in Chile, 58, 59, 60, 61, 64, 202; monitoring of Cubans by, 27, 104, 135, 140, 141, 266, 279–80, 315 (n. 139); and Pinochet regime, 246, 248, 249–50; propaganda operations by, 12, 38, 48, 93, 94, 130, 253, 272; support to opposition parties, 48, 89, 90, 182–83, 205, 206, 274. *See also* United States—covert action by

Chain, Carlos, 209

Chile: navy of, 219, 220, 234, 237, 238, 240, 273, 274

—economy and economic relations of, 14, 15, 20, 35, 88–89, 116–17, 118, 120, 131, 145, 147, 152, 156, 157, 162, 176–77, 180, 189; trade with Cuba, 82, 133–34, 171, 200, 269, 271; trade with United States, 177

—Embassy (in Washington), 86, 93, 103, 112, 193; burglary of, 179, 202

—foreign policy of: anti-imperialist nature of, 14, 77, 84, 112, 119, 213, 230, 260; avoiding confrontation with United States, 14, 16–17, 77–79, 83–84, 87, 110, 111, 118, 119, 122, 146, 155, 176–77, 201, 215–16; establishing relations with Cuba, 2, 14, 65–66, 71, 82, 92; foreign policy team, 79; "healthy realism" of, 78–79, 81–82, 85, 105; historiography on, 13–14; "ideological pluralism" of, 3, 75, 104, 116, 145, 261–62; lack of cohesion in, 13, 153, 155, 156, 181, 192, 217; and negotiations with U.S., 15, 155–56, 180–81, 182, 192, 201–3, 210–11, 215; new diplomatic and commercial relationships of, 113–14, 116, 261; persuasion as tool of, 84, 105; policy choices, 74–75, 76–77; pragmatic and cautious approach of, 78–79, 80–81, 83, 91; relations with Latin America, 6, 75, 81, 84, 94–97, 102–3, 113–14, 116, 144–45, 213, 216; toward Soviet bloc, 76, 80, 84, 116–18, 122–23, 157–58, 178–79, 196–98, 199, 201–2; Third World appeals by, 14, 75, 82–83, 113–16, 151, 158–60, 163–64, 263; winning international support, 13–14, 17, 104, 112, 113, 144, 151, 159–60, 194–95, 198–201, 262

—Left: arming of, 146, 225, 226, 233, 235–36; Cuba's relations with, 12, 30, 31, 32, 55–56, 71, 133, 139, 140, 144, 154, 155, 160, 208, 232, 233, 234; divisions among, 12, 18, 20, 22, 142–43, 178, 246, 270; far Left, 30, 145, 177, 234–35, 271; unprepared for coup, 184–85, 221, 243–44, 246. *See also* Unidad Popular

—military and armed forces of, 12, 59, 146–47, 152, 236, 220, 221, 271; as architect of coup, 17, 221, 241, 242, 243, 244; attempt to purchase arms for, 56, 84, 111, 274; Brazilian relations with, 17, 18, 128, 184–85, 194, 228, 251, 273, 274; brought into UP government, 184, 208, 210; divisions within, 206, 220, 223–24, 226–27; illusions in, 142, 185, 239, 271, 337 (n. 112); politicization of, 184, 219, 229–30; size of, 239; U.S. doubts about, 8–9, 206–7, 223, 225; U.S. monitoring of, 130, 183; U.S. support for, 18, 70, 75, 90–91, 248. *See also* Coup preparations

Chilean Road to Socialism (La Vía Chilena), 4, 7, 17, 18, 55, 74, 75, 107, 182, 197; Allende's commitment to, 5, 33, 110, 113, 142, 218, 260, 274, 275; Cuban view of, 12, 31, 50, 51, 64, 65, 71–72, 171, 230, 274; and deepening class conflict, 145; fight for international acceptance of, 5, 33, 97, 118–19, 189; growing fragility of, 107–8, 132, 145, 153, 173, 184, 190, 210, 270–71, 273; illusions in, 5, 104; international impact of, 21, 63–64, 104, 257, 261–62; responsibility for failure of, 7–8, 221, 271–72, 273; Socialist Party attacks on, 270; Soviet view of, 177–78, 191, 221, 230; U.S. hostility to, 8, 50, 60–61, 63, 64, 130, 272

"Chile syndrome," 252

China, People's Republic of, 35, 39, 41, 80, 108, 116, 117, 150, 157, 159, 169, 191, 210, 211, 217, 219, 230–31, 257, 258, 269

Christian Democrat Party. *See* Partido Demócrata Cristiano

Cienfuegos crisis (1970), 77, 298 (n. 14)

Colburn, Forrest, 16, 33, 289 (n. 67)

Cold War, inter-American, 16, 18, 19, 22, 47, 51, 170, 213, 255, 265, 266, 277, 281; Chile as theater of, 9, 151, 176, 185, 186; defined, 1–2; and détente, 3–4, 62–63, 150, 187; as framework for U.S. policy, 4, 50, 64, 85, 105, 151, 259, 261; illusions about ending of, 3, 118, 150, 258; indigenous origins of, 6; as Nixon perspective, 8, 123, 187, 188, 258–59, 260; as rarely "cold," 256

Colombia, 22, 24, 27, 40, 96, 108, 113, 115, 116, 123, 135, 149, 169, 188, 211

Communist movement, international, 20, 113, 269

Communist Party: Bolivian, 25; Chilean (*see* Partido Comunista de Chile); Cuban, 23, 208; Indonesian, 233; Italian, 231, 269; Polish, 28–29, 172; Portuguese, 269; Soviet, 80, 172, 197; Venezuelan, 24

Confederación Democrática (CODE), 204, 205, 207

Connally, John, 120, 121, 146, 162; Latin American trip of, 150, 166–69, 173–74, 187, 188, 293

Contreras, Manuel, 250

Contreras Bell, Miria (La Paya), 52, 53, 54, 185

Copper, 138, 145, 197, 199, 271; alternative markets for, 117, 198, 289 (n. 66); and Chile's dependency, 20, 34–35; nationalization of, 35, 75, 77, 78, 83, 84, 85–86, 88, 107, 110, 111, 112, 120, 162, 181; U.S. mining companies and, 15, 112, 156, 180, 182, 202, 210, 249, 308 (n. 20). *See also* "Excess profits" ruling; Nationalization of copper

Cordones industriales, 183

Corea, Gamani, 188

Corvalán, Luis, 140, 145, 184, 200, 231; and coup preparations, 134, 183, 239; fight for release of, 268; trip to USSR and Eastern Europe, 196–97

Council of Mutual Economic Assistance (COMECON), 116, 123, 173, 260–61

Coup (Sept. 11, 1973), 17, 230, 240; Allende during, 221, 240, 241–42, 243, 260, 274, 275; Castro on options during, 246; Cuban Embassy attacked during, 18, 221, 242–43, 244, 245, 254, 273, 333 (n. 7), 338 (nn. 137, 152); as defeat for Cuba, 266; international impact of, 221, 252, 253, 262, 266; military's declaration during, 222; national stadium as torture center during, 18, 274; as repudiation of socialism, 222, 260; responsibility for, 7, 17, 220–21, 238, 246, 253–54, 271–72, 273; troop movements prior to, 239; U.S. foreknowledge of, 238. *See also* Pinochet regime

Coup preparations, 12, 56, 218, 219, 238; Brazil and, 184–85, 186, 220, 228, 250, 273; Chilean Left and, 134–35, 146, 207, 234–37, 239, 246, 271; concern for Cuban involvement in, 11, 219, 221, 254, 273; Cuban Embassy and, 141, 233, 234, 240–41; Cuban, 155, 232, 234; Cuban warnings to Allende about, 133, 139, 140–42, 184, 186, 199–200, 209, 218, 231, 254, 274; divisions in military over, 206, 220, 223–24, 226–27; motivations of, 271, 272–73; and Tanquetazo, 225, 230; U.S. doubts about, 130–31, 206, 207, 218, 220, 223, 225, 226, 227, 228; U.S. encouragement of, 51, 59, 61, 207,

218, 220–21, 228, 229, 247, 253; U.S.
monitoring of, 8, 183, 220, 223–26, 239,
273; warnings about, 183
Crimmins, John, 57, 86, 91, 98, 100, 120,
278
Cuba, 6, 15, 172–73, 185, 219; advice, 72,
80, 156, 278–80, 281; and Africa, 3, 10,
18, 268, 287 (n. 22); Allende's security
bolstered by, 4, 50, 52, 53–55, 65, 106,
135–36; Allende's ties to, 14, 16, 21, 30,
34, 35–36, 37–38, 71, 81, 105, 185, 199,
238, 260; Allende victory celebrated in,
49, 51–52, 71; arming of Chilean Left
by, 135, 140, 146, 155, 233–34, 255; and
Bolivia coup, 126, 168; Brazil and, 92,
95, 127, 129, 273; as challenge to U.S.
domination, 23–24, 35–36, 264; Chile
as celebrated cause in, 133, 199–200;
Chile's reestablishment of relations
with, 2, 65–66, 71, 267; Chile's trade
agreements with, 82, 133–34, 171, 200;
Cienfuegos crisis (1970), 77, 298 (n. 14);
and Cold War 2, 24, 47, 186, 257, 266;
conflicting views about role of, 10–11,
13; coup defense preparations by, 11,
184, 187, 209, 218, 221, 232–33, 235, 254;
diplomatic isolation of, 2, 26, 28, 31, 53,
66, 92–93, 97, 134, 267; on lessons of
Chile coup, 269–70; Mexico and, 170;
MINREX Latin American Department
in, 171; and Peru, 26, 92, 134, 169, 170–
71, 267; Pinochet regime's break with,
222, 245; Pinochet's role unanticipated
by, 12, 221, 239; pragmatic shift by, 2,
26, 27, 28–30, 47, 64, 65, 92, 139, 168,
267–68; propaganda attacks against, 12,
48, 70, 93, 136–38, 139, 154–55, 219, 232–
33, 246, 253, 320 (n. 23); reintegration
in Latin America of, 2, 92–93, 132, 134,
147–48, 171, 173, 267; relations with
Chilean Left, 12, 30, 31, 32, 55–56, 71,
139, 140, 146, 153, 154, 155, 160, 184, 197,
208, 233, 234, 274; respect for Allende
leadership by, 11, 12, 55, 72, 208–9, 232,
274; revolutionary example of, 10, 13,
20–21, 35–36, 47, 71, 81, 132, 144, 261,
273; revolutionary internationalism of,
23, 37, 53, 267–68; security apparatus
of, 53; and Soviet Union, 28, 29, 30, 134,

149, 158, 173, 191, 198, 260; support for
revolution in Latin America by, 18, 22,
23, 24–25, 27, 31, 38, 72, 92, 266, 267,
287 (n. 22), 288 (n. 52); U.S. views of and
relations with, 4, 10, 24, 40, 63, 76, 82,
86, 112, 123, 124, 150, 151, 167, 173, 259,
264, 267, 268; view of Chilean Road in,
4, 12, 52, 56, 71–72, 104, 110, 133, 152,
230, 234, 239, 254
— Embassy, 134, 137, 138, 140, 231, 241,
336 (n. 76); attack on during coup,
18, 221, 242–43, 244, 254, 273, 333
(n. 7), 338 (nn. 137, 152); departure
of personnel after coup, 245, 246,
254, 266; establishment of, 66;
military preparations by, 141, 234,
240–41; paramilitary attacks on, 233;
vulnerability of, 141, 240
See also Castro, Fidel

Davis, Nathaniel, 142, 144–45, 156, 157,
205, 210, 215; and bilateral negotiations,
162, 182, 193–94, 210, 211–12; and
Chilean coup, 218, 223, 226, 227,
228, 229, 238, 243, 252; on Chilean
opposition and military, 204, 205, 207,
227; and Pinochet regime, 247, 248, 249,
250, 251
Debray, Régis, 20, 25; interview with
Allende, 34, 35, 53, 77
Debt negotiations, 156, 157, 159–60,
161, 162–63, 179–80, 194, 202, 203–4,
226
De la Flor, Miguel, 174
Del Canto, Hernán, 155
Departamento General de Liberación
Nacional (DGLN), 54, 66, 155, 170,
171–72, 267, 269
Dependency, 22, 44, 158, 192, 223, 237;
Allende call for ending, 14, 32–33, 35,
81, 118, 195; Chile's, 20, 34–35, 152, 188,
190, 192, 210, 248, 261, 263–64; and
Dependency Theory, 44
Détente, 5, 39, 74, 119, 121, 150, 152, 211,
256, 268, 284 (n. 3); Castro critique of,
172–73, 257–58; with China and USSR,
108, 150, 217; illusions in, 3, 14, 80,
118, 150, 258; not applicable to Latin
America, 3–4, 10, 62–63, 150, 187, 191,

economic dependency, 22, 34–35, 39, 40, 44, 81; foreign ministers conference (1969), 43–44; Left's divisions within, 20, 22, 71; military dictatorships in, 4–5, 46, 98–99, 260–61; national bourgeoisie in, 267; nationalism in, 23, 25–26, 44–45, 46, 70, 71, 72, 120, 161, 212–13; political refugees, 6, 17, 185, 186, 251; revolutionaries and revolutionary prospects in, 2–3, 21, 23–25, 27, 31, 36, 50, 72, 103, 126, 173, 176, 185; and Third World, 115; U.S. imperialism in and sphere of influence, 6–7, 23–24, 33, 77, 80, 84, 109, 252, 264–65; U.S. investments in, 35, 46, 85, 164, 247; U.S. military assistance to, 100, 125, 127; U.S. paternalism toward, 9, 42–43, 105, 124, 151–52, 187, 213, 214–15, 216; U.S. policy toward, 4–5, 10, 17, 18, 26, 39–40, 44–47, 50, 58, 63–64, 68–70, 71, 74, 94, 98–99, 103, 106, 118, 124–25, 128–30, 147, 150, 151, 164–67, 170, 175–76, 188, 214, 259–61, 265, 272. *See also* Cold War, inter-American; Organization of American States

Leigh, Gustavo, 238
Leonov, N., 310 (n. 47)
Letelier, Orlando, 86, 111, 123, 153, 157, 161, 164, 169, 175–76, 184, 189, 237, 278, 300 (n. 44); on avoiding confrontation with the United States, 78, 111, 146, 155, 160, 176–77, 179, 215, 264; becomes ambassador to U.S., 79, 86–87; becomes defense minister, 237; becomes foreign minister, 215, 226; and bilateral negotiations, 156, 179, 180–81, 182, 203, 204, 211–12; Davis discussions with, 194, 212; on détente, 118, 150, 151, 178, 187, 211; Kissinger discussions with, 87, 98, 111, 121, 122, 179; as misguided about U.S. policy, 87, 98, 118, 131–32, 179; and nationalization program, 86, 111–12, 113; at OAS meeting, 215–16; and Pinochet, 247; on possible Nixon-Allende meeting, 193–94; on Soviet Union, 178, 192–93

Malley, Robert, 33
Marambio, Max, 55, 245, 246, 293 (n. 29)

Marshall, Arturo, 228
Martner, Gonzalo, 181
Marxism, 13, 20, 26, 27, 57, 58, 67, 89, 121, 144–45, 151, 165, 166–67, 175, 187, 208; of Allende, 33, 80–81, 200; of Castro and Cuba, 23, 172, 270; military plotters' fear of, 184, 210, 229–30, 237, 253
Matus, Carlos, 181
Media, 51, 153, 180, 227; anti-Cuba campaign in, 136–38, 154–55, 232–33, 253, 254; opposition control of, 155; U.S. funding of, 70, 89, 130, 154, 206, 272
Médici, Emílio Garrastazu, 98, 126–30, 147, 149, 166, 167, 173, 176, 187, 257, 264, 298 (n. 4)
El Mercurio, 59, 154
Merino, José Toribio, 219, 220, 229–30, 237, 238, 254
Mexico, 41, 53, 67, 86, 92, 96, 97, 151, 169–70, 176, 187, 188, 190, 194, 219, 265, 278
Meyer, Charles, 45, 58, 83, 95, 130, 272; Allende meetings with, 6, 66–67; in bilateral negotiations, 203
Millas, Orlando, 177, 178–79
Ministry of the Interior (Cuba), 53, 54
Miret, Pedro, 134
Mitchell, John, 59
La Moneda presidential palace, 47, 74, 111, 142, 232, 238; attack on during coup, 239, 240, 241, 242, 243, 254, 255, 260, 275
Monje, Mario, 25
Monroe Doctrine, 259
Montero, Raúl, 237, 238
Moorer, Thomas, 62
Movimiento de Acción Popular Unitario (MAPU), 13, 181, 204–5, 210, 234; Cuba's relations with, 56, 233; military preparation of, 135, 233, 336 (n. 79)
Movimiento de Izquierda Revolucionaria (MIR), 32, 105, 153, 185, 204, 273; Allende and, 32, 53, 79, 136, 143, 154, 160, 171, 270; Castro and, 139–40, 144, 266; CIA propaganda around, 130; during coup, 240, 241, 242, 243; Cuba's relations with, 32, 55–56, 154, 155, 160, 186, 208, 233, 234, 245; formation and history of, 31–32; and GAP, 55, 135, 136,

154; military preparations by, 135, 155, 233, 246
Muñoz, Heraldo, 21

Nachmanoff, Arnold, 89, 99, 124, 125
Nationalism. *See* Third World—nationalism
Nationalization of copper, 84, 107, 110, 300 (n. 44); Allende commitment to, 35, 77, 262; and bilateral negotiations, 180; compensation decision around, 156; Cuba's advice on, 308 (n. 18); Frei's measures for, 35; international campaign to justify, 111–12; U.S. response to, 85–86, 88, 109, 110, 119, 120, 121, 155–56, 310 (n. 54). *See also* "Excess profits" ruling
National Party. *See* Partido Nacional
National Security Council (NSC), 58, 63, 68, 69, 88, 91, 93, 124, 162; Decision Memorandum 93 of, 69–70. *See also* Senior Review Group
Negotiations, bilateral U.S.-Chilean, 15, 192, 201, 215, 263–64; account of, 182, 191–92, 203, 210–11; Chilean split over, 181, 190; collapse of, 211–12; Kissinger offer of, 121–22; Letelier and, 156, 177, 179, 180–81, 211–12; U.S. aims in, 182, 188–89, 202–3
Neruda, Pablo, 191
Netto, Manso, 129
New International Economic Order (NIEO), 14, 263
Nixon, Richard, 27, 39, 41–42, 45–46, 59, 63, 64, 65, 66, 67, 78, 83, 84, 87, 106, 109, 110, 114, 119, 120, 156, 158, 162, 163, 187–88, 191, 202; Allende seen as threat by, 9, 49, 56, 188; Allende's possible meeting with, 176, 193–94; and Brazil, 69, 98, 99–100, 125, 126–28, 129–30, 167, 187, 247, 256, 264; Cold War perspective of, 8, 47, 50, 123, 187, 188, 258–59, 260; and détente with China and USSR, 3, 108, 118, 150, 172, 178, 217, 260; favors covert action in Chile, 4, 56, 57, 60–62, 63, 64, 69; Latin America trips of, 40, 41, 151, 214; Letelier meets, 86–87; lobbying of European governments by, 61, 296 (n. 65); reelection of, 180, 190, 192, 201;

and responsibility for Chile coup, 7, 246, 251, 253; on U.S. Latin America policy, 4, 9, 10, 39, 40–41, 44, 45, 46, 50, 69, 70, 106, 132, 143, 150, 151, 166, 169, 170, 175, 188, 213–14, 215, 272; view of Latin America and Latin Americans, 40–41, 42, 44, 47, 68, 69, 93, 105, 124, 151–52, 187, 218; and Watergate, 202, 213, 229. *See also* United States—foreign policy of
Nixon Doctrine, 106, 124, 128
Non-Aligned Movement, 114, 237, 262; Chile and, 14, 82, 223, 263
North Korea, 41, 116, 159, 245–46

Ochoa, Arnaldo, 140
Olivares, Augusto, 139
Oña, Luis Fernández, 36, 37, 38, 49, 52, 56, 66, 141, 231, 232, 233, 278–79; Allende and, 238; during coup, 243, 244, 338 (n. 152); on Cuban diplomats, 27, 336 (n. 76); on GAP, 55; sent to Chile, 54
Operation Condor, 2, 5, 250
Operation Pan America, 40
Organization of American States (OAS), 35, 43, 93, 99, 161, 162, 258; Allende on, 81; Chilean addresses to, 97, 211, 212, 213, 215–16; and Cuba, 2, 4, 31, 66, 92, 147, 171, 267
Organization of Latin American Solidarity (OLAS), 36, 73
Otero, Lisandro, 66, 320 (n. 23)
Ovando, Alfredo, 26

Packard, David, 62
Panama, 22, 26, 90, 94, 267
Paraguay, 5, 10, 115, 127, 228
Paramilitaries, rightist, 55, 56, 107, 139, 153, 228, 244, 323 (n. 85); and coup, 236, 242; U.S. funding of, 183, 227
Pardo, Pablo, 103
Paredes, Eduardo "Coco," 155
Paris Club, 163, 179–80, 202–4, 226
Partido Comunista de Chile (PCCh), 32, 35, 102, 183, 239, 271; Allende siding with, 13, 154; attacks on "ultraleftism" by, 153, 178, 270; after coup, 268, 269; during coup, 243, 244; Cuba's relations with, 30, 55, 56, 71, 132, 139, 140, 239; military preparations by, 134, 135, 140,

Schneider, René, 51, 59, 62, 228
School of the Americas, U.S. Army, 90, 312
   (n. 89)
"Second Declaration of Havana" (Castro),
   23, 36
Senior Review Group (SRG), National
   Security Council, 70–71, 88, 99, 120,
   175; Action Plan to prevent Allende
   inauguration, 62, 295 (n. 49); on Latin
   America policy, 124–25; support to
   Chilean military by, 90–91
Sepulveda, José Maria, 232
Shlaudeman, Harry, 225
El Siglo, 243
Siracusa, Ernest, 125
Socialism. *See* Chilean Road to Socialism
Socialist Party. *See* Partido Socialista
Soto, Oscar, 198
Southern Command (SOUTHCOM), 100
Southern Cone. *See* Latin America
Soviet Union, 20, 33, 35, 48, 49, 56, 70, 77,
   80, 93, 111, 123, 159, 161, 168, 175, 183,
   190, 191, 210, 233, 256, 274 ; Afghanistan
   invasion by, 268; arms sales by,
   117–18, 220, 221, 247, 310 (n. 47); breaks
   relations with Pinochet regime, 268–69;
   Castro's trip to, 172, 173; Chilean
   Embassy of, 178, 230, 239, 244, 245; on
   Chilean Road to Socialism, 170, 177–78,
   198, 199, 230; Chile's economic ties
   with, 75, 76, 116–18, 122, 123, 157–58,
   199, 202, 219, 262; courting of Latin
   America nationalists by, 30, 151, 165,
   174, 220, 221, 260–61; Cuba's relations
   with, 24, 28, 29, 30, 134, 149, 173, 196,
   268, 279; and détente, 3, 4, 149, 150, 192,
   217, 258, 284 (n. 3); divisions within,
   over Chile, 197–98; Foreign Ministry
   of, 204, 206, 208, 230; limitations of
   support to Chile, 4, 12, 80, 177, 178, 183,
   186, 191, 192–93, 198–99, 204, 222–23,
   260–61; Nixon's trip to, 108; reluctance
   to confront U.S., 2, 150, 193, 196–98,
   264; sees Latin America as in U.S
   sphere, 24, 80, 128; ties with right-wing
   dictatorships, 260–61; U.S. view of, 9,
   44, 62, 99, 109, 123, 124, 125, 162, 169,
   252, 259
Spenser, Daniela, 10

Strikes: by miners, 145, 210, 226, 227, 233,
   248, 249, 271, 274; by truckers, 182–83,
   184, 186, 197, 274
Stroessner, Alfredo, 127

Tanquetazo (June 29, 1973), 225, 230, 231,
   235, 236–37, 274
Teitelboim, Volodia, 30, 71, 138
Thieme, Roberto, 228
Third World, 3, 20, 28, 33, 34, 98, 163, 169,
   178, 188, 206, 223, 252, 256, 260–61, 263;
   Chile's growing prestige in, 104, 151,
   161, 182, 222–23, 262; Chile's outreach
   to, 13–14, 82, 84, 108, 113, 114–16, 153,
   158–60, 190, 194–95, 203, 222, 237, 262;
   Cuba's ties with, 54, 172, 258; divisions
   within, 164, 262–63; revolution in, 16,
   34, 289 (n. 67); U.S. and, 14–15, 108, 109,
   119, 120, 121, 132, 151, 152, 162, 175, 202,
   252, 264
—nationalism: of Left and Right, 188,
   252–53; U.S. opposition to, 44–45, 109,
   120, 121, 132, 212–13; U.S. toleration of,
   165–66, 216–17, 265
   See also Dependency; Non-Aligned
   Movement
Timossi, Jorge, 138, 238, 244
Tomás Moro (Allende home), 169, 232,
   236, 239, 245
Tomic, Radomiro, 38, 226
Torres, Juan José, 26, 125, 126, 167
Torrijos, Omar, 26
Tricontinental Conference (1966), 36
Tropas Especiales (Cuba), 54, 55, 66, 136,
   233, 336 (n. 76)
Trujillo, Rafael, 40
Tupamaros, 27, 97, 174; in exile in Chile,
   185, 251, 260

Ulianova, Olga, 198
Unidad Popular (UP): and approaching
   coup, 134, 207, 234–37, 239, 271; class
   loyalty to, 205, 218; Cuban advice to
   and influence on, 13, 70, 140; divisions
   within, 13, 108, 142–43, 178, 181, 204–5,
   270; heterogeneous nature of, 3, 13,
   76; international hostility to, 9, 74–75,
   77, 107; international prestige of, 13,
   73, 104, 114, 133, 144–45, 151, 159–60,

222–23; lack of direction within, 208, 217; and Latin American revolutionary movements, 105, 185; 1970 electoral campaign, 47, 49–50, 70, 73, 74, 105; 1971 electoral campaign, 90; 1972 convention of, 153–54; 1973 electoral campaign, 18, 205, 207; and opposition parties, 90, 108; U.S. efforts to weaken, 70; and wealth redistribution, 90, 104, 145. *See also* Allende, Salvador; Chile—Left

United Kingdom: actions against Chile by, 61, 295–96 (n. 65); Chilean Embassy of, 97, 137, 158

United National School System (ENU), 209, 210

United Nations: Economic Commission for Latin America, 20

—Conference on Trade and Development (UNCTAD), 14, 82–83, 102, 104, 114–15, 116, 151, 159–60, 169, 170, 175, 262; Allende's hopes for, 153, 158; Cuban delegation at, 172; United States and, 161, 162, 163–64, 165

—General Assembly: Allende's speech to, 190, 194–95; Almeyda's speech to, 108, 114, 134

United States: Air Force, 125; Treasury Department, 8, 119, 120, 121, 146, 150, 156, 162, 166, 168–69

—Congress, 78, 95–96, 100, 129, 215, 249, 251; hearings on ITT, 202, 211; investigates covert action in Chile, 252; passes González Amendment, 156–57

—covert action by, 7, 15, 58, 62–63, 65, 70, 106, 202, 205, 225, 252, 255, 278, 279–80; contacts with military, 70, 90–91, 130, 183; Covert Action Program, 70–71, 76, 89; propaganda campaigns, 12, 38, 48, 70, 93, 130, 272; support to opposition media, 70, 89, 130, 154, 272; support to opposition parties, 48, 70, 89–90, 130, 183, 186, 205, 272, 274; support to paramilitaries, 183, 227; Tracks I and II, 50–51, 57, 58–60, 295 (n. 49). *See also* Central Intelligence Agency; 40 Committee

—Defense Department, 7, 8, 58, 62, 69,

90, 100, 125, 168; Defense Intelligence Agency (DIA), 225–26, 227, 247

—Embassy (in Santiago), 60, 145, 167, 178, 225, 228; and coup, 238, 239, 243, 247

—foreign policy of: and Allende electoral victory, 9, 48, 49–51, 56–58, 64, 158, 271–72; anti-Allende consensus of, 8, 56, 98, 191; bilateral negotiation aims, 15, 182, 188–89, 202–3; and Brazil, 4, 8, 10, 68–70, 74, 92, 94–96, 98–102, 103, 106, 125, 126–30, 147, 151, 165–66, 167–68, 214, 216, 228, 250; Cold War framework of, 4, 50, 64, 85, 105, 151, 259, 261; "cool but correct" approach of, 66, 69, 71, 72, 74, 88, 120, 147; Cuba as challenge to, 23–24; détente with China and USSR, 108, 150, 217; divisions within Nixon administration around, 58–59, 64, 65, 91, 119, 132, 146, 147, 162–63; duplicitous diplomacy of, 16, 64–65, 86–87, 91, 98, 109, 121–22, 163; economic pressure as tool of, 122, 155–57, 226, 271, 272; encouragement of Chile coup, 51, 59, 61, 207, 220–21, 228, 246–47, 253–54; flexibility of tactics, 18, 151, 272; hiding of aims in, 14–15, 57, 74, 162, 202; for Latin America, 4–5, 10, 17, 18, 26, 39–40, 44–47, 50, 58, 63–64, 68–70, 71, 74, 94, 98–99, 103, 106, 118, 124–25, 147, 150, 151, 164–67, 170, 175–76, 214, 259–61, 265, 272; military dictatorships supported, 4–5, 46, 125; military interventions in Latin America, 22, 26–27; paternalism toward Latin America in, 9, 42–43, 105, 124, 151–52, 187, 213, 214–15, 216; and Peru, 46, 60, 68, 77, 93–94, 169, 170, 174–75, 176, 214, 215, 216, 324 (n. 108); and Pinochet regime, 18, 247, 248–49; and responsibility for Allende ouster, 7–8, 17, 221, 253, 271–72, 273; shifts in, 15, 99, 100, 175–76; Third World nationalists tolerated, 165–66, 216–17, 265; Vietnam and China as preoccupations of, 5, 14, 39, 57, 74, 78, 91, 101, 102, 217, 251, 291 (n. 98). *See also* Nixon, Richard

—State Department, 8, 29, 51, 92, 103, 114, 156, 161–62, 168, 194, 225, 226, 229,

278; advocates caution, flexibility, and
"damage limitation," 56, 58, 61, 65,
67–68, 86, 91, 119, 123, 130, 161, 162–63,
165, 213; Agency for International
Development of, 88; and Allende
election victory, 56, 57, 58, 63, 64;
and Brazil, 98, 100, 129, 130; Bureau
of Intelligence and Research of, 92,
194, 279; and Cuba policy, 92–93, 150;
Inter-American Bureau of, 8, 45, 57,
58; Kissinger and, 65, 120; on Latin
American policy, 42, 45, 48, 124, 165,
168, 213, 216; and NSC, 91; and Pinochet
regime, 247, 251; and reassurances, 111;
and Treasury Department, 156, 162
Urrutia, Javier, 118, 299 (n. 21), 310 (n. 48),
312 (n. 73)
Uruguay, 5, 10, 17, 24, 40, 97, 101, 103,
104, 115, 128–29, 147, 166, 185, 234, 251;
Frente Amplio defeat in, 125, 126–27,
130; Tupamaros in, 27, 173–74

Vaky, Viron Peter, 39, 62, 93, 278
Valdés, Gabriel, 39, 44, 79, 291 (n. 100),
299 (n. 24)

Vásquez Carrisoza, Alfredo, 113
Velasco Alvarado, Juan, 26, 104, 170, 216
Venezuela, 22, 24, 27, 36, 40, 67, 68, 163,
176, 267
La Vía Chilena. *See* Chilean Road to
Socialism
Vietnam: Allende trip to, 34; and Chile,
166, 191, 194, 198, 200, 211, 217–18, 244,
260; North, 41, 116, 159, 197; South, 159,
262; U.S. war in, 5, 14, 20, 24, 36, 39, 56,
57, 74, 78, 91, 101, 103, 149, 172, 173, 182,
195, 251; and Vietnam Syndrome, 252
Vuskovic, Pedro, 181, 186

Walters, Vernon, 7, 127–28, 249–50, 259,
280; memorandum on Chile by, 63–64,
69, 99
Warren, Ray, 206, 207, 224–25
Washington Post, 5, 103, 130, 159
Watergate, 179, 202, 213, 229, 251
Wimert, Paul, 61
World Bank, 88, 226

Zhou Enlai, 230–31, 269

The New Cold War History

Tanya Harmer, *Allende's Chile and the Inter-American Cold War* (2011).

Alessandro Brogi, *Confronting America: The Cold War between the United States and the Communists in France and Italy* (2011).

Gregg Brazinsky, *Nation Building in South Korea: Koreans, Americans, and the Making of a Democracy* (2007).

Vladislav M. Zubok, *A Failed Empire: The Soviet Union in the Cold War from Stalin to Gorbachev* (2007).

Stephen G. Rabe, *U.S. Intervention in British Guiana: A Cold War Story* (2005).

Christopher Endy, *Cold War Holidays: American Tourism in France* (2004).

Salim Yaqub, *Containing Arab Nationalism: The Eisenhower Doctrine and the Middle East* (2003).

Francis J. Gavin, *Gold, Dollars, and Power: The Politics of International Monetary Relations, 1958–1971* (2003).

William Glenn Gray, *Germany's Cold War: The Global Campaign to Isolate East Germany, 1949–1969* (2003).

Matthew J. Ouimet, *The Rise and Fall of the Brezhnev Doctrine in Soviet Foreign Policy* (2003).

Pierre Asselin, *A Bitter Peace: Washington, Hanoi, and the Making of the Paris Agreement* (2002).

Jeffrey Glen Giauque, *Grand Designs and Visions of Unity: The Atlantic Powers and the Reorganization of Western Europe, 1955–1963* (2002).

Chen Jian, *Mao's China and the Cold War* (2001).

M. E. Sarotte, *Dealing with the Devil: East Germany, Détente, and Ostpolitik, 1969–1973* (2001).

Mark Philip Bradley, *Imagining Vietnam and America: The Making of Postcolonial Vietnam, 1919–1950* (2000).

Michael E. Latham, *Modernization as Ideology: American Social Science and "Nation Building" in the Kennedy Era* (2000).

Qiang Zhai, *China and the Vietnam Wars, 1950–1975* (2000).

William I. Hitchcock, *France Restored: Cold War Diplomacy and the Quest for Leadership in Europe, 1944–1954* (1998).